BIOGRAPHICAL REGISTER OF THE

CONFEDERATE CONGRESS

BIOGRAPHICAL REGISTER

OF THE

CONFEDERATE CONGRESS

Ezra J. Warner and W. Buck Yearns

LOUISIANA STATE UNIVERSITY PRESS

BATON ROUGE

ISBN 0–8071–0092–7
Library of Congress Catalog Card Number 74–77329
Copyright © 1975 by Louisiana State University Press
Manufactured in the United States of America

Designed by Albert Crochet. Set in Times Roman
by Graphic Composition, Inc., Athens, Georgia.
Printed on Warren Olde Style paper and bound
by Kingsport Press, Inc., Kingsport, Tennessee.

To our wives

CONTENTS

ILLUSTRATIONS

Following page 42

Exterior View of the Virginia State Capitol, 1862

Meeting Room of Confederate House of Representatives in Virginia State Capitol

The Confederate Senate in open session at Montgomery, Alabama

Signees of the Permanent Confederate Constitution

Mississippi Congressional Delegation, 1860

Representative Clifford Anderson, North Carolina

Representative John B. Baldwin, Virginia

Senator Robert W. Barnwell, South Carolina

Representative John R. Baylor, Texas

Representative Elias Cornelius Boudinot, Cherokee Nation

Senator Clement C. Clay, Jr., Alabama

Senator Henry Stuart Foote, Tennessee

Senator Landon Carter Haynes, Tennessee

Representative Benjamin L. Hodge, Louisiana

Senator R. M. T. Hunter, Virginia

Senator Herschel V. Johnson, North Carolina

Senator Robert W. Johnson, Arkansas

Senator Waldo P. Johnson, Missouri

Representative Willis B. Machen, Kentucky

Representative Henry Marshall, Louisiana

Representative William Porcher Miles, South Carolina

Senator William Elliott Simms, Kentucky

Senator Edward Sparrow, Louisiana

Representative George Graham Vest, Missouri

Senator Louis T. Wigfall, Texas

ACKNOWLEDGMENTS

No Work of this nature can be assembled without substantial contributions from many people to whom, collectively, the authors are greatly indebted for their time and trouble. The following individuals and institutions have shown extraordinary generosity, and our special thanks are due them:

Warren Akin, Cartersville, Ga.; Alabama State Department of Archives and History, Montgomery; Elizabeth Alexander, P. K. Yonge Library of Florida History, University of Florida, Gainesville; Mrs. Samuel Altshuler, Tucson, Ariz.; Robert Lanier Anderson, Macon, Ga.; Arkansas Historical Commission, Little Rock; Elizabeth Ball, Rutherford County Library, Rutherfordton, N.C.; Mrs. Douglas A. Barnett, Morganton-Burke Library, Morganton, N.C.; Mr. and Mrs. M. Cook Barwick, Atlanta, Ga.; James R. Bentley, Curator of Manuscripts, Filson Club, Louisville, Ky.; Edmund Berkeley, Jr., Curator of Manuscripts, University of Virginia Library, Charlottesville; Susan Borden, Wayne County Public Library, Goldsboro, N.C.; E. W. Bowers, Clarksville, Tex.; Mrs. Thomas H. Bowles, Little Rock, Ark.; Gladys Bracy, Tennessee State Library and Archives, Nashville; Joyce Bragg, Muskogee Public Library, Muskogee, Okla.; Jane Brand, Department of Archives and History, Charleston, W. Va.; Marshall M. Brice, Staunton, Va.; Alice Clapp Brown, Gainesville, Fla.; Mrs. Gordon Brown, Henderson, Tex.; Stacy L. Brown, Muskogee, Okla.; Margaret W. Browne, Dalton Regional Library, Dalton, Ga.; Sewell Brumby, University of Georgia Library, Athens; Wanda S. Campbell, Bladen County Historical Society, Elizabethtown, N.C.; Central Florida Regional Library, Ocala; John R. Chambliss, Rocky Mount, N.C.; Louise J. Chandler, R. T. Jones Memorial Library, Canton, Ga.; Margaret L. Chapman, Florida Historical Society, Tampa; Hope M. Cinquegrana, University of Virginia Library,

Charlottesville; Walton C. Clark, Chevy Chase, Md.; Mrs. Frank Cline, Hot Springs, Ark.; George M. Cochran, Staunton, Va.; Mrs. Roy J. Cochran, Huntsville, Ala.; C. F. W. Coker, Department of Archives and History, Raleigh, N.C.; Kenneth Coleman, University of Georgia, Athens; Marguerite B. Cooley, Director, Department of Library and Archives, Phoenix, Ariz.; E. Merton Coulter, University of Georgia, Athens; Mrs. Hugh B. Cox, Historical Alexandria Foundation, Alexandria, Va.; Mrs. Thomas H. Crass, Gadsden, Ala.; T. W. Crigler, Jr., Macon, Miss.; Kenneth Crouch, Bedford, Va.; Mrs. W. E. Crown, Clearwater, Fla.; Joseph H. Croxton, Lancaster, S.C.; Martha R. Cullipher, Washington and Lee University, Lexington, Va.; Raymond J. Curran, Towson, Md.; Charles H. Cuthbert, Petersburg, Va.; Mrs. Richard M. Cutts, The Plains, Va.; Wayne Daniel, El Paso Public Library, El Paso, Tex.; Mrs. Henry G. Dashiell, Smithfield, Va.; Jo Cille Dawkins, Archivist, Mississippi Department of Archives and History, Jackson; Angie Debo, Marshall, Okla.; Donald N. Denson, Ocala, Fla.; Jack L. Dial, Superintendent of Municipal Cemeteries, San Antonio, Tex.; Mrs. Harry Dietz, Newton County Library, Covington, Ga.; Dorothy Dodd, Tallahassee, Fla.; John Frederick Dorman, Washington, D.C.; Eleanor L. Eanes, Emporia, Va.; Mrs. William M. Eaves, Bristol, Tenn.; John F. Echols, Atlanta, Ga.; Eufaula Heritage Association, Eufaula, Ala.; Mahlon T. Everhart, Hachita, N.M.; Nancy McCullers Ferguson, Raleigh, N.C.; Sara Ferguson, Marion County Historical Commission, Ocala, Fla.; Suzanna Foley, College of William and Mary, Williamsburg, Va.; Urline P. Foster, Talladega, Ala.; Mrs. Temple Fraker, Knoxville, Tenn.; Mrs. Ragsdale Garrison, Detroit, Tex.; Chester F. Geaslen, Fort Wright, Ky.; Sarah C. Gillespie, Emory University Library, Atlanta, Ga.; Dorothy Glasser, Tennessee State Library and Archives, Nashville; Margaret Godley, Savannah Public Library, Savannah, Ga.; William M. Goza, Clearwater, Fla.; Mary Preston Gray, Bristol, Va.; Martin H. Hall, University of Texas, Arlington; Virginius C. Hall, Jr., Virginia Historical Society, Richmond; Collin B. Hamer, Jr., New Orleans Public Library, New Orleans, La.; Alfred J. Hanna, Rollins College, Winter Park, Fla.; Marvin L. Harper, Tuscaloosa, Ala.; Allie E. Harris, Moulton Public Library, Moulton, Ala.; Carol H. Harris, Jacksonville Public Library, Jacksonville, Fla.; Edward P. Harris, Snow Hill, Md.; Carroll Hart, Director, Georgia Department of Archives and History, Atlanta; Walter C. Hartridge, Savannah, Ga.; Lilla M. Hawes, Director, Georgia Historical Society, Savannah; T. R. Hay, Locust Valley, N.Y.; Susie Henderson, Museum of New Mexico, Santa Fé; Harley P. Holden, Harvard University Library, Cambridge, Mass.; Jeanne Hollis, Bradley Memorial Library, Columbus, Ga.; Eleanor W. Hooks, Smithfield, N.C.; Mrs. Oliver Howard, State Historical Society of Missouri, Columbia; Mrs. Phil D. Huff, Laurens County Library, Laurens, S.C.;

Frances Imon, Hugo, Okla.; E. L. Inabinett, South Caroliniana Library, University of South Carolina, Columbia; Mrs. Frank S. James, Newport Beach, Ga.; John Melville Jennings, Virginia Historical Society, Richmond; Charles P. Johnson, Georgia Historical Society, Savannah; Edward N. Johnson, Bureau of Archives and Records Management, Tallahassee, Fla.; Mrs. A. Waldo Jones, Vinings, Ga.; Mrs. Charlie Jones, La Jolla, Ga.; Mrs. Paul Jones, Grove Hill, Ala.; Thomas J. Jones, Superintendent, Magnolia Cemetery, Charleston, S.C.; Nathan A. Josel, Jr., Memphis Public Library, Memphis, Tenn.; J. A. C. Keith, Warrenton, Va.; the late William A. Keleher, Albuquerque, N.M.; Mary R. Kensinger, H. B. Stamps Memorial Library, Rogersville, Tenn.; Spencer B. King, Mercer University, Macon, Ga.; Gladys Krone, Fort Smith Public Library, Fort Smith, Ark.; Mrs. R. O. LaFollette, Handley Library, Winchester, Va.; Buxton L. Layton, New Orleans, La.; E. B. Long, University of Wyoming, Laramie; Harold Love, Dalton, Ga.; Lisabeth Lovelace, El Paso Public Library, El Paso, Tex.; Evangeline Lynch, Louisiana State University Library, Baton Rouge; C. L. McAlister, Cleveland, Tenn.; Robert M. McBride, Tennessee Historical Society, Nashville; Royce McCrary, University of Georgia Library, Athens; Anne McDonnell, Kentucky Historical Society, Frankfort, Ky.; Mrs. F. W. McIntire, Paducah, Ky.; Sybil McRay, Chestatee Regional Library, Gainesville, Ga.; Mrs. P. M. Marchman, Lexington, Ga.; W. G. Massey, Smithfield, N.C.; Winifred Maxwell, Lexington, Ga.; Mrs. Ronald Melton, Tallahassee, Fla.; Elizabeth R. Merrill, Vigo County Public Library, Terre Haute, Ind.; Donald W. Meyer, Superintendent, Bellefontaine Cemetery, St. Louis, Mo.; Larry Mitchell, North Carolina College, Dahlonega, Ga.; Mobile Public Library, Mobile, Ala.; Mrs. R. L. Montague, Urbanna, Va.; Montgomery Public Library, Montgomery, Ala.; Robert N. Mullin, South Laguna, Calif.; Susan Naulty, Huntington Library, San Marino, Calif.; Mrs. William T. Nelson, Alexandria, Va.; Lee Nesbitt, Henderson, Tex.; Maud Neville, Paris, Tex.; S. H. Newman III, University of Texas Library, El Paso; Sadie R. Norwood, Greenville County Public Library, Emporia, Va.; Mrs. G. I. Nystrom, Atlanta, Ga.; Wiley C. Owen, Director, Carnegie Library, Rome, Ga.; Katherine M. Owens, Centenary College, Shreveport, La.; Malcolm G. Parker, Librarian, Louisiana State University Library, Shreveport; Mrs. R. H. Patterson, Covington, Ga.; Patty Paul, Division of State Library Services, Tallahassee, Fla.; Lucille Peacock, Aberdeen, Miss.; Dorothy E. Pittman, University of Georgia Library, Athens; Michael F. Plunkett, University of Virginia Library, Charlottesville; William C. Pollard, College of William and Mary Library, Williamsburg, Va.; Mrs. P. B. Price, Austin, Tex.; Ellinor Ramsay Putzel, Salisbury, N.C.; Cooper K. Ragan, Houston, Tex.; E. Alex Rankin, Chattanooga, Tenn.; Kenneth W. Rapp, United States Military Academy, West Point, N.Y.;

Roy D. Ridgway, Augusta County Historical Society, Staunton, Va.; Ben Ritter, Winchester, Va.; Margaret C. Rouse, Gadsden Public Library, Gadsden, Ala.; Rose C. Ruffin, Petersburg Chamber of Commerce, Petersburg, Va.; Henry W. Rupp, Baltimore, Md.; Milton C. Russell, Virginia State Library, Richmond; E. Forrest Sanders, Las Cruces, N.M.; Mahala Saville, Oxford, Miss.; Martin F. Schmidt, Louisville Free Public Library, Louisville, Ky.; Lemuel C. Shepherd, La Jolla, Ga.; Alene Simpson, Oklahoma Historical Society, Oklahoma City; Mrs. Urban Smith, Pulaski, Tenn.; William G. Smith, Washington, D.C.; Dena Snodgrass,' Jacksonville, Fla.; Mrs. Harry E. Spencer, Copiague, N.Y., Robert H. Spencer, Salem, Va.; JoAnne P. Stratton, Cobb County Public Library, Marietta, Ga.; Mrs. Fred Swaney, Holly Springs, Miss.; Virginia E. deTreville, Richmond County Historical Society, Augusta, Ga.; Lee S. Trimble, Jr., Director, Dalton Regional Library, Dalton, Ga.; Mamie G. Tucker, Chattanooga, Tenn.; Mrs. Drouett Vidrine, Ville Platte, La.; Richard E. Walker, Gettysburg College, Gettysburg, Pa.; Mary Bondurant Warren, Danielsville, Ga.; Ruth Warren, Mobile Public Library, Mobile, Ala.; Mrs. Williams C. Wickman, Jr., Hanover, Va.; Horace G. Williams, Anderson County Historical Society, Anderson, S.C.; Mrs. Slade Willingham, Macon, Ga.; Mrs. J. T. Wilson, Dawsonville, Ga.; Waverly K. Winfree, Virginia Historical Society, Richmond; Mary Wolf, Alexandria, Va.; H. T. Wood, Indianapolis, Ind.; Mrs. William C. Wood, Columbia, Mo.; J. Russell Woodard, Mercer University Library, Macon, Ga.; E. Winston Woolfolk, Bowling Green, Va.; Herman Work, Staunton, Va.; David Wyatt, Winston-Salem, N.C.

INTRODUCTION

FEW MEMBERS of the Confederate Congress have come down to posterity boasting the illustrious image of such men as Charles Sumner, Ben Wade, Zachariah Chandler, and Thad Stevens of the United States Congress. Perhaps this is so because they very often languished in postbellum obscurity, their names cherished—if at all—only in a Southland laid waste by war and reconstruction as the carpenters who nailed together the framework of a lost cause. They were a little like supporting actors in a play who appeared, performed their roles, and then drifted almost unnoticed into the wings while the generals held center stage.

Even the manner of their coming together was hurried, unorthodox, improvised, and not a little controversial. When the seven states of the lower South were in the process of severing themselves from the Federal Union during the winter of 1860–1861, no one doubted that they would immediately reunite into a southern confederacy. The South Carolina secession convention took the first formal step toward this end when it appointed commissioners to hurry to the other state conventions to urge them also to secede and to invite them to send delegates to Montgomery, Alabama, on February 4 to form such a union. When the conventions of Georgia, Alabama, Florida, Mississippi, Louisiana, and Texas adopted their ordinances of secession, they accepted South Carolina's invitation and followed her example of electing two delegates at large and one from each old United States congressional district, an arrangement paralleling the states' existing representation in the Federal Congress.[1] None of these states held a popular election for delegates to Montgomery, even after that convention resolved itself into the Provisional Confederate Congress. Vacancies were filled either by the state con-

[1] Florida's convention gave up after two ballots, and assigned the task of selecting her three delegates to Governor M. S. Perry.

ventions or by the legislatures or, failing that, by the president of the convention itself subject to future approval. The "Georgia project," fathered by Thomas R. R. Cobb, proposed on February 5 that the convention write a provisional constitution, elect a president, and decree that "all legislative powers herein granted (under the constitution) shall be vested in this Congress . . . until otherwise ordained," a presumptuous program, speedily initiated, which irritated many people back home, but which, considering the exigencies of the times, rendered any other action impracticable. Thus came into being the Provisional Confederate Congress and with it a new nation.

When Arkansas, North Carolina, Tennessee, and Virginia seceded in the spring of 1861 and requested admission into the Confederacy, they were received on equal terms and assigned their proportionate representation in Congress. Except for that of Tennessee, each of their conventions then elected its delegation to the Confederate Congress. Tennessee called for an election simultaneous with that of the regular United States election scheduled for that year. On the first Thursday in August, Tennessee Unionists and secessionists went together to the polls and made their choices. Pro-Confederate candidates in the mountainous first and second districts lost so badly that they declined seats in the Confederate Congress. In the third and fourth districts Confederate candidates also lost to their Unionist opponents but still took their seats in Richmond.[2] Rump Confederate governments in Kentucky and Missouri received the same generous reception and representation. The avowedly secessionist Missouri legislature, then in session in Neosho, elected its congressmen, while the Russellville convention, which allegedly had taken Kentucky out of the Union, chose theirs. Arizona Territory, embracing the southern half of present day Arizona and New Mexico, and the Indians of the Cherokee, Choctaw, and Creek/Seminole nations also seceded and each was assigned one nonvoting representative. The Arizona representative was elected by a handful of voters assembled in convention at Tucson; the Indian nations chose theirs in general council.

Succeeding congresses under the soon-adopted regular Constitution were theoretically to be elected by popular vote, but in those states or parts of states occupied by Federal troops, the results were hardly representative of the sentiments of such areas, the "voters" being mainly refugees and members of the armed forces.

Both the provisional and regular Confederate constitutions differed little from that of the United States. The principal distinctions, some of which were admittedly an improvement on the old model, were that Congress was

[2] Curiously enough, Hamilton County voted three to two for the Union while the city of Chattanooga went two to one for secession.

xvi

forbidden to appropriate money save at executive request unless by a three-fourths vote of both houses, that the executive be empowered to veto individual items in an appropriation bill, and that the institution of chattel slavery was expressly recognized instead of being acknowledged by indirection, as was the case in the older document.

For the first few months of its existence the Provisional Congress met in the old State Capitol in Montgomery, convening in the Alabama House of Representatives chamber from February 4, 1861, until adjournment of the second session on May 21. But Montgomery could never compensate for the paucity of its accommodations and all but burst at the seams from the crush of legislators, officeholders (and seekers), and visitors. Accordingly, it was determined to move the capital of the putative new nation to Richmond. There, in a room especially prepared for it in the Virginia State House designed by Thomas Jefferson (whose grandson would soon be the Confederate secretary of war), the third and subsequent sessions of the Provisional Congress and all the sessions of the Regular Congress met until final adjournment was moved on March 18, 1865, two weeks prior to the fall of the city.

The room itself was pleasant and airy in summer, about twelve by twenty-five yards in size, with the speaker's chair in the center opposite the entrance. In winter a large stove in the rotunda provided inadequate heat, and chilly members sometimes kept their hats on for warmth. The walls, unfortunately, were bare, the chairs uncushioned, and the desks "slashed with pocketknives." Visitors sat in small galleries at each end, and members sitting under them frequently complained about not hearing well there.

When Congress became bicameral under the permanent Constitution, the House retained these quarters and the Senate was left to shift for itself. Its regular place of meeting was on the third floor in a dingy room which had been improvised by combining the adjutant general's room with an adjoining one. It was cramped and drafty, with only a rail to separate senators from spectators. It proved so unsatisfactory that whenever the Virginia Senate was not in session the Confederate Senate moved downstairs into its chamber across the rotunda from that of the House. Standing committees engaged suites of rooms around the city, but unless they could lease them in public buildings they were overcharged unmercifully. Congress once contemplated buying the Exchange Hotel for its varied uses but found the price of $175,000 too high.

In May, 1861, Congress ordered elections to be held on the first Wednesday in November for representatives to the First Congress of the permanent government. Elections were to be conducted under the constitutions and laws of the several states, but Congress added that if any unforeseen contingency arose the old United States election laws would apply. As noted,

xvii

the seven original states of the Confederacy had sent to Montgomery two delegates at large and one for each of its congressional districts. The permanent Constitution ordered a census to be taken within the next three years and specified that when this was done each state would have one representative for each fifty thousand residents. Until then each of the seven states was assigned a specific number of seats in the House on the basis of one for each ninety thousand residents according to the United States census of 1860. As other states entered, Congress assigned them representation on the same basis. Under this plan every state except South Carolina received at least one additional representative and consequently had to redistrict itself. During the summer and fall of 1861, therefore, all states were redistricted either by act of their state legislatures or by act of their conventions. In 1863 South Carolina finally redistricted itself in order to obtain a fairer representation in the Second Congress, although it did not gain an additional seat. Congress had granted Missouri thirteen representatives, but for some reason the rump Neosho legislature chose to divide the state into only seven districts, the same number which it had had in the Federal Congress. The accompanying map exhibits the number of congressional districts and their boundaries after redistricting.

The migratory nature of nineteenth-century Americans is amply demonstrated by the birthplaces and states represented by the 267 individuals who were the Confederacy's lawmakers from 1861 to 1865. Arkansas, Florida, Missouri, Texas, and the territories had no congressmen born within their borders, whereas 67 were born in Virginia. The latter state also had the largest delegation (35) and was the state whose representatives were all natives. Thus 32 Virginians represented other states of the Confederacy. Georgia claimed 39 natives, 27 of whom were members of its congressional delegation of 32. North Carolina followed with 37 native sons, and its congressional representatives numbered 27 who were born within the state out of a total of 32 who served in one of the three congresses. Kentucky's native sons included only 16 who represented the state out of a total of 22, but furnished a large proportion of Missouri's delegation of 13. Only 4 representatives came from foreign lands: Ford (England), Lander (Ireland), Memminger (Germany), and Sparrow (Ireland); the birthplace of 1 representative (Macwillie) is unknown. Of the 4 northern-born members, Conrow and Sexton came from Ohio and Indiana respectively; the other 2, Ingram and Sanderson, came, rather singularly, from the Green Mountains of Vermont. The table below sets forth in detail the number of representatives from each state, those born in each state (or country), and those who were natives of the states which they represented. The number of congressional districts per state is shown in parentheses.

Two other phenomena of some significance are reflected by the foregoing

xviii

STATE	REPRESENTATIVES 1861/1865	NATIVES	NATIVE REPRESENTATIVES
Alabama (9)	24	12	5
Arkansas (4)	11	0	0
Florida (2)	11	0	0
Georgia (10)	32	39	27
Kentucky (12)	22	31	16
Louisiana (6)	11	4	4
Mississippi (7)	21	5	2
Missouri (7)	13	0	0
North Carolina (10)	27	37	23
South Carolina (6)	15	28	13
Tennessee (11)	23	31	14
Texas (6)	17	0	0
Virginia (16)	35	67	35
Territories (4)	5	0	0
Scattering	0	13	0
	267	267	139

table: the disproportionate number of individuals who occupied seats from some states versus those who represented others, and the relatively large representation from occupied states such as Missouri, Kentucky, and Tennessee. It can be seen that during the life of the Confederacy Georgia, with ten congressional districts, sent no less than 29 different men to Montgomery and Richmond, while Louisiana sent only nine from its four districts, senators being excluded in both instances. The large turnover in Georgia, paralleled to a great extent in North Carolina, resulted principally from the running battles conducted by governors Joe Brown and Zebulon Vance with Jefferson Davis, which fostered a growing disillusionment with the war. The fact that nearly one-fourth of the members of Congress at any given time represented states wholly or in part occupied by Federal troops and/or unsympathetic to the secession cause is one measure of the futility with which the Congress operated, particularly after the executive branch of the government was established. Aside from routine business, where "politics as usual" was the order of the day, an examination of the *Journal of the Confederate Congress* is apt to remind one of a group of medieval theologians debating the question of the number of archangels that could be accommodated on the head of a pin. The Congress, it must be confessed, was a classic example of the parliamentary system, in which energies are squandered in intrigue and bombast. Jefferson Davis was jealous of his prerogatives and was not disposed to brook interference with them. Furthermore, his curiously rigid mentality was incapable of accommodating itself to what he deemed to be the whims of opposition members holding views contrary to his own. Accordingly, while the emergency lasted (which embraced the entire life of the Confederacy), Congress had little to do but either approve and implement administration policy or occupy its time with endless debate over minutiae.

An examination of the ages, occupations, and slaveholdings of members seems to be in order; therefore, the following figures are offered. All of these analyses tend to contradict some commonly accepted notions such as the conservatism of the old versus the young, and the cherished belief that the secession movement was the creation of a clique of slave nabobs. Of the 267 members of Congress in 1860, 11 were over sixty; 55 were between fifty and sixty; 101 were between forty and fifty; 89 were between thirty and forty; 9 were under thirty; and the ages of 2 are not known.

If there is one fact which can be asserted with reasonable certainty about these 267 men, who hailed from sixteen different states and foreign countries, and ranged in age from seventy-one (Thomas Fearn) down to twenty-five (Elias Boudinot), it is that age had nothing to do with their attitudes, their beliefs, their politics, or their espousals of one side or the other of the questions at issue. Perhaps for that reason Alexander and Beringer in their exhaustive computer analysis of roll-call votes in *The Anatomy of the Confederate Congress* made no effort to correlate age with voting postures.

To rigidly define the occupations of members is not so simple, since many men had two or more vocations. The vast majority, however, 213 of the 267, had one thing in common: they were either practicing attorneys or had studied law. There were also 41 men who pursued agriculture to the exclusion of other vocations, five who were journalists, two doctors, a clergyman (S. H. Ford), and an educator (William Porcher Miles). On the other hand 108 of the lawyers also engaged in farming or planting and 11 others followed such varied pursuits as financier, teacher, journalist, and merchant, while Warren Akin of Georgia combined the duties of a clergyman with his legal practice and farm activities. And during the course of the war William Porcher Miles, hitherto a popular but impecunious schoolteacher and mayor of Charleston, and briefly a member of the U.S. Congress, married an heiress and found himself the owner of broad acres in (West) Virginia and Louisiana.

If lawyers by sheer numbers dominated the councils of the Confederacy, as they have since time immemorial dominated the Federal Congress, it cannot be said that large slave owners were in the majority. The slavehold-

xx

ings of 24 members are unknown; however, 21 are recorded as owning no slaves, and more than 40 others owned 5 or less. While 122 members possessed from 6 to 50 Negroes, only 7 could in all conscience be classified as tycoons, 5 of them being Louisiana sugar planters. They were Henry Marshall with 201 slaves, Alexandre de Clouet with 275, John Perkins, Jr., with 340, Edward Sparrow with 460, and Duncan F. Kenner with 473. Charles Munnerlyn of Georgia was the owner of 216 blacks, and the seventh large holder was Robert M. Jones, delegate from the Choctaw Nation who was himself a full-blooded Choctaw. Jones admitted to owning 227 Negroes in 1860, although the total on his several plantations along Red River is said to have been more nearly 500. But none of these men could compare with the really large slave owners; Wade Hampton, later to be a Confederate lieutenant general, at the same time was reputed to be the master of more than 2,000 black people on his vast estates in South Carolina and Mississippi. The figures given here are probably not wholly accurate since they reflect the census of 1860, wherein the number of Negroes owned by an individual generally indicates only those on his home plantation (his place of residence). If he had slaves in other counties or states, they might be separately enumerated, and thus not be included above. Nevertheless, it is rather apparent that the members of the Confederate Congress did not constitute a mere convention of slave nabobs whose sole purpose was to maintain the Negro in bondage, which is not to say the question of slavery was not an issue—and in later years *the* issue—of the Civil War.

The more one studies the careers of the members, the more one is impressed by the fact that in not a few cases neither they nor their descendants nor even local historians attached great importance to their service in the Confederate Congress. How different was the distinction attached to having been a Confederate officer—particularly a general! Several members, indeed, subsequently omitted mention of their service or even denied it in authorized biographical sketches. Others seem to have gone to their graves unhonored and unsung, with the result that data of the most basic nature has been difficult, if not impossible, to come by. Marcus H. Macwillie—whose name has come down to us in such variants as Malcolm H. McWillie—a delegate from the Arizona Territory, emerged from total obscurity in 1860 by way of a brief notice in the Mesilla (N.M.) *Times* offering his legal services, and dropped completely out of sight with the collapse of the Confederacy in 1865; not even his age or his birthplace is on record.

No systematic effort to take or assemble a gallery of photographs of members was ever made in Richmond, as was done by Brady in Washington; accordingly, the authors were faced with the evident impractability of attempting to gather anything like a complete collection of portraits, a task which could well be the lifetime avocation of an avid student of the period.

The photographs accompanying the text are intended to be representative not only of the members themselves but of the surroundings in which they worked and some of the documents they wrote.

Where the basic biographical information has been derived from published and generally accessible works, the sources of such information are not given in the notes. In such cases the reader will understand that the information is derived from standard items in our bibliography, such as recognized biographies, the *Biographical Directory of the American Congress, The Dictionary of American Biography,* the *National Cyclopedia of American Biography,* the *Journal of the Confederate Congress*, and so on.

Much the same can be said for certain primary sources. First and foremost, particularly in sketches of persons whose names do not appear in standard biographies, information from the decennial United States censuses beginning with the Seventh Census of 1850 (when each member of a household was for the first time enumerated individually) must be recognized as a cornerstone. Without this priceless research tool, obscure historical figures would long since have faded into permanent oblivion. The authors have also researched carefully the official records of the secession conventions and the state legislatures, and they have read twenty-eight Confederate newspapers for the duration of their publication. The compressed nature of the biographical sketches has made it impractical to cite these sources unless they are quoted directly.

With these few comments, the authors are encouraged to hope that what follows will provide a greater insight into the lives and activities of the 267 members of the Confederate Congress than is generally available in other specialized compilations of a similar nature.

BIOGRAPHICAL REGISTER OF THE

CONFEDERATE CONGRESS

WARREN AKIN[1] (Georgia) was born in Elbert County, Georgia, on October 9, 1811. After a limited education in Elbert County and one term in a Walton County school, he began clerking in a store in Monroe. When Aiken was eighteen he succumbed to the excitement of the gold rush in Cherokee County and worked there in the fields for several years. While not mining he studied law, and he was admitted to the bar in 1836. He opened an office in Cassville—his first partner was A. R. Wright (*q.v.*)—and soon he had a moderately successful practice. He also owned a small plantation near Cassville.

Akin frequently preached at the local Methodist church and gained considerable renown for being audible a mile away. He was always interested in politics—in 1840 he was a Whig presidential elector, and in 1850 he was a member of the Nashville convention, which probably preserved the Union by adopting the "Georgia Platform" with its features of compromise. In 1860 Akin was an unsuccessful candidate for governor on the Constitutional Union ticket, defeated by Joseph E. Brown.

Akin opposed secession but supported the Confederacy when Georgia left the Union. He was in the legislature from 1861 to 1863 and was the only man to hold that speakership in his first term. In the fall of 1863 Akin campaigned for a seat in the Confederate House of Representatives on a promise of full support to President Davis and won a clearcut victory. Before going to Richmond he moved his family to Oxford and later to Elberton to avoid the path of Sherman's army.

For a newcomer Akin participated actively in the proceedings of Congress, though generally by means of minor amendments and routine resolutions. He was a close friend of Jefferson Davis and, after a long talk with him on January 9, 1865, was convinced that only Davis could save the Confederacy. A week later, when Congress was establishing the office of general-in-chief for Robert E. Lee, Akin proposed that the new position should not encroach on the president's authority, though the amendment failed. The only emergency power that Akin refused to grant the central government was the right to suspend the habeas corpus freely.

After the war Akin resumed his law practice in Bartow County. He died at Cartersville on December 17, 1877, and is buried in the family lot at the cemetery in Cassville.[2]

[1] Bell I. Wiley (ed.), *Letters of Warren Akin, Confederate Congressman* (Athens, Ga., 1959), Introduction.
[2] The authors are indebted to Akin's grandson, Warren Akin of Cartersville, Ga., for information on the place of interment.

CLIFFORD ANDERSON[1] (Georgia) was born on March 23, 1833, in Nottoway County, Virginia. He was orphaned at the age of twelve soon after his father lost his considerable fortune. Four years later Clifford moved to Macon, Georgia, and worked in his brother's law office. In his spare time he read intensively and obtained a broad classical education without the benefit of a teacher. In 1850 he began studying law under Robert S. Lanier. Two years later he established a partnership with Lanier that lasted over forty years. Anderson was always vitally interested in local and state affairs. In 1856 he was elected city judge, but he resigned after two years. In 1859 he was elected as a Whig to the state house of representatives. In the election of 1860 he supported the Constitutional Union party, and even after Lincoln's election he opposed secession; but after observing the course of South Carolina toward secession, on December 14 he signed a statement with other prominent citizens of Macon demanding the immediate secession of Georgia.

When fighting began Anderson enlisted as a private. He soon was elected lieutenant in the Floyd Rifles and then was promoted to brigade inspector on General Wright's staff. As a result of his conduct in the Gettysburg campaign he was considered for promotion, but before any action was taken he resigned to seek a place in the Confederate Congress. In October, 1863, he unseated the incumbent, Augustus H. Kenan, a close friend of Jefferson Davis.

As one of the youngest members of the Second Congress, Anderson seldom participated in debate. Most of the few bills and amendments that he proposed were designed to remedy certain inequalities in the tax and impressment laws. In the last stages of the Confederacy he opposed peace negotiations and voted to arm the slaves. He generally supported efforts made by other congressmen to fill the army's thinning ranks, and he accepted the president's dictates regarding army organi-

4

zation and diplomacy. Otherwise he almost always refused to extend the powers of the central government beyond the limits set by the First Congress. He openly repudiated, however, the obstructionist tactics of Governor Joseph E. Brown.

After the war, Anderson resumed his law practice in Macon. In 1876 he was chairman of the state Democratic executive committee. In 1880 he was elected state attorney general and was repeatedly reelected to that position for the next ten years. When Mercer University moved to Macon, Anderson became one of its first professors of law. In 1893 Governor William J. Northen appointed him to a committee to codify the laws of Georgia, a task Anderson completed after two years of intense work. Anderson died on December 19, 1899, and is buried in Rose Hill Cemetery in Macon.[2]

[1] William J. Northen (ed.), *Men of Mark in Georgia* (6 vols., Atlanta, 1907–12), III, 191–94.

[2] Information on Anderson's interment was provided by Robert Lanier Anderson, Jr., of Macon, Ga.

JAMES PATTON ANDERSON (Florida), a native of Tennessee, was born in Franklin County on February 16, 1822.[1] He was graduated from Jefferson College (one of the predecessor institutions of Washington and Jefferson) in Canonsburg, Pennsylvania, in 1842, and then studied law in Frankfort, Kentucky. After being admitted to the bar, he practiced in Hernando, Mississippi, until 1846; then, after raising a company, he commanded the Second Battalion Mississippi Rifles during the Mexican War with a rank of lieutenant colonel. After a term in the Mississippi legislature, he was in 1853 appointed by President Pierce United States marshal for Washington Territory, which he was later elected to represent as its delegate to Congress. Declining an appointment as territorial governor in 1857, Anderson moved to Florida the same year and established a plantation, Casabianca, near Monticello.

As a member of the Florida convention of January, 1861, Anderson voted for immediate secession and was then appointed delegate to Montgomery.[2] He attended sessions of the Provisional Congress for only about three weeks and took an active part only in seeing that the law establishing a court of admiralty and maritime jurisdiction at Key West was properly written. He resigned on April 8, 1861, to accept the colonelcy of the First Florida Infantry. Anderson's initial service was with General Braxton Bragg at Pensacola. Promoted brigadier general on February 10, 1862, he fought gallantly at Shiloh and commanded a division at Perryville. His brigade especially distinguished itself at

5

Murfreesboro. Again in divisional command at Chickamauga and Chattanooga, he was promoted major general to rank from February 17, 1864. In command of the district of Florida during the first part of the Atlanta campaign, he was recalled to the Army of Tennessee in time to participate in the battles of Ezra Church and Jonesboro and was severely wounded at Jonesboro. He rejoined the Army in North Carolina and surrendered with it at Greensboro.

After the war General Anderson conducted a farm paper in Memphis and later was collector of state taxes for Shelby County. He died at Memphis on September 20, 1872, and is buried there in Elmwood Cemetery.

[1] See Mrs. J. P. Anderson (transcriber), "Autobiography of Gen. Patton Anderson, C.S.A.," *Southern Historical Society Papers*, XXIV (1896), 57–70, and Anderson's autobiography in the *Biographical Directory of the American Congress*. The author of Anderson's life in the *Dictionary of American Biography* gives February 12 as his birth date and states that he studied and practiced medicine, not law, in Hernando, Mississippi. But see the 1860 federal census of Jefferson County, Florida, wherein Anderson listed his occupations as lawyer and agriculturist.

[2] After two inconclusive ballots taken in an effort to elect three delegates to Montgomery, the Florida convention asked Governor Madison Perry to appoint them, subject to convention approval. Accordingly, the governor recommended Anderson, Jackson Morton, and James B. Owens, all of whom were confirmed by the convention with little opposition. See the *Journal of the Florida Secession Convention*, 75–85.

ARCHIBALD HUNTER ARRINGTON (North Carolina) was born on November 13, 1809, on his father's plantation at Hilliardston in Nash County, North Carolina. He attended academies at home and in Louisburg and then studied law. He began practicing in Nash County and also engaged in planting. He soon became one of the wealthiest men of his district; the census of 1860 valued his estate at over $300,000. Arrington served as a Democrat in the United States House of Representatives from 1841 to 1845, but he failed to be reelected for a third term. During the secession crisis in the winter of 1860–1861 he was a strong Unionist. However, as a member of the convention which convened after Lincoln's call for troops he voted to secede. In November, 1861, he and Josiah Turner waged a heated personal contest for a seat in the Confederate House of Representatives and Arrington won a narrow victory.

In Congress Arrington asserted himself only to improve the pay and care of enlisted men. His position on other legislation was one of the most balanced there. He voted for the first conscription law, but opposed further extensions. He favored shortening the list of occupations exempt from military service, but he felt justified in exempting all men in state employment. He also approved the principle of destroying

6

property to keep it from the enemy, but he wished to limit the kinds of property that could be destroyed. Arrington's position on other matters followed much the same line. The only major powers that he attempted to withhold from the central government were heavy taxation and the forced funding of inflated currency. This moderation won him few friends in his war-weary district. In November, 1863, he lost decisively in a return engagement with Turner.

In 1866 Arrington was a delegate to the Union national convention. Thereafter he took no active part in politics. He died at his home on July 20, 1872, and was interred in the family graveyard on his plantation.

THOMAS SAMUEL ASHE (North Carolina) was born in Orange County on July 19, 1812, into a family which had been prominent in North Carolina since the early eighteenth century. His parents soon moved to Alabama, but he returned to North Carolina to attend the famous Bingham School in Orange County. In 1832 he was graduated from the University of North Carolina and began to study law in Hillsboro under Chief Justice Thomas Ruffin (q.v.). In 1836 he began practicing in Wadesboro. Ashe served two terms as a Whig member of the legislature, and in 1848 the legislature elected him district solicitor for four years. Meanwhile he had bought and was managing a small plantation. In February, 1861, his county elected him a Unionist delegate to a proposed constitutional convention, but the convention call was defeated. After Lincoln's call for volunteers in April, however, North Carolina quickly ordered such a convention and Ashe was now elected as an immediate secessionist. In November he was elected a representative to the Confederate Congress.

In Congress Ashe opposed quietly but firmly every major effort to enlarge the powers of the central government at the expense of the states or of individuals. He made a particular effort to restrict conscription, feeling that "Congress has no power to conscribe any officer of a State, unless the State Legislature shall deliver him to be liable to service in the Confederate army."[1] Nevertheless Ashe believed that the Confederacy could win its independence without such legislation and deplored the Reconstructionist sentiment developing in North Carolina. In 1863 he campaigned for reelection on these terms and lost to an avowed peace candidate. In December, 1864, his position received statewide sanction when he was elected Confederate senator over Edwin G. Reade (q.v.), but the war ended before his term began.

In 1868 Ashe was the Conservative candidate for governor even though Reconstruction legislation prevented him from voting, but he lost to W. W. Holden. In 1872 he was elected as a Democrat to the United States House of Representatives. As a member of the judiciary committee he made a name for himself in exposing fraud and corruption under "Grantism," but after two terms he deferred to the widely accepted principle of rotation in office. In 1878 he was elected associate justice of the state supreme court and served until his death in Wadesboro on February 4, 1887. He is buried in East View Cemetery.

[1] Thomas S. Ashe to Zebulon B. Vance, April 24, 1863, in Miscellaneous Correspondence, John T. Pickett Papers, Library of Congress, Washington, D.C.

JOHN DeWITT CLINTON ATKINS (Tennessee) was born in Henry County, Tennessee, on June 4, 1825. He was educated at a private school in Paris, Tennessee, and at East Tennessee College in Knoxville, from which he was graduated in 1846. Atkins then studied law and was admitted to the bar; but he never practiced, preferring farming and politics to the courtroom. He was successively a member of the Tennessee House of Representatives, the Tennessee Senate, and the United States House of Representatives, meanwhile serving as a Democratic presidential elector in 1856. In 1861, after a brief period of service in the Confederate army as lieutenant colonel of the Fifth Tennessee infantry, Atkins was elected Ninth District representative to the Provisional Congress and continued, by reelection to both Regular Congresses, to represent Tennessee in the Confederacy until the end of the war.[1]

In the First Congress Atkins chaired a special committee to investigate railroad frauds, and in the Second Congress he chaired the standing Committee on Ordinance. Atkins believed that "the Army was our government"[2] and that Congress' main duty was to man and supply it. He proposed several cuts in the list of class exemptions, and in 1864 he voted to draft men fifty-five years old. In 1865 he suggested giving poor whites a vested interest in victory by buying 100,000 Negroes and giving them as enlistment bonuses, which would seem to refute the theory advanced by some historians that slavery was not the cause of the Civil War. As early as March, 1862, he tried to investigate Albert Sidney Johnston for his failures in defending Tennessee. On matters less directly related to the war, Atkins was not particularly cooperative with the administration. He never sanctioned suspensions of the writ of habeas corpus nor legislation regulating business activities, and he frequently found fault with the president's cabinet selections and with his handling of diplomacy.

After the war, as Tennessee emerged from the Reconstruction

period, Atkins was elected to five more consecutive terms in the Federal Congress (1873–1883), and in 1884 he was again a presidential elector on the Cleveland-Hendricks ticket. He served for three years as commissioner of Indian affairs under Cleveland, resigning in 1888 to run unsuccessfully for United States senator. He then returned to his farm near Paris, Tennessee, and lived there until, fully retired, he moved into Paris proper. He died there on June 2, 1908, and was buried in City Cemetery.

[1] With two-thirds of Tennessee in Union hands by election time for the Second Congress, Governor Isham P. Harris called a convention to meet at Winchester on June 12, 1863, to nominate a congressional ticket. There was little opposition to this slate and all nominees were elected on a common ballot devised by Congress and providing that each voter vote for one representative from each of the eleven congressional districts. The vote was small and mainly from army camps.

[2] Richmond *Daily Enquirer*, January 27, 1864.

WILLIAM WAIGSTILL AVERY (North Carolina), the son-in-law of John Motley Morehead (*q.v.*), was born in Burke County, North Carolina, on May 25, 1816. He came from a long line of Puritan forebears, the first of whom emigrated from England to Massachusetts in 1631; another came from England to North Carolina in 1769. Avery was graduated from the University of North Carolina at Chapel Hill in 1837 and, after studying law, was admitted to the bar two years later. Between 1842 and 1860 he was elected to the state legislature on five different occasions, and in 1860 he was head of the North Carolina delegation to the Democratic national convention in Baltimore, Maryland. During the same period he had built up an important law practice. He was a member of the North Carolina secession convention, which in May, 1861, elected him a delegate at large to the Provisional Confederate Congress.

In Congress he deferred almost completely to the administration and strongly supported its designs to strengthen the newly formed nation. The only significant exception was his dislike of the produce-loan program, an attitude which seems to have been widespread among Davis supporters. Beyond his congressional duties, Avery's special interest, amounting to a crusade, was to see that North Carolina received its fair share of general officers. In September, 1861, the Democratic party endorsed him for the Confederate Senate, but after two weeks of stalemate the legislature compromised on William T. Dortch (*q.v.*), whose secessionist leanings had not been as pronounced as Avery's. In the summer of 1864, while the star of the Confederacy waned, Avery was engaged in repelling the incursion of wandering guerrillas from

9

Tennessee when he was mortally wounded and brought to his home in Morganton, North Carolina, to die. The third of his father's sons to be killed in action while fighting for the Confederate cause, Avery died on July 3, 1864, and was buried in the Avery family cemetery near Morganton.

LEWIS MALONE AYER[1] (South Carolina) was born on November 12, 1821, at his father's plantation, Patmos, near Barnwell, South Carolina. He attended several academies and in 1838 enrolled in South Carolina College. After two years there he studied for two more at the University of Virginia and Harvard Law School, finishing there in 1842. He began practicing law in Barnwell, but in 1846 he accepted a plantation from his father and turned to agriculture. In 1848 Ayer was overwhelmingly elected as a Democrat to the General Assembly, and was returned by reelection until 1856. Meanwhile he was a brigadier general in the militia and in 1856 took a company to Kansas to support the slave interests there. In 1860 Ayer was elected to Congress but chose instead to attend the state secession convention, where he advocated immediate disunion. In November, 1861, Ayer defeated D. F. Jameson, president of the secession convention, in a contest for the Confederate House of Representatives. In 1863 he won reelection, this time over Robert Barnwell Rhett (q.v.).

Though Ayer had campaigned on the grounds that to elect Rhett would be to make war on the Confederacy, the two had similar viewpoints. Ayer demanded an aggressive war and never condoned peace negotiations, but he adamantly refused to give the central government sufficient authority. He was especially conservative in finance—his chief concern—and one might question his appointment as chairman of the Committee on the War Tax. In December, 1863, he suggested that the profitable tax-in-kind be abandoned, and he considered the repudiation of redundant currency to be ruinous and absurd. His own solution to the Treasury's problems was a half-billion-dollar bond issue with interest guaranteed by higher export duties. In a similar vein Ayer opposed the "monstrous" efforts to give the government more control over manpower, over army personnel and organization, and even over the habeas corpus in the most extreme situations.

Ayer spent three years after the war as a cotton merchant in Charleston while his plantation was being repaired. When he returned to Barnwell in 1868, now owner of the entire eight thousand acres of Patmos, his former slaves were still there, and Ayer was the first man in his district to rent land to Negroes. In the same year he became an

10

ordained Baptist minister. To avoid Radical Reconstruction, he accepted calls to Texas and Tennessee, returning in 1876 to accept a pastorate in Anderson. Three years later he established a female seminary there and operated it until 1887. In that year he became a professor at Patrick Military Institute and taught until his death on March 8, 1895. Ayer is buried in the (Old) Silverbrook Cemetery[2] in Anderson.

[1]*Cyclopedia of Eminent and Representative Men of the Carolinas of the Nineteenth Century* (2 vols.; Madison, Wis., 1892), I, 488–90.
[2]Information on Ayer's interment was provided by Horace G. Williams, Anderson County Historical Society, Anderson, S.C.

JAMES McNAIR BAKER[1] (Florida) was born in Robeson County, North Carolina, on July 20, 1821.[2] He was graduated from Davidson College in 1844; he then studied law in Lumberton and practiced there for a year. His health, however, forced him to seek a different climate, and in 1847 he rode on horseback the entire distance to Florida and began practicing in Old Columbus, a now abandoned village on the Suwannee River, seventy miles east of Tallahassee. He soon moved to Alligator, Florida, and was instrumental in having its name changed to Lake City. Within the decade Baker had achieved prominence as a specialist in land law. He also acquired and operated a fair-sized plantation. Baker's first public service was as a delegate to the Whig national convention of 1852 in Baltimore, Maryland. In 1856 he was an unsuccessful candidate for Congress on the American party ticket. Baker served as solicitor of the eastern circuit of Florida from 1853 to 1859 and as judge of the same circuit for the next three years. During the secession crisis he was a confirmed Unionist and supported the Bell-Everett presidential ticket.

In November, 1861, the legislature elected Baker a Confederate senator on the forty-first ballot. He drew only a two-year term, but in 1863 he won reelection unanimously. In the Second Congress he was chairman of the Committee on Public Lands. Baker left the formulation of the major pieces of legislation to others and concerned himself chiefly with the routine but necessary matters of administration. He was especially diligent in establishing the guidelines on postal routes, judicial districting, sequestration procedures, and pay scales. Baker's voting record indicates basic approval of the administration's war policies; but it also shows a strong belief that several of these policies damaged the economy of the interior Confederate districts. It was for this reason that he disliked heavy taxes, impressments, strict control over commerce, arming the slaves, and the conscription of skilled labor.

11

At the close of the war Baker returned to his law practice in Lake City. In 1866 he was appointed associate justice of the state supreme court, but he was forced off the bench when Florida began congressional Reconstruction in 1868. Soon afterward Baker moved to Jacksonville where he quickly rebuilt his law practice. In 1876 he was a member of the state Democratic Executive Committee which led the redemption of the state for the Conservatives. In 1881 Baker was appointed judge of the fourth judicial circuit and held the position until ill health forced his resignation in 1890. He died at home in Jacksonville on June 20, 1892, and is buried in Evergreen Cemetery.[3]

[1] Francis P. Fleming (ed.), *Memoirs of Florida . . . by Rowland H. Rerrick* (2 vols., Atlanta, 1902), I, 424; hereinafter cited as Rerrick, *Memoirs of Florida*.

[2] Rerrick, *Memoirs of Florida*, I, 424, gives Baker's birth date as July 20, 1822. The *National Cyclopedia of American Biography*, V, 88, gives the birth date as July 22, 1821. Baker's grave marker gives the birth date as July 20, 1821, and this date has been used.

[3] Information on Baker's place of interment was provided by Dena Snodgrass, Jacksonville Historical Society, Jacksonville, Fla.

JOHN BROWN BALDWIN (Virginia) was born at Spring Farm, Staunton, Virginia, on January 11, 1820. After attending the local public schools and Staunton Academy he entered the University of Virginia in 1836 for three more years of study. He then read law with his father and began practicing in Staunton in 1841. In 1846 Baldwin won a seat in the house of delegates as a Whig. There his advocacy of a "mixed basis" of representation (i.e., based on person and property as opposed to the "white basis" which his district preferred) caused him to lose his race for reelection. During 1860 and 1861 he worked untiringly for peace, both in support of the Bell-Everett ticket and as a member of the Union delegation which went to Washington to seek some sort of compromise with President Lincoln that would prevent hostilities.

As a member of the Virginia convention of 1861 Baldwin voted against disunion, but when his state seceded he accepted the position of inspector general of the state volunteers. When these were merged with those of the Confederacy in August he took the field as colonel of the Fifty-second Virginia Infantry, and saw active service in West Virginia. While at the front Baldwin was elected over two opponents to the Confederate House of Representatives. In 1863 he won reelection over former Governor John Letcher.

The fertile Shenandoah Valley comprised much of Baldwin's district, and no congressman better reflected the economic trials of his constituents. Baldwin's primary aim was to give the Confederacy the means to protect such exposed districts and at the same time preserve their productive capacities. For instance, he supported conscription once it became an established policy, but he sought the exemption of numerous classes of producers. He was willing for the government to commandeer for army labor any number of slaves and free Negroes, except those producing food or forage. Baldwin approved strict currency controls and on May 3, 1864, suggested doubling the tithe on agriculture. But he considered all impressments unfair levies upon farmers. He constantly badgered the House and the War Department about inequities and malpractices in the system, particularly when he became chairman of the Special Committee on Impressments. Only on habeas corpus did he take consistent and doctrinaire opposition against conferring power upon the central government.

In October, 1865, Baldwin was again elected to the General Assembly. As speaker, he formulated the rules of procedure still in use and known as Baldwin's Rules. In 1868 he was president of the state Conservative convention, then chairman of the Virginia delegation to the Democratic national convention. In the same year, however, he declined the Democratic nomination for governor. When Baldwin died on September 30, 1873, the places of business in Staunton were closed and all the church bells were rung in his honor.[1] He is buried in Thornrose Cemetery there.[2]

[1] This information was furnished by Marshall M. Brice of Staunton, Va.
[2] According to George M. Cochran of Staunton, Va.

ETHELBERT BARKSDALE (Mississippi), a brother of Brigadier General William Barksdale, C.S.A., and a brother-in-law of Representative James B. Owens of Florida (*q.v.*), was born in Smyrna, Tennessee, January 4, 1824. He came to Mississippi with his family in 1837. He adopted the profession of journalism and at the age of twenty-one was the editor of the *Democrat* in Yazoo City. Subsequently he was editor of the *Mississippian* and the *Clarion*, both published in Jackson. He was a delegate to the Democratic national convention in Charleston in 1860; in the fall of 1861 he was elected to the First Regular Confederate Congress and was easily reelected in 1863.

Barksdale had not been an original secessionist but, once committed, he came to be regarded as "the leader of the Administration party in the House."[1] A frequent and forcible debater, his forte was the introduction of controversial bills, and he once expressed his willingness to "throw aside the Constitution" if necessary. In the First Congress he led the movement to suspend habeas corpus and even to impose martial law. He naturally sided with President Davis on such

13

questions as the draft, exemptions from service, and a tax increase on agricultural products. In the waning days of the Confederacy he headed a select committee to augment the armed forces and, a month before final adjournment, introduced a bill authorizing Davis to arm slaves; he subsequently read the favorable response of General Robert E. Lee on the subject from the House floor.

At the end of the war Barksdale resumed the editorship of the *Clarion*, and during the Ames administration he called loudly for the governor's impeachment. He was again a delegate to the Democratic conventions of 1868, 1872, and 1880. In 1882 he was elected to the United States Congress; he was reelected in 1884 but unsuccessfully sought reelection in 1886. Barksdale then operated a plantation, Oak Valley, in Yazoo County, where he died on February 17, 1893. He is buried in Greenwood Cemetery in Jackson.

[1] Edward A. Pollard, "The Confederate Congress," *Galaxy,* VI (1868–69), 755. Barksdale's widow deposited material in the Mississippi State Archives which has been of assistance in reconstructing his career.

ROBERT WOODWARD BARNWELL (South Carolina), who served in the Confederate Congress from the day it convened in Montgomery until the day it dissolved in Richmond, was born on one of the several Barnwell plantations near Beaufort, South Carolina, on August 10, 1801, a scion of one of the leading families of the state. After obtaining a preparatory education in Beaufort and Charleston, he entered Harvard, where he graduated summa cum laude in 1821. He was a member of the South Carolina House of Representatives in 1826, and a member of Congress from 1829 to 1833. Meanwhile he was one of the signers of the celebrated Nullification Ordinance of 1832. Three years later he became president of what is now the University of South Carolina, which was greatly expanded during his administration. Barnwell retired from this post in 1841 because of ill health and returned to his plantation, where he resided until he was appointed in 1850 to fill the unexpired term of John C. Calhoun in the United States Senate.

A moderate rather than an extreme states' righter, Barnwell was a member of South Carolina's secession convention; was one of three commissioners appointed to treat with President Buchanan; and in February, 1861, was named to the Southern Convention in Montgomery of which he was elected temporary chairman, and which resolved itself into the Provisional Confederate Congress. Here he was responsible for his delegation's support of Jefferson Davis for president; Davis, in turn, obligingly offered Barnwell the state portfolio, which

Barnwell declined. He was later elected to the Confederate Senate, where he remained until the end. Barnwell was chairman of the Senate Committee on Finance and was soon considered one of the administration's strongest supporters; the perceptive Mrs. Chesnut once observed that "Only Mr. Barnwell stands by Jeff Davis."[1] But she was partially deceived by Barnwell's unruffled demeanor and by his close attention to routine matters, for in fiscal matters he was quite conservative, preferring low taxes, no price and currency controls, and the immediate audit of state claims against the Confederacy, all of which represented an antiadministration viewpoint. He also argued that Congress should encourage rather than discourage the planting of cotton. However, on army matters and on affairs clearly executive in nature, the central government had few stronger friends. As late as 1865 he was one of two senators opposed to creating the office of general-in-chief lest it threaten Davis' authority.

Barnwell was ruined by the war, his property destroyed, and his Negroes expropriated. In 1865 he moved to Greenville, in the western part of the state, and the same year he was appointed chairman of the faculty of the University of South Carolina. However, in 1873 he was removed by the Negro-Carpetbagger legislature, and for the next four years he conducted a girls' school in Columbia. When the state was redeemed in 1877, Governor Wade Hampton, a former Confederate lieutenant general, appointed Barnwell librarian of the university, a post which he occupied until his death in Columbia on November 5, 1882. He is buried in St. Helena's Churchyard in Beaufort.

[1] Mary Boykin Chesnut, A Diary from Dixie, ed. Ben Ames Williams (Boston, 1949), 164.

WILLIAM TAYLOR SULLIVAN BARRY (Mississippi), a lifelong resident of Mississippi, was born in Columbus on December 10, 1821, and died there on January 29, 1868. He was graduated from Yale College in the class of 1841, studied law, and practiced in Columbus for several years. From 1849 to 1851 he was a member of the Mississippi legislature. Barry also owned plantations in Oktibbeha and Sunflower counties. He lived for a time in Sunflower County, presumably so he could be elected to Congress in 1852 from his temporary residence; thus he did not have to run against William Barksdale, who represented the Columbus district. He was again a member of the legislature, and its speaker, in 1855. Barry was a full-bore, proslavery, immediate secessionist, and he withdrew from the 1860 Democratic national convention in Charleston because the platform did not expressly deny the power of the federal government to legislate against slavery. He presided over Mississippi's secession convention, which in turn sent him to the Provisional Congress.

There, in keeping with the sentiments of his Mississippi colleagues, he advocated such extreme measures as reopening the African slave trade and by constitutional enactment prohibiting any state from abolishing slavery without the unanimous consent of the others. He advocated giving the president unlimited powers to raise volunteers for the army, the nonrecognition of United States patents, and complete commercial independence for the Confederacy. Barry did not seek election to the Regular Congress; instead he recruited the Thirty-Fifth Mississippi Infantry and was made its colonel. With it he was captured and paroled at Vicksburg, shot through the lung at Allatoona in the course of the Atlanta campaign, and finally captured upon the surrender of Fort Blakely near Mobile on April 9, 1865—the same day Lee surrendered at Appomattox. Following the war Colonel Barry practiced law in Columbus. He was buried there in Odd Fellows Cemetery. His wife was a daughter of Thomas Fearn (*q.v.*).

FRANCIS STEBBINS BARTOW (Georgia) was born September 6, 1816, at Savannah, Georgia. He was educated at Franklin College (predecessor of the University of Georgia) and at Yale Law School. He later studied law under Judge John McPherson Berrien, whose daughter Bartow married. Originally a Whig in politics, he became a member of the American or Know-Nothing party in 1856 and the next year was defeated for a seat in Congress from the First District. Also in 1856, Bartow had gained some knowledge of military affairs by becoming captain of the Oglethorpe Light Infantry, a militia company composed of the scions of Savannah's leading families. By 1860 Bartow had become a Democrat and a leading secessionist. He was also, aside from his law practice, a large planter and slaveholder, owning eighty-nine Negroes according to the federal census of that year. He took a prominent part in the proceedings of the Georgia secession convention, and when the state seceded and allied itself to the Confederacy, he was elected a member of the Provisional Congress.

As captain of the Oglethorpes, Bartow was one of the detachment which seized Fort McAllister, near Savannah, and while a member of Congress he offered his company's service to President Davis—his was said to be the first company tendered for the war. Bartow divided his time between Congress and the field. In Congress he devoted himself almost entirely to his duties as chairman of the Committee on

Military Affairs. He was so convinced that secession would be peaceful that, paradoxically, he wished to accept volunteers for no more than sixty days, and it was only upon the persuasion of the president that he agreed to twelve-month enlistments. From his scattered votes on other matters Bartow seemed to believe that no further emergency action was needed and that the Confederacy would subsist upon tariff revenue.

Meanwhile, the Oglethorpes were made a part of the Eighth Georgia Infantry, with Bartow as colonel, and entrained for the seat of war in Virginia. Their first service was in the army of General Joseph E. Johnston in the lower Shenandoah Valley from whence they proceeded to Manassas. On July 21, 1861, while in command of a demibrigade consisting of the Seventh and Eighth Georgia Infantries, Bartow, while in the act of rallying his men on the Henry House Hill, was almost instantly killed by a rifle ball. His last words were: "They have killed me, boys, but never give up the field." His body was taken to Savannah for burial in Bonaventure Cemetery.[1]

[1] A sketch of Bartow, neither fully complete nor entirely accurate, is to be found in Northen (ed.), *Men of Mark in Georgia*, III, 115–18.

NATHAN BASS (Georgia) was born October 1, 1808, certainly in Georgia, and probably in Putnam County, whence his parents had moved from Virginia. He is said to have been educated at Mount Pleasant Academy, the location of which is unknown to the Georgia Historical Society, but which may have been in the hamlet of Mount Pleasant in Wayne County.[1] Shortly after 1840 Bass took his family, including two stepdaughters, to the newly opened Floyd County in northwest Georgia, where they were listed as early settlers of Rome. After acquiring land and slaves in Floyd County, Bass moved with his family in 1851 to Macon in Bibb County, where he came to be regarded as one of the wealthiest men in Georgia—his personal property in Bibb County alone was worth $351,000 in 1860 and his real estate was worth $251,000. Besides this, he retained ownership of his land and Negroes in Floyd County, and an undetermined interest in plantation lands in Barbour County, Alabama.[2]

As a Union Democrat, Bass was for years active in politics as well as in civic affairs. He served as vice-president of the Cotton Planters' Convention of the Southern States in 1851; and five years later he was appointed chairman of the Kansas Aid Meeting, formed to combat the abolitionist movement and to lend assistance to proslavery settlers in the new territory. As president of the Cotton Planters' Association,

Bass presided at the inaugural of the Belgian Fair in Macon. When Georgia seceded the next year, he went with his state despite his Union principles. When Eugenius A. Nisbet (*q.v.*) resigned from the Provisional Congress, Bass, without his knowledge, was chosen to succeed him. Bass took his seat January 14, 1862, and thus served only until adjournment on February 17. During his brief tenure he took little part in lawmaking but apparently had confidence in Jefferson Davis; he granted the War Department whatever use of manpower it requested. His few votes on other matters, however, indicate that he opposed any control by the Confederate government over the economy. He made no effort to seek election to the Regular Congress.

In the remaining course of the war Bass was prominent in supporting various civic enterprises while two of his sons served in the Confederate army. At its termination he was, of course, ruined by inflation, the expropriation of his slave property, and the subsequent decline of the southern economy. By 1872 he had moved back to Rome, Georgia, where he lived, bereft of his former land holdings, in a sort of genteel poverty until his death there on September 22, 1890, at the age of eighty-two. He was buried in Myrtle Hill Cemetery in Rome, with his wife and several of his sons and daughters.

[1] His father, John H. Bass, left a will in Putnam County, and Nathan was a resident of the county as early as 1820. (Information provided by Mrs. Slade Willingham, Washington Memorial Library, Macon, Ga.)

[2] Bass enjoys the unusual distinction of having been enumerated twice in the 1860 federal census: once in Bibb County (Macon), and once in Floyd County (Rome). He owned considerable land and slaves in both counties and is sometimes supposed to have been two different men.

FELIX IVES BATSON (Arkansas) was a native of Tennessee, born September 6, 1819, probably in Dickson County, but he moved at an early age to Humphreys County, where he lived near Waverly. It may be assumed that he gained his early education in the local schools; it is not known where he studied law or was admitted to the bar, nor when he went to Arkansas. He was one of Clarksville's first lawyers, and in 1853 he was made judge of the fourth judicial circuit. Five years later he was elevated to the Arkansas supreme bench.

Batson was an early secessionist, and as a member of both the March and May, 1861, conventions he voted for disunion.[1] In November he won election to the First Regular Congress over Hugh F. Thomason (*q.v.*) on the grounds of having been the stronger secessionist. He won reelection in 1863, although he was absent from Congress from December, 1863, until November, 1864, missing two entire sessions. Batson seldom interjected his opinions during debate, but from the first he was willing to grant almost any authority to the central government to protect his exposed state. During 1862 and 1863 when much of Arkansas was still in Confederate hands, he tried to reserve for it a fair number of state employees and local defense troops. During the Second Congress, when the state was largely overrun by the enemy, his only significant difference of opinion with the administration was his opposition to arming the slaves.

When the war was over, Batson resumed his law practice in Clarksville for the few years that were left to him. His only child, a daughter, had married Jordan E. Cravens, a colonel in the Confederate army who would serve three terms in the U.S. Congress after the Reconstruction period ended. Judge Batson died in their home in Clarksville on March 11, 1871, and was buried in Oakland Cemetery.

[1] On January 15, 1861, the Arkansas General Assembly called for an election on February 18 for delegates to a convention to be held on March 4. This convention decided against secession. After the firing on Sumter and Lincoln's call for volunteers, the president of the convention reassembled it on May 6, and it then adopted an ordinance of secession. David Y. Thomas, *Arkansas in War and Reconstruction, 1861–1874* (Little Rock, 1926), 52–81.

JOHN ROBERT BAYLOR (Texas) was born July 20, 1822, in Paris, Kentucky. His education was limited to the local schools of Bourbon County, and at the age of seventeen he went to Texas where, in the following year, he took part in the campaign against the Comanches under Colonel J. H. Moore, an early-day Texas Indian fighter. In 1853 Baylor was elected to the Texas legislature, but soon afterwards he was appointed agent to the same Comanches with whom he had contested. He and the state Indian superintendent disagreed on policies and Baylor was dismissed. In 1859, at the head of a group of like-minded ranchers, he forced the abandonment of the Brazos Indian reservation and the removal of its inhabitants to Indian Territory.

While making his home on a ranch near Weatherford, Texas, Baylor was a delegate to the state secession convention. He then joined the Confederate army and, as lieutenant colonel of the Second Texas Mounted Rifles, captured El Paso and the surrounding area and was appointed governor of the Confederate Territory of Arizona, with headquarters at Mesilla, New Mexico. As such he was in charge of Indian policy, and as an old Indian fighter he operated on the principle that the only good Indian was a dead one. The plains tribes were savagely depredating on Americans and native Mexicans alike at the time, and Baylor proposed a policy of total extermination in an open

19

letter to Jefferson Davis, which, although heartily supported by virtually everybody personally involved (except, of course, the Indians), resulted in his dismissal as governor. Baylor then returned to Texas to vindicate himself and in 1863 overwhelmingly defeated Malcom D. Graham (q.v.), the proadministration incumbent, in a race for a seat in the Second Regular Congress. While he was a member, he consistently voted to restrict Davis' functions as commander-in-chief and against the imposition of martial law, but otherwise he supported the war effort zealously. Although he was a silent member, his voting record indicates a determination to use the last resources of the Confederacy and to oppose any and all peace overtures.

After the war Baylor lived for a time in San Antonio but finally settled in Montell, Texas, a small community northwest of Uvalde, where he died on February 6, 1894, and where he is buried. The Baylors were an independent lot, highly motivated by the fancied slight; Baylor's brother, Colonel George W. Baylor of the Second Texas Cavalry, killed General John A. Wharton in an affray at a Houston hotel room only three days before Lee's surrender.

CASPAR WISTAR BELL (Missouri) was born in Prince Edward County, Virginia, February 2, 1819, descended on both sides of his family from distinguished revolutionary forebears.[1] He received his early education from private tutors, and in 1837 he was graduated with high honors from the College of William and Mary. Two years later he was graduated in law from the University of Virginia. Bell emigrated to Missouri in 1843 and located in Brunswick, Charlton County, to practice his profession. Until 1860, he was a prominent member of the bar in that largely slaveholding section of Missouri lying along the Missouri River, but he held no public office.

When the Missouri convention refused to secede from the Union after Lincoln's call for volunteers in April, 1861, Governor Claiborne Jackson called an extra session of the General Assembly to "repel invasion." The convention itself reassembled in July and declared Jackson deposed. Jackson then convoked at Neosho the secessionist members of the General Assembly and this rump legislature passed an act of secession on October 28, 1861—hardly to be construed as an expression of the sentiments of the majority of Missouri voters. It then proceeded to appoint seven representatives and two senators to serve in the Confederate Congress until an election could be held.[2] Bell was appointed as one of the seven representatives and duly made his way to Richmond, virtually a congressman without a constituency, as were his Missouri and Kentucky colleagues. In the absence of any arrangement for an election until May, 1864, when he was defeated by a handful of soldier and refugee votes in a farcical poll set up by Congress, Bell continued to occupy a seat in the House. He distinguished himself by a total lack of regard for President Davis, and was identified in some quarters as a disciple of Henry S. Foote, whose dislike of Davis amounted to monomania. Bell voted almost invariably to override the president's vetoes, to restrict his appointive powers, and in one instance to publish certain embarrassing presidential correspondence. On the other hand, he was a strong Confederate except in the matter of suspending the writ of habeas corpus. While serving in Congress he wrote a "Missouri Column" for the Richmond *Examiner*.

When he returned to Brunswick in 1867, having practiced law for a year in Danville, Virginia, Bell was without means and had to start a whole new career. Being favorably known in his community, he renewed his old practice, was successful, and was even elected prosecuting attorney of his judicial district, a post whose duties he discharged to the satisfaction of all concerned. In the spring of 1861, Bell served briefly as adjutant general of a division of the Missouri State Guard, from which he derived the honorific of "General" in later life. He died in Brunswick on October 27, 1898, and was buried there in Douglas Cemetery.

[1] The spelling of Bell's given names and the date of his birth are taken from his monument in Douglas Cemetery, Brunswick. These do not agree with some published sources.

[2] The designee from the Seventh Congressional District, one Dr. Hyer, chose never to take his seat, with the result that southeastern Missouri went unrepresented in the First Congress. By the time R. A. Hatcher (*q.v.*) took his seat in the Second Congress, Senator R. L. Y. Peyton (*q.v.*) had died and his successor, George G. Vest (*q.v.*), was transferred from the House to the Senate. Thus at no time did the state have its full complement of representation in Congress.

HIRAM PARKS BELL[1] (Georgia) was born on a small farm in Jackson County, Georgia, on January 19, 1827. For a number of years he helped his father on the farm, obtaining only six months of schooling in that time. But when he was twenty he borrowed money and attended the academy in Cumming for two years. Bell then taught school for two more years in Ellijay and studied law in his spare time. He was admitted to the bar in 1849 and began practicing in Cumming. By his first wife he was a brother-in-law of George N. Lester (*q.v.*). Bell's first public office was as a Whig member of the Georgia secession convention, in which he strongly opposed disunion. But when Georgia seceded, Bell accepted a commission to hurry to Tennessee and persuade its government to follow suit. Bell was elected to the Georgia Senate in October, 1861, but resigned after one year and raised a company which became Company I of the Forty-third Georgia Regiment. He eventually attained the rank of colonel of that regiment. In December, 1862, Bell was wounded at Chickasaw Bayou near Vicksburg and eventually had to resign his commission. In October, 1863, he was elected to the Confederate House of Representatives.

In his autobiography Bell reported that he and several other Georgians reached Richmond determined to force the president to open peace negotiations. Meanwhile he opposed most efforts made in Congress to adopt new war measures or to extend existing ones. In particular Bell aligned himself with those who decried what they considered to be class legislation. First he attempted to speed the settlement of claims against the Confederacy; next he proposed a change to only ad valorem taxation in order to avoid inequities; and finally he sought to end completely the impressment of farm produce. Bell left Congress a month before it ended to take his family to safety.

After the war Bell's law practice became one of the largest in his district. In 1868 and 1876 he was a Democratic elector, and in 1872 and 1876 he was elected to Congress. In Congress his foremost interest was to secure financial legislation benefiting the South, particularly for railroad development in north Georgia. Bell lost his race for reelection in 1878, and his last political service was in the state senate from 1898 to 1901. Here he was chairman of a joint committee to revise those parts of the Georgia constitution dealing with taxation. Bell died in Atlanta on August 16, 1907, and is buried in the Cumming cemetery.

[1] Northen (ed.), *Men of Mark in Georgia*, III, 226–30.

MARK HARDEN BLANDFORD[1] (Georgia) was born of well-to-do parents in Warren County, Georgia, on July 13, 1826. After a good academic education near home he entered Mercer University, but he soon decided to concentrate upon the law and began reading under Robert Hardeman in Clinton. He was admitted to the bar before his eighteenth birthday, and a special act of the legislature was necessary before he could practice. Blandford opened his first office in Hamilton in 1844, but he soon moved to Tazwell where he practiced until the war with Mexico began. He then volunteered and served for almost a year as a sergeant in the First Georgia Regiment. When the war ended Blandford settled in Buena Vista and quickly developed a large law practice as well as a thriving mercantile business.

When Georgia seceded, Blandford raised and was elected captain of

22

a company which became part of "the bloody Twelfth" Georgia Regiment. In the battle of McDowell, Virginia, he was so severely wounded that his right arm had to be amputated. On April 29, 1863, and before Blandford's wound had completely healed, President Jefferson Davis appointed him a judge in the Confederate military court with the rank of lieutenant. That October, Blandford was a candidate for the Confederate House of Representatives and easily defeated the incumbent.

In Richmond, Blandford worked to keep the army at full strength if at all possible. On November 7, 1864, he proposed to end all exemptions from military service and to give the president complete use of all manpower. Nor was Blandford often inclined to limit the president's hand in other executive matters. He was convinced, however, that the central government already had too much control over the economy. He did everything possible to reverse this trend, suggesting that Congress repeal its ban on the importation of luxuries and that it restrict impressments only to agents appointed specifically for that purpose. Blandford remained at his post in Richmond until the last day of Congress.

After the war Blandford resumed his law practice in Buena Vista, but he moved to Columbus in 1869. In 1872 the Georgia legislature elected him an associate justice of the supreme court, where he served for the next eight years. On his retirement Blandford returned once more to private practice, working until his death in Columbus on January 31, 1902. He is buried in Linwood Cemetery.[2]

[1] Northen (ed.), *Men of Mark in Georgia*, III, 296–98.
[2] Information on the place of Blandford's interment was provided by Jeanne Hollis, Bradley Memorial Library, Columbus, Ga.

THOMAS STANHOPE BOCOCK (Virginia) was born May 18, 1815, in that part of Buckingham County which is now Appomattox. He was educated largely by his brother Willis (later attorney general of Virginia), save for two years at Hampden-Sydney College, from which he was graduated in 1838. Having studied law and been admitted to the bar under the tutelage of Willis, Thomas Bocock was elected to the Virginia General Assembly at the age of twenty-seven. After a term as county commonwealth's attorney, he went to the United States House of Representatives in 1847. He remained there until Virginia passed its secession resolution, serving as chairman of the Committee on Naval Affairs for a decade, and running as the Democratic candidate for the speakership against John Sherman in the celebrated contest of 1859–1860, when a compromise candidate was finally elected on the forty-fourth ballot.

Bocock was a member of all three Confederate Congresses and was elected speaker of both the First and Second Regular congresses by unanimous votes. Because of his speakership he seldom participated in debate unless some legislative procedure was under discussion. For the most part he voted to uphold and strengthen administration policies. But during 1862 and 1863 his congressional district, removed from the seat of war, was vulnerable to impressment, high taxes, and other types of economic regimentation, all of which he opposed as being oppressive to his constituents. Subsequently, however, he reconciled himself to the necessity for sacrifice and opposed only the administration's request to arm slaves. In January, 1865, he headed the Virginia delegation which waited upon President Davis to advise him that the House wanted confidence in the cabinet and was prepared to pass a resolution to that effect, an errand which constructively came to naught, except for the voluntary resignation of Secretary of War Seddon.

After the war, as a moderate Conservative, Bocock took a leading part in the so-called Readjuster Movement, advocating a compromise between outright repudiation of Virginia's Confederate debt and total assumption. Meanwhile his law practice prospered, and he himself was greatly in demand as a speaker and presiding officer of government and party functions. He died at his estate, Wildway, near Appomattox Court House, August 5, 1891, and was buried in the family cemetery there.

MILLEDGE LUKE BONHAM (South Carolina) was born at Red Bank (now Saluda), South Carolina, on December 25, 1813, of a family which could trace its American origins to the *Mayflower* pilgrims. He attended academies in Edgefield and Abbeville. He then enrolled in South Carolina College, from which he graduated in 1834. He began studying law, but he took time off in 1836 to act as adjutant general of the South Carolina brigade in the Seminole War. He began practicing law in Edgefield in 1837 and later added planting to his interests, but he once again succumbed to his zest for war, serving as lieutenant colonel in the Mexican War. Bonham's political life began in 1840 when he was elected as a states' rights Democrat to the legislature. After serving there for four years, he was district solicitor from 1848 to 1857. He was then elected to Congress to fill the unexpired term of his cousin, Preston Brooks, who has resigned after caning Charles Sumner so brutally. Bonham was reelected and remained in Congress until South Carolina seceded. An early secessionist, he accepted the appointment

24

as commander of the South Carolina army around Charleston. In April he became a brigadier general in the Confederate army and saw considerable action in Virginia. In November, 1861, he was elected to the Confederate House of Representatives and resigned his commission the following January.

As a congressman Bonham was almost exclusively interested in army affairs. His chief goal was to prevent Congress from stripping the states of their manpower. Rather than extend the draft age to forty-five he proposed a call upon the states for their quota of 300,000 men, to be called up only when needed. He also favored an exceptionally long exemption list. But on other subjects Bonham supported the central government so vigorously that some accused him of an *"entente cordial"* with the administration. He was particularly ready to give the government broad controls over the economy, and he was one of the few Carolinians ever to vote to suspend the writ of habeas corpus.

Bonham resigned on January 17, 1863, upon his election as governor. At the expiration of this two-year term he was reappointed brigadier general of cavalry, and he fought under Joseph E. Johnston in the face of Sherman's march through the Carolinas. After the war Bonham resumed his law practice and also began planting. He was in the legislature again from 1865 to 1867 and was a delegate to the national Democratic convention of 1868. In 1876 he reentered politics once more when he became an active participant in the "Red Shirt" activities to restore white supremacy. Bonham became railroad commissioner in 1878 and served until his death. He died at Sulphur Springs, North Carolina, on August 27, 1890. He is buried in Elmwood Cemetery, Columbia, South Carolina.

ALEXANDER ROBINSON BOTELER (Virginia) was born May 16, 1815, at Shepherdstown, Virginia, now West Virginia. His mother having died when he was four, he grew up in his maternal grandmother's house in Baltimore and received his early education there. He was graduated from Princeton in 1835, and soon after, having married, he returned to his birthplace to live. Boteler's primary interest was in his father's farm, Fountain Rock, but he also devoted time to politics, a universal preoccupation of the day, and in 1852 he was a presidential elector on the Whig ticket. After the dissolution of the Whig organization, he joined the Know-Nothings and went to Congress in 1859 under the American party label.

In the crisis of 1860–1861 Boteler was an avowed cooperationist and made a powerful speech in behalf of the Union on the House floor. But when his state convention voted for secession, he accepted appointment to the Provisional Congress and narrowly won election to the First Regular Congress over several rivals. He served as a member or chairman on several standing committees, but his principal concern was the reconquest of his congressional district, two-thirds of which became a part of West Virginia when that state was established by act of the United States Congress. To strengthen the Confederacy at almost any cost for this purpose, he seldom opposed administration measures or favored bills limiting the administration's authority. In minor matters he favored more state control over local defense units and opposed the policy of complete repudiation of Treasury notes not exchanged by a certain date. When not in Richmond, Boteler served, with the rank of colonel, on the staff of General Thomas J. Jackson. He also acted as a sort of liaison officer between the often touchy Stonewall and his administrative superiors, as well as the civil authorities, until Jackson's death. After that event he was for a time on the staff of General Jeb Stuart, having been decisively defeated for reelection to Congress in the fall of 1863.

Following the war Boteler continued to be active in public life: he was West Virginia's commissioner to the Philadelphia Centennial Exposition in 1876, a member of the Tariff Commission by appointment of President Arthur, and an official of the Department of Justice in later years. He was also the author of several historical treatises as well as an artist of some talent. Colonel Boteler died May 8, 1892, in Shepherdstown and was buried there in Elmwood Cemetery.

ELIAS CORNELIUS BOUDINOT (Cherokee Nation), whose family name was actually Watie, was the son of a full-blooded Cherokee father[1] and a white mother, and he was the nephew of General Stand Watie, C.S.A. He was born near the site of Rome, Georgia, on August 1, 1835, and was thus the youngest member of the Confederate Congress. He grew up and was educated in New England among his mother's relatives. After a year spent working as a civil engineer with an Ohio railroad, he settled in Fayetteville, Arkansas, where he studied law and was admitted to the bar in 1856. He also engaged in newspaper work and in 1860 was elected chairman of the Arkansas Democratic state central committee. Boudinot then moved to Little Rock and the following year acted as secretary of the secession convention.

After the secession of Arkansas, Boudinot went to the Indian Territory and aided his uncle in raising a regiment for the Confederate cause in the Cherokee Nation, a regiment in which he rose to the rank of lieutenant colonel. On August 21, 1861, the Cherokee legislature declared for secession, stipulating that their first congressman should be elected in whatever manner the principal chief should determine. Boudinot was probably elected by the tribal council. He did not take his seat until October 9, 1862. A year later he was appointed a "corresponding member" of the Committee on Indian Affairs without the privilege of voting, in line with the various treaties concluded by the Confederacy with the Cherokees, Choctaws, Chickasaws, Seminoles, and Creeks (the Five Civilized Tribes), whereby each nation was promised a nonvoting representative.[2] Boudinot was the only Indian representative who placed a broad interpretation on the rights of a "nonvoting" congressman, for he occasionally proposed amendments to bills affecting the Indians. He also introduced bills providing for the clarification of procedures governing Indian elections and for systematizing the distribution of money and supplies to them under treaty obligations.

After the close of the war Colonel Boudinot took a prominent part in negotiations with the government leading to the restoration of tribal rights to the Cherokees, who were threatened with forfeiture by reason of their adherence to the Confederacy. He also was an exponent of many advanced ideas for his people, including education, the breakup of tribal fetishes, and the allotment of lands in severalty, views which were not popular with the Indians and which earned him the enmity of many. Boudinot then spent a number of years in Washington. During the later years of his life he resided in Fort Smith, Arkansas, practicing law and farming in the Territory. He died at his residence in Fort Smith on September 27, 1890, and was buried in Oak Grove Cemetery there.

---

[1] Boudinot's father, also named Elias, was born in Georgia among his people, the Cherokees. He was sent by missionaries to be educated at the mission school in Cornwall, Connecticut, and while there adopted the name of the benefactor of the school, the revolutionary statesman Elias Boudinot.

[2] The treaties did not define the rights and privileges of these delegates; accordingly, President Davis placed in the hands of Congress the onus of determining whether, and on what grounds, the Indian delegates should be admitted. The Committee on Indian Affairs suggested that they should be permitted to propose and discuss measures in which their nation "is particularly interested," and this rule of thumb was tacitly adopted.

WILLIAM WATERS BOYCE (South Carolina) was born October 24, 1818, in Charleston, South Carolina. After receiving his early education in private academies there, he attended South Carolina College (now the University of South Carolina) and the University of Virginia at Charlottesville. He then studied law and was admitted to the bar in 1839.

Boyce began the practice of law in Winnsboro, and from that place he was elected to the state house of representatives. From 1853 until December 21, 1860, when he withdrew upon the secession of his state, Boyce served in the U.S. House of Representatives, having been elected as a states' rights Democrat. After secession he was elected to all three Confederate Congresses without opposition; he was certainly one of the few, if not the only member, who could claim this distinction. In the Second Congress he was chairman of the Committee on Naval Affairs. For much of the war he supported a surprisingly strong central economic program; his primary reservation in military matters was his desire to keep large numbers of men in local defense duty. However, his demand for "Audacity! *Audacity*! *AUDACITY*!" was dampened by his conviction that President Davis was both incompetent and "puffed up with his own conceit." Boyce wished Congress to preempt control over foreign policy; he allowed Davis few discretionary powers in military matters; and he opposed the suspension of habeas corpus primarily because it placed arbitrary power in the wrong hands. To circumscribe Davis further, Boyce secured a constitutional prohibition against the reelection of a president, and he later proposed the office of general-in-chief and a committee on the conduct of the war. After his "cabal" to remove Davis failed, Boyce in 1864 published a dramatic open letter urging the president to call a convention of all the states of the old Union to discuss peace. When this failed, he remained prominent in peace circles until the end. Boyce, who had owned twenty-seven Negroes and property valued at nearly sixty thousand dollars in 1860, was wiped out by the war, and in 1866 he moved to Washington, D.C., where he practiced law until he retired a few years before his death. He died at his country home, Ashland, in Fairfax County, Virginia, February 3, 1890, and was buried in the Episcopal Cemetery at Winnsboro, South Carolina.

ALEXANDER BLACKBURN BRADFORD (Mississippi), one of the older members of the Congress, was born June 2, 1799, in Jefferson County, Tennessee. After a common-school education he read law in Knoxville and then settled in Jackson, Tennessee, where he was immediately elected attorney general of the circuit. He was sent to the state senate in 1837, but in the meantime he served in the Creek War of 1836 and, being a major general of Tennessee militia, commanded the Second Tennessee Regiment. In 1839 Bradford moved to Holly Springs, Mississippi, to practice law. He was a member of the Mississippi legislature on several occasions but, being of the Whig persuasion, failed to be elected to higher office. When the Mexican War broke out, Bradford was elected major of the celebrated First Mississippi Rifles, whose colonel was Jefferson Davis. He was distinguished for intrepidity, particularly at Buena Vista, and on his return was voted a sword by the state.

Bradford was a member of the Mississippi House of Representatives in 1861 and, upon the resignation of Alexander M. Clayton (*q. v.*) from the Provisional Congress on May 11, was elected by his colleagues to fill Clayton's unexpired term. However, he could not take his seat until December 5, and the legislation enacted in the last three months of the Provisional Congress tended toward adjustment rather than innovation. Bradford was willing to temporize on most of his states' rights convictions and to support the administration's program of moderate centralization. He did not seek reelection. He was again a member of the Mississippi legislature in 1863 and 1864, representing Bolivar County, where he had established a plantation, Bradford Place, in 1852. He apparently lived there, occasionally practicing law, until his death on July 10, 1873. General Bradford was buried in Hillcrest Cemetery at Holly Springs.

BENJAMIN FRANKLIN BRADLEY (Kentucky) was born about a mile and a half from Georgetown, Scott County, Kentucky, on October 5, 1825. He received an academic education at Georgetown College and then studied law at Transylvania University in Lexington, receiving a degree in 1846. After practicing briefly in his hometown, he assisted in recruiting a company of the Third Kentucky Volunteers for the Mexican War and served first as regimental and then as brigade adjutant until the end of the war. He then returned to Georgetown and resumed his practice. In 1854 Bradley moved to Chicago, where he resided until the beginning of the Civil War. If anyone allied himself to the Confederacy on principle, it was Bradley. He owned no Negroes, was a native of a border state, and had lived for seven years in a northern city, enjoying a lucrative legal practice. Nevertheless, he hurried South and was soon organizing troops for the southern cause. In 1862 he became major of the First Battalion of Kentucky Mounted Riflemen, a command which took part in the West Virginia campaign. While on sick leave he was elected, on February 10, 1864, to be Kentucky's Eleventh District congressman. Like the elections in Missouri, such mandates were somewhat ephemeral, since the provisional Confederate government of Kentucky was based in Macon, Georgia, and had decreed an election to be held by general ticket with each voter voting for one candidate in each of the twelve districts. Nominations were made whenever a group of soldiers and/or civilians agreed on a slate for write-in votes. When Bradley reached Richmond, he was convinced that the recovery of his state from the Federals justified any extremity. As a rule he refused to take part in debate, voted to limit discussion, and voted to give the army whatever it needed. Like most border-state congressmen, Bradley would never consider peace negotiations. In 1868 he was elected clerk of the Scott County circuit court, an office which he held for twelve years. In 1889 Major Bradley was elected to the Kentucky Senate from the counties of Scott, Woodford, and Jessamine. He died at his residence in Georgetown on January 22, 1897, and was buried in Georgetown Cemetery.

ANTHONY MARTIN BRANCH (Texas) was born in Buckingham County, Virginia, July 16, 1823, and was graduated from Hampden-Sydney College in 1842. Five years later he went to Huntsville, Texas, where he formed a law partnership with Henderson Yoakum. Through Yoakum, Branch became an intimate acquaintance of General Sam Houston and was named both executor of Houston's will and guardian of his children. He was elected district attorney in 1850 and a representative to the eighth legislature in 1859. In November, 1861, Branch was elected to the state senate, but on March 20, 1862, he enlisted in the Confederate army and a month later became captain of Company A, Twenty-first Texas Cavalry. In 1863, while still in the army, Branch was nominated for Congress by a citizens' committee angered by Peter W. Gray's (*q.v.*) support of a measure exempting overseers from the army, and he won a decisive victory at the polls. During his congressional career he was first and last an uncompromising exponent of states' rights, concentrating his attention almost exclusively on parochial matters. He worked to prevent Texas manpower from being drained away toward the eastern armies and opposed any interference by Richmond in the Texas economy except for the levying of money taxes. He was particularly dedicated to curbing the powers of General E. Kirby Smith, commanding general of the Trans-Mississippi Department, who had become virtually a dictator in his domain, sometimes referred to as Kirby Smithdom. After the war Branch was elected to the Thirty-ninth and Fortieth U.S. Congresses, but he was refused his seat on both occasions because of his previous Confederate affiliation. He was an active participant in Reconstruction politics and one of the incorporators of the Central Transit Company; however, his life was cut short by yellow fever, and he died in Huntsville on October 3, 1867. He was buried in Oakwood Cemetery there.

ROBERT JEFFERSON BRECKINRIDGE, JR. (Kentucky) was born September 14, 1833, in Baltimore, Maryland, where his father was pastor of the Second Presbyterian Church. One of his brothers was a colonel in the Confederate army; another adhered to the Union and rose to be, after the Civil War, a major general in the United States Army. The family were Kentuckians of Virginia descent.[1] R. J. Breckinridge was a member of the class of 1850 at Centre College, Danville, Kentucky, but did not graduate, instead taking his degree at the University of Virginia in 1852. After spending a couple of years in the U.S. Coast Survey, he began to study law at Danville and in 1856 was graduated from the law department of Transylvania University in Lexington, where he practiced until the outbreak of the Civil War. He raised a company of the Second Kentucky (Confederate) Mounted Infantry, and served with it until February 5, 1862, when he resigned, having been elected to represent the Eleventh Congressional District in the First Regular Congress.[2] He soon found his new duties dull and took extended leaves. During such sessions as he attended, he showed marked interest only in matters of army organization. On one occasion he proposed that volunteers continuing in service by conscription be permitted to reenlist in any company of their choice, but this would have created enormous confusion and the proposal was defeated. He opposed compulsory funding of Treasury notes, asserting it would deprive the refugee class of their subsistence. Otherwise the administration could depend upon his support. He declined to run for reelection; instead, at the termination of the congressional session in February, 1864, he reentered the army as colonel of a cavalry regiment raised in Kentucky. According to his service record in the National Archives, Breckinridge was captured in Woodford County, Kentucky, February 22, 1865, although Long's *The Civil War Day by Day*[3] does not mention an action in Kentucky on that day. He was imprisoned in the Ohio Penitentiary and on Johnson's Island until the end of the war, after which he settled on a farm near Stanford, in Garrard County, Kentucky. He was indicted for treason in the U.S. District Court at Frankfort on November 6, 1861, and his disabilities were not removed until March 9, 1871, by an act of Congress. In 1873 he went to New York with the idea of practicing law, but he soon returned to Danville, Kentucky, and in 1876 was elected judge of a seven-county common-pleas court. Judge Breckinridge continued to live in Danville until his death on March 13, 1915. He was buried in Lexington Cemetery at Lexington, Kentucky.[4]

[1] A first cousin was John Cabell Breckinridge, vice-president of the United States under Buchanan and later a Confederate major general and secretary of war. R. J. Breckinridge, Sr., does not seem to have actively espoused either side.

[2] According to the law of Congress of December 21, 1861, the Confederate provisional

government of Kentucky divided the state into twelve congressional districts and called for an election for representatives to the First Congress. Voting places were provided and elections were held in counties within the then Confederate lines.

[3]Everett B. Long, *The Civil War Day by Day* (New York, 1971).

[4]*The Biographical Encyclopedia of Kentucky* (Cincinnati, 1878); H. Levin (ed.), *The Lawyers and Lawmakers of Kentucky* (Chicago, 1897); Lexington Cemetery to Ezra J. Warner, December 6, 1970.

ROBERT RUFUS BRIDGERS (North Carolina) was born on November 28, 1819, on a small farm in Edgecombe County, North Carolina. He was graduated first in the class of 1841 at the University of North Carolina. In the same year he became licensed to practice law and opened an office in Tarboro. Bridgers had a gift for politics and between 1844 and 1861 he served four terms in the state house of representatives as a Democrat. But business was his chief interest. During the 1850s he organized a bank in Tarboro, bought extensive cotton lands, and promoted a railroad connecting Tarboro with the Wilmington and Weldon Railroad of which he became director in 1861. The same year Bridgers was planning to go to Louisiana to plant sugar, but national affairs seemed so gloomy that he remained in North Carolina and worked for secession. During the Civil War Bridgers developed iron mines and manufactories in western North Carolina, his High Shoals property supplying the state with nails and plows and becoming one of the largest mills in the Confederacy. In November, 1861, he won an uncontested seat as a Confederate congressman.

In Richmond, as could be expected, Bridgers' foremost interest was in the economy. His few legislative proposals generally aimed to encourage manufacturing. In February, 1863, he asked the Ways and Means Committee to consider penalizing speculation and profiteering. Behind the scenes he worked fruitlessly to have Congress encourage cotton production and use it as a basis for money and credit. Bridgers believed, however, that inflation curbs and impressment depressed the economy unnecessarily and opposed both programs. Where the economy was not involved he usually accepted administration leadership. In 1863 Bridgers barely won reelection, and in the Second Congress he revealed a set of attitudes more in accord with North Carolina's war weariness. Most important, he abandoned his efforts to bolster the economy, and the only administration policy that now received his unqualified endorsement was its refusal to suggest peace negotiations to the United States.

After the war Bridgers devoted himself to his business interests. In 1865 he began a twenty-year service as president of the Wilmington and Weldon, which renewed operations with thirteen pieces of rolling stock and eventually became the Atlantic Coast Line. He was also president of the Columbia and Augusta, which continued the Wilmington and Weldon southward. For many years he was president of the Navassa Guano Company, noted for years for its high-quality fertilizer. Bridgers died in Columbia, South Carolina, on December 10, 1888, and was buried in St. James's churchyard in Wilmington.

JOHN WHITE BROCKENBROUGH (Virginia) was born December 23, 1806, in Hanover County, Virginia. He attended William and Mary College at Williamsburg and the University of Virginia at Charlottesville before commencing the study of law at Winchester. He began practice in Hanover County and was soon afterwards elected the commonwealth's attorney. In 1834 he moved to Rockbridge County, and in 1837 he published two volumes of reports containing the decisions of Chief Justice John Marshall in the United States Circuit Court, which were for many years regarded as one of the cornerstones of a Virginia law library.

In 1845 Brockenbrough was appointed by President Polk judge of the United States Court for the Western District of Virginia, a jurisdiction which comprised all of what is now West Virginia. He held the office until 1861, when he was made Confederate States judge for the same district. During the sixteen years of his tenure in the United States court, not one of his decisions was overruled by the Supreme Court. In February, 1861, Judge Brockenbrough was elected by the Virginia legislature as one of the five "peace commissioners" who met in Washington in an attempt to avert civil war. The following June he was elected to the Provisional Confederate Congress, in which he served on the Committee on Judiciary. He was primarily interested in establishing the routine forms of government for the new nation and introducing resolutions and bills on naval construction, gunpowder manufacture, judicial appointments, and other such matters. Having been an early advocate of southern independence and a representative of a district quickly threatened by Federal invasion, he enthusiastically supported all major administration programs. He chose not to run for election to the Regular Congress and instead accepted the judicial appointment.

Judge Brockenbrough had been a trustee of Washington College (now Washington and Lee University) since 1852, and in 1865 he was made rector of the board, an office in which he was instrumental in securing General Robert E. Lee for the presidency of the institution. For many years, he also conducted the Lexington Law School, which in 1866 became affiliated with Washington College. Judge Brockenbrough died in Lexington on February 20, 1877, and was buried there in Jackson Memorial Cemetery.

WALKER BROOKE (Mississippi) was a native of Virginia, born near Winchester on December 25, 1813. He attended the public schools in Richmond, Virginia, and Georgetown in the District of Columbia and then was graduated from the University of Virginia in 1835. After admission to the bar he began practice in Lexington, a small, county-seat town in central Mississippi. He was elected to the lower house of the Mississippi legislature in 1848 and to the state senate in 1850 and 1852. When Henry S. Foote resigned from the United States Senate in order to become governor of the state, Brooke was elected to fill his unexpired term and served from March 11, 1852, until the inauguration of Franklin Pierce on March 4, 1853. He was not a candidate for reelection and resumed his law practice in Lexington. He moved to Vicksburg in 1857, however, and was subsequently identified with that city. Before and during the Mississippi secession convention, of which he was a member, Brooke, a longtime Whig, was an avowed disciple of cooperation with the federal government. However, when his efforts were unavailing, he voted to secede. Even then he proposed to submit the ordinance to the people for ratification—also to no avail. He was then elected to the Provisional Congress. Brooke was an energetic chairman of the Committee on Patents and took an active interest in a variety of other matters. He was a vigorous Confederate nationalist and had few reservations about increasing the authority of the central government. It was Brooke's suggestion to the Committee on Finance that led to the valuable produce loan program, but his proposal that the Post Office Department need not be self-supporting was roundly defeated. He ran twice for the Confederate Senate but was both times defeated, presumably because south Mississippi already had one senator (Albert G. Brown [*q.v.*]). After his congressional service he was appointed a member of the permanent military court of the Confederate states. Brooke did not long survive the war; he died in Vicksburg on December 18, 1869, and was buried in Vicksburg Cemetery.

ALBERT GALLATIN BROWN (Mississippi), United States congressman and senator, governor of Mississippi, and Confederate senator, was born in Chester District, South Carolina, on May 31, 1813. He was a far more important figure under the aegis of the United States than he was under that of the Confederacy, or in the postbellum years when his moderate stance on Reconstruction was odium to his old constituents.

34

A measure of this relative importance can be gleaned from the standard account of Brown's life in the *Dictionary of American Biography*, which devotes three columns to his life antebellum and fifteen lines to the twenty years thereafter. When Brown was ten, his parents emigrated to the then almost new state of Mississippi, settling in what is now Copiah County. He was educated at Mississippi College and at Jefferson College in Washington, Mississippi. He then studied law and, after admission to the bar, began his practice in Gallatin, a now extinct town near Hazelhurst, before he had attained legal age. Meanwhile, on the strength of his six months of military training at Jefferson College, he was elected colonel of the Copiah County militia at the age of nineteen, and was promoted brigadier general a year later.

In 1835 Brown commenced a political career which would continue almost without interruption for thirty years. He served in the legislature from 1835 to 1839, in Congress from 1839–1841, was judge of the superior court in 1842–1843, governor of Mississippi for two terms, 1844–1848, then in Congress again from 1847 to 1853. The following year he was elected to fill a vacancy in the United States Senate and served until he withdrew on January 12, 1861. The Mississippi legislature chose him its senior senator for a four-year term in November, 1861. Before that he had recruited a company of the Eighteenth Mississippi Infantry, of which he was captain, and which he took into battle at First Manassas.

In the Confederate Senate Brown was chairman of the Committee on Naval Affairs in both congresses. Before secession he tended more toward sectionalism than the theory of strict states' rights, and now the survival of the Confederacy was, in his eyes, the *sine qua non*. He believed that Congress possessed almost unlimited war powers and, on December 10, 1863, introduced a dramatic series of resolutions calling for total commitment to victory. In their support he would "save the country first, and settle constitutional constructions afterwards."[1] At different times he introduced bills restricting cotton production, drafting all men capable of bearing arms, establishing a volunteer navy for privateering, and drafting and emancipating 200,000 slaves. In the postwar period Brown advised the people of his state "to meet Congress on its own platform and shake hands"; in other words, to submit to the inevitable, a policy which might have reaped untold benefits, but which, instead, elicited scorn and derision. He never again ran for office but devoted himself to farming near Terry, in Hinds County, Mississippi, where he died on June 12, 1880. He was buried in Greenwood Cemetery, Jackson, Mississippi.

[1]*State of the Country, Speech of Hon. A. G. Brown, of Mississippi, in the Confederate Senate, December 24, 1863.*

ELI METCALFE BRUCE (Kentucky) was a native of Kentucky, born near Flemingsburg on February 22, 1828. He was brought up on his father's farm, was educated in the neighborhood schools, and at the age of nineteen became a clerk in a dry-goods store in Maysville. Later he was a partner with his uncle in a pork-packing plant in Cincinnati, and from 1854 to 1859 he engaged with another uncle in the manufacture of pig iron near Terre Haute, Indiana. In 1859 Bruce sold his interest in the iron business and reengaged in pork-packing; he soon established a chain of packing houses on the Wabash, Missouri, and Mississippi rivers, with his headquarters at St. Louis. In 1861, having determined to cast his lot with the South, Bruce closed his packing plants in the North and changed his base of operations to Chattanooga, Tennessee; Augusta, Georgia; and other southern points. According to Ed Porter Thompson,[1] Bruce became the Confederacy's main source for supplies of all kinds: buying blockade runners, exporting cotton to bring back war materials, and engaging in a wide range of other activities. Early in 1862 he was elected Ninth district congressman by the Confederate element in Kentucky, and he was reelected two years later by the soldier and refugee vote. As an important member of the Committee on Ways and Means, Bruce's greatest concern was for the Confederacy's tottering financial structure; and his public and private interests sometimes overlapped. He speculated at one time in the inauspicious Erlanger loan, but he soon withdrew his investments and was exonerated by a congressional investigation which he had himself asked for. On money matters he was a conservative; he also criticized government interference in the economy in all its aspects, but he fervently advocated carrying the war to the enemy, supported all requisite legislation, and in 1862 implored President Davis to take the field personally. At the close of the war Bruce went to Washington and obtained a presidential pardon from Andrew Johnson. He then proceeded to New York and took over the operation of the Southern Hotel at 673 Broadway, where, it is said, no former Confederate ever found a want of hospitality, whatever his financial condition. Bruce died there suddenly, of heart disease, on December 15, 1866. He was first buried in Linden Grove Cemetery in Covington, Kentucky; his remains were moved in 1917 to Highland Cemetery in nearby Fort Mitchell.[2]

---

[1] Ed Porter Thompson, *History of the Orphan Brigade* (Louisville, 1898).

[2] Aside from the printed source noted, the authors are greatly obligated for information to George S. Bruce, Houston, Tex., a grandson of Eli M. Bruce, and to Chester F. Geaslen, Fort Wright, Ky., an authority on the history of Cincinnati and vicinity.

HORATIO WASHINGTON BRUCE (Kentucky), no discernible relation to Eli Metcalfe Bruce (*q.v.*), was born near Vanceburg in Lewis County, Kentucky, on February 22, 1830. His father was a lawyer, merchant, farmer, and mill-owner who had represented his county in the legislature. The younger Bruce was educated at private schools in Lewis County and in Manchester, Ohio, but never had any college training, despite which he engaged in a variety of practical occupations before studying law and being admitted to the bar in Flemingsburg at the age of twenty-one. He occupied a number of positions of trust in Fleming County in subsequent years and in 1855 went to the legislature, as had his father thirty years before. In 1856 Bruce was elected commonwealth's attorney for the six-county Tenth Judicial District. The same year he married a sister of the future Confederate general Ben Hardin Helm, whose wife was, in turn, a half-sister of Mrs. Abraham Lincoln. After moving to Louisville in 1858, he practiced law in partnership with his brother-in-law in that city. Bruce was defeated for Congress at the special election of 1861, running on a states' rights ticket, but later in the year he was a member of the so-called Southern Conference at Russellville, Kentucky, and the later "Sovereignty Convention," held in November, which voted Kentucky out of the Union, and established a provisional government under which the state was admitted to the Confederacy. In January, 1862, he was elected Seventh District representative to the First Regular Congress, and two years later he was returned by the soldier and refugee vote.

In all respects Bruce was probably an exemplar of southern sentiment in his state. Serving in Congress until the collapse of the Confederacy, Bruce seldom interfered with the administration's program of mobilizing the country's economic resources. He granted the army whatever manpower the War Department requested, begged his fellow members not to meddle in army reorganization, refused to criticize cabinet members and commanding generals, and occasionally promoted legislation to ease the lot of the rank and file. In December, 1864, when the Confederacy was tottering toward oblivion, he submitted a resolution setting forth the uselessness of making peace offers to the United States. Bruce accompanied the presidential party to Danville after the fall of Richmond in 1865 and on to Augusta, Georgia, before determining to make his way to Washington and have a settlement with the United States government. He learned there of his pardon and proceeded to Louisville to resume his law practice. He was successively circuit judge of the Louisville district, chancellor of the chancery court, and professor of law at the University of Louisville. In 1880

Judge Bruce became general counsel for the Louisville and Nashville Railroad, a position he occupied until his death in Louisville on January 22, 1903. He is buried in Cave Hill Cemetery.[1]

[1] Bruce's life has been largely reconstructed from *The Biographical Cyclopedia of the Commonwealth of Kentucky* (N.p., 1896); the *Biographical Encyclopedia of Kentucky*; and Thompson, *History of the Orphan Brigade*. Information on Bruce's place of burial was provided by Cave Hill Cemetery in a letter to Ezra J. Warner, December 9, 1970.

HENRY CORNELIUS BURNETT (Kentucky), a native of Virginia, was born in Essex County on October 5, 1825,[1] but moved with his parents to Kentucky in early childhood. He attended the common schools and an academy in Hopkinsville, studied law and was admitted to the bar in 1847, and began practice in Cadiz, Kentucky. From 1851 to 1853 Burnett was clerk of the Trigg County circuit court. In 1854 he was elected as a Democrat to the Thirty-fourth Congress and to the three succeeding congresses and served from March 4, 1855, until December 3, 1861, when he became the only Kentucky congressman to be expelled for his open secessionist sentiments. Meantime he had served as president of both the Kentucky Southern Conference at Russellville in October and the "Sovereignty Convention" the following month, which passed an ordinance of secession and organized a provisional state government. Soon after, its executive council appointed Burnett first a commissioner to the Confederate Congress, then a provisional congressman, and finally a senator.[2] In the Second Congress he was chairman of the Senate Committee on Claims and was a vigorous advocate of postponing the settlement of most claims until after the war. His main interest, however, was in army matters. After Bragg's invasion of Kentucky in 1862 failed so miserably, Burnett worked to create bands of partisan rangers to assist in reclaiming the state; meanwhile, he recommended drafting all men capable of bearing arms and putting in the field all noncombatants and replacing them with older and disabled men. He was a warm friend of President Davis and supported Davis' program enthusiastically; the only exception to his loyalty was the sponsorship in September, 1862, of a bill exempting everyone exempted by state law. Burnett was one of the only three members of the Kentucky delegation to serve in all three Confederate Congresses. After the war he went home, resumed his law practice, and worked to restore the Democratic party's control of the state. He died in Hopkinsville on October 1, 1866, four days before his forty-first birthday, and was buried in East End Cemetery in Cadiz.

[1] *Appleton's Cyclopedia of American Biography* (6 vols.; New York, 1898) incorrectly records his name as Henry *Clay* Burnett.

THEODORE LEGRAND BURNETT (Kentucky), a member of all three Confederate Congresses, of which he was one of the last survivors, was born November 14, 1829, in Spencer County, Kentucky, southeast of Louisville. He was a graduate of both the liberal arts and law departments of Transylvania University in Lexington and was admitted to the Kentucky bar in 1846, according to two different biographical compendiums.[1] In 1847, after some brief service in the Mexican War, Burnett began practice in Taylorsville, in his native county; the same year, he was elected county attorney, an office which he occupied for a year or two before returning to private practice. When the secessionist Kentucky government was recognized by the Confederate Congress, Burnett was appointed a representative to that body. He attended the Provisional Congress for only one day, but a scattering of Kentucky voters returned him from the Sixth District to both succeeding congresses, in which he was chairman of the Committee on Pay and Mileage. In 1862 he pressed for an investigation into the loss of Fort Donelson, but generally he played a rather passive role as congressman. He supported the vigorous measures introduced by others, although in the last year of the war he seems to have become disillusioned with President Davis' qualifications as commander-in-chief. He voted several times to instruct Davis as to whom to place in high command, and he consistently refused to give the War Department the emergency control over army personnel and organization that it requested—attitudes most unusual for a Kentucky congressman. When the war ended Burnett returned to Taylorsville, but in 1866 he moved to Louisville, and in 1870 he was elected city attorney, an office whose title was subsequently changed to corporation counsel and to which he was repeatedly reelected. When he died in Louisville on October 30, 1917, the Louisville *Times*, in reporting his demise the following day, stated that he was "thought to be the last surviving member of the Confederate Congress." This qualified assertion, although untrue, points up the fact that an era had almost ended. Judge Burnett was interred in Cave Hill Cemetery.

[1] *Biographical Encyclopedia of Kentucky*; Levin (ed.), *Lawyers and Lawmakers of Kentucky*.

SAMUEL BENTON CALLAHAN (Creek and Seminole nations), a delegate from the Creek and Seminole nations, was born January 26, 1833,

39

in Mobile, Alabama. His father is said to have been a prominent white man, his mother one-quarter Creek. He was educated in Texas and engaged in newspaper work there before going to Indian Territory in 1858. Here he established a ranch and apparently used his one-eighth-Creek blood to become a Creek citizen. Callahan enlisted in the First Creek Regiment in 1861 and became one of its captains. The treaties concluded by the Confederacy with the Creeks and Seminoles provided that they should jointly elect a nonvoting representative to the Congress. The time and place of Callahan's election does not appear, but he took his seat in Congress on May 30, 1864. The records exhibit that he participated in proceedings only twice: once he introduced a bill calling for the annuities due the Seminoles to be paid in cotton; on another occasion he helped all the tribes to exchange their old Treasury notes and bonds for new ones at face value. In the postwar years until his death after Oklahoma had been admitted to the Union, Captain Callahan was a prominent man in the Territory and in the affairs of the Creek Nation, besides conducting a farm and ranch in the neighborhood of Okmulgee, Oklahoma. He was at various times clerk of the House of Kings, auditor of the Creek Nation, clerk of the supreme court, a justice of the supreme court in 1891, and in 1896 representative of the Creek Nation in Washington. At another time he served as superintendent of the Creek boarding school at Wealaka, Oklahoma. Callahan's residence during those years is variously reported as Okmulgee, Cusseta, and Muskogee. He died in Muskogee on February 17, 1911, and was buried there in Greenhill Cemetery.[1]

[1] The principal sources for Callahan's life are: Luther B. Hill, *A History of the State of Oklahoma* (2 vols., Chicago, 1909), II, 322, and *Chronicles of Oklahoma* (Autumn, 1955), 314–15, an appendix to an article written about his daughter by Carolyn Thomas Foreman.

JOSIAH ADAMS PATTERSON CAMPBELL (Mississippi), one of the last survivors of the Confederate Congress, was born at Camden, South Carolina, on March 2, 1830. He attended school in Abbeville and in Lawrenceville, Georgia, and completed his education at Davidson College in North Carolina. About this time (1845) his parents moved to Madison County, Mississippi, and he began the study of law, being licensed to practice in June, 1847, when he was but seventeen years of age. The following year he commenced practice in Kosciusko, Mississippi, which continued to be his residence until the war. Campbell represented Attala County in the legislature in 1851 and again in 1859 when he was House speaker, and in 1861 he was a member of the Mississippi secession convention. The latter body sent him to the Provisional Congress as one of Mississippi's seven delegates. There he was given committee assignments which required special talent for attention to detail. He worked dutifully, but his continuing interest seemed to be in the problems of territorial organization. He conceded the need for new grants of power to the central government, but it was primarily at his insistence that local defense units be confined to duty within their respective states, a common attitude among congressmen from the lower South.

After being decisively defeated in a bid for election to the First Regular Congress, Campbell entered the army as captain of the "Campbell Guards," which became Company K of the Fortieth Mississippi, a regiment of which he in turn became lieutenant colonel. He was wounded at the Battle of Corinth in October, 1862, but returned to duty in time to take part in the Vicksburg campaign, although he was not in the city itself. Subsequently, with the rank of colonel of cavalry, he performed staff duty until the end of the war. In the immediate postwar period Campbell was elected to the position of circuit judge, but his office was later declared vacant and he moved to Canton, Mississippi, in 1869 and resumed law practice. After the return of home rule he was appointed to the Mississippi supreme court, where he served for eighteen years, the last nine as chief justice. By the time of his death in Jackson, Mississippi, on January 10, 1917, newspaper obituaries referred to him as the "Nestor of the Mississippi Bar." [1] Judge Campbell was buried in Greenwood Cemetery in Jackson.

[1] Jackson *Daily News*, January 11, 1917, which also asserts he was "Sole Surviving Member of the First Confederate Congress," a completely erroneous statement, since both Roger A. Pryor of Virginia and Jehu A. Orr of Mississippi (!) were both still living.

ALLEN TAYLOR CAPERTON (Virginia) was born at the family estate Elmwood near Union, Monroe County, Virginia (now West Virginia), on November 21, 1810. He attended public school in Union and in Huntsville, Alabama; studied for a time at the University of Virginia; and eventually was graduated from Yale College in 1832. He then studied law in Staunton and returned to Peterstown in Monroe County to practice. He later acquired a large plantation in the county. Between 1841 and 1861 Caperton served as a Whig for six years in the Virginia House of Delegates and for four years in its senate. He was a delegate to the Whig national convention of 1848 and a member of the state constitutional conventions of 1850 and 1861. As a member of the latter he opposed secession until Lincoln's call for volunteers in April; he then voted for disunion. In January, 1863, a distinguished field of five candidates sought the place in the Confederate Senate made vacant by the death of W. B. Preston (*q.v.*). A split in the Democratic majority of the General Assembly enabled Caperton to win on the twentieth ballot.

In the Confederate Senate Caperton served as chairman of the Committee on Accounts. Like his predecessor, he considered maintaining home-front productivity and efficiency as important as creating an ever-larger army. His personal dislike of President Davis magnified this regard for local interests. The result was that Confederate authority fared badly at Caperton's hands. Had his will prevailed, conscription, impressment, habeas corpus suspensions, and monetary policy would have been hedged and restricted almost to the point of uselessness. He showed equal concern for the yeoman farmer. Caperton wanted to tax money and bonds rather than land; he argued that military substitution favored the wealthy; and he warned that arming the slaves would lead to their emancipation. During the last months of the Confederacy he voted to dictate foreign policy to the president and to ask him to reshape the cabinet.

After the war Caperton was active in enlisting outside capital to develop West Virginia's coal, iron, timber, and farmlands. He also became a director of the James River and Kanawha Canal Company. In 1874 Caperton was elected as a Democrat to the United States Senate and served until his death in Washington, D.C., on July 26, 1876. He was interred in Green Hill Cemetery in Union, West Virginia.

DAVID WILLIAMSON CARROLL (Arkansas) was born March 11, 1816, in Baltimore, Maryland, a lineal descendant of that Daniel Carroll who aided in drafting the United States Constitution, and whose farm was the site of the city of Washington. David W. Carroll was educated at St. Mary's College, Baltimore, and went first to Arkansas in 1836 as an employee of the surveyor general's office in Pine Bluff. Two years later he returned to Maryland and farmed for some years before again moving to Arkansas to teach school for a year. In 1846 he was appointed a deputy clerk of the United States District Court, and at the rather advanced age of thirty-two he was admitted to the bar. Carroll served in the Arkansas legislature, was land-agent at Pine Bluff, and in 1860 was prosecuting attorney for the Pine Bluff District. In the spring of 1862 he organized a company which became part of the Eighteenth Arkansas Infantry, of which he was elected colonel, and with which he served at Fort Pillow and Corinth. Both stations were plague spots, and Carroll became so ill he was forced to resign his commission in August, thereby escaping the fate of his successor, who was mortally wounded at the Battle of Corinth in October.

Exterior View of the Virginia State Capitol, 1862

Meeting Room of Confederate House of Representatives in Virginia State Capitol

Howell Cobb presiding over the Confederate Senate in open session at the capitol, Montgomery, Alabama.

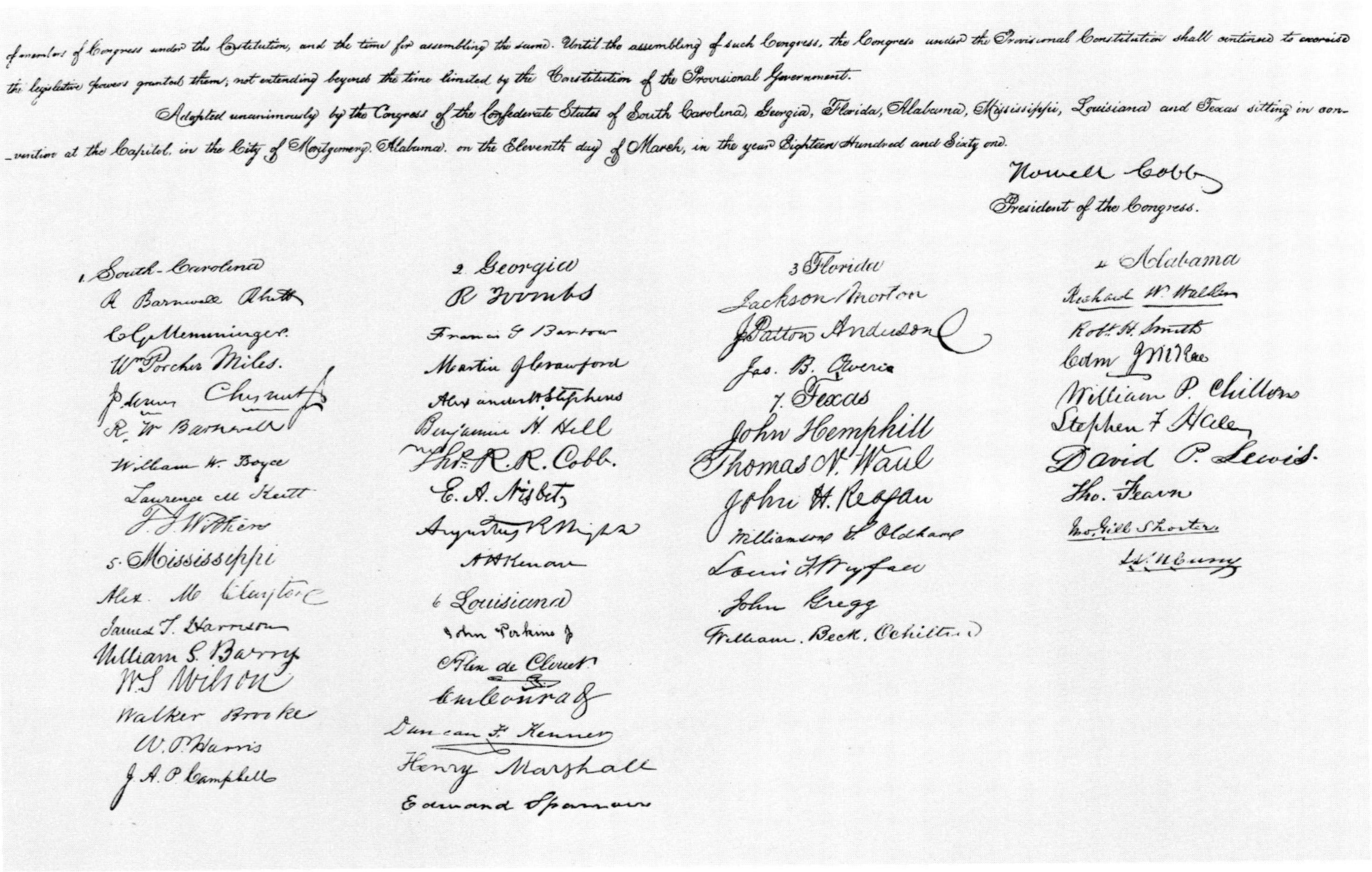

The top paragraph (partially legible):

... members of Congress under the Constitution, and the time for assembling of said Congress, the Congress under the Provisional Constitution shall continue to exercise the legislative powers granted them, not extending beyond the time limited by the Constitution of the Provisional Government.—

Adopted unanimously by the Congress of the Confederate States of South Carolina, Georgia, Florida, Alabama, Mississippi, Louisiana and Texas sitting in convention at the Capitol, in the City of Montgomery, Alabama, on the Eleventh day of March, in the year Eighteen Hundred and Sixty one.—

Howell Cobb
President of the Congress.

1 South Carolina
R. Barnwell Rhett
C.G. Memminger
Wm Porcher Miles
James Chesnut
R. W. Barnwell
William W. Boyce
Laurence M. Keitt
T. J. Withers

5 Mississippi
Alex. M. Clayton
James T. Harrison
William S. Barry
W.S. Wilson
Walker Brooke
W.P. Harris
J.A.P. Campbell

2 Georgia
R. Toombs
Francis S. Bartow
Martin J. Crawford
Alex. H. Stephens
Benjamin H. Hill
Thos. R. R. Cobb
E. A. Nisbet
Augustus R. Wright
A.H. Kenan

6 Louisiana
John Perkins Jr
Alex. de Clouet
Charles M. Conrad
Duncan F. Kenner
Henry Marshall
Edward Sparrow

3 Florida
Jackson Morton
J. Patton Anderson
Jas. B. Owens
J. Stocas
John Hemphill
Thomas N. Waul
John H. Reagan
Williamson S. Oldham
Louis T. Wigfall
John Gregg
William Beck Ochiltree.

4 Alabama
Richard W. Walker
Robt. H. Smith
Colin J. McRae
William P. Chilton
Stephen F. Hale
David P. Lewis
Tho. Fearn
J. L. M. Curry
J. L. Pugh

Signees of the Permanent Confederate Constitution

Mississippi Congressional Delegation, 1860.
From top to bottom: (left) Reuben Davis, Lucius Q. C. Lamar,; (center)
Jefferson Davis (senator), Albert Gallatin Brown (senator), William
Barksdale; (right) Otho R. Singleton, John J. McRae.

Representative Clifford Anderson, North Carolina

Courtesy of Georgia Department of Archives and History, Atlanta

Representative John B. Baldwin, Virginia

Courtesy of Virginia State Library

Senator Robert W. Barnwell, South Carolina

Courtesy of University of South Carolina Library, Charleston

Representative John R. Baylor, Texas

Courtesy of University of Texas Library, Austin

Representative Elias Cornelius Boudinot,
Cherokee Nation

Courtesy of Oklahoma Historical Society, Oklahoma
City

Senator Clement C. Clay, Jr., Alabama

Courtesy of Alabama Department of Archives and
History, Montgomery

Senator Henry Stuart Foote, Tennessee

Senator Landon Carter Haynes, Tennessee

Courtesy of Virginia State Library

Representative Benjamin L. Hodge, Louisiana

Courtesy of Olive Hodge, Shreveport

Senator R. M. T. Hunter, Virginia

Senator Herschel V. Johnson, North Carolina

Courtesy of Georgia Department of Archives and
History, Atlanta

Senator Robert W. Johnson, Arkansas

Courtesy of Arkansas History Commission

Senator Waldo P. Johnson, Missouri

Courtesy of State Historical Society of Missouri

Representative Willis B. Machen, Kentucky

Courtesy of the Filson Club, Louisville

Representative Henry Marshall, Louisiana

Courtesy of Henry Marshall Furman, Shreveport

Representative William Porcher Miles, South
Carolina

Courtesy of University of South Carolina
Library, Charleston

Senator William Elliott Simms, Kentucky

Courtesy of the Filson Club, Louisville

Senator Edward Sparrow, Louisiana

Courtesy of Mrs. Frank Voelker, Sr., Lake Providence

Representative George Graham Vest, Missouri

Courtesy of State Historical Society of Missouri

Senator Louis T. Wigfall, Texas

Courtesy of University of Texas Library, Austin

In 1864 after August H. Garland's (*q.v.*) election to the Confederate Senate, Carroll was appointed to fill the vacant House seat, which he occupied from January 11, 1865, until the final adjournment of Congress on March 18. The pace of legislation during these last weeks was so rapid that Carroll's role was largely that of a spectator. Nevertheless, he attended faithfully and supported all the desperation measures of the period except high taxation and the arming of slaves. He was even willing to let the Confederacy take over the various state militia bodies and impress state-owned property, and he never voted for any peace proposal. In 1866 Carroll became probate judge of Jefferson County, Arkansas, but was dispossessed in 1868. After the reclamation of the state from the Carpetbag regime, during which period he had practiced law, he became chancellor of the state in 1878, serving for many years. On June 24, 1905, in his ninetieth year, Judge Carroll died in Little Rock and was buried in Calvary Cemetery there.[1]

[1] The principal sources for information about Carroll's career are John Hallum, *Biographical and Pictorial History of Arkansas* (Albany, N.Y., 1887) and the *Arkansas Gazette*, June 24, 1905.

ROBERT LOONEY CARUTHERS (Tennessee) was born in Smith County, Tennessee, July 31, 1800. He became a clerk in a country store at the age of seventeen and afterwards studied law and was admitted to the bar in 1823. He was then successively clerk of the state house of representatives, clerk of the chancery court of Smith County, and editor of the *Tennessee Republican* before moving to Lebanon, Tennessee—which would afterward be his home—in 1826. Caruthers then went on to be state's attorney for five years, a member of the state house of representatives, the founder of Cumberland University in Lebanon in 1842 and of its law department in 1847, presidential elector, congressman, and justice of the supreme court of Tennessee from 1852 until the beginning of the Civil War.[1]

In 1861 Judge Caruthers was a member of the peace convention in Washington which attempted to avert the war. In later years he seems not to have been particularly proud of his Confederate connection, for there is no mention of it in his biographical sketch in the *Biographical Directory of the American Congress*. Nevertheless, after Tennessee had joined the Confederacy, Judge Caruthers was elected to the Provisional Congress from the Fifth District. During his half-year there he seldom voiced his opinions, attended irregularly, and did not attend at all after December, 1861. In his voting he supported all the administration's programs to put the Confederacy on a war basis except the

43

produce loan. In October, 1861, Judge Caruthers was a strong candidate for the Senate of the First Regular Congress, but he lost to Landon C. Haynes on the thirty-second ballot.

In 1863—Governor Isham G. Harris being ineligible by law to succeed himself—Judge Caruthers was elected governor of Tennessee. However, because of the occupation of the state by Federal forces, he could not be inaugurated and never assumed the duties of the office. Harris continued as nominal governor until the close of the war and the collapse of the Confederacy, a period during which the gubernatorial power was exercised by Andrew Johnson, military governor by authority of Abraham Lincoln. Judge Caruthers then became professor of law at Cumberland University, a position which he occupied with distinction until his death in Lebanon on October 2, 1882. He was buried in Cedar Grove Cemetery.

[1] He was also one of the most affluent men in Tennessee in 1860, possessing property worth $400,000, including 119 Negroes. (See U.S. Census, Wilson County, Tenn.)

HENRY COUSINS CHAMBERS (Mississippi) was a native of Limestone County, Alabama, born there on July 26, 1823. His father, who had served on the staff of Andrew Jackson as a surgeon during the early Indian Wars, was briefly one of Alabama's U.S. senators; he died when Chambers was two years old. Chambers received an excellent education for the day and time, graduating with honors in 1843 from what is now Princeton University. He then moved to Rankin County, Mississippi, to engage in planting, and in 1854 he went to Coahoma County. He also owned land in the adjoining county of Bolivar. He was sent to the legislature in 1859, and in 1860 he was a presidential elector for the ticket of Breckinridge and Lane. Chambers vied for a seat in the First Regular Confederate Congress and in October, 1861, the race became so heated that he forced his opponent into a duel—rifles at fifty paces—and killed him. Perhaps for this reason he had no opposition when he sought reelection to the Second Congress in 1863.

Chambers soon established himself as a strong nationalist. As early as September, 1862, he voiced the hope that the concept of individual state defense had been abandoned. As an administration stalwart, upon whom the president depended, he proposed or advocated a number of unpopular but necessary measures, such as that exempting certain overseers, but drastically limiting the numbers exempt from military service and making those exempt pay five hundred dollars. In early 1864 he introduced two severe impressment programs which failed to win support. Only in his opposition to forced funding of the national debt and to arming slaves did his ultra convictions falter. At the close of the war Chambers returned to his plantation in Bolivar County and devoted himself to agricultural pursuits during the few years that were left to him. He died at a Mississippi River steamboat landing known as Carson's, in Bolivar County, May 1, 1871, and was buried in Elmwood Cemetery, Memphis, Tennessee.

JOHN RANDOLPH CHAMBLISS [1] (Virginia) was born on March 4, 1809, in Sussex County, Virginia, where his family had been residing since 1624. After an academic education he began teaching school nearby, meanwhile continuing his own studies in private. He then studied law in Winchester for a little over a year [2] and afterward attended William and Mary for the school year 1828–1829. He was admitted to the Greensville County bar in 1830 and began practicing in Hicksford (now Emporia). By 1860 Chambliss had also acquired a moderate-sized plantation. Chambliss soon became heavily involved in community affairs. He helped found what is now Main Street Baptist Church, whose membership included both whites and blacks. He then became the first superintendent of schools for his county. He also served on numerous commissions for local development, particularly those related to internal improvements. In 1845 Chambliss was appointed commissioner in chancery, serving until 1849 when he was elected commonwealth attorney for his county. He was a member of the Virginia constitutional conventions of 1850–1851 and of 1861. He was elected to the latter as a Unionist, but by April he had turned secessionist. Until this time he had been a Whig but had chosen not to become involved in state politics. When war began Chambliss, who had earlier served for a brief time as a colonel in the state militia, helped accumulate equipment for companies raised in the county. In November, 1861, he won a decisive victory over several other candidates for a seat in the Confederate House of Representatives.

In Richmond Chambliss' primary concern was with army matters. He believed conscription totally wrong, but once it was in effect he worked for as large an army as possible. He also wished to give it more flexibility by letting the War Department determine both exemptions and promotions. In February, 1864, he argued that agriculture was flourishing and saw the adoption of his proposition to end the exemption of overseers. Chambliss' cooperation with the war effort was equally good on other matters, for he condoned almost complete Confederate control over production, currency, transportation, and prices. It was only on habeas corpus suspension that he denied significant emergency authority to the central government. He considered running for reelection in 1863 as an opponent of conscription but soon withdrew his name.

Once the war had ended Chambliss took the oath of allegiance and helped prepare instructions for the guidance of the county police to restore law and order. Afterward he worked diligently to rebuild the county's economy. He himself was debt-ridden for much of his remaining life. He died on April 3, 1875, and is buried in the graveyard back of his old home site[3] in Emporia alongside his eldest son, General John R. Chambliss, C.S.A., who was killed in action in 1864.

[1] Most of the biographical information on Chambliss was provided by Eleanor L. Eanes and Sadie R. Norwood of Emporia, Va.; Suzanne Foley of the Library of William and Mary College, Williamsburg, Va.; and John R. Chambliss of Rocky Mount, N.C.

[2] The statement on his law study is from Chambliss' obituary in the Petersburg (Va.) *Index*, April 5, 1875.

[3] The family burial plot is in the yard of the home of Mr. and Mrs. H. C. Pruett.

JAMES CHESNUT, JR. (South Carolina) was the youngest of thirteen children whose father owned more than three thousand acres of land and hundreds of Negroes. He was born at Camden, South Carolina, January 18, 1815. Like his father and many other well-born southerners of the time, James, Jr., received his college education at Princeton, where he was graduated in the class of 1835. From 1840 until 1858, in addition to supervising his plantation property, Chesnut was almost continuously a member of the South Carolina legislature, both as representative and senator. He had also studied law and been admitted to the bar, but his practice was distinctly secondary to his political activities. He was president of the state senate from 1856 to 1858, when he was elected to the United States Senate. As an extreme states' rights Democrat and defender of slavery, with considerable reputation as an orator, Chesnut was a leader of the southern bloc bent on taking the southern states out of the Union. He resigned his seat in the Senate even prior to the secession of his state, so that he could participate in the proceedings of the South Carolina convention and aid in drawing up the ordinances of secession.

Chesnut was in due course elected to the Provisional Congress, where he was chairman of the Committee on Naval Affairs, for reasons not apparent. He preferred his duty as aide to General Beauregard, however, to that of a legislator, and after his defeat for the Senate in November, 1861, he missed the last three months of Congress. His first concern as congressman was to see that the Confederacy had a large and properly equipped army. Beyond that, despite his warm friendship with President Davis, Chesnut begrudged further intrusions into local affairs, particularly in financial matters. He also, in writing the two Confederate constitutions, proposed to include the right of secession and to leave with Congress the decision of a ban on the foreign slave trade.

In October, 1862, Chesnut became an aide on the staff of President Davis with rank of colonel of cavalry. On April 23, 1864, he was promoted brigadier general and placed in charge of the South Carolina reserves. After the war General Chesnut played a prominent part in the Reconstruction politics of the state, and stood next in importance only to former generals Wade Hampton and Matthew C. Butler in the fight to redeem South Carolina from the Carpetbag regime. His wife, Mary Boykin Chesnut, wrote the revealing and informative *Diary from Dixie*, a virtual primer of wartime Richmond and life in the plantation South. General Chesnut died at his home in Camden on February 1, 1885, and is buried in a family cemetery near there.

WILLIAM PARIS CHILTON (Alabama) was born near Elizabethtown, Kentucky, on August 10, 1810. His parents died when he was but a child and little is known about his early life save that his education was meager and that at the age of seventeen he was making a living by teaching. He studied law for three years in Nashville, Tennessee, and in 1831 moved to Alabama, where he opened a law office in Talladega. In 1839 Chilton was elected as a Whig to the state legislature, and in 1840 and 1844 he was active in the presidential campaigns of Harrison and Clay. He was defeated for Congress in 1843. In 1846 Chilton moved to Tuskegee, Alabama, where he conducted a law school until, the following year, he was elected by a Democratic legislature to be a justice of the Alabama Supreme Court. He was chief justice from 1852–1856, when he retired to resume his law practice. In 1859 he was elected state senator from Macon County.

Like most Whigs, Chilton was opposed to secession, but when the die was cast he went with his state. By this time he had taken up residence in Montgomery and from there was sent to the Provisional Confederate Congress. He was reelected to both Regular Congresses. His colorful language and oratorical ability made him a favorite with the galleries, and his delegation considered him its most industrious member. He chaired the Post Office Committee in all three congresses, that of the Quartermaster's and Commissary departments in the First, and that of Flag and Seal in the Second. It was his committee report on February 21, 1861, which advised the Post Office Department that it could become self-sustaining only by cutting services to a minimum. Generally Chilton advocated such strong war measures that William W. Boyce (*q.v.*) once accused him of wanting to raise "the black flag," but on two questions he took a more conservative viewpoint, introducing proposals to exempt farmers and mechanics from military service, and opposing on constitutional grounds those parts of the draft and currency laws which seemed to violate previous contracts with individuals. Chilton found himself, like most southerners, in greatly reduced circumstances after the war; but reengaging in his law practice proved fruitful, and by the time of his death in Montgomery on January 20, 1871, he was again comfortably situated. He was buried in Montgomery in the Old Division of Oakwood Cemetery.

JAMES STONE CHRISMAN (Kentucky) was born in Monticello, Kentucky, September 14, 1818. He died there July 29, 1881, and was buried in a private cemetery on his farm near this southern Kentucky county seat. After attending the common schools of the neighborhood, and helping on his father's farm, he studied law, was admitted to the bar at the advanced age of thirty-one, and commenced practice in Monticello. Except for his one election to Congress in 1852, Chrisman's track record as a politician was largely that of a loser. He was twice an unsuccessful candidate for the state house of representatives and twice defeated for the office of presidential elector, and in 1854 he unsuccessfully contested the election to Congress of the man who defeated him for reelection. Nevertheless, in January, 1862, Chrisman was elected Fifth District congressman by the Confederate sympathizers in his bailiwick. Two years later the soldier and refugee vote returned him to Congress. Few members demonstrated a greater willingness to sacrifice local and personal interests to the central government, even allowing for the fact that Kentucky members were more often than not of this persuasion. For the sake of victory he sanctioned any financial measure, any tampering with individual rights, control over all manpower, to say nothing of regimentation of the entire Confederate economy. And he refused to instruct the president or criticize his appointees. It was only in his adamant stand against arming slaves that Chrisman withheld his support. For his own part he sought only to see that Confederate soldiers were well treated in northern prisons and exchanged as quickly as possible. After the collapse of the Confederacy Chrisman returned to his home in Monticello and resumed his law practice. From 1869 to 1871 he was a member of the state house of representatives.

JEREMIAH WATKINS CLAPP (Mississippi), a native of Virginia, was born September 24, 1814, in Abingdon. He was educated at Hampden-Sydney College, where he was graduated in law in 1836. After practicing in Abingdon for a time, he went to Holly Springs, Mississippi, in 1841. There he soon built up a large practice in partnership with John W. C. Watson (*q.v.*), much of it involving work in Memphis, forty miles northwest, with the result that he maintained residences in both places until after the Civil War. In 1854 Clapp was a delegate to the Charleston convention, and in January, 1861, he was a member of the Mississippi secession convention. Since he had advocated immediate secession after Lincoln's election the preceding November, his course was predictable. In the fall of the year he defeated by a narrow margin Jehu A. Orr (*q.v.*), representative in the Provisional Congress, for a seat in the First Regular Congress, but he was in turn decisively beaten for reelection by Orr in 1863. During the two years of his tenure Union forces gradually took over the northeast Mississippi district which he represented, and he generally supported legislation aimed to strengthen the central government and the War Department. On March 21, 1862, he introduced an important bill to compel the destruction or removal of property in the path of the enemy. He objected, however, to drafting men over thirty-five, feeling that older men should be kept at home for productive labor and emergency military duty. His special legislative interest was to keep vice and fraud out of the army and to see that financial legislation was free of inequities. From 1852 to 1867 Clapp was a trustee of the University of Mississippi, and for fifty years he was an elder of the old Second Presbyterian Church of Memphis. After the war he made his home there and at a summer home in Hardin County, Tennessee. He died in Memphis, September 5, 1898, and was buried in Elmwood Cemetery.

JOHN BULLOCK CLARK (Missouri), whose career is sometimes confused with that of his son of the same name, was born in Madison County, Kentucky, April 17, 1802. After attending such schools as the county afforded, he studied law and was admitted to the bar in Fayette, Missouri, in 1824. His record is a typical frontier success story: clerk of the Howard County courts, 1824–1834; colonel of volunteers in the Black Hawk War; major general of Missouri militia; member of the state house of representatives; and member of the United States Congress from 1857 until he was expelled by resolution on July 13, 1861. That October the rump Neosho legislature chose Clark to serve in the Provisional Confederate Congress, and then elected him to a two-year term in the Senate of the First Regular Congress.[1] At the end of his term, Governor Thomas C. Reynolds, whose authority extended just so far as the spot upon which he was standing, refused to reappoint Clark because of the latter's alleged extracurricular activities in Richmond, which were said to include mendacity, drunkenness, and the attempted seduction of General Albert Pike's mistress. Clark, who had hung around the Confederate capital after the end of the First Congress, hoping for a reappointment to the Senate, was "elected" over Caspar W. Bell to the House of Representatives by a handful of soldier and refugee votes from the so-called Third Missouri Congressional District, and was thus the only Missourian to attend the first session of the Second Congress.

Even though Clark may not have fairly represented a majority of the people of Missouri, he worked unceasingly for the interest of the West. To protect it from Union guerrilla bands, he attempted to keep home-guard units intact and to suspend the draft in endangered districts. A special project was to permit the raising of Confederate partisan bands to operate, virtually at discretion. He invariably supported the principle of promotion based on seniority and seldom voted to give President Davis appointive powers. For these reasons the sensitive chief executive marked Clark as an enemy. On the other hand, when the interests of his area were not directly affected, Clark supported almost all the emergency legislation requested by the administration. At the close of the war Clark returned to his home in Fayette, Missouri, where, after his disabilities had been removed, he practiced law until his death on October 29, 1885. His son, John Bullock Clark, Jr., was a Confederate brigadier general, and served five terms in Congress postbellum.[2]

[1] Cf. above sketch of C. W. Bell for Missouri's method of choosing delegates to the Confederate Congress.
[2] Cf. Ezra J. Warner, *Generals in Gray: Lives of the Confederate Commanders* (Baton Rouge, 1964), 52.

WILLIAM WHITE CLARK (Georgia) was born near Augusta, Georgia,[1] on September 23, 1819.[2] In 1838 he enrolled in the Covington Manual Labor School, his expenses being paid by an older brother. Upon his brother's death Clark was thrown upon his own resources and began reading law. In a short while he was admitted to the bar and began a practice in Covington which lasted more than forty years. From 1858 to 1862 Clark was in partnership with Jefferson Lamar. In 1867 he formed another partnership with James M. Pack. Clark himself was considered one of the foremost trial lawyers of his circuit and amassed a considerable fortune. By 1860 he was worth more than eighty thousand dollars. When the Manual Training School moved to Oxford and became Emory College, Clark bought the abandoned property and converted the main building into an elegant colonial home, Clark Grove.[3] In addition he bought and farmed land near Covington and even speculated in Texas farmland. In 1841 Clark was elected to the state house of representatives for one term but thereafter took no part in state politics.[4]

In October, 1861, Clark was elected a representative to the Confederate Congress as a professed friend of the Davis administration. In Congress he considered conscription "fraught with tyranny and injustice," but he supported with enthusiasm most other wartime programs. From his position on the Committee on the Quartermaster's and Commissary departments, however, Clark made every effort to safeguard the home front's productive capacity. He never approved drafting overseers, and he proposed the exemption of most artisans and mechanics, arguing that it was ridiculous to suppose that lame soldiers could perform such labor. Clark also worked successfully to exclude perishable goods from the tax in kind because they usually spoiled while awaiting shipment. He lost reelection in 1863 to a far stronger states' rights man.

After the war Clark resumed his law practice and continued his interest in community affairs. In 1869 he was a member of the board of trustees which reactivated the Southern Masonic Female College in Covington. He was also a member of the mercantile firm of Clark, Rosser and Company, and he occasionally lent money at interest.[5] In 1873 Clark was elected a director of the Georgia Railroad and Banking Company and remained in the position until 1878.[6] In 1883 he went to Baltimore for medical treatment and died there on August 6. His body was returned home and interred in Covington City Cemetery.[7]

[1] This information was provided by Sewell Brumby, University of Georgia Law Library, Athens.

[2] This information was taken from the W. W. Clark family Bible and provided by Mrs. Harry Dietz, Newton County Library, Covington, Ga.

[3] This information was provided by Virginia E. deTreville, Richmond County Historical Society, Augusta, Ga.

[4] This information was provided by Mrs. Harry Dietz. The statement on Clark's property holdings is taken from his will, also provided by Mrs. Dietz.

[5] This information was provided by Mrs. Harry Dietz.

[6] This information was provided by Virginia E. deTreville, Richmond County Historical Society, Augusta, Ga.

[7] This information was provided by Mrs. Harry Dietz.

CLEMENT CLAIBORNE CLAY, JR.[1] (Alabama) was born near Huntsville, Alabama, on December 13, 1816. After graduating from the University of Alabama in 1834 he became private secretary to his father, Governor C. C. Clay, and editor of the Huntsville *Democrat*. He then earned a law degree from the University of Virginia in 1839 and began practicing in Huntsville. He later acquired and operated a plantation. In 1843 he married Virginia C. Tunstall, who later became "one of the brightest ornaments"[2] in the United States and Confederate capitals. Clay served for three years in the legislature and for three more as county judge; he was then elected to the United States Senate in 1853. He remained there until Alabama seceded, distinguishing himself as an ardent exponent of state sovereignty and nullification, an expert in finance, and, after Lincoln's election, an advocate of secession.

On the organization of the Confederate government President Davis offered Clay the post of secretary of war, but Clay declined and secured instead the appointment of Leroy P. Walker. In November, 1861, Clay overcame a combination of former Unionists and Whigs and was chosen Confederate senator on the tenth ballot.

Clay's biographer states that as senator he played a "watchdog and efficiency role."[3] He was chairman of the Committee on Commerce and of a joint committee to investigate the Navy Department, the latter resulting in a whitewash. He was one of Jefferson Davis' closest friends and was recognized as an administration supporter. But he was equally close to Wigfall and Yancey, two of the president's harshest critics. The fact that Clay preserved these ties bespoke the confidence that these and other Confederate leaders had in his integrity. Clay favored vigorous measures to mobilize the Confederacy for war, and most of his bills were aimed at this goal. But with characteristic independence he voted against most of President Davis' major nominations and often sought to force Davis' hand in diplomacy. On January 18, 1863, Clay precipitated the liveliest debate of the session by proposing to remove from the Supreme Court bill all appellate jurisdiction over state courts. He had drawn only a two-year term and in November lost his bid for reelection.[4]

In April, 1864, Clay was sent to Canada as a member of a mission to undertake informal peace negotiations with the United States. He remained in Canada for a year but ultimately despaired of success and returned just as the war ended. On hearing that he was accused of plotting raids from Canada and of conspiring to assassinate Lincoln, Clay surrendered rather than attempt flight. He was taken to Fort Monroe with Davis and others and confined for nearly a year. He was finally released without an opportunity to defend himself. Broken physically by confinement and years of asthma, Clay spent the remaining years quietly in his law practice. He died near Gurley in Madison County on January 3, 1882, and is buried in Maple Hill Cemetery in Huntsville.

[1] Clay used the designation *Junior* simply to distinguish himself from his father, Clement Comer Clay.
[2] *DAB*, IV, 170.
[3] Ruth K. Nuremberger, *The Clays of Alabama: A Planter-Lawyer-Politician Family* (Lexington, Ky., 1958), 196.
[4] *Ibid.*, 224–27.

ALEXANDER MOSBY CLAYTON (Mississippi) was born January 15, 1801, in Campbell County, Virginia. As a boy he had little formal schooling, but he read law in Lynchburg, was admitted to the bar, and began practice in Fredericksburg in 1823. A year or two later, newly married, he moved to Clarksville, Tennessee. Andrew Jackson appointed Clayton United States judge for the Arkansas Territory in 1832, but he served little more than a year, resigning because of poor health. In 1837 he moved to Mississippi and purchased a large tract of land near the present town of Lamar, which became his home for the rest of a long life. In 1842 Clayton was elected to the High Court of Errors and Appeals, a post he occupied for nine years. Franklin Pierce appointed him U.S. consul in Havana in 1853, but he served only a few months because of a yellow-fever epidemic which carried off, among others, his secretary.

Clayton had been a delegate to the Nashville convention of 1850, and to the Democratic national convention in Baltimore in 1860 when Mississippi selected him as a delegate to the secession convention which convened in January, 1861. Like the majority of his colleagues he had favored immediate separation after the election of Lincoln, and he took an active part in drawing up the ordinance of secession. The convention sent him to the Provisional Congress, where he quickly demonstrated his willingness to face the problem of making a new nation and, as chairman of the Committee on the Judiciary, was responsible for placing in the Confederate Constitution the same guarantees to the states as existed in the U.S. Constitution. He also figured prominently in devising the rather novel Confederate judiciary system. He resigned from Congress on May 11, 1861, to accept an appointment as Confederate district judge for the state of Mississippi.

After the war Judge Clayton was elected a Mississippi circuit judge but was removed in 1869 by the resolution of Congress which declared all civil offices vacant in the states of Virginia, Mississippi, and Texas.

53

He then continued to practice law and manage his plantation. He was for years a director of the Northern Bank of Mississippi in Holly Springs, one of the organizers of the Mississippi Central Railroad (now part of the Illinois Central), and an incorporator of the University of Mississippi, whose first president of the board of trustees he became in 1844, and on whose board he served at intervals until his death. He died at Woodcote, his plantation near Lamar, on September 30, 1889, in his eighty-ninth year and was buried in Hillcrest Cemetery, Holly Springs.[1]

[1] Much of the data on Clayton's career was supplied by Mahala Saville of Oxford, Miss., a retired reference librarian at the University of Mississippi Library.

DAVID CLOPTON (Alabama), descendant of a prominent Virginia planter family, was born on September 29, 1820, in Putnam County, Georgia, where his father was practicing medicine. After attending several county schools and Edenton Academy, he was graduated with honors from Randolph-Macon College in 1840. He then read law in Macon, Georgia, for a year and commenced practicing in Griffin. In 1844 Clopton moved to Tuskegee, Alabama, and built a successful law practice there. He also engaged in farming on a small scale. Despite his written protest he was nominated in 1858 for Congress on the Democratic ticket, winning after one of the most exciting contests in Alabama history. A strong secessionist, Clopton resigned when Alabama seceded and enlisted as a private in the Twelfth Alabama Infantry, rising to a captaincy. In November, 1861, he was elected to the Confederate House of Representatives without opposition, but he won reelection in 1863 only after a close race.

In the Second Congress Clopton was chairman of the Committee on the Medical Department. In lawmaking Clopton was generally exceedingly wary of comprehensive grants of power to the central government, but he never displayed the truculence of so many strict constructionists. In particular, when Congress or the president had a limited objective in mind, generally an economic one, he readily made concessions to the emergency. Thus Clopton voted to let the government control all commerce, draft speculators, nationalize specie, and arm the slaves. Most of his own suggestions sought to moderate major programs already in existence, particularly conscription and taxation. On January 19, 1863, he proposed to hand over to the states as ordinary criminals all Union soldiers captured and accused of atrocities.

After the war Clopton moved to Montgomery and for a time lived quietly, but in 1874 he was one of the leaders in bringing an end to

Radical Reconstruction in Alabama. In 1878 he was persuaded to seek a place in the state legislature, which he won by a majority of eighteen hundred votes in a county with a Republican majority of over three thousand. For his overwhelming victory he was chosen speaker of the house. Clopton refused reelection, however, largely owing to his often expressed distaste for legislative duties. In 1884 he accepted an appointment as associate justice of the state supreme court, the only public office that he had ever genuinely desired, and remained on the bench until his death. Clopton's third wife was Mrs. Virginia Clay, widow of C. C. Clay, Jr. (*q.v.*)[1] Clopton died in Montgomery on February 5, 1892, and is buried in Oakwood Cemetery there.

[1] She wrote her celebrated *Belle of the Fifties* under the name of Virginia Clay-Clopton.

MICHAEL WALSH CLUSKEY (Tennessee) was born in Savannah, Georgia. The exact date of his birth is uncertain; his parents, both natives of Ireland, were married on or about August 15, 1831, the date of their marriage license,[1] and Michael was baptized on May 11, 1832.[2] When the boy was about fifteen, the family moved to Washington, D.C., where the father practiced as an architect. In 1852 Cluskey was appointed postmaster of the national House of Representatives, an office which he held until 1859. Meanwhile, he wrote a treatise entitled *The Political Text-Book or Encyclopedia Containing Everything Necessary for the Reference of the Politicians and Statesmen of the United States*. The book was popular—the ninth edition was published in Philadelphia in 1860. Cluskey moved to Memphis in 1859 and bought an interest in the *Avalanche*, an extreme states' rights paper, which he sold early in 1861. When the war broke out, he entered the Confederate army and served on the staff of General Preston Smith with the rank of lieutenant colonel until he was severely wounded at the Battle of Shiloh. After the death of David M. Currin (*q.v.*) in March, 1864, Tennessee citizens in army camps all over the country chose Cluskey as his replacement. In Richmond Colonel Cluskey quickly identified himself with the die-hard faction. Until the very end he remained at his post and supported every suggestion that might prolong the struggle. He had no patience with those who did otherwise. He introduced the resolution to expel Henry S. Foote (*q.v.*) when the latter went north on his one-man mission for peace; and on March 16, 1865, two days before Congress adjourned for the last time, Cluskey asked the Speaker of the House to order the arrest of any member absent without leave. Some time after the war he moved to Louisville, Kentucky, where he aided in editing the Louisville *Ledger*, an ultra paper which was founded in 1871; he also served on the board of the first public library. Cluskey had never fully recovered from the wound received at Shiloh, and on January 13, 1873, he died at his home in Louisville. He is buried in Mount Olivet Cemetery in Washington, D.C., in an unmarked grave.[3] Cluskey also edited the *Speeches, Messages, and Other Writings of the Hon. Albert G. Brown* (1859), which contains seventy-two documents deemed indispensable to students of the political history of the antebellum period.

[1] Chatham County, Georgia, Index to Marriages, 1806–51, courtesy of Walter C. Hartridge, Savannah.
[2] Register II (1816–38) of the Parish of St. John the Baptist, Savannah, courtesy of Walter C. Hartridge.
[3] According to Mr. Hartridge, a grandson of Julian Hartridge, member of the Confederate Congress from Georgia's First District.

HOWELL COBB (Georgia), one of the ablest men of the antebellum South, was born in Jefferson County, Georgia, on September 7, 1815. His family, "by reason of its wealth, social prestige and the ability of its members, occupied a secure position in the small group of planters who dominated . . . political life" in the southern states before the Civil War.[1] After his graduation from the University of Georgia at Athens in 1834, his marriage to the daughter of another wealthy Georgia planter freed him to devote his life to public affairs. Cobb was admitted to the bar in 1836, and the next year was elected by vote of the legislature to the ofce of solicitor general of the Western Circuit, comprising the northeastern counties of Georgia. This area, strongly pro-Union in sentiment, populated by small farmers who owned few slaves, came to be known as Cobb Country, and his followers as Cobb Democrats, *i.e.*, Union Democrats.

Cobb served in Congress from 1843 to 1851, and upon the organization of the House of Representatives in 1849 was elected speaker on the sixty-third ballot, principally because of support from the northern wing of the Democratic party. In 1851, with the Whigs and Cobb Democrats arrayed against the southern rights Democrats, Cobb was overwhelmingly elected governor of Georgia. In 1855 he was reelected to Congress, and in 1857 he was appointed secretary of the treasury by President Buchanan. However, when Lincoln was elected president, Cobb advocated immediate secession. In February, 1861, he was sent to the Montgomery convention and at once elected its presiding officer. He might have been elected president of the Confederate states had it not been for his devotion to the Union and the "tag ends of old party animosities clinging to him." [2] Because of his position, Cobb took almost no active role in lawmaking. It was not long, however, before he was considered "in the coalition against Jeff Davis." He readily granted the Confederacy the routine powers of government, even voting for appeal from state to Confederate courts, but he saw no need for innovation. He opposed taxation, objected strenuously to more than minimum interference with state troops, and was particularly reluctant to broaden any executive powers. Cobb, however, was more shortsighted than recalcitrant, for he later bitterly denounced the obstructionist policy of Georgia's Governor Brown.

Early in 1862, having been defeated for election to the Regular Congress by Augustus H. Kenan, Cobb took the field as a soldier, and was appointed a brigadier general to rank from February 12, 1862, and a major general from September 9, 1863. He rendered some distinguished field service, but his most important contribution was as commander of the district of Georgia, where, as representative of the administration, he strove to resolve the differences between Davis and Brown. After the war General Cobb practiced law in Macon and was an uncompromising opponent of Radical Reconstruction. He died on October 9, 1868, at the rather early age of fifty-three, while on a business trip to New York, and was buried in Oconee Hill Cemetery in Athens, near the grave of his brother T. R. R. Cobb (*q.v.*).

[1] R. P. Brooks in *DAB*, IV, 241.
[2] Bruce Catton, *The Coming Fury* (New York, 1961), 210.

THOMAS READE ROOTES COBB (Georgia), like his older brother Howell Cobb (*q.v.*), was born on his father's estate, Cherry Hill, in Jefferson County, Georgia, April 10, 1823. He followed his brother at the University of Georgia and after graduation there studied law and was admitted to the bar in 1842. To his great talent as an advocate and constitutional lawyer was attached a prodigious capacity for work; few men of his years wrote so many books. Cobb edited twenty volumes of Georgia Supreme Court reports (1849–1857), prepared *A Digest of the Statute Laws of the State of Georgia* (1851), and compiled a new state criminal code (1858–1861). In addition he wrote two books on the institution of slavery and was a prolific contributor of newspaper articles. Cobb was a leader in the secession movement after the election of Abraham Lincoln, and was credited by at least one contemporary, Alexander H. Stephens (*q.v.*), for being the moving force in taking Georgia out of the Union.

In January, 1861, the Milledgeville convention appointed Cobb a delegate to the provisional congress of the Confederacy. In that body he was chairman of the Committee on Printing, but his vast knowledge of constitutional law led him to more fundamental work. It was his idea for the Montgomery convention to become the Provisional Congress. He also wrote much of the legislation on naturalization and the judiciary. Generally, Cobb accepted the need to place the Confederacy on a sound fiscal basis, and the idea of an export duty on cotton was his. He would not, however, give the War Department more than nominal control over state militia units or their officers. By August, 1861, both his own brother Howell and seven of his wife's brothers, sons of the chief justice of the Georgia Supreme Court, were in the army, and T. R. R. Cobb did not so much resign from Congress as retire to recruit "Cobb's Legion," which he led with distinction during the battles of the Seven Days, at Second Manassas, and in the Maryland campaign which culminated at Sharpsburg. He was promoted from colonel to brigadier general on November 1, 1862. Little more than a month later, on December 13, while defending with his brigade the "sunken road" at the battle of Fredericksburg, he was struck in the thigh by a rifle ball and bled to death in a matter of minutes in a nearby house being used as a field hospital. He is buried in Oconee Hill Cemetery in Athens, Georgia.

CHARLES FENTON COLLIER[1] (Virginia) was born at his mother's ancestral home in Petersburg, Virginia, on September 27, 1817.[2] After a good academic education he attended Washington College and the University of Virginia for a year each. Then, after the fashion of wealthy southern men, he studied at Harvard. He returned from that institution in 1848 and began practicing law in Petersburg when he was not yet twenty-one. After practicing for a year, Collier began planting in Prince George County at Silver Bluff, formerly an experimental farm of Edmund Ruffin.[3] In 1852 Collier won a seat in the house of deputies as a Democrat and served for two terms. At his father's request, Collier returned to his law practice in Petersburg in 1857, but he continued to manage his plantation. In 1859 he began another four-year service in the house of deputies. Though Collier opposed secession, once Virginia had joined the Confederacy he loyally supported the new nation. When Roger Pryor (*q.v.*) resigned his place in the Confederate Congress, Collier won a three-man race for the position by a small plurality; one of his opponents was James A. Seddon (*q.v.*).

While still in the Virginia Assembly, Collier had publicly thanked Jefferson Davis for superb leadership, and during his first months in

Congress he gave the president uncritical support. But by 1863 he "saw his error"[4] and decided that Congress should participate more in decision-making. Collier had supported both conscription laws of 1862, but during 1863 he fought to exempt more men for vital service at home. He also decided belatedly that only Congress should designate areas where the habeas corpus should be suspended. In 1862 he voted to increase taxes and to legalize impressment; later, he opposed the severe tax law of February, 1864, and argued against postponing the settlement of claims for property illegally impressed. On the other hand, Collier continued to respect executive leadership where local interests were not immediately concerned. In 1863 Collier lost his race for reelection to Judge Thomas Gholson (*q.v.*).[5] At the last of the war he was one of the volunteer defenders of Petersburg and saw active combat.

In 1866 Collier was elected mayor of Petersburg in a poll for whites only, but in 1868 he was removed from office under the Reconstruction laws of Congress. In the same year he was elected president of the Petersburg Railroad Company and held office for four years. Collier was elected mayor again in 1888 and served for five consecutive terms. Meanwhile he had rebuilt his law practice and remained a prominent figure until his death. After several months of painful illness he took his own life on June 29, 1899.[6] He is buried in the Blandford Church Cemetery.[7]

[1] Most of the information on Collier is taken from *The City of Petersburg, Virginia: The Book of Its Chamber of Commerce* (Petersburg, Va., 1894), 103.

[2] The date of Collier's birth was supplied by Harley P. Holden, Harvard University Library, Cambridge, Mass.

[3] Collier's obituary in the Petersburg (Va.) *Index* of June 30, 1899, names this plantation Shell Banks, but Ruffin's early estate was named Silver Bluff.

[4] *Southern Historical Society Papers*, LXVII, 173.

[5] During the campaign Collier claimed that Gholson had continued to hold court during the race and had gained unfair advantage thereby. When Gholson refused a rerun, Collier gave in gracefully.

[6] Obituary, Petersburg (Va.) *Index*, June 30, 1899.

[7] This information was furnished by Charles H. Cuthbert, Petersburg, Va.

ARTHUR ST. CLAIR COLYAR (Tennessee) was born June 23, 1818, in Washington County, Tennessee. When he was quite small, his family moved to middle Tennessee, settling first in Coffee County. There, when only ten years old, Colyar joined a temperance society; at his death he had been a Son of Temperance for eighty years. He received a meager common-school education and became a schoolteacher in Franklin County, meanwhile reading law in his spare time. He was admitted to the bar in Winchester, Tennessee, in 1846.

Colyar was an ardent Whig in overwhelmingly Democratic Franklin County; he also had very definite opinions; the combination would on occasion prove highly combustible. Colonel Colyar—as he was always called, although the reason is not discernible—was a staunch Union man and, during the months leading up to the state's secession from the Union, made numerous loyalist addresses. However, when the state went out in June, 1861, he at once accepted the situation and became an ardent supporter of the Confederate cause. In August, 1863, Colyar was elected without opposition to the Second Regular Congress as representative from the Third District. In that body he was considered a dependable, although not brilliant, legislator. He was wont to accept the administration's leadership in army matters but frequently found fault with its management of the home front. As a member of the Ways and Means Committee he opposed economic controls, and he thought that the currency could be stabilized by taxation. He voted to double the tithe on agriculture and in May proposed heavy taxes on profits and corporation property, the latter to be assessed at its gold value. He deemed the conscription of skilled artisans and the impressment of slaves to be equally foolish, and he deplored habeas corpus suspensions. Near the end of the war Colyar joined those who were trying to force President Davis to reshuffle his commanding generals and to open peace negotiations.

When the war was over Colonel Colyar made his home in Nashville and resumed his law practice. In the 1850s he had become associated with the Sewanee Mining Company, a small coal operation to which a railroad was to be built. Subsequent to the war he expanded this property into the Tennessee Coal, Iron and Railroad Company, the first large-scale industrial complex in the South to be developed by northern capital. At one point Colyar owned the company lock, stock, and barrel, which should have made him a rich man, but in 1881 he gave over control to New York interests, and he died only moderately affluent. Always a civic figure, he was instrumental in locating the University of the South at Sewanee, and when he died in Nashville on December 13, 1907, the *Tennessean* devoted much of its front page and its lead editorial to his passing. He was buried in Mount Olivet Cemetery.[1]

[1] Colyar is universally referred to as "Colonel" both in his lengthy obituary in the *Tennessean* and in a biographical piece which ran in three parts in the *Tennesse Historical Quarterly* in 1953. Neither source, however, even hints as to the provenance of the title.

CHARLES MAGILL CONRAD (Louisiana), whose maternal grandfather was a colonel of the Continental Line, was born at Winchester, Virginia, December 24, 1804. His family moved to Louisiana during his boyhood and he received his early education at a private school in New Orleans. He later studied law there and was admitted to practice in 1828. In accord with the custom of the times, Conrad developed an early interest in politics; he also, as was customary, killed his man in a duel. Originally a Jackson supporter, he split with Old Hickory on the bank issue and joined the Whigs. He had been a member of the Louisiana legislature for several terms when he was appointed to the United States Senate in 1842 to fill an unexpired term, but he was defeated the following year for reelection. Four years later, however, he went to Congress and served until President Fillmore in 1850 appointed him secretary of war, an office he filled until the end of the administration. Conrad was a moderate on the slavery issue and during the presidential campaign of 1860 supported the ticket of Bell and Everett.

In January, 1861, the Louisiana convention chose Conrad as a delegate to the Provisional Confederate Congress, and he was twice reelected, serving until the collapse of the government in 1865. While chairman of the Committee on Naval Affairs he became bitterly critical of Secretary of the Navy Mallory, going so far as to propose abolishing Mallory's office and consolidating it into the War Department. Mallory believed that this hostility was personal rather than public and arose from the loss of Conrad's property on the coast of North Carolina, seized by the Federals in the course of Burnside's expedition.[1] He was otherwise a staunch supporter of President Davis, whom he regarded as the proper source for all wartime legislation, and publicly stated that the conduct of the war should be left to Davis and his generals, an attitude not shared by all of his colleagues. Upon returning home in 1865 he found his estate confiscated and himself proscribed. Nevertheless, he resumed the practice of law and in time accumulated means with which to support his family. He died in New Orleans, February 11, 1878, a few days after suffering a stroke while testifying before the United States Circuit Court, and was buried in the Girod Street Cemetery.[2] His wife was a great-niece of George Washington.

[1] Stephen R. Mallory to his wife, August 21, 31, 1862, in Mallory Papers, Southern Historical Collection, University of North Carolina, Chapel Hill.

[2] When the Girod Street Cemetery was demolished in 1957, the remains of the Conrad family were removed to Hope Mausoleum in St. John Cemetery. Leonard V. Huber to Ezra J. Warner, February 7, 1972.

AARON H. CONROW (Missouri), whose middle name is not known, even to his granddaughter,[1] was one of the few men of northern birth in the Confederate Congress. He was also one of the comparatively few who served in all three congresses. He was born near Cincinnati, Ohio, June

19, 1824, spent part of his boyhood near Pekin, Illinois, and then moved with his parents to Ray County, Missouri. By dint of his own efforts he obtained a fair education and taught school himself part of the time. He then studied to become a lawyer, and was appointed judge of the first probate court established in Ray County. From 1857 to 1861 Conrow was prosecuting attorney of the fifth judicial circuit of the state. A strong and early secessionist, he was instrumental in recruiting and equipping the first company raised in Ray County for Confederate service, and held a colonel's commission in the Missouri State Guard, an organization which he had helped to create while a member of the legislature in 1860.

Conrow was elected to the Provisional Congress by the Neosho legislature[2] and in 1864 won reelection by the soldier and refugee vote at polling places scattered all over the Confederacy but concentrated in Texas, where most Missouri troops were at the time stationed. The "election," in which not more than three thousand votes were cast for all seven congressional districts, was largely a popularity contest. Conrow began his service in Congress as a quiet, firm friend of the administration and supported it even more zealously as the war progressed. First hoping that the Confederacy would control Missouri, he opposed the president's accepting militia units or single volunteers, but when this hope vanished, he placed no reservations on his advocacy of total war, constantly advocating both the extension of the draft age and the curtailment of the exemption list. Later he voted in favor of the president's taking over all the state militias. At the close of the war, along with General M. M. Parsons[3] and two members of his staff, Colonel Conrow went through Mexico to California to obtain a ship to England, where his party had sent gold for safekeeping. On August 15, 1865, in the vicinity of China, on the San Juan River, in the state of Nuevo Leon, they were set upon by Juarista irregulars, and all in the party, with the exception of Conrow's Negro servant, were killed. According to one story, the bodies were thrown into the San Juan River; another account states that local peasants buried them near the spot where they were slain. In any event, the location of Conrow's remains is unknown.

[1] Mrs. Harry E. Spencer to Ezra J. Warner, October 20, 1971.
[2] See the above sketch of C. W. Bell for Missouri's method of choosing delegates to the Confederate Congress.
[3] See Warner, *Generals in Gray*, 228–29

WILLIAM MORDECAI COOKE (Missouri) was a Virginian, born at Portsmouth on December 11, 1823. He was descended from that Mordecai Cooke who patented lands in Virginia in 1650. Receiving his early education from private tutors, Cooke was graduated in law from the University of Virginia at the age of twenty, whereupon he at once moved to St. Louis to practice. In 1849 he moved to Hannibal and was elected judge of the court of common pleas, but in 1854 he returned to St. Louis. Cooke was a disciple of Calhoun and a strong proslavery man; when Lincoln was elected he became an active secessionist, and was sent by Governor Claiborne Jackson as a special commissioner from Missouri to confer with President Davis. Before his election to the Confederate Congress by the Neosho legislature, he served on Jackson's staff with the rank of colonel at the battles of Boonville and Carthage, and on the staff of General Sterling Price at Wilson's Creek. Cooke was elected First District representative in the Provisional Congress with the understanding that he would serve until an election was held,[1] but for some reason his name does not appear in some lists of members of the Provisional Congress, although his membership therein is attested to by colleagues in that body who pronounced eulogies upon the occasion of his death. He is included in all lists of members of the First Regular Congress, with his name usually misspelled *Cook*. He was ill during much of his tenure and, except for a bill on January 31, 1862, "to encourage enlistments . . . in the state of Missouri," introduced no bills, resolutions, or petitions. He objected only to the imposition of a tariff, seems to have disliked Secretary of the Navy Mallory, and was reluctant to grant President Davis greater control over the selection of independent militia officers. Otherwise, during his brief congressional career he seems to have approved of the modest legislation enacted. Colonel Cooke died on April 14, 1863, at the residence of relatives in Petersburg, Virginia, leaving a wife and seven minor children in St. Louis. His body was later taken there for burial in Calvary Cemetery.

[1] See the above sketch of C. W. Bell for Missouri's method of choosing delegates to the Confederate Congress.

FRANCIS BURTON CRAIGE (North Carolina), a native and lifelong resident of North Carolina, was born March 13, 1811, near Salisbury in Rowan County. After attending a private school in Salisbury, he went on to the University of North Carolina at Chapel Hill, from which he was graduated in 1829. For the next three years he was editor and publisher of the *Western Carolinian*; he then studied law, was admitted to the state bar in 1832, and began practice in Salisbury. From 1832 to 1834 Craige was one of the last borough representatives in the state house of representatives. In 1852 he was elected as a Democrat to the first of four successive terms in the United States Congress. In 1861 Craige was a delegate to the North Carolina secession convention, and as such he wrote and introduced the Ordinance of Secession, which was adopted verbatim. Soon after, the convention chose him as a delegate to the Provisional Confederate Congress, in which body he took his seat July 23, 1861. While there he supported the work under way to strengthen the central government for all-out war. His advocacy of higher taxes was the strongest in the North Carolina delegation. His only important reservations to preparedness were his opposition to the produce loan and, later, his conviction that the new controls over state militia so gratuitously conceded to the president in the enthusiasm of May should be partially revoked and restored to the states. Craige declined to run for election to the Regular Congress and, so far as is known, took no further part in public life. He resumed his law practice and, while attending the courts of Cabarrus County, died there suddenly in Concord, the county seat, on December 30, 1875. His remains were brought back to Salisbury for burial in Old English Cemetery.

MARTIN JENKINS CRAWFORD (Georgia) was born March 17, 1820, on his father's plantation in Jasper County in the heart of Georgia's black belt. After attending Brownwood Institute and Mercer University in Macon, he studied law and was admitted to the bar at the age of nineteen by special act of the Georgia legislature. He practiced for a time in Hamilton, Georgia, and represented Harris County in the legislature from 1845 to 1847; in 1849 he moved to Columbus, Georgia, his home for the rest of his life. In the immediate antebellum years Columbus was a hotbed of secession, a climate which suited Crawford exactly. He was a delegate to the Nashville convention in 1850 and, after ten months' service as judge of the superior courts of the Chattahoochee circuit, went to Congress in 1855 as a vocal, though unfailingly courteous, champion of southern rights. He remained in Congress until he withdrew on January 23, 1861, four days after his state passed an ordinance of secession. The Georgia convention then chose Crawford as a delegate to the Provisional Congress.

Though he was one of the Confederacy's peace commissioners to the United States and afterwards recruited the Third Georgia Cavalry and became its colonel, Crawford attended Congress with fair regularity. He was one of the strongest high-tax advocates there, but he granted the central government other emergency powers with great reluctance. He even proposed to end the president's right to appoint field-grade officers and he opposed both the produce loan and any aid to railroad construction. Crawford based his campaign for election to the Regular Congress on the dangers inherent in the government's buying the entire cotton crop, and he was soundly defeated. Meanwhile, he had maintained his military ties and after a year of cavalry service joined the staff of General Howell Cobb (q.v.), with whom he was associated until the end of the war, trying to reconcile the differences between President Davis and Governor Joseph E. Brown. Crawford's property was destroyed by the war, but, being only forty-five, he resumed his law practice and continued to be prominent in Georgia public affairs until his death. In 1875 he was again appointed judge of the Chattahoochee circuit, and in 1880 he was appointed associate justice of the Georgia Supreme Court by Governor Alfred H. Colquitt, a former Confederate brigadier. Judge Crawford died in Columbus on July 23, 1883, and was buried in Linwood Cemetery there.

JOHN WATKINS CROCKETT (Kentucky), the son of a farmer, was born in Jessamine County, Kentucky, on May 17, 1818. His grandfather, colonel of a Virginia regiment during the Revolution, emigrated to Kentucky in 1782 and was prominent in erecting the state government. The younger Crockett was educated in the local schools of Jessamine and in Hancock County, Illinois, where his sister resided. In 1839 he commenced the study of law in Hopkinsville and was admitted to the bar in Paducah where he practiced until shortly before the war. He then moved to Henderson, the home of his second wife. Crockett was a member of the "Sovereignty Convention" at Russellville, after which he was elected Second District representative to Congress. He had a low opinion of Congress' role during wartime; he deemed debate largely a waste of time and proposed to ban the discussion of military defeats lest it cause dissension. Once he took a long leave of absence, asserting that he could do more good in Kentucky than in Richmond. Notwithstanding this attitude, he advocated comprehensive wartime legislation. He particularly wanted to take the fight to the enemy and was the first House member to propose extending the draft age to forty-five. Crockett's only antiadministration bias was the conviction that making Treasury notes legal tender or forcing people to exchange them for new notes would do nothing but create disaffection on the home front. He did not seek reelection in 1864. After the war he returned to Henderson and resumed his law practice, devoting his energies thereto until 1872 when failing health caused him to leave the bar and take up residence in Madisonville. There he died on June 20, 1874.

He is probably buried in one of two unmarked graves in one of the Ingram lots in Fernwood Cemetery, Henderson, where his wife, mother-in-law, and father-in-law are buried.[1]

[1] Jackie S. Combest (Superintendent of Cemeteries, Henderson, Ky.) to Ezra J. Warner, June 4, 1971.

MARCUS HENDERSON CRUIKSHANK[1] (Alabama) was born in Autauga County, Alabama, on December 12, 1826, the son of a young Scotsman who had settled there in 1822. The father soon died and the family moved to Mardisville in Talladega County, where Marcus attended neighborhood schools and took a classical course at the academy. When old enough, he began reading law in the office of Lewis E. Parsons of Talladega; he also studied history in Parsons' home. After completing his studies Cruikshank entered into a partnership with his mentor in 1847. He also operated a small farm in the county. Cruikshank served as a register in chancery for several years and was a number of times chosen mayor of Talladega. In 1855 he bought half interest in the *Alabama Reporter*, the leading Whig paper in east Alabama, and was connected with it for the remainder of his life. Cruikshank himself was an active Whig and frequently canvassed the eastern part of the state. In 1860 he campaigned vigorously for the Bell-Everett ticket, and upon Lincoln's election he warned against secession and predicted that it could not succeed.

During the early war years Cruikshank operated a saltworks in Clarke County in addition to his other occupations. In 1863 he took advantage of war weariness and disaffection to contest Curry's bid for reelection to the Confederate Congress. As a "Peace party" candidate and a reputed Reconstructionist Cruikshank won easily by more than a two-to-one majority in Talladega, the home of both candidates.

In the Second Congress, Cruikshank was chairman of the Committee on Enrolled Bills. On the second day he proposed to repeal the act suspending the writ of habeas corpus. Thereafter he demonstrated unwavering hostility to the war and even to the Confederacy, not even suggesting viable alternatives to measures which he opposed. There was no area of legislation in which he was remotely willing to ask greater sacrifices of the people, and he voted for every peace proposal introduced.

In the Alabama provisional government following the war Cruikshank was appointed commissioner for the relief of the destitute, a position he held for three years. He then returned to journalism and the law and followed both industriously until his death. On October 10,

1881, while riding, he was thrown from his horse and died instantly. He is buried in Clark Hill Cemetery in Talladega.[2]

[1] This information was taken from Cruikshank's biographical folder in the Department of Archives and History, Montgomery, Ala.
[2] Information on the place of interment was provided by Urline P. Foster, Talladega Public Library, Talladega, Ala.

DAVID MANEY CURRIN (Tennessee) was born in Murfreesboro, Tennessee, November 11, 1817. He was graduated from Nashville University at the age of seventeen, after which he read law, and at twenty-one he was a Democratic candidate for the legislature. Although defeated, he won considerable distinction as a speaker and in 1844 was a presidential elector for James K. Polk. In 1849 Currin removed to Memphis, which became his permanent home and where he became a prominent politician. He was elected to the legislature in 1851 and was on another occasion an unsuccessful candidate for the United States Congress. After Tennessee seceded, Currin was elected to the Provisional Congress from the Tenth District and to the two Regular Congresses from the Eleventh.[1] In all three elections he had only slight opposition. Generally Currin left the initiative in legislation to others, although in August of 1861 he secured an appropriation for the construction of two ironclads to defend the rivers near Memphis. During the first year of the war he tried to deny the president the use of any troops except those offered by state governors. Soon, however, military necessity forced him to abandon his hopes of local defense. This change of heart, plus his concurrent record, made Currin one of the stronger nationalists in Congress. It was only in his continued preference for free trade that he retained part of his earlier localism. Currin died suddenly in Richmond on March 25, 1864, before taking his seat in the Second Congress. He was buried in Elmwood Cemetery, Memphis.[2]

[1] Tennessee had had ten representatives in the Federal Congress and elections to the Provisional Congress were held accordingly. The state was allocated eleven representatives subsequently, and the legislature redistricted in October, 1861.
[2] *Charter Rules, Regulations, and By-laws of the Elmwood Cemetery Association of Memphis* (Memphis, 1874), a compendium of lot owners and prominent occupants, is the principal authority for Currin's career. The dates of Currin's birth and death were taken from the monument in Elmwood.

JABEZ LAMAR MONROE CURRY (Alabama) was born on the borderline between Georgia and South Carolina, on the banks of the Savannah River, near Double Branches, Lincoln County, Georgia, on June 5, 1825. Although he had a notable career as a politician and diplomat, this aspect of his life was far overshadowed by his accomplishments in the field of education. He may well be said to be the father of universal public education in the states of the old Confederacy in the postwar years. After moving with his father to Talladega County, Alabama, in 1838, Curry was graduated from what is now the University of Georgia at Athens, studied law at Harvard, was admitted to the Alabama bar, and commenced practice at Talladega. He was briefly a private in the Mexican War, resigning because of ill health, and in 1847, 1853, and 1855 he was elected to the Alabama legislature. A Buchanan elector in 1856, he was elected the same year to the U.S. Congress, serving until January 21, 1861, when, upon the secession of his state, he withdrew. He was at once elected to the Provisional Confederate Congress, the only consistent Democrat in the entire Alabama delegation, and was elected to the Regular Congress in November without opposition. In the First Congress he chaired the Committee on Commerce and a special committee to draw up the House rules. Curry was a young and ambitious activist who tied his career to the administration and after Fort Sumter proposed that President Davis command the army in person. He also established himself as an unofficial watchdog over finances and as a strong Confederate nationalist, an attitude not inconsistent with his proadministration bias. His only reservation was his concern lest conscription drain too many men from production at home. The stirring "Address of Congress" of February 17, 1864, exhorting support for the war, was largely his handiwork. However, his support of the central government had cost him his congressional seat in August, 1863, and in November he failed to win Clement C. Clay's senatorial toga.

During the balance of the war Curry served on the staffs of Generals Joseph E. Johnston and Joseph Wheeler with the rank of lieutenant colonel of cavalry. When the war ended Curry embraced theology and became a Baptist preacher. He was chosen president of Howard College in Birmingham, Alabama, in 1865, and in 1868 he was made a professor at Richmond College (now the University of Richmond), a post which he occupied until 1881. Rutherford B. Hayes is said to have offered Curry a place in his cabinet, and Grover Cleveland appointed him minister to Spain, where he served from 1885 to 1888. Again in 1902, Theodore Roosevelt sent him back to Madrid as ambassador extraordinary to represent the United States upon the occasion of the "coming of age" of Alfonso XIII. But these honors were "a mere interlude in the man's essential career." From 1866, when the South lay in ashes, Curry, as the agent first of George Peabody of Boston, and later of the Slater Fund, laid the foundation for the equal education of black and white children in the states south of the Mason and Dixon line. His principal achievements were the establishment of state normal schools for both races in twelve southern states; a system of public schools in every city and town; the influencing of state legislators to establish adequate rural schools; and the dissemination of enormous amounts of educational literature which he had himself written. At the time of his death near Asheville, North Carolina, February 12, 1903, Curry had no superiors in the field of general education and few, if any, peers. By his own request he was buried in Hollywood Cemetery, Richmond.

STEPHEN HEARD DARDEN (Texas) was a native of Fayette County, Mississippi, where he was born on November 19, 1816. At the time of the Texas War for Independence in 1836 he went to Texas as a member of a volunteer company and remained there as a clerk in the office of the comptroller. In 1841 he purchased land on the Guadalupe River in Gonzales County. As a state senator in 1861 Darden opposed secession, but when it was an accomplished fact, he enlisted in the army and served in Hood's Texas Brigade. After resigning from service because of ill health, he was appointed colonel of a battalion of state troops for home guard duty on the Gulf Coast in 1863, and when John A. Wilcox (*q.v.*) died the following year, Governor Lubbock ordered a special election to fill the unexpired term. Darden won and took his seat on November 21, 1864. Unlike his predecessor, Darden disapproved of the continuous growth of the central government's emergency powers. As an army veteran, he recognized the need for higher taxes, a larger army, and a powerful commander-in-chief, but at the same time he opposed further inroads into state and personal rights. His voting record exhibits his conviction that such matters as taxation-in-kind, federal control over production and transportation, and the taking of slaves for any purpose, were outside the jurisdiction of Congress and the president. When the Carpetbag era ended, Darden served six years as state comptroller, during which time Texas bonds returned to par. Although retired for age in 1881, he continued to occupy a number of public posts: superintendent of public buildings and grounds in 1884, chief clerk of the comptroller's department in 1887, and secretary of the Texas Veterans Association from 1886 until his death. Darden died in Wharton, Texas, on May 16, 1902, and was buried in the State Cemetery at Austin.

EDMUND STROTHER DARGAN (Alabama) was born in Montgomery County, North Carolina, on April 15, 1805. His background of rural poverty and the early death of his father forced him to be self-taught, but he eventually acquired a fair classical education and in 1828 he began reading law in Wadesboro. The next year he walked to Washington, Alabama, was admitted to the bar, and began teaching school and practicing law. In 1833 Dargan moved to Montgomery for better opportunities, then to Mobile to be district judge for a year. In the next years he was elected mayor of Mobile, was twice elected to the General Assembly, and in 1845 was a Democratic representative to Congress. In the discussions on terminating the joint occupation of Oregon, Dargan suggested the compromise with Great Britain that was eventually adopted. Dargan declined renomination and in 1847 was elected to the Alabama Supreme Court, becoming chief justice two years later. His sound judgment and personal eccentricities made him the most picturesque justice in Alabama history, but he resigned in 1852 and returned to his practice. By 1850 he had a large practice and owned a small plantation. After Lincoln's election Dargan worked for immediate disunion, and in the secession convention he opposed submitting the ordinance of secession to a popular referendum. In November, 1861, he was elected to the Confederate House of Representatives over two strong opponents.

In Congress Dargan's mannerisms and piercing calls of "Mr. Cheer-man" attracted instant attention, and in the summer of 1863 he drew a bowie knife on Henry S. Foote (q.v.) for calling him a "d——d rascal."[1] Dargan was chairman of the Special Committee on the Foreign Cotton Loan set up to scrutinize the Erlanger Loan negotiations. He began his term in Congress enthusiastic about the Confederacy's prospects and seldom subordinated national to local needs. He condoned martial law though believing it to be unconstitutional, proclaimed that conscription had saved the nation, and advocated emancipation if it would gain foreign recognition. As a member of the Committee on the Judiciary he directed most of his own suggestions from the floor toward improving the administration of justice in Confederate courts. By mid-1863 Dargan had become discouraged about the prospects of victory, but he never became a defeatist. He declined to seek reelection.

After the war Dargan practiced law in Mobile and took no further part in politics. He died there on November 24,[2] 1879, and is buried in Magnolia Cemetery.

[1] Pollard, "The Confederate Congress," 754–55.
[2] The *Biographical Directory of the American Congress* erroneously gives Dargan's date of death as November 22. The Mobile County Board of Health records confirm the date cited by the *DAB* and Thomas M. Owen's *History of Alabama and Dictionary of Alabama Biography* (4 vols.; Chicago, 1921).

ALLEN TURNER DAVIDSON (North Carolina), a native of western North Carolina, was born May 9, 1819, in Haywood County on Jonathan's Creek. His mother was a member of the Vance family. Allen attended the local schools and clerked in his father's general merchandise store. Later he studied law and, after being admitted to the bar in 1845, moved to Murphy in Cherokee County, where he remained sixteen years and served as county solicitor. He was also president of the Miners and Planters Bank. In May, 1861, the North Carolina secession convention elected Davidson a member of the Provisional Congress, and in October of that year he won election to the First Regular Congress over the two opponents.

In Richmond Davidson readily granted the Confederacy full control over diplomacy, commerce, and transportation, but any efforts made in Congress to encroach very far on state or individual rights met his quiet but steady opposition. In most instances his policy was to grant the administration its early and moderate requests but to resist further grants of authority. After 1861, in fact, Davidson made few concessions to the emergency in matters of army and finance and none at all where individual liberties were concerned. However, even this moderation did not suffice to appease his disaffected constituents in 1863, when North Carolinians, particularly those in the western part of the state, were becoming more and more disillusioned with the war and the Confederacy. In the election of that year Davidson lost his congressional seat to George W. Logan (*q.v.*), a peace-at-any-price candidate.

In 1865 Davidson moved from Murphy to Franklin, in Macon County, where he resumed his law practice. Four years later he moved once again, this time to Asheville, which would be his home for the remainder of a long life. He was for many years president of the Merchants and Miners Bank there and he continued to practice law until 1885, when he retired. Davidson died in Asheville, January 24, 1905, at the age of eighty-five, and was buried in Riverside Cemetery.

GEORGE DAVIS (North Carolina) was born in New Hanover (now Pender) County, North Carolina, March 1, 1820, scion of a family which had been living in the Cape Fear district for more than a century. He was graduated at the head of his class from the University of North Carolina at the age of eighteen and in due course was admitted to the bar and established his practice at Wilmington, where he soon attained a considerable reputation. Always a zealous member of the Whig party, Davis came close to being nominated for governor in 1848, although he never sought political office. Like most members of his party he was a strong Union man in 1860 and was a member of the so-called Peace

Conference in Washington in February, 1861; however, he sub-sequently repudiated the recommendations of that body, terming them dishonorable.

In May the secession convention elected Davis as one of two dele-gates at large to the Provisional Congress, and in September he won a seat in the Senate on the twenty-fifth ballot, but he drew only a two-year term and in 1863 was defeated for reelection by William A. Graham (*q.v.*). In the Senate he was chairman of the Committee on Claims. Davis soon became such a strong supporter of the administra-tion that other former Whigs in the North Carolina congressional dele-gation considered him a "camp follower of the precipitators" (*i.e.*, of those who brought on the war).[1] Perhaps it would be fairer to say that he was one of North Carolina's strongest Confederate nationalists. Most of the bills that he introduced aimed to create as large and effec-tive an army as possible, and except for his extreme conservatism in financial matters he withheld no important powers from the central government. In fact, he was one of only four senators willing to give a supreme court appellate jurisdiction over state courts. Jefferson Davis, with his characteristic compulsion to reward loyal lame ducks, had appointed George Davis Confederate attorney general; the latter re-signed his Senate seat shortly before his term ended. He served hon-estly and faithfully until the end of the war in an office which admittedly was not of the first importance, and then he attempted to flee the country by way of Florida but was arrested at Key West and confined in Fort Hamilton until January 1, 1866. He thereupon took the oath of allegiance and returned to his law practice in Wilmington. In later years he enjoyed marked success, particularly as counsel for the Atlantic Coast Line system. In 1878 he was offered the chief justiceship of the North Carolina Supreme Court, which he is said to have declined for pecuniary reasons. Davis died in Wilmington, February 23, 1896, and was buried there in Oak Dale Cemetery.

[1] John A. Gilmer to William A. Graham, June 5, 1862, in William A. Graham Papers, North Carolina Department of Archives and History, Raleigh.

NICHOLAS DAVIS, JR. (Alabama) was born in Athens, Alabama, January 14, 1825. His father, Nicholas Davis, Sr., a native of Virginia, had been a captain in the War of 1812. The younger Davis was educated in his native state but completed his legal studies at the University of Vir-ginia. During the Mexican War he was commissioned a lieutenant of the Thirteenth United States Infantry, with which he served for a time under General Zachary Taylor. After the war he was admitted to the bar and established his practice in Athens, the county seat of Limestone, on the Tennessee border. In 1851 he was elected to represent his county in the Alabama legislature. Two years later he moved to Huntsville in neighboring Madison County, where he was elected solicitor, an office which he held for five years.

In 1860 Davis was a Douglas elector, stumped north Alabama in opposition to secession, and was elected to the secession convention of 1861 as a Union delegate, maintaining to the bitter end that the convention had no authority to take the state out of the Union without a vote of the people. Nevertheless, when the convention after long debate voted for secession, he abided by the decision, and when Thomas Fearn (*q.v.*) resigned his seat in the Provisional Congress, Davis accepted election to that body as Fearn's successor. Davis did not take his seat until April 29, 1861, and the record reveals that he was present on only ten occasions, meanwhile establishing no significant bias. He did not stand for election to the Regular Congress. He was soon made lieutenant colonel of the Nineteenth Alabama Infantry, but declined the commission, later commanding a battalion for a short time. At the close of the war Davis refused to take the oath of allegiance, and his property suffered correspondingly. He reengaged in the practice of law, specializing in criminal cases, but hardly survived the Reconstruction era, dying in Huntsville on November 3, 1875.[1] He was buried there in Maple Hill Cemetery.

[1] Owen, *History of Alabama*, III, 467, records Davis' death in 1874; however, both Davis' grave marker and Francis Bernard Heitman, *Historical Register of the United States Army from Its Organization September 29, 1789, to September 29, 1889* (2 vols.; Washington, D.C., 1903) I, 359, attest to the date's being 1875.

REUBEN DAVIS (Mississippi), no relative of the Confederate president, was born in Winchester, Tennessee, January 18, 1813, but moved with his family to northern Alabama when he was a small boy. He was early inclined to become a lawyer, but his father, who felt that it was impossible for a lawyer to "enter the kingdom of Heaven," persuaded him to study medicine under his brother-in-law, a physician of Monroe County, Mississippi. It is a commentary on the medical and legal professions of the day that Davis briefly practiced medicine at the age of eighteen, but forsook it in order to open a law office in Athens, Mississippi, at the age of nineteen. He soon moved to Aberdeen, where his success at the bar was brilliant from the beginning. In 1835 he was elected district attorney of the Sixth Judicial District, and by the time he was twenty-six he had saved twenty thousand dollars from his fees. He was defeated for Congress as a Whig in 1838, but in 1842 he was appointed a justice of the High Court of Errors and Appeals, a post in which he served for only a few months.

During the Mexican War Davis was elected colonel of the Second Mississippi Volunteers, but owing to ill health he saw no actual fighting. He was a member of the Mississippi legislature from 1855–1857 and was then elected as a Democrat to Congress, taking his seat on December 7, 1857, and withdrawing, with his colleagues, in January, 1861. He had believed for years that war between the North and the South was a foregone conclusion, and because of this freely expressed viewpoint he was regarded in many circles as a proslavery fire-eater. For a short time he was a brigadier general of Mississippi state troops, but in November, 1861, he was elected to the First Regular Congress. Despite his being recorded absent at a startling number of roll calls, he made his antiadministration bias apparent in his opposition to a number of measures, including the vital issue of conscription. He attempted to abolish the Committee on Military Affairs, of which he was a member, and ultimately resigned from it in protest. In 1863 he ran unsuccessfully for governor of Mississippi on a platform bitterly critical of Confederate war policy, and the following year he resigned from Congress before the expiration of his term. It may be remarked here that in the brief account of his life submitted to the United States congressional directory Davis omitted mention of his career in the Confederate Congress, preferring to make note of his few months of army service. During the Reconstruction era he was firmly committed to a policy of repression toward the former slaves; the principal landmark of his postwar career was his record as a criminal lawyer. In two hundred capital cases in which he acted as defense counsel, not one defendant went to the gallows. Davis died in Huntsville, Alabama, October 14, 1890, and was buried in Odd Fellows Cemetery in Aberdeen.[1]

[1] See Reuben Davis, *Recollections of Mississippi and Mississippians* (Boston, 1889). See also *Biographical Directory of the American Congress 1774–1961* (Washington, D.C., 1961).

JAMES BAIRD DAWKINS (Florida), son of Elijah Dawkins who had been a major in the War of 1812, was born in Hancocksville, Union District, South Carolina, on November 14, 1820. After a preparatory education he entered the University of South Carolina and received his bachelor's degree in 1840. He then studied law at home and began practicing in Union Courthouse.[1] Sometime during the 1840s, Dawkins moved to Gainesville, Florida, where he built a large double log house and opened a law office nearby. His practice grew rapidly in the next few years and he also acquired a small plantation in the county. In 1856

Dawkins became solicitor for the Suwanee, or eastern judicial, circuit and served until 1861. In late 1860 he was elected to the United States House of Representatives,[2] but by this time he was a strong secessionist and never took his seat. Instead he represented Alachua County in the Florida secession convention where he was a member of the Committee of Thirteen which wrote the ordinance of secession. In November, 1861, he was elected to the Confederate House of Representatives.

During his year in Congress Dawkins confined himself to presenting resolutions of the Florida legislature and petitions from private citizens. He opposed Congress' attempts to preempt control over local transportation and commerce, but otherwise he seemed to be strongly in favor of vigorous wartime legislation. In the fall of 1862 Dawkins was elected judge of the Suwanee circuit and on December 8 he resigned his place in Congress. He held the judgeship until the end of the war.

After the war Dawkins continued to live in Gainesville. In 1866 he was a delegate to the national Conservative convention in Philadelphia and served on the Committee on Organization.[3] He was forced out of politics during Radical Reconstruction, but in 1877 he was appointed judge of the Fifth Judicial Circuit.[4] He held the position until his death in Gainesville on February 12, 1883. He is buried in the old Gainesville Cemetery.[5]

[1] This information was provided by E. L. Inabinett, South Caroliniana Library, University of South Carolina, Columbia.
[2] This information was provided by the Department of State, Division of Archives, History, and Records Management, Tallahassee, Fla.
[3] New York *Times*, August 15, 1866.
[4] This information was provided by Elizabeth Alexander, P. K. Yonge Library, University of Florida, Gainesville.
[5] The location of Dawkins' place of interment was provided by Mrs. W. E. Crown, Clearwater, Fla.

ALEXANDRE de CLOUET (Louisiana) was born in St. Martin Parish, Louisiana, on June 9, 1812, and was educated at Bardstown, Kentucky, and Georgetown College in the District of Columbia. He then made an extended tour of Europe, during which he visited his French relatives, before returning home to study law. Exchanging a law career for the life of a planter, he settled in Lafayette Parish and was markedly successful, accumulating a considerable fortune. He was elected to the legislature in 1837 as a Whig and was that party's candidate for governor in 1849. De Clouet just as zealously espoused the Democratic cause after the Whigs passed out of existence; he was elected a member of the Louisiana secession convention in 1861, which in turn elected him one of six members of the Provisional Confederate Congress from the state at large. He signed the Confederate Constitution but was an almost silent member of Congress, attending sessions faithfully but rarely making himself heard. He supported the war effort in toto, save for his opposition to the proposal to allow companies to volunteer directly into Confederate service, instead of through the state militia organizations, perhaps because de Clouet himself was a brigadier general of the Louisiana militia. In November, 1861, he was nominated for election to the Confederate Senate, but lost to T. J. Semmes (*q.v.*) by a vote of sixty-four to fifty. After the war de Clouet managed to retain his plantation and worked energetically to retrieve his fortunes, which had been badly shattered. At the same time, he was among those who sought to reclaim the state from the Carpetbag regime. Upon the election of former Confederate General F. R. T. Nicholls as governor in 1876, de Clouet retired from public life to the quiet of his plantation home near Bayou Vermilion. He died there June 26, 1890, and was buried in St. Martin de Tours Cemetery in St. Martinville.

DANIEL COLEMAN de JARNETTE (Virginia) was born at Spring Grove Manor near Bowling Green, Virginia, on October 18, 1822.[1] He studied under a tutor for several years and then attended Bethany Collge (now in West Virginia). After completing his education he became a planter and followed that occupation for the remainder of his life. He served as a Democrat in the state house of delegates from 1853 to 1858 and in the United States House of Representatives from 1859 to 1861. He was reelected to the latter, but had been an early secessionist and went with Virginia when it left the Union. In November, 1861, De Jarnette won a seat in the Confederate House of Representatives over three other candidates, and in 1863 he defeated James Barbour for reelection.

De Jarnette was a strong Confederate nationalist during his terms in the House. He supported all conscription bills except those aimed at Marylanders,[2] and toward the last he advocated giving commanding generals full charge of conscription in their districts. De Jarnette wished Congress to specify only a few exemptions from military service and let the secretary of war detail the remainder either to the army or to productive labor. He thought it best to leave decisions on army organization and officer selection to the War Department. De Jarnette's position on economic legislation was even more extreme. He would place no limits upon the right of the government to regulate foreign commerce, restrict staple crop production, destroy endangered property, punish speculation, or control the movement of gold and silver. He demurred only at moving slaves from the field to the army and taxing civilians already suffering from enemy depredations. This latter circumstance was the only matter on which he took much initiative in legislation. While De Jarnette was no peace advocate, on January 30, 1865, he offered a resolution and a brilliant supporting speech contending that France's "invasion" of Mexico might constitute a basis for the joint defense of the Monroe Doctrine by the United States and the independent Confederacy.

In 1871 De Jarnette was one of the arbitrators appointed to define the boundary line between Maryland and Virginia. He died at White Sulphur Springs, West Virginia, on August 20, 1881, and is buried in the family cemetery at Spring Grove.

[1] Lyon G. Tyler (ed.), *Encyclopedia of Virginia Biography* (5 vols.; New York, 1915), III, 40, gives different birth and death dates from those given in the *Biographical Directory of the American Congress*. The De Jarnette family Bible confirms the dates in the latter volume. This information was provided by E. Winston Woolfolk, Bowling Green Public Library, Bowling Green, Va.

[2] De Jarnette's eulogy of the loyalty of Marylanders provoked an editorial from Edward A. Pollard of the Richmond *Daily Examiner* claiming that De Jarnette wished to exempt Marylanders from military service because his district profited from the smuggling between the two states. A bitter correspondence resulted and a duel was narrowly averted when both men were arrested and brought to court. Richmond *Daily Examiner*, January 21, 28, 1864.

WILLIAM HENRY DeWITT (Tennessee) was born in Smith County, Tennessee, October 24, 1827. After attending the local elementary schools, he was a student at Berea Academy near Chapel Hill, Tennessee, and then studied law and was admitted to practice in 1850. He combined schoolteaching with practicing law until 1856 when he settled in Carthage, Tennessee, which was his residence until 1875. From 1855 until 1857 DeWitt represented Smith, Macon, and Sumner counties in the legislature as a member of the Know-Nothing party, having previously been a Whig. Later he would join the Democratic ranks. In 1861 he was elected to the state convention which considered secession, but defeated it by popular vote. Later that year, after Tennessee entered the Confederacy, DeWitt was elected as Fourth District delegate to the Provisional Congress.[1] He participated in formulating a workable law sequestering enemy property, a matter of particular interest in the border states, and he consented to give the president wide latitude in raising troops from these states. The only major program before Congress of which he disapproved was the produce loan, which proposed to use staple crops (mainly cotton) as a basis for credit. He did not stand for election to the Regular Congress. DeWitt continued to practice law in Carthage until 1875, when he moved to Chattanooga. He served as special judge in the Fifth Chancery Division in 1872 and in 1876 was a delegate to the state Democratic convention. High in the hierarchy of the Masonic Order, De Witt died in Chattanooga on April 11, 1896, and was buried there in Forest Hills Cemetery.

[1] By Tennessee law United States elections were held on the first Thursday in August, under which law provisional Confederate congressmen were also to be elected. In the Fourth Congressional District both Confederates and Unionists nominated candidates, resulting in the election of DeWitt and Andrew J. Clements by the opposing parties. Each claimed to be the only legal candidate, with the somewhat bizarre result that each took his seat in his respective Congress.

JAMES SHELTON DICKINSON[1] (Alabama) was born on January 18, 1818,[2] in Spotsylvania County, Virginia. Three years later the family moved to Clarke County, Alabama, and settled near Grove Hill. Dickinson attended the academy in Grove Hill, then taught school for a year. In 1840 he returned to Virginia to enter the university law school, from which he was graduated in 1844. In the same year he married his first cousin, Mary F. Dickinson, of Louisiana County, Virginia. In 1845 Dickinson began practicing law in Grove Hill and soon had a thriving career. He also acquired and managed a plantation of several hundred acres. In 1853 Dickinson was elected as a Democrat to the state senate for a two-year term; there he was made chairman of the Committee on Finance and Taxation.[3] In 1860 he was a Breckinridge elector, and upon Lincoln's election he advocated the secession of Alabama. When war began he raised and equipped a company at his own expense, though he did not serve with it.

In August, 1863, Dickinson won a close race over three opponents to succeed E. S. Dargan (*q.v.*) in the Confederate House of Representatives. His lack of much previous legislative experience probably explains his general abstinence from debate, but he attended regularly and until the last day. In contrast to much of his delegation, Dickinson did not represent a protest vote. His district was threatened and he opposed certain impressment and militia laws which would drain away Alabama's resources for use elsewhere. Otherwise he supported almost any attempt to strengthen the Confederacy. He was one of the few who advocated doubling the tithe on agriculture and requisitioning state governors for all soldiers absent from the army without leave.

After the war Dickinson resumed his law practice in Grove Hill. For the remainder of his life he abstained from active politics and devoted his extra energies to church work and to the Order of the Sons of Temperance. He died on July 23, 1882, in Grove Hill and is buried in a family lot adjoining the old Grove Hill Cemetery.[4]

[1] Owen, *History of Alabama*, III, 488.

[2] This is the date given in Owen, *History of Alabama*, and also inscribed on Dickinson's gravestone. The date is smudged in the census of 1860 and has been erroneously read as 1816.

[3] William Garrett, *Reminiscences of Public Men in Alabama, for Thirty Years* (Atlanta, 1872), 601.

[4] Information on the place of interment was provided by Mrs. Paul Jones of Grove Hill, Ala.

WILLIAM THEOPHILUS DORTCH[1] (North Carolina) was born on a farm near Rocky Mount, North Carolina, on August 23,[2] 1824. After attending the local schools and Bingham School in Hillsboro, he began studying law at the age of seventeen under B. F. Moore in Halifax. Two years later he received his license and opened an office in Nashville. At the age of twenty he was elected county attorney. In 1848 Dortch moved to Goldsboro, where he also became county attorney. Over the next ten years he also engaged extensively in planting. Between 1852 and 1860 he served four terms as a Democrat in the General Assembly, being elected Speaker of the House in 1860. During the winter of 1860–1861 he acted with the immediate secessionists, but at the same time he expressed such strong attachment to the Union as to discredit himself somewhat with that group. This was probably why the Whig-dominated legislature of 1861 resolved a close contest for a Confederate senatorship by turning to Dortch as a compromise appointment.

In the Senate Dortch was chairman of the Committee on Engrossment and Enrollment. He was a personal friend of Judah P. Benjamin and often acted as an intermediary between him and Governor Vance. In his legislative capacity Dortch supported all major programs designed to strengthen the Confederacy. He differed from extremists, however, in his refusal to disregard local interests completely. For instance, he wished to pay better prices for impressed produce, to guarantee the habeas corpus when military status was in question, and to make inflation curbs a little less arbitrary. A majority of his own suggestions were made to keep production and state government in satisfactory operation. But where local interests were not concerned, few congressmen were more dedicated Confederates. He was also North Carolina's strongest opponent of peace negotiations.

Dortch emerged from the war almost bankrupt; his law library was lost and much of his property destroyed when Sherman's army occupied Goldsboro. For the next decade he labored to recoup his fortunes and eventually rebuilt his law practice into the most lucrative in the state. He had similar success with his plantation. Dortch served in the state senate from 1879 to 1885 and was president of that body in

1879. In 1877 he had been appointed a director of the state-owned North Carolina Railroad, and in 1880 he was one of the leaders in the legislature against the sale of the line to a group of northern investors. In 1881 Dortch was appointed chairman of a commission to revise the North Carolina Code. This was a monumental task, since the revisal had to incorporate so many fundamental changes in the law, but it was successfully completed after two years' work. Dortch died in Goldsboro on November 21, 1889, and was buried in Willow Dale Cemetery.[3]

[1] R. D. W. Connor et al., North Carolina Biography (Chicago and New York, 1919), V, 343-45.
[2] Connor et al., North Carolina Biography, V, 345, mistakenly gives Dortch's birth date as August 3, 1824. Other records, including his gravestone, give August 23, 1824, as his birth date; this information was provided by Susan Borden, Wayne County Public Library, Goldsboro, N.C.
[3] Information on the place of Dortch's interment was provided by Susan Borden.

LUCIUS JACQUES DUPRÉ (Louisiana) was born April 18, 1822, in St. Landry Parish, Louisiana. He was graduated in belles lettres from the University of Virginia and received a law degree from that institution in 1842. Subsequently he also obtained a law degree from the University of Louisiana, now Tulane. Dupré practiced law in Opelousas and in 1853 was elected judge of the Fifteenth Judicial District, comprising three parishes. In 1861 he was a member of the constitutional convention, and soon after he enlisted as a private in the Eighteenth Louisiana Infantry. In November he won an uncontested race from the Fourth District to the First Regular Congress, and he was reelected in 1863 by a narrow plurality over two opponents. In the Second Regular Congress he was chairman of the Committee on Printing. He was a staunch supporter of the administration and believed that Congress could best serve by enacting the president's requests and by permitting him to direct the war without interference. His primary interest was in financial matters; in this field he was extremely conservative. He opposed high taxes and penalties on speculation and, in order to combat inflation, proposed that Treasury notes be made legal tender. He advocated the equalization of salaries, the prompt payment of claims against the government, and the provision of better supplies to the army rather than higher pay. Shortly after taking his seat he was made chairman of a special committee to ascertain if military commanders were practicing proper economy. When Congress finally adjourned in March, 1865, Dupré returned to his home in Opelousas. He died there on March 5, 1869, and was buried with his ancestors in an unmarked grave in the St. Landry Church Cemetery.

JOSEPH HUBBARD ECHOLS (Georgia) was born in Washington, Georgia, on December 25, 1816, of wealthy Wilkes County parents. He entered Randolph-Macon College in Virginia in 1836 but transferred the next year to Franklin College in Athens, Georgia.[1] He was graduated in 1848 despite being placed on probation for leaving school for two months in 1838 to volunteer in the campaign against the Cherokee Indians of north Georgia.[2] By this time the family had moved to Lexington and had purchased extensive lands in Oglethorpe County. Echols read law in Lexington under Joseph Henry Lumpkin and was admitted to the bar in 1841. After practicing law for four years Echols turned to the ministry and became a licensed Methodist minister in 1845. He served in several nearby circuits and for two years was stationed in Washington, Georgia. In 1850 Echols was appointed professor of mathematics at Madison Female College and the next year he began a service of four years as its president. In the mid-1850s, however, he inherited all his father's property as an only son and returned to Lexington to manage it. In 1861 Echols was elected to the Georgia Senate. He was unable to stem Georgia's rush toward secession, but his Unionism apparently did him credit, for one of the first military units raised in his county was the Echols Artillery.[3] In October, 1863, he won a clear-cut victory over W. W. Clark (*q.v.*) as a representative to the Confederate Congress.

Echols reached Richmond convinced that the Confederacy's resources were exhausted and that victory was hopeless. He considered laws demanding further sacrifices worse than useless and threatened to resign if they were continued. Echols' few suggestions aimed to provide better subsistence for the families of soldiers. His most unique proposal was a resolution asking the army and the navy to observe the Sabbath better. He worked quietly for peace during his tenure and left Congress shortly after the failure of the Hampton Roads peace conference.

After the war Echols devoted himself primarily to managing his three thousand acres of farmland,[4] though for some years he was senior member of the firm of Echols and Company, cotton merchants of Augusta. Though he held no regular pastorate, he remained prominent in local Methodist circuits and the census of 1880 gives his chief occupation as "minister of the Gospel." Echols was in very bad health during his last years and in his last months suffered from dropsy. He died in Lexington, Georgia, on September 23, 1885, and is buried in the Echols family plot of the Beth-Salem Presbyterian Church cemetery.[5]

[1] This information was taken from Echols' obituary in the *Wesleyan Christian Advocate*, October 14, 1885, and provided by Sarah C. Gillespie, Robert W. Woodruff Library, Emory University, Atlanta, Ga.

[2] Information provided by Dorothy E. Pittman, University of Georgia Library, Athens, Ga.
[3] Information provided by Winifred Maxwell, Lexington, Ga.
[4] Records of Deeds, AA 95, 97, for Oglethorpe County, Lexington, Ga.
[5] Information provided by Mrs. P. M. Marchman, Lexington, Ga.

JOHN MILTON ELLIOTT (Kentucky) was born on the banks of the Clinch River in Scott County, Virginia, May 20, 1820, but in childhood moved to Morgan County (now Elliott County), Kentucky, where he received his early schooling. He was graduated from Emory and Henry College at Emory, Virginia, in 1841, after which he studied law. Elliott was admitted to the Kentucky bar in 1843 and began practice at Prestonsburg, Kentucky, a county seat which would be his home for most of his life. In 1847 he was a member of the state house of representatives, and in 1852 he was elected as a Democrat to the first of three consecutive terms in Congress. He was not a candidate for renomination in 1858, and returned home the following year to resume his law practice.

In 1861 Elliott was again a member of the legislature and in December he was elected by the executive council of the provisional state government to the Provisional Confederate Congress. He was elected Twelfth District congressman to the two succeeding congresses by Confederate sympathizers, soldiers, and refugees. In the First Congress, Elliott was chairman of the Committee on Enrolled Bills. Though he seldom participated in House debate, Elliott's legislative leanings are obvious. During the winter of 1861–1862 he fought unsuccessfully the laws delegating to the president the power to strip outlying areas of their local defense troops. But once Kentucky had been irrevocably lost to the enemy the only significant concession that he withheld from the central government was the imposition of genuinely heavy taxes in 1864, feeling that such an impost would deprive refugee Kentuckians of much of their remaining wealth. Following the war he again resumed his law practice in Prestonsburg, and in 1868 he was elected to the office of circuit judge, serving until 1874. Two years later Elliott was appointed a justice of the Kentucky court of appeals, the state's highest tribunal.

On March 26, 1879, Justice Elliott was shot and instantly killed in front of the ladies' entrance to the Capitol Hotel in Frankfort by Colonel Thomas Buford of Henry County, Kentucky, a brother of General Abraham Buford. Buford claimed in extenuation of his deed that his sister, against whom judgment had been rendered and reaffirmed in a land case by the whole court, and who had died six years previously,

82

"had been robbed and murdered by the decision." Elliott was buried in the State Cemetery at Frankfort.[1]

[1] Quite naturally, the assassination of Elliott became a cause celebre of the newspapers of the day. The weapon was a double-barreled shotgun. Buford at one time contemplated killing Chief Justice Pryor as well but changed his mind. He killed Elliott because "He gave me a Judas kiss; he came to me after the decision and said 'Colonel, I did all I could for you.' I knew this was a lie. I killed Elliott to try my case. Last week I was down by Henry [County] and knelt on my sister's grave and swore to gain this suit or die with her." The reaffirmation of the decision against the sister's estate, of which Buford was the administrator, came only a few days before the murder. (Louisville *Courier-Journal*, March 27, 1879, quoted by Martin F. Schmidt, Head, Kentucky Division, Louisville Free Public Library, in a letter to Ezra J. Warner, June 22, 1972.) Elliott's birth date is herein given as May 16. The *Biographical Directory of the American Congress* gives it as May 20.

GEORGE WASHINGTON EWING (Kentucky), a lifelong resident of Logan County, Kentucky, was born on a farm near Adairville, within rifle shot of the Tennessee border, on November 29, 1808.[1] He was the youngest of ten children born to Robert Ewing, a brigadier general of the Kentucky militia during the War of 1812, and a grandson of Robert Ewing I, who emigrated from Ireland to Virginia in the first half of the eighteenth century. He is said to have been "educated at Russellville and Princeton Colleges, and at the age of twenty-one commenced the study of law."[2] He then practiced law at Russellville, county seat of Logan, until the beginning of the Civil War, meantime representing his county in the legislature for seven terms.

After the secessionist Kentucky government was recognized by the Confederacy, Ewing, a lifelong Whig who had become a Democrat in 1860, was appointed to the Provisional Congress and was elected from the Fourth District to the next two congresses by the few thousand voters able to reach polling places. As a congressman he seldom voted to give the president new appointive powers, and he supported several resolutions advising Davis to make changes in the cabinet and in the field. On the other hand he approved every significant effort made in Congress to strengthen the government's hand. His only important demonstration of initiative came on January 31, 1865, and arose from a conflict of interest between congressmen from districts overrun by the enemy and certain representatives from districts which would be affected by the strong war measures advocated by the first group. Ewing posed the question of whether these men were entitled to their seats and tried to instruct the Committee on the Judiciary to rule on the matter. His measure, largely a matter of self-interest, and intensely embarrassing to the whole government, was at length tabled. After the surrender, he made his way to a farmhouse in North Carolina, where, according to one biographer, he purchased a pardon from the Federal government for the sum of one thousand dollars, after which he returned home. He lived thereafter on his four-hundred-acre farm near Adairville, where he died May 20, 1888. He was buried in the Old Red River Meeting House Cemetery nearby.

[1] According to his grave marker and to J. H. Battle, W. W. Perrin, and G. C. Kniffin, *Kentucky: A History of the State* (Louisville, 1885), Ewing was born on November 29; however, Edward Coffman, *The Story of Logan County* (Nashville, 1962), records the date as November 22.

[2] Battle, Perrin, and Kniffin, *Kentucky*, 841.

JAMES FARROW[1] (South Carolina) was born at Laurens (Court House), South Carolina, on April 3, 1827,[2] into a family whose American antecedents began in Virginia in 1608. After attending Laurens Male Academy, he entered South Carolina College and was graduated in 1847. He then studied law with W. D. Simpson (*q.v.*) and began practicing in Spartanburg in 1849. In 1856 Farrow won a seat in the General Assembly in order to prevent the withdrawal of state support from his college. As a compliment to his gallant fight, he became the youngest man until that time ever elected to its board of trustees. Farrow remained in the General Assembly until 1862 as a National Democrat and was a delegate to the Democratic national convention of 1856. In the state convention of 1852 Farrow had maintained the right of secession; when Lincoln was elected president, he demanded immediate and separate state action. In 1861 and 1863 he was elected to the Confederate House of Representatives by large majorities.

In Congress Farrow was an excellent example of South Carolina moderation. Except for his dislike of habeas corpus suspension, he sanctioned all the basic programs designed to strengthen the central government. On the other hand, his record indicates his unwillingness to extend them as far or as fast as the administration desired. He was also one of the more insistent defenders of Congress' equality with the president in policy-making during wartime. His own special project was to see that hospitalized soldiers received adequate care and quick furloughs. Farrow also introduced several bills of peculiar interest: that the tax on manufactures should be paid in kind; that soldiers should be recruited from foreign nations; and that resolutions asking for the ages of clerks should not apply to lady clerks.

In 1865 Farrow was elected to the United States Congress, but he and his colleagues were refused seats there. In 1870 he moved to Kansas City, Missouri, where he was elected city judge. However, he returned to South Carolina in 1875 and accepted a position as president of Laurens Female College. After a successful administration, he resumed his law practice. Farrow served one more term in the legislature; he died on July 3, 1892. He is buried in the Laurens Cemetery.

[1] Phileman Berry Waters (comp.), *A Genealogical History of the Waters and Kindred Families* (Atlanta, 1902), 92, 93.
[2] Farrow's birth date was provided by E. L. Inabinett, South Caroliniana Library, University of South Carolina, Columbia.

THOMAS FEARN (Alabama), one of the few physicians who were members of the Confederate Congress, and its dean in terms of age, was born in Pittsylvania County, Virginia, on November 15, 1789, during the first administration of General George Washington. He received his early education in Danville, Virginia; then attended Washington College (now Washington and Lee); and was graduated from the Old Medical College in Philadelphia in 1810. He settled in Huntsville, Alabama, that same year and began to practice medicine. He served in the War of 1812 and against the Creeks in 1814, and during this period he dressed the wounds of Andrew Jackson, who later appointed him "surgeon's mate" in charge of a hospital at Huntsville. For three years after 1818 Dr. Fearn studied in Europe, after which he returned to Huntsville and practiced until 1837. In the meantime he engaged in a number of successful commercial ventures, and served in the state legislature and on the board of trustees of the University of Alabama. He also received honorary degrees from both Rutgers College and Transylvania University. His articles on medicine were widely copied in medical journals in this country and in foreign countries. He was a director of banks, railroads, turnpike companies, and canal companies, and altogether was perhaps the leading citizen of northern Alabama. He is also said to have been the first man on this continent or in Europe to recognize the properties of quinine, and to use it accordingly; he made his own quinine from the bark of the cinchona tree.

Dr. Fearn was a staunch Union man who even after Lincoln's election advised against secession. But when Alabama left the Union in January, 1861, he accepted an appointment to the Provisional Confederate Congress and took his seat on February 8; at the same time he published an open letter explaining that he was convinced that secession had been necessary. He attended the sessions of Congress only a few days and then left the business of lawmaking to others. He resigned because of ill health on April 29, 1861, the day the second session convened in Montgomery, and he died in Huntsville on January 16, 1863, and was buried in Maple Hill Cemetery there. Dr. Fearn was the father-in-law of Colonel W. T. S. Barry (*q.v.*) of Columbus, Mississippi, and the grandfather of Colonel Matthew Forney Steele, whose *American Campaigns* became a West Point and army textbook in later years.

HENRY STUART FOOTE (Tennessee), who has been aptly characterized as the "Vallandigham of the South"[1] was born in Fauquier County, Virginia, February 28, 1804. He was graduated from Washington College in 1819, studied law, and was admitted to practice at Richmond in 1823. Foote soon moved to Alabama and then to Mississippi, residing in a number of places while practicing law and at times editing newspapers. According to his obituary in the Nashville *Daily American* on May 21, 1880, he had no equal as a criminal lawyer in Mississippi.

After holding a number of minor political offices, Foote was elected to the United States Senate by the Mississippi legislature in 1847, and he alone among Mississippi congressmen strongly supported the compromise measure of 1850. He and Jefferson Davis, the other Mississippi senator, were bitterly antagonistic on this question as well as on the abstract right of secession, both publicly and privately, an antagonism which once, at least, led to blows. Even though the legislature censured Foote for his advocacy of the Compromise of 1850, he surprised everybody by defeating Davis for the governorship of the state in 1853, a victory attributed to his great ability as a stump speaker. Foote was an uncompromising Union man, and the victory of the states' rights faction during his term of office caused him to move temporarily to California in 1854. He returned in 1858 but, being out of step with his former constituents, decided to move to Nashville, Tennessee. Paradoxically, although he was a bitter opponent of secession, he accepted election to the First Regular Confederate Congress from Tennessee's Fifth District, in November, 1861, and two years later he won reelection over strong opposition. In the First Congress he was chairman of the Committee on Foreign Affairs and of special committees to investigate military losses and illegal arrests. In the second he chaired a special committee on illegal impressments. An uncompromising foe of Davis, whom the president considered to be his "only open assailant in Congress," Foote was a one-man committee on the conduct of the war, repeatedly urging an offensive war, demanding military information and battle reports, investigating defeats, and ordering no less than thirty inquiries, eleven alone for fraud in the Quartermaster's and Commissary departments. On numerous occasions he instructed Davis on foreign affairs, sought to dismiss top officials, proposed to abolish the War Department, and was in general a thorn in the side of the administration, fighting it viciously on almost every issue except control over the economy.

Early in 1865, Foote, who had been in favor of accepting the terms of peace offered by Lincoln in 1863 and 1864, went North on a peace mission of his own and was expelled from Congress for his efforts. Coolly received by the Federal authorities, he departed for Europe. Later he resided in Washington and struck up a friendship with Grant, who made him superintendent of the New Orleans Mint. Foote died at his home in Nashville on May 19, 1880, and was buried in Mount Olivet Cemetery. Possessed of a violent temper, which involved him in numerous personal encounters, he was also endowed with a degree of literary skill, which resulted in the publication of three books valuable from an historical standpoint, especially his *Casket of Reminiscences*.

[1] See Charles S. Sydnor in *DAB*, VI, 501. Clement L. Vallandigham, an Ohio congressman, was virulently "anti-Republican" and antiwar, and actively supported the southern element and the disloyalists in his area. He was finally expelled to the Confederacy by Lincoln.

SAMUEL HOWARD FORD (Kentucky), one of the few foreign-born members of the Confederate Congress, as well as one of its few ordained ministers, was born February 19, 1819, in London, England. He was brought to the United States in childhood by his father, a pioneer Baptist preacher of central Missouri. The younger Ford was licensed to preach in 1840 and was ordained in 1843. During the next thirty years he was pastor of a succession of churches in Missouri, at Memphis, and at Louisville. During his seven years as pastor of the Central Baptist Church in Memphis, he is said to have increased the membership from 75 to 450 and to have constructed a $75,000 church building. In 1853 Dr. Ford began editorial work, and in the same year he began publication of *Ford's Christian Repository*. His wife aided in his editorial work and was herself the author of five books. In the fall of 1861 Dr. Ford left Louisville and allied himself with the Confederacy. In December the executive council of the Kentucky Confederate government appointed him to the Provisional Congress. During his brief service he opposed both giving the president greater use of local defense forces and depriving the governors of much of the power to appoint militia officers. Where local interests such as the tariff and railroad construction were less involved, Ford consented to strengthen central authority. He did not run for election to the Regular Congress. Ford refugeed after his term in Congress, first in Memphis and then in Mobile. When the war ended, he returned to Memphis and continued publication of the *Christian Repository*. Subsequently he moved to St. Louis, where he conducted the paper until his death and wrote a number of books on ecclesiastical history in general and Baptist history in particular. At the age of eighty-six Dr. Ford died in St. Louis on July 5, 1905, and was buried in Bellefontaine Cemetery.[1]

[1] Ford's life has been mainly reconstructed from the *Missouri Historical Review*, I, 152; and J. H. Spencer, *A History of Kentucky Baptists from 1769 to 1885* (Cincinnati, 1885), II, 191–92.

THOMAS MARSH FORMAN (Georgia) was born at Nonchalance, his father's estate on Wilmington Island near Savannah, Georgia, on January 4, 1809. His father was Joseph Bryan and his mother was Delia Forman, daughter of General Thomas Marsh Forman of Maryland. Young Thomas bore the name of Thomas Forman Bryan until 1846 when, by act of the Maryland legislature, his name was changed so that he could profit from the provisions of his grandfather's will. This change resulted in his five eldest children being named Bryan and the two youngest Forman. His father had died when Thomas was three years old; he was adopted by his grandfather and educated at St. Mary's College, Baltimore. He then commenced planting at the family home on Wilmington Island but sold the place in 1831 and bought Broughton Island in the Altamaha River in McIntosh County.

In 1847, Forman was elected to the Georgia state senate, his only public office. The 1860 census found him in Savannah (Chatham County), owner of an estate worth more than a hundred thousand dollars in that county alone. After the death of Francis S. Bartow (*q.v.*) the Georgia delegation to the Provisional Congress tendered the place to Forman, and he took his seat on August 7, 1861. As a congressman he worked uncompromisingly to insure the Confederacy's independence. At the first opportunity he proposed free trade with any nation at peace with the Confederacy, and to back this stratagem he wanted the government to buy the entire 1861 cotton crop. When Congress began trying in December to induce twelve-months volunteers to reenlist, Forman proposed to strike out such bribes as furloughs and the right to reelect their officers, fearing that the army would become disorganized. His only resistance to administration policy was his refusal to vote money for railroad construction. He sought election to the Regular Congress but was badly defeated by Julian Hartridge (*q.v.*). At this point Forman retired into the relative obscurity from which he had briefly emerged. "A typical Southern planter, who enjoyed the warmest attachment of all who knew him,"[1] Forman died on September 27, 1875, at his residence in Brunswick, Georgia, and was buried there in Oak Grove Cemetery.

[1] Information on Forman, whose name is uniformly misspelled *Foreman* in most published sources, and who is frequently indexed as "Thomas Forman Bryan" in genealogical material, derives in the main from James B. Heyward, *The Genealogy of the Pendarvis-Bedon Families of South Carolina, 1670–1900* (Atlanta, 1905), courtesy of the Georgia Historical Society, and from Mrs. Marvin F. Engel of St. Simons Island, Ga., who kindly undertook to seek out and identify Forman's grave and to copy the inscription thereon.

THOMAS JEFFERSON FOSTER[1] (Alabama) was born in Nashville, Tennessee, on July 11, 1809, his parents having moved there from Virginia by way of Bardstown, Kentucky. In 1836 Foster married Virginia Prudence Watkins, daughter of a wealthy planter of Lawrence County, Alabama, and soon afterward he moved to Alabama and began planting on his wife's estate near Moulton. As his planting efforts prospered Foster also developed numerous manufacturing interests and by 1860 he had become wealthy. Foster was a strong Whig, though he never sought office before 1861. He also opposed secession firmly, and after Lincoln's election he urged a conference of the southern states to seek redress within the Union. When war began, however, Foster entered service as colonel of an organization of Alabama troops known as Foster's Regiment, which later became the Twenty-seventh Alabama Infantry. He realized the strategic importance of the Tennessee River in Confederate defenses and worked under General Tilghman in locating and building Fort Henry. While still on active duty at Fort Henry, Foster was elected in November, 1861, to the Confederate House of Representatives over three opponents, including the incumbent. He won reelection in 1863 without opposition.

As a congressman Foster was primarily interested in promoting the economic development and fiscal stability of the Confederacy. In March, 1862, he introduced a comprehensive bill to promote industry and mining, and he worked continuously to exempt from military service men in industry and agriculture. His solution to inflation was a bill making Treasury notes legal tender and punishing extortioners, but he saw the bill die in committee. Foster's voting record on other economic matters places him on the side of all strong legislative policies except high taxes. Since Foster's district was occupied by enemy forces during the last half of the war he generally supported whatever military measures seemed necessary to redeem it. Even though he believed the draft to be unconstitutional he confessed that he would "burn the

Constitution" to save the Confederacy. And though he owned almost two hundred slaves, in 1865 he voted to arm and then free them.

In 1865 Foster was elected to the United States Congress over two strong opponents, but he was denied his seat because of his support of the Confederacy. In 1867 he moved to Kentucky where he died on February 24, 1887.[2]

[1] Owen, *History of Alabama*, III, 606.

[2] The authors have been unable to follow Foster after he moved to Kentucky. Owen gives Kentucky as Foster's last place of residence. Marcus J. Wright, *General Officers of the Confederate Army* (New York, 1911) states that Foster died in Lawrence, Ala., but the Alabama census records for 1870 and 1880 do not show Foster as a resident of Lawrence County. Foster's obituary in the Moulton (Ala.) *Advertiser*, February 24, 1887, states that he died "at home," but does not indicate whether he was at home in Alabama or Kentucky. No burial site has been found.

THOMAS W. FREEMAN (Missouri), whose middle name cannot be determined, was born in Anderson County, Kentucky, in 1824, according to *Bench and Bar of Missouri*, a source which also states that "this lawyer was well known to the people of southwestern Missouri." After a common-school education, he began the study of law in Lawrenceburg, Kentucky (seat of Anderson County), and was admitted to the bar in 1847. Two years later he moved to Marysville, California, in the Mother Lode country, where he built up something of a reputation as a criminal lawyer in surroundings eminently suited to such talents. In 1851, however, Freeman returned to Missouri and settled in Bolivar, in Polk County, where he was elected circuit attorney.

During the tumultuous early months of 1861 Freeman was a strong secessionist, and the Neosho legislature chose him as Sixth District representative in Congress. He served in the Provisional and First Regular congresses and was badly defeated in 1864 for reelection by Peter S. Wilkes, mainly, it may be supposed, because Wilkes was in the army and the election was largely a popularity contest in which most of the voters were Missouri soldiers stationed in Texas.[1] His voting record affords the only indication of his political views, since he offered no ideas of his own. Except for denying the president the right to accept single volunteers, and opposing repudiation of the old Confederate Treasury notes which would deprive westerners of their remaining currency, he supported the entire body of war measures proposed by the administration. During his service in Richmond, his wife and three children were in Texas, and it is interesting to note that he made two long trips there to see them, the journey taking almost a month each way. Freeman survived the war by only a few months, dying of a "bilious fever" in the Southwestern Hotel in St. Louis on October 24, 1865. He is buried in an unmarked grave in Bellefontaine Cemetery.

[1] See the above sketch of C. W. Bell for Missouri's method of choosing delegates to the Confederate Congress. Freeman's name, like that of his colleague W. M. Cooke, does not appear on many lists of members of the Provisional Congress. See the sketch of Cooke above.

THOMAS CHARLES FULLER (North Carolina) was born on February 27, 1832, to a prosperous merchant in Fayetteville, North Carolina. The father soon died and the family moved to Franklin County in 1835. After preparatory studies in Louisburg, Fuller entered the University of North Carolina in 1849. He left after three years, however, and entered the employ of a Fayetteville merchant. In 1855 he began studying law under Judge Richmond M. Pearson, and he opened an office in Fayetteville the next year. As a Union Whig, Fuller opposed secession as unwise and unconstitutional, but at Lincoln's call for troops he enlisted in the First North Carolina Infantry. After six months he raised a battery of artillery and was elected its first lieutenant. In the summer of 1863 Fuller resigned his commission to campaign for a seat in the Confederate House of Representatives. Both his opponents had been secession Democrats, and Fuller won an easy victory on the tide of discontent sweeping North Carolina.

Fuller's extreme youth probably accounts for his reticence as a congressman. He seems also to have been the least wealthy congressman, for the census of 1860 shows him as having no property. Nevertheless his voting record indicated a conviction that the Confederacy's demands upon the states and individuals had reached their limits. The only program that he consented to augment even slightly was the excise tax, and here inflation made the increase minimal. At every opportunity Fuller voted to undo controls which had been placed over individuals and to retract powers conferred upon the executive during emergencies. The few suggestions that he made attempted to correct inequities in the tax and habeas corpus laws. At every opportunity Fuller urged President Davis to begin negotiations based on Confederate independence. By 1865 he was privately working for separate state negotiations.

Fuller was elected to the United States Congress in 1865 but was not seated. In 1868 he was defeated in another bid for a congressional seat, and in 1872 he lost a race for Democratic elector. He never again sought public office, but he took part in every campaign for years. Meanwhile he was developing one of the state's best law practices. In 1873 Fuller

91

moved to Raleigh, where his chief reputation was made as defense counsel in criminal cases. In 1891 President Harrison made him a justice of the court of private land claims established to determine titles to land acquired from Mexico. Fuller died in Raleigh on October 20, 1901, and was buried at Oakwood Cemetery.[1]

[1] Information on Fuller's place of interment was taken from the graveyard files of the Department of Archives and History, Raleigh, N.C.

DAVID FUNSTEN[1] (Virginia) was born on October 14, 1819, in Clarke County, Virginia. After attending the Alexandria Boarding School he entered Princeton and was graduated from there in 1838. He then studied law and began practicing in his native county. In 1844 Funsten was elected to the Virginia House of Delegates and served one term.[2] In 1852 he moved to Alexandria where he practiced law until the commencement of the war. When fighting broke out he was appointed lieutenant colonel of the Seventeenth Virginia Infantry, and in October, 1862, he was commissioned colonel of the Eleventh Infantry. However, Funsten had been severely wounded earlier that year at the Battle of Seven Pines and soon was forced to obtain a discharge from the army.[3] When William Smith resigned his seat in the Confederate House of Representatives, Funsten won an easy victory at the regular election in May, 1863, both to complete Smith's term and also to serve in the Second Congress. By this time Funsten's district was occupied by Union forces and most of the voters were soldiers and refugees from the district who cast their votes in army camps.

In the Second Congress Funsten was chairman of the Special Committee Relative to Compensation for Patents. As representative of the district adjacent to Washington, D.C., he was one of Virginia's extremists. He supported the broadest conscription laws, even those including free Negroes and slaves. He also conceded to the president extraordinary powers to appoint officers and to reorganize army units however he chose. From the first Funsten supported heavier taxation, particularly on farm produce. He opposed the tax law of June 14, 1864, because of its weak response to Secretary of the Treasury Memminger's pleas. Funsten also favored stronger antiinflation action, frequent suspensions of the writ of habeas corpus, the impressment of railroads and precious metals, and the impressment of planters' surpluses, all to little avail. The legislation that Funsten proposed dealt mainly with improvements in army organization, and his most innovative idea was to organize disabled soldiers for special services.

Funsten never completely recovered from the effects of his army wounds and was unable to cope with a severe attack of pneumonia. He died at Howard near Alexandria on April 6, 1866, leaving a widow and nine of the thirteen children that had been born to them. He is buried in Ivy Hill Cemetery.[4]

[1] Most of the personal information on Funsten was furnished by Mrs. Hugh B. Cox, Historic Alexandria Foundation, Alexandria, Va.

[2] The authors have been unable to ascertain Funsten's politics. It might be helpful to know that in 1844 his county went Democratic, and in the secession convention of April, 1861, it was represented by a Unionist. See *Niles National Register*, January 4, 1845, p. 276; Henry T. Shanks, *The Secession Movement in Virginia, 1847–1861* (Richmond, 1934), 206.

[3] During the winter of 1862–63 Funsten's oldest son was visiting his father in winter quarters and was killed when the building that he and some soldiers were constructing for Colonel Funsten collapsed.

[4] This information was furnished by Mary Wolf, Ivy Hill Cemetery, Alexandria, Va.

BURGESS SIDNEY GAITHER[1] (North Carolina) was born in Iredell County, North Carolina, on March 16, 1807. After an academic education near home he attended the University of Georgia irregularly, but he eventually decided to study law under his brother. He was licensed to practice in 1829 and in the same year opened his office in Morganton. Gaither was clerk of court in Burke County for the next six years, but his first important political experience was as a delegate to the constitutional convention of 1835. His vigorous work for the Whig party soon attracted attention, and in 1841 President Tyler made him superintendent of the mint at Charlotte, a position he held until 1843. Gaither was later offered the first superintendency of the mint at San Francisco but preferred to remain in North Carolina. Between 1844 and 1860 he was elected to the state senate on three different occasions, and from 1844 to 1852 he was solicitor for the Seventh Judicial District. In 1851 and 1853 Gaither sought a place in the United States House of Representatives, but he could not overcome the Democratic majority in his district at that time. In 1860 he supported the Constitutional Union party for the avowed purpose of saving the Union, but at Lincoln's call for volunteers he became an active secessionist. In November, 1861, Gaither won an uncontested race for the Confederate House of Representatives. Two years later he easily won reelection.

In Congress Gaither loyally supported the central government whenever the Confederacy's jurisdiction was clear. He was the only North Carolinian there in favor of arming the slaves and one of two who did not try to force President Davis to begin peace negotiations. But Gaither feared that a "consolidated military depotism" was developing. He resisted as vigorously as the rest of his delegation any program

93

that might sacrifice the states' interests or that might encroach on the constitutional rights of individuals or states. Most of his own bills, for instance, aimed to preserve each state's control over its available manpower. This balanced position made Gaither an effective voice in Congress. He was chairman of a special committee to investigate the loss of Roanoke Island, and his report led to the resignation of Secretary of War Judah P. Benjamin. During March of 1863 Gaither led the defense when North Carolina's loyalty was impugned during debate.

After the war Gaither devoted himself to his lucrative law practice and to his work as a Son of Temperance. He died in Morganton on February 23, 1892, and was buried in the First Presbyterian churchyard.[2]

[1] Samuel A. Ashe *et al.* (eds.), *Biographical History of North Carolina: From Colonial Times to the Present* (8 vols.; Greensboro, N.C., 1905–17), II, 93–98.
[2] Information on Gaither's place of interment was provided by Mrs. Douglas Allen Barnett, Morganton-Burke Library, Morganton, N.C.

ERASMUS LEE GARDENHIRE (Tennessee) was born in Livingston, Overton County, Tennessee, November 12, 1815. After attending the local schools, he spent two years at Clinton College in Smith County, studied at home one year, then studied law and was admitted to the bar in 1839. However, he did not begin practice at once, but taught school and acted as principal of Livingston Academy for several years. He commenced his law practice in 1844 and from 1849 to 1851 represented five central Tennessee counties in the state senate. In 1851 Gardenhire moved to Sparta, Tennessee, where he edited the *Mountain Democrat* in addition to his legal work. In 1853 he was an unsuccessful candidate for Congress on the Democratic ticket, but in 1856 he was both a delegate to the National Democratic convention and an elector on the ticket of Buchanan and Breckinridge.

In November, 1861, Gardenhire was elected Fourth District representative to the Confederate Congress. During his two years' service he debated infrequently and offered few suggestions as to pending legislation. He accepted executive dominance as a war necessity and balked only at the plan to repudiate inflated currency and replace it with new notes. Outside Congress Gardenhire worked with a few others on the futile plan to induce the states of the Northwest to ally themselves with the Confederacy. He was not a candidate for reelection to the Second Congress. In 1877 Gardenhire was appointed to the state arbitration court, serving one year. Prior to that time he had served another two years in the lower house of the state legislature (1875–1877). He

94

later was a member of the Commission of Referees for western Tennessee. Judge Gardenhire had moved to Carthage, Tennessee, in 1876, and he died there on April 4, 1899.[1]

[1] The authors of this work were fortunate to find that the Tennessee State Library and Archives were concurrently compiling a biographical register of all members of the Tennessee legislature, which resulted in much valuable material being made available. Particular assistance in this connection was given by Gladys Bracy, Research Technician, and Robert M. McBride, Recording Secretary, Tennessee Historical Society, Nashville.

AUGUSTUS HILL GARLAND (Arkansas), younger brother of Rufus King Garland (*q.v.*) and youngest member of the Provisional Confederate Congress, was born in Tipton County, Tennessee, June 11, 1832. The year after his birth his parents moved to Arkansas; after his father's death he was brought up in his stepfather's residence in Washington, Arkansas, where he obtained his early education in a private school. He later attended St. Mary's College at Lebanon, Kentucky, and was graduated from St. Joseph's College at Bardstown. After teaching school for a time, Garland studied law and was admitted to the Arkansas bar at the early age of eighteen. In 1856 he moved to Little Rock, and in 1860 he was a presidential elector on the ticket of Bell and Everett.

An original opponent of secession, Garland was considered by some to be unsound on the slavery question, but after Lincoln's call for volunteers in April, he shifted his ground and worked actively for separation in the May convention.[1] He was then chosen one of Arkansas' five delegates to the Provisional Congress, all of whom were elected at large. In November he won the Third District seat in the First Regular Congress in an election subsequently contested by his opponent. A year later he unsuccessfully sought the Senate seat of Robert W. Johnson (*q.v.*), but in 1863 he was easily reelected to the House. On November 8, 1864, upon the death of Senator Charles B. Mitchel (*q.v.*), he was appointed to fill out Mitchel's unexpired term, thus serving prior to his thirty-third birthday in all capacities in the legislative branch of the Confederate government from first to last. In the second Congress Garland was chairman of the House Committee on Territories and Public Lands and, as an advocate of strong emergency measures, was considered one of the president's ablest young supporters. While he proposed to make Treasury notes legal tender, to permit the detail of soldiers for civilian duty, and to draft 500,000 men for the army, his main interest focused on the protection of personal rights, and he was a member of the Committee on the Judiciary in all three congresses. He vigorously advocated bills to establish a supreme court, a court of claims, and measures to prevent delay in the judicial process. Perhaps his strongest motivation as a legislator was his abhorrence of martial law; his and Burgess S. Gaither's (*q.v.*) minority report of May 28, 1864, was one of the most compelling statements against suspension of the writ of habeas corpus ever penned in the Confederacy.

Immediately following the close of hostilities Garland became active in reconstructing his state and his class. First securing a pardon from President Johnson, he successfully argued and overturned an act of Congress which debarred from practice before the United States Supreme Court all those who had borne arms against the government or accepted office in a government hostile to it. This was the so-called "Iron-Clad Oath"; Garland maintained it was a bill of attainder and ex post facto to boot, and he was upheld. In 1867 he was elected to the Senate but was denied his seat. After the Democrats reclaimed the state, he was elected governor of Arkansas, and two days later he was elected to the United States Senate for the second time, taking his seat on March 4, 1877. He resigned on March 9, 1885, to become attorney general in Cleveland's first cabinet. When he retired from this office at the end of the presidential term, Garland continued to practice law in the capital. He died suddenly on January 26, 1899, while arguing a case before the supreme court, and was buried in Mount Holly Cemetery, Little Rock.

[1] See above sketch of Felix I. Batson, Note.

RUFUS KING GARLAND (Arkansas), elder brother of Augustus Hill Garland, and whose cousins were successively the wives of Simpson H. Morgan (*q.v.*), was born in Tipton County, Tennessee, May 22, 1830. He was taken to Arkansas in childhood and grew up in his stepfather's home in Washington, county seat of Hampstead. His education was obtained in a local private school and at St. Joseph's College in Bardstown, Kentucky. Garland was elected to the Arkansas legislature in 1858 and was reelected up to and including the called session of 1861, which met to consider the question of secession. Like his brother, R. K. Garland had been a strong Union Whig, but in the May session, after Lincoln's call for troops, he voted to take Arkansas out of the Union. He then organized a company of troops, became its captain, and served with it until after the fall of Vicksburg. In the summer of 1863, thoroughly disillusioned with the conduct of the war, he canvassed the Second Congressional District and defeated Grandison D.

Royston (*q.v.*) in his bid for reelection. As a congressman Garland seldom missed an opportunity to censure a cabinet member, limit the authority of President Davis, or zealously guard the rights of states and individuals. His military background, however, made him entirely sympathetic with the armies in the field, and bills to maintain them were almost the only ones which he would support involving the extension of Confederate authority. For instance, in sharp contrast to his avowed opposition to the administration (which in turn was in sharp contrast to his brother's position), Rufus Garland, on February 22, 1865, voted to double the tax on agricultural products, a virtual act of heresy by a Trans-Mississippian at that time. After the close of the war Garland settled down on his farm at Prairie de Anne, then in Hempstead County (now Nevada). A delegate to the 1874 constitutional convention, he left the Democratic party in 1879 to espouse the Greenback cause, and in 1882 he ran unsuccessfully for governor. Garland died on December 12, 1886, at his home and was buried in Prescott, county seat of Nevada County.

MUSCOE RUSSELL HUNTER GARNETT (Virginia) was born into a prominent family at Elmwood, Essex County, Virginia, on July 25, 1821. He was a nephew of Robert M. T. Hunter (*q.v.*). Garnett was first tutored at home and then attended the academy opened for his benefit on the family estate by his father.[1] Next he attended the University of Virginia for a year, followed by two more years of private study at home. In 1840 he returned to the university for two years of further study and received his law degree in 1842. Garnett began practicing in Essex County in 1842, but he continued a rigorous program of self-education in preparation for a career in politics. In 1850 he published *The Union, Past and Future*, which deplored governmental centralization and argued that the South would thrive if it seceded. The popularity of this work, which was one of the earliest competent analyses of the relation of slavery to the federal government, led to his election to the state constitutional convention of 1850, where he advocated a mixed basis of representation based on person and property. Garnett was a delegate to the Democratic national conventions of 1852 and 1856. He served in the state House of Delegates from 1853 to 1857, where he headed the Committee on Finance. Then came four years in Congress, where he earned a reputation as a protagonist of slavery, strict construction, and financial conservatism. By this time he was also a successful planter with extensive holdings. Long a secessionist, Garnett entered the Virginia convention of 1861 in time to vote for disunion. In November he won a close race for the Confederate House of Representatives.

In Congress Garnett continued his interest in finance. He also weighed carefully how all laws might affect his productive district. He accepted the moderate tax program before Congress in 1862 but afterward opposed both higher taxes and a broader tax base. In March, 1863, he tried to lighten agriculture's burden by seeking a ruling that taxes on land, slaves, and property were direct and must be apportioned among the states on the basis of population. Garnett had long advocated low tariffs and now voted for free trade and against prohibiting the import of luxuries. He exercised similar vigilance on other matters. He urged retroactive pay for property impressed, and was one of the few completely opposing the destruction of any property to prevent its capture. He sanctioned conscription but wished to retain the long exemption list set early in 1862. By contrast, Garnett endorsed fully the president's dictation of foreign affairs and the War Department's judgment in army matters.

In 1863 Garnett lost his race for reelection to R. L. Montague (*q.v.*). He contracted typhoid during his last days in Congress and died at home on February 14, 1864. He was buried at the family cemetery on his estate.

[1] James M. Garnett, "Biographical Sketch of Hon. Muscoe Russell Hunter Garnett," *William and Mary College Quarterly*, XVIII (1909–10), 17–37, 71–89.

LUCIUS JEREMIAH GARTRELL (Georgia) was born in Wilkes County, Georgia, on January 17, 1821, into a prosperous planter family. He attended Randolph-Macon College from 1838 to 1841 and the University of Georgia for one more year. But before graduating he began reading law under Robert Toombs (*q.v.*) and was admitted to the bar in 1842. After practicing in Wilkes for a year, Gartrell was elected solicitor general and then judge of the northern judicial circuit. In 1854 he moved to Atlanta. Gartrell was originally a Whig, but he was of such states' rights convictions that he soon switched to the Democrats. He served in the legislature from 1847 to 1851. In 1849 he introduced the noted Southern Rights Resolution, expressing the most extreme southern position on the slavery controversy then before Congress. The next year he stumped the state against Toombs, Stephens, and Cobb (*q.q.v.*) in opposition to the proposed Clay Compromise. He carried his radicalism to Congress in 1857, was an early secessionist, and resigned when Georgia seceded. When war began, Gartrell organized the Seventh Georgia Regiment and was elected its colonel. At

First Manassas, Gartrell's sixteen-year-old son was killed and Francis S. Bartow (*q.v.*) died in Gartrell's arms.[1] In November, 1861, Gartrell easily won a seat in the Confederate House of Representatives.

In Congress Gartrell was chairman of the Committee on the Judiciary, and in this capacity he tried unsuccessfully to enable cabinet members to discuss on the floor of Congress matters pertaining to their departments. He caused a stir in 1863 when he went before the Georgia legislature and praised both President Davis and the administration. His voting record confirms this support, and its strength is indicated by the variety and the nature of the legislation which he proposed: to make Treasury notes legal tender, to end all military substitutions and exemptions, to draft all employees in the executive departments, to nationalize the textile industry, and to let the president suspend the habeas corpus when public safety required it.

Gartrell did not seek reelection, and on August 22, 1864, he was reappointed in the army with the rank of brigadier general. He organized four regiments of reserves into Gartrell's Brigade and did good service in opposing Sherman's march into South Carolina. He was wounded near Coosawatchie.

After the war Gartrell became the premier criminal lawyer in Atlanta. He was a member of the state constitutional convention of 1877, and in 1882 he waged an unsuccessful race against A. H. Stephens (*q.v.*) for the Democratic gubernatorial nomination. He died in Atlanta on April 7, 1891, and is buried in Oakland Cemetery.

[1] There is another possible explanation of Gartrell's decision to leave the army. His major wrote Alexander H. Stephens that morale and discipline in Gartrell's regiment was so bad that the commanding general planned to call a court martial to investigate the situation. John Dunwoody to A. H. Stephens, November 27, 1861, in Alexander H. Stephens Papers, Manuscripts Division, Library of Congress, Washington, D.C.

MEREDITH POINDEXTER GENTRY (Tennessee) was born September 15, 1809, in Rockingham County, North Carolina. When he was four years old his father, a wealthy planter, moved to Williamson County, Tennessee, where the younger Gentry's education was limited to a log schoolhouse. He read widely, however, in his father's library and in the newspapers of the day—particularly the congressional debates. In 1835 he was elected to a seat in the legislature, an office which he held until his election to Congress in 1838. He served six nonconsecutive terms in Congress and, although he was a large slaveholder, was a moderate on the slavery question and an opponent of secession. But with the election of Lincoln he veered the other way, and after the attack on Sumter he reluctantly became a secessionist. Gentry was elected to the First

Regular Confederate Congress by the voters of the Sixth District in November, 1861. He was considered for the speakership of the House but lost in the balloting to Thomas S. Bocock of Virginia (*q.v.*). At first Gentry preferred to maintain the army by increasing the calls upon the states for volunteers, but by the fall of 1862 he had become an enthusiastic supporter of conscription. He missed most of the roll calls on other important matters and for some reason did not attend the last two sessions of the First Congress; nor did he stand for reelection. In fact, Gentry was much more of a figure in the United States Congress, where he had been an intimate of Clay, Webster, and Calhoun, than he was in the Confederate Congress. He advocated secession only as a temporary expedient, and was not generally in sympathy with the policies of the Richmond government. Gentry did not long survive the war; he died in Nashville on November 2, 1866, and was buried in Mount Olivet Cemetery.

THOMAS SAUNDERS GHOLSON (Virginia) was born in Gholsonville, Virginia, on December 9, 1808. He attended secondary school in Oxford, North Carolina, then entered the University of Virginia and graduated in 1827. After studying law he practiced for several years in his home county of Brunswick. In 1829 he married his cousin Cary Ann Gholson. In 1840 he moved to Petersburg and entered a partnership with his brother, soon becoming prominent in the practice of both civil and criminal law. Gholson was active in civil affairs. He helped found and support the Petersburg public library. For several years he was president of the Bank of Petersburg and was interested in railroad development in the state. In 1859 he was appointed judge of the Fifth Judicial Circuit of Virginia and served until his election to the Confederate Congress. In 1863 the voters rejected C. F. Collier (*q.v.*) and chose Gholson in his place, his large majority of the army vote giving him a total majority of twenty-nine.[1]

Judge Gholson's lack of legislative experience[2] probably kept him from focusing his attention on any particular matter while in Congress, but there were few stronger advocates of emergency war legislation. In February, 1865, he instructed the Committee on Military Affairs to consider placing all able-bodied men in the army. He also wished to increase the powers of General-in-Chief Robert E. Lee and to give the War Department the right to take over all state militia. To make the best use of the economy Gholson favored almost total wartime control over the Confederacy's currency, produce, and transportation facilities. Nor did he hesitate to let the president suspend the right of habeas

100

corpus where it seemed necessary. As late as February 1, 1865, Gholson saw no cause for despondency and vigorously opposed arming the
"licentious and fanatical" [3] Negroes, his only significant disagreement
with the Davis administration.

After the war Gholson and his son-in-law formed a cotton and tobacco commission house in Liverpool, England. En route from there,
he died in Savannah, Georgia, on December 12, 1868, and was buried in
the Blandford Church Cemetery in Petersburg.

[1] Collier contested the outcome of this election. See, in this volume, the Collier
biography, Note 5.

[2] He was an active Whig but held no other elective office.

[3] *Speech of Hon. Thos. S. Gholson, of Virginia, on the Policy of Employing Negro
Troops and the Duty of All Classes to Aid in the Prosecution of the War* (Richmond, 1865).

JOHN ADAMS GILMER (North Carolina) was born in Guilford County,
North Carolina, on November 4, 1805. For several winters he attended
near-by academies and worked the remaining months on his father's
farm. At the age of seventeen he began teaching school in South
Carolina, but he eventually studied law under Archibald D. Murphy
and began practicing in Greensboro in 1832. By the start of the Civil
War he had the largest practice in his part of the state and also engaged
in planting. In politics Gilmer was an active Whig. In 1846 he began a
ten-year service in the state senate, gaining recognition as a champion
of state aid to railroads and as an opponent of agitation of the slavery
issue. Gilmer's forcefulness and wit earned him such popularity that in
1856 the Know-Nothing party, into which most North Carolina Whigs
had gone, nominated him for governor. He campaigned vigorously in a
hopeless contest and emerged with his popularity unscathed. Gilmer
was a representative to Congress from 1857 to 1861, winning further
favor with moderates by his opposition to the southern strategy on the
Kansas-Nebraska question. At the urging of William H. Seward and
others President-elect Lincoln offered him a place in his cabinet, but
Gilmer declined when Lincoln could not convince him that the Republican party was not hostile to the South. As late as February, 1861,
Gilmer distributed thousands of antisecession pamphlets over North
Carolina; he voted for secession in the May convention only because of
Lincoln's call for troops.

In November, 1863, Gilmer won an uncontested race as representative to the Confederate Congress. He was chairman of the Committee
on Elections, a post he had held under the United States. His most
constructive work was his effort to secure the broadest tax and monetary policies with the least infringement on individuals and states,

101

surely a difficult task. Otherwise Gilmer tried to halt and even to reverse the accretion of powers to the central government. His only concessions to the emergency were his approval of certain measures aiming to improve the efficiency of existing laws; for instance, a better allocation of manpower between the army and production. Though not a Reconstructionist, Gilmer was an active peace advocate. He was instrumental in persuading President Davis to send a delegation to Hampton Roads to discuss peace with Abraham Lincoln. When the conference failed Gilmer proposed a diet to represent the independent Confederacy and the United States.

After the war Gilmer supported President Johnson's Reconstruction program and attended the national Union convention of 1866. He died at his residence in Greensboro on May 14, 1868, and was interred in the Presbyterian Church cemetery.

JOHN GOODE (Virginia) was born on May 27, 1829, in Bedford County, Virginia, of family stock which had been in Virginia since the seventeenth century. He attended New London Academy, graduated from Emory and Henry college in 1848, and then studied at the Lexington Law School. Goode began practicing in Liberty in 1851 and was elected to the General Assembly the same year, beginning a half-century of distinguished service within the Democratic party. In 1860 Goode urged secession if Lincoln were elected, and when that occurred he worked for disunion both before and as a member of the secession convention. When war broke out Goode enlisted in the Second Virginia Cavalry, participating in the Battle of First Manassas. Subsequently he became a colonel on the staff of General Jubal Early. In November, 1861, while still at the front, he was elected to the Confederate House of Representatives and was reelected in 1863, though he refused to campaign on either occasion.

Goode was one of the most innovative Virginians in Congress and bent his energies primarily to army matters. At first he opposed conscription, but soon he became one of its leading exponents. In January, 1865, he even tried to end the president's power to detail some soldiers to civilian duties. Goode also chaired a special committee which advised that commanding generals administer the draft laws in their respective districts. Later he voted to arm, but not free, the slaves. To keep the army at top efficiency, Goode advocated equally comprehensive use of the Confederacy's facilities and resources. He placed great reliance on impressment. In the First Congress he suggested forcing producers to sell their surplus to the government at impressment prices; in the Second, he headed a committee to investigate impressing meat from speculators. Obviously Goode had President Davis' complete confidence. In March, 1865, upon being summoned to Davis' office, Goode assured the president that Virginians would gladly make far greater sacrifices if called upon.

After the war Goode moved to Norfolk, where he became a noted criminal lawyer. He remained active in politics, serving in the legislature in 1866, in the "Whig and Democratic Convention" in 1867, and as a perennial delegate to Democratic national conventions. Goode was elected to Congress for five straight terms, being chairman of the House Committee on Education. After finally being defeated for a sixth term in 1884, he moved to Washington, D.C., and was United States solicitor general for one year only, since the Senate refused to confirm his nomination. In 1898 Goode became president of the state bar association, but his highest honor was his unanimous selection as president of the constitutional convention of 1901–1902. His *Recollections of a Lifetime*[1] is a sensitive account and contains his more important addresses. He died in Norfolk on July 14, 1909, and was buried in Longwood Cemetery, Bedford, Virginia.

[1] John Goode, *Recollections of a Lifetime* (New York, 1906).

MALCOLM DUNCAN GRAHAM (Texas) was born in Autauga County, Alabama, on July 6, 1827. He received a college education at Transylvania University in Lexington, Kentucky, and also studied law there. On his return to Alabama he located in Wetumpka, and in 1853 he was appointed clerk of the state house of representatives. The following year he emigrated to Texas, settling in Henderson. Graham was a state senator in 1857, and the next year he was elected attorney general of the state on the ticket with Sam Houston as governor. He was a Breckinridge elector in 1860, and after the secession of Texas he raised a regiment for the war. Soon after, however, he won a seat in the First Regular Congress in a campaign which his friends conducted while he remained with his regiment. Graham was an unassertive representative, his only significant proposal being an unsuccessful attempt to exempt from military service all men on the Texas frontier. He disliked most taxes and condemned the high-handed use of martial law frequently employed by commanders in the Trans-Mississippi Department. Otherwise he supported aggressive action on the part of Congress and the president. In the summer of 1863 he stumped his district for reelection as an administration supporter, but he lost to the popular John R. Baylor (*q.v.*), whose political posture in the Confederate Congress was exactly the opposite of Graham's. Graham was then appointed a judge advocate with the rank of colonel, and while enroute from Richmond to Texas he was captured attempting to cross the Mississippi River. He was imprisoned at Johnson's Island in Lake Erie until February, 1865, when he was exchanged. After the war Graham resided in Montgomery, Alabama, practicing his profession and involving himself in the political struggles of the Reconstruction era. In 1876 he was elected chairman of the executive committee of the Conservative Democrat party, and in 1877 he declined consideration for the governorship of Alabama. He died in Montgomery on October 8, 1878, and was buried in Oakwood Cemetery.

WILLIAM ALEXANDER GRAHAM (North Carolina) was born on September 5, 1804, in Lincoln County, North Carolina. He attended local academies, then entered the University of North Carolina and graduated in 1824. He next studied law under Chief Justice Thomas Ruffin (q.v.) and in 1826 began practicing in Hillsboro, where he soon became a recognized leader of the bar. He also acquired and operated a small plantation. But Graham's chief interest was politics. He served as a Whig in the General Assembly from 1833 to 1840, as a United States senator for the next three years, and as governor from 1843 to 1849. Graham's service was always identified by interest in public education and in internal improvements. As a legislator he introduced the bill that established a system of common schools for North Carolina. As governor he vigorously promoted state aid for railroad development. In 1849 President Fillmore named him secretary of the navy, where he was instrumental in sending Commodore Perry to Japan and in sending an expedition to explore the Amazon River. He resigned to become Whig candidate for vice-president in 1852, but this was not a Whig year. In 1860 Graham opposed secession so vehemently that he was a presidential possibility on the Constitutional Union ticket, and as a member of the Washington Peace Convention and of the North Carolina secession convention he worked for the Union. However, after Lincoln's call for volunteers to quell the rebellion Graham reversed his position. Five of his sons became Confederate officers.

In November, 1862, Graham foiled George Davis' (q.v.) bid for reelection to the Confederate Senate and took his place in that body at the beginning of the Second Congress. Richmond gossips correctly observed that his election was a "rebuke to military usurpation."[1] Graham refused to support experiments in reorganization that might

104

demoralize the army; otherwise he opposed virtually all of President Davis' legislative programs: habeas corpus suspensions were unconstitutional; drafting slaves destroyed the meaning of the Confederacy; curtailing military exemptions would ruin the home front; controlling state vessels in foreign commerce reduced imports by half; the frequency of presidential vetoes revealed a would-be despot; and so on. Most of his own bills sought to ease the tax and funding burdens on civilians. Graham inevitably became a leader in the peace movement, and by March, 1865, he was advising separate state negotiations for the best reconstruction terms available.

Graham was elected to the United States Senate in 1866, but was not allowed to take his seat. Thereafter he was North Carolina's beloved elder statesman. He was a trustee of the Peabody Fund until his death. Graham died on August 11, 1875, at Saratoga Springs, New York, while arbitrating a boundary dispute between Maryland and Virginia. He was buried in the Presbyterian Church cemetery in Hillsboro.

[1] John B. Jones, *A Rebel War Clerk's Diary at the Confederate States Capital*, ed. Howard Swiggett (2 vols.; New York, 1861), I, 199.

HENRY GRAY (Louisiana), a native of South Carolina, was born in Laurens District, January 19, 1816, and was graduated from what is now the University of South Carolina at the age of eighteen. After studying law and being admitted to the bar, he settled in Winston County, Mississippi, where he was for several terms district attorney. Gray then served a term in the Mississippi legislature, and in 1848 ran unsuccessfully for Congress on the Whig ticket. Upon his removal to Bienville Parish, Louisiana, in 1851, he changed his political allegiance to the Democrats and, while establishing a formidable reputation in the field of criminal law, found time to engage in agriculture and in the politics of his newly adopted state. In 1860, as a member of the Louisiana legislature, he failed by but one vote of election to the United States Senate, his opponent being Judah P. Benjamin.

When Mississippi seceded early in the following year, Gray enlisted as a private in a regiment from that state, but was persuaded by Jefferson Davis (an intimate friend) to organize a Louisiana regiment, the Twenty-eighth Infantry, of which he was elected colonel. Gray took a prominent and praiseworthy role in the battles of Mansfield and Pleasant Hill, being at times in brigade command. Upon the death of Benjamin Lewis Hodge (*q.v.*) on August 12, 1864, Governor Henry W. Allen called a special election for October 17 to fill the vacant seat. Gray, a wholly involuntary candidate who was on duty with his command, only learned after the fact of his easy victory over an opponent who endorsed the administration of General E. Kirby Smith of the Trans-Mississippi—an index to Smith's popularity in north Louisiana. He took his seat on December 28, 1864. Paradoxically, Smith had promoted Gray to brigadier general in an order issued April 15, 1864, and in the dying days of the Confederacy Davis made his appointment official; the Senate confirmed the nomination on the day of its final adjournment. During his brief congressional service Gray opposed any sort of peace negotiation and voted in favor of every desperation measure proposed. However, he also voted to dismiss his old opponent Benjamin as secretary of state, to restrict the presidential powers of Davis, and to invest General Lee with supreme authority. He served one term in the Louisiana Senate immediately after the war, after which he retired into almost complete seclusion. His last years were spent at the home of his daughter near Coushatta, Louisiana, where he died December 11, 1892. General Gray was buried in Springville Cemetery there.

PETER W.[1] GRAY (Texas), was born in Fredericksburg, Virginia, December 12, 1819, one of twelve children. His father went to Texas in 1835, and the younger Gray migrated to the then Republic in 1838 and began the study of law in his father's office in Houston. He also served in the Texas army and in 1841 succeeded his father as district attorney. After being active in city politics, he represented Harris County in the house of the first legislature and in the senate of the fourth, after the admission of Texas to the Union. He was elected district judge in 1854 and served until the outbreak of the Civil War.

In November, 1861, Gray won a decisive victory to the First Regular Confederate Congress as a candidate from the district embracing Houston. While in Richmond he was the most vigilant guardian of Texas' economic interests. He secured a separate branch of the Treasury Department for the Trans-Mississippi region, and when Congress decided against direct taxation, which most Texans preferred, Gray labored unsuccessfully to rely more heavily on export duties. At the same time he proposed that the ban on cotton exports not apply to shipments into Mexico. He also took a leading part in writing sequestration laws, presumably because of the great amount of Texas land in the hands of northern owners. On most other matters Gray was a nationalist; as early as March, 1862, he suggested that the Confederacy take "absolute control" over all railroads. It was his support of conscription and of overseer exemption from military service that caused him to lose his race for reelection to A. M. Branch (q.v.) in 1863. The

106

following year he was appointed fiscal agent of the Trans-Mississippi Department by President Davis.

After the war Gray resumed his successful law practice. Although suffering from tuberculosis, he was appointed a justice of the Texas Supreme Court in 1874, but he had to resign two months later because of his health. He died in Houston October 3, 1874, and was buried in Glenwood Cemetery. Two years later the Texas legislature named Gray County in the Panhandle in his honor. One of his sisters was the wife of Brigadier General Claudius W. Sears, C.S.A.

[1] According to collateral descendants and other students of Texiana, Gray adopted the initial W. because all his brothers had middle names and he had none.

JOHN GREGG (Texas) was born in Lawrence County, Alabama, September 28, 1828, but moved to La Grange, Alabama, in boyhood. He was educated in La Grange College, after which he studied law in Tuscumbia. Emigrating to Fairfield, Texas, in 1852, he established a practice there and in 1856 was elected district judge. In 1861 Gregg was elected to the secession convention, which in turn chose him as a member of the Provisional Confederate Congress, where he was appointed chairman of the Committee on Claims. It was his suggestion to have the permanent Constitution stipulate that federal officers residing or acting solely within a particular state be subject to impeachment by the legislature of that state. Otherwise he generally supported legislation strengthening the central government, and was the only Texas delegate to approve the ban on cotton exportation except through Confederate seaports. After the Battle of First Manassas in July, Gregg gave up his seat in Congress to recruit the Seventh Texas Infantry, although he never formally resigned and the vacancy was not filled. The following February he and his regiment had the bad luck to be in Fort Donelson and were surrendered. After parole and exchange, he was promoted brigadier general to rank from August 29, 1862. His brigade was assigned to Hood's division of Longstreet's corps, and was part of the "wedge" driven into the Union line at Chickamauga. Gregg was severely wounded in the battle. After his recovery he was assigned to command Hood's old Texas Brigade, which he led with conspicuous gallantry at the Battle of the Wilderness and during the Richmond campaign which followed in the summer of 1864. After five months of almost continuous fighting, during which he had two horses killed under him and his brigade suffered frightful casualties, the intrepid Gregg was killed in action on the Charles City Road below Richmond on the morning of October 7, 1864. He is buried in Odd Fellows Cemetery in Aberdeen, Mississippi.

STEPHEN FOWLER HALE (Alabama), a native of Kentucky, was born in Crittenden County on January 31, 1816. He was graduated from Cumberland University and moved to Alabama about 1837; there he taught school in Greene County for a year while he read law. He subsequently graduated from the law department of Transylvania University at Lexington, Kentucky, and located in Eutaw, Alabama, to practice. In 1843 Hale was elected to the legislature from Greene County, and in 1846 he served as lieutenant of the First Alabama Infantry in the Mexican War. He was defeated in a race for Congress in 1853, running on the Democratic ticket, but was again elected to the legislature in 1857 and in 1859.

When the ordinance of secession was adopted in January, 1861, Hale was appointed commissioner to Kentucky by Governor Moore, and later that month he was elected to the Provisional Confederate Congress in Montgomery. He recognized the need for haste in establishing a strong and solvent government and even proposed that the permanent Constitution go into effect as soon as elections could be held. Later he suggested that the permanent Constitution invest Congress with the authority to permit appeals from state to Confederate courts and that Congress place an export tax on all forest and field products (which would, of course, include cotton), both of which were too ultra for acceptance. The only significant power which Hale attempted to withhold from the central government was the right to enlist volunteers and appoint officers independently of the state governors.

Instead of seeking election to the Regular Congress, Hale entered the army as lieutenant colonel of the Eleventh Alabama Infantry. In the course of the Peninsular Campaign he transferred temporarily to the Ninth Alabama, which he led at the Battle of Seven Pines, but then he returned to his old regiment which he commanded at Gaines's Mill during the Battle of the Seven Days. Here he was wounded on June 27, 1862; his wound was not at first considered consequential, but it caused his death at Richmond on July 18, 1862.[1] Colonel Hale was buried in Mesopotamia Cemetery in Eutaw.

[1] Both the Ninth and Eleventh Alabama infantries were in Wilcox's brigade of Longstreet's division. Hale was only reported "wounded" at Gaines's Mill in official reports and probably succumbed to infection in a day when asepsis was unknown.

THOMAS BURTON HANLY (Arkansas) was born June 9, 1812, in Nicholsonville, Kentucky. It is not known where he was educated or where he was admitted to the bar; however, he went to Arkansas in 1833 and settled in Helena, where he began practice. He was described as a vigorous, aggressive character who made either devoted friends or bitter enemies. In the years before the Civil War Hanly served in both branches of the legislature and as county, probate, circuit, and supreme court judge. He was an early exponent of secession and was labeled by a contemporary as the ablest disunionist in the May, 1861, convention which made Arkansas a member of the Confederacy. In November of that year he won election to the First Regular Congress and was reelected in 1863. In the beginning of his congressional career he opposed virtually every major program to strengthen the central government, being especially hostile to execution of the draft laws. But by 1864 he recognized the need for desperation measures and supported every sort of bold innovation. Condemning Secretary of the Treasury Memminger as incompetent and accepting the financial situation as hopeless, Hanly advocated doubling the tax on agriculture, ending all classes of exemptions from army services, impressing everything needed to continue the war, drafting slaves, and even attempting to extend the draft into enemy-held territory. There were few emergency powers he would deny the president, and he savagely pounded the president's chief critic, Henry S. Foote of Tennessee, in a committee brawl over administration policy. After the war he practiced law in Helena until his retirement in 1872. Judge Hanly died at his residence in Little Rock on June 9, 1880, and was buried there in Maple Hill Cemetery.

THOMAS ALEXANDER HARRIS (Missouri), a native of Warren County, Virginia, gave his age as seventeen years and four months upon entrance to the Military Academy on September 1, 1843. The year of his birth, 1826, is confirmed by the inscription on his marker in Cave Hill Cemetery, Louisville, Kentucky. His father moved to Missouri when Harris was a boy, and he grew up there. He did not graduate from West Point but withdrew in May, 1845, after which he studied law and was admitted to the bar. He was well known as a lawyer and budding politician in northeastern Missouri when he was appointed a second lieutenant of the Twelfth U.S. Infantry for Mexican War service in 1848, but he was mustered out without seeing action. For a time he was then a soldier of fortune in South and Central America, but about 1856, after marrying a sister of Admiral D. D. Porter of later Civil War fame, Harris settled in Hannibal, Missouri. The Neosho "legislature" chose him to represent the Second District until an election was held and he served during the Provisional and First congresses.[1] As a member of the Committee on Military Affairs he was especially interested in the welfare of soldiers and their families. In an effort to keep western soldiers at home to control guerrilla warfare, he opposed giving the president any troops not voluntarily offered by state governors; and he fought the draft for the same reason. Otherwise Harris was one of the readiest to give the government and the army any additional powers they requested. Nevertheless, by 1864 he had alienated President Davis by constantly badgering him to promote Major General Sterling Price, decidedly not one of the chief executive's favorite generals. In Richmond, Colonel Harris, as he was known (his rank derived from the Missouri State Guard), was a celebrated *bon vivant* and was defeated for reelection in 1864 by the soldier and refugee vote, which went heavily in favor of the "Sobriety and Morality" candidate, Nimrod L. Norton (*q.v.*). After the war Harris pursued a number of occupations, including life insurance agent and newspaperman, before settling in Louisville in the 1870s. He was appointed assistant secretary of state of Kentucky in 1880 and continued to reside in or near Louisville until his death in Pewee Valley, Kentucky, April 9, 1895.

[1] See the above sketch of C. W. Bell for Missouri's method of choosing delegates to the Confederate Congress.

WILEY POPE HARRIS (Mississippi), a relative of George Washington on his father's side and of Lieutenant General Wade Hampton, C.S.A., on his mother's side, was born near Holmesville, Mississippi, November 9, 1818. After attending schools in Columbus and Brandon, and the University of Virginia, he graduated from the law department of Transylvania College in Lexington, Kentucky, and in 1840 began practice in Gallatin, Mississippi, a now extinct town, then the county seat of Copiah County. He was appointed and then elected circuit judge of the Second District, serving from 1844 to 1850; despite being the youngest he was reputed to be the ablest judge in the state. From 1853 to 1855 he was a Democratic member of Congress.

Harris was elected to the Mississippi constitutional convention of 1861 as a straight-out secessionist, and that body chose him unanimously on the first ballot as a delegate to the Provisional Congress. At Montgomery he was recognized as preeminent in the Mississippi delegation, and few men tried to give the new nation more momentum. He even advocated dispensing with a provisional government and going directly into general elections. To fill the treasury he proposed a duty on all exports and a tax on slaves. With considerable vision he suggested giving the president control over telegraph lines, dividing the Confederacy into four military districts, and offering reenlistment bonuses to volunteers. He opposed, however, the president's use of state troops for special service, a privilege which he felt had been abused. Judge Harris did not run for election to the Regular Congress; he instead retired to private life at his home in Jackson, where he had moved in 1855, and continued the practice of law. In his later years Judge Harris was the acknowledged Nestor of the Mississippi bar, renowned alike for his legal learning and sparkling wit. He was a member of the constitutional convention of 1890 and chairman of one of its committees. The following year, on December 3, 1891, he died in Jackson and was buried there in Greenwood Cemetery.

JAMES THOMAS HARRISON (Mississippi), a lineal descendant of Benjamin Harrison, signer of the Declaration of Independence, was born near Pendleton, South Carolina, on November 30, 1811. His father had been a battery commander in the War of 1812 and later comptroller general of the state of South Carolina. The son received a common-school education and attended the University of South Carolina, from which he was graduated in 1829. He then studied law under James Louis Petigru, a staunch Unionist and undisputed leader of the state bar for nearly forty years. Harrison moved to Macon, Mississippi, in 1834 and two years later settled permanently in Columbus, Mississippi, which would be his home for the rest of his life. As a local leader in that area of northeast Mississippi lying along the Alabama line, he was sent by the Mississippi secession convention to the Provisional Congress in Montgomery, Alabama, in January, 1861. He soon wrote to his wife, "There will be no halting or backing down—no attempt at reconstruction."[1] As a congressman he faithfully adhered to this belief. He seldom missed a day in attendance, obligingly acceded to the leadership of the Davis administration, and volunteered few suggestions of his own. Only in rare instances did he even cater to local interests—and then on matters of secondary importance. In short, his congressional career was neither particularly inspired nor inspiring. At the conclusion of his term he did not run for election to the Regular Congress but returned home to his practice. After the war and prior to the imposition of a military regime upon the prostrate state, Harrison was elected to the U.S. Congress but was refused admission. He continued to practice law in Columbus until his death there on May 22, 1879. He was buried in Friendship Cemetery.

[1] James Thomas Harrison to his wife, February 17, 1861, in James Thomas Harrison Papers, Southern Historical Collection, University of North Carolina Library, Chapel Hill.

111

JULIAN HARTRIDGE (Georgia) was born on September 9, 1829, on Daufuskie Island,[1] Beaufort District, South Carolina. His father was a prominent merchant[2] who sent his son to Chatham Academy in Savannah, Georgia, and then to Brown University. After graduating in 1848 Hartridge studied law at Harvard Law School for two years and then read law in Savannah. He was admitted to the bar in 1851 and opened an office in Savannah. Hartridge served as solicitor general of the eastern judicial circuit of Georgia from 1854 to 1858, then in the legislature as a Democrat for one term. As a member of the Democratic national convention of 1860 he was a strong Breckinridge supporter. After Lincoln's election Hartridge worked for the secession of Georgia, and when war began he entered the army as a lieutenant in the prestigious Chatham Artillery. While in service, he was nominated for a place in the Confederate Congress by a convention of prominent men from his district. He easily defeated the incumbent, T. M. Forman (*q.v.*), without campaigning, but two years later he won reelection by a bare plurality over two other rivals.

Hartridge was one of the best speakers in the Confederate House of Representatives and generally used this talent to strengthen his new nation. Only occasionally did he cater to local pressures. In October, 1864, a governors' conference held in Augusta asked Congress to remove all commercial restrictions on vessels owned by the states. As chairman of the Committee on Commerce in the Second Congress, Hartridge introduced such a resolution but could not get favorable action from Congress until March, 1865. To calm Georgia's discontent with the progress of the war Hartridge also worked for the dismissal of secretaries Mallory and Memminger (*q.v.*) and of General Braxton Bragg. Beyond that it was only on matters of suspending habeas corpus and arming slaves that Hartridge stood in direct opposition to major administration programs.

Hartridge confined himself to his law practice during Reconstruction, then returned to politics. He was made chairman of the State Central Committee of the Democratic party in 1870. In 1872 he was a presidential elector, and in 1872 and 1876 he was a delegate to the national party conventions. He declined a place on the state supreme court bench because his health had begun to fail, but in 1875 he allowed himself to be elected to the United States House of Representatives. He served until his death in Washington, D.C., on January 8, 1879. He is buried in Laurel Grove Cemetery in Savannah.

[1] The information in the *Biographical Directory of the American Congress* that Hartridge was born in Savannah is incorrect. His grandson, Walter C. Hartridge of Savannah, has researched the matter and has verified Daufuskie Island as his birthplace.

[2] Northen (ed.), *Men of Mark in Georgia*, III, 446.

ROBERT ANTHONY HATCHER (Missouri) was born February 24, 1819, in Buckingham County, Virginia. He attended private schools in Lynchburg, Virginia, then studied law and was admitted to the bar in Kentucky. He began to practice in 1847 in New Madrid, Missouri, which would be his residence for the next thirty years. Hatcher was circuit attorney for several years and a member of the state house of representatives in 1850 and 1851. At the beginning of the Civil War Hatcher crossed the Mississippi River to Tennessee and enlisted in the Confederate army from that state. He rose to the rank of major and A.A.G., served on the staffs of Generals A. P. Stewart and H. D. Clayton, and was repeatedly commended by these officers for his bravery and efficiency.

While still in the army Hatcher was elected over two opponents in the spring of 1864 as congressman from the Seventh District. In Richmond he seldom interjected an opinion during debate, but his voting record stamped him as Missouri's most conservative representative. While a strong nationalist on matters directly related to taxation and the army, Hatcher valued more than his colleagues the importance of the home front. His exemption list was short, but it included everyone in state employment, agriculture, and manufacturing; he would let the government impress railroads but not specie and take slaves temporarily for labor but not permanently as soldiers; and he condoned the enrollment of all state militia. However, requisitioning deserters from state governors violated his concept of personal freedom.

In 1872 Hatcher, who returned to Missouri after the war, was elected to the first of three consecutive terms in the U.S. Congress, serving until 1879. During this period he moved his residence from New Madrid to Charleston, where he died December 4, 1886. He was buried there in Odd Fellows Cemetery.[1]

[1] See the *Biographical Directory of the American Congress*; the Charleston (Mo.) *Enterprise*, December 10, 1886; and *Official Records, passim*.

LANDON CARTER HAYNES (Tennessee) was born in the east Tennessee county seat of Elizabethton on December 2, 1816. After attending the local schools, he graduated as valedictorian of his class from Washington College and then studied law in the office of T. A. R. Nelson, a noted east Tennessee jurist and uncompromising supporter of the Union. Haynes was admitted to the bar in 1841, but he began his career as a Methodist preacher. He later farmed and practiced law at Jonesboro and was elected to the legislature in 1845. In 1847 he won election to the state senate, and in 1849 he was Speaker of the House. In 1844 he was an elector for James K. Polk, and he performed the same function for the Breckinridge ticket in 1860.

In October of 1861 the Tennessee General Assembly chose Haynes a Confederate senator on the first ballot for a term of six years, probably because of his residence. In the First Regular Congress he was chairman of the Committee on Engrossment and Enrollment. During his three years in the Senate Haynes worked primarily to put the Confederacy's economy on a war basis. He proposed bills to encourage manufacturing, exempt skilled labor, regulate impressment, and attempt to encourage the writing of more productive tax laws. On these and other programs Haynes granted the central government in essence whatever powers it requested, provided the legislation did not arbitrarily violate state and individual rights. He sanctioned conscription, but not of state officials; he wanted a supreme court, but one without appellate jurisdiction over state courts; he believed in impressment, but only at market prices; and he would be willing to let the army destroy private property, but he refused to urge planters to raise only food crops. On strictly army matters Haynes generally deferred to President Davis' wishes, though he liked few of the president's top appointments and felt that the war was being mismanaged. When the end came, Haynes felt himself at a distinct disadvantage in east Tennessee, many of whose residents had been bitter Union partisans; accordingly he made his home in Memphis thereafter and continued his law practice. He died in Memphis on February 17, 1875, and was first buried in Elmwood Cemetery there. Twenty-seven years later his remains were moved to the cemetery in Jackson, Tennessee, the home of his eldest son.[1]

[1] Haynes's career has been reconstructed from research on members of the Tennessee General Assembly conducted by the Tennessee State Library and Archives.

JOSEPH BROWN HEISKELL (Tennessee) was born in Knoxville, Tennessee, November 5, 1823. His father was editor of the *Register*, the oldest paper published in the state. The younger Heiskell graduated from East Tennessee College (now the University of Tennessee) at the age of seventeen, studied law, and was admitted to the bar. He began practice in Madisonville, Tennessee, in 1844. About 1847 he moved to Rogersville, Tennessee, and engaged in practice in a number of upper east Tennessee counties. He ran for the state senate in 1858 and was elected, representing Hawkins, Hancock, and Jefferson counties. But it was in the codification and reporting of the statutes and decisions of

114

the Tennessee courts that he received his primary distinction. Heiskell was a staunch Union Whig in politics, but when Lincoln called for volunteers he cast his lot with the Confederacy. Curiously and confusingly, the Tennessee secession ordinance provided that the state should elect its delegates to the Provisional Confederate Congress on the same date in August prescribed for United States elections. In the First Congressional District Heiskell was nominated on the pro-Confederate ticket to run against T. A. R. Nelson, who was running on the Union ticket for reelection to the U.S. Congress. Heiskell received only half as many votes as his opponent and declined to take his seat in Richmond. Nelson, on the other hand, was seized by Confederate authorities while attempting to make his way to Washington and was imprisoned in Richmond for a time. In November after the ground rules had been perfected, Heiskell was elected to the First Regular Congress from a district Union in sentiment and already wholly in Union hands and in 1863 won reelection, both times without opposition. He favored an aggressive war and supported most of the emergency measures before Congress. During 1862 he was active in trying to develop Confederate industry, particularly that relating to ordnance material. In 1863 he turned his attention to laws protecting Confederate citizens behind enemy lines; he particularly objected to funding old currency because of the hardship it would bring to such people, unable as they were to participate in such an exchange. In 1864, while temporarily at his home in Rogersville, Heiskell was arrested by Federal authorities and confined until the close of the war. At this point, the sentiment in east Tennessee being decidedly anti-Confederate, Heiskell, like many others of his persuasion, moved to Memphis, which would be his home thereafter. He was a member of the constitutional convention of 1870 and the same year was appointed attorney general and reporter of the state, an office which he held for eight years. *Heiskell's Reports*, which he edited, form a cornerstone of Tennessee jurisprudence to this day. Heiskell died in Memphis in his ninetieth year on March 7, 1913, and was buried in Elmwood Cemetery.[1]

[1] See material gathered by the Tennessee State Library and Archives for a proposed *Biographical Directory of the Tennessee General Assembly*.

JOHN HEMPHILL (Texas) was a native of South Carolina, born in Chester District on December 18, 1803. He was graduated from Jefferson College (now Washington and Jefferson) in 1825; studied law and was admitted to the bar; and began practice in Sumter, South Carolina. Hemphill was an extreme states' righter of the old school, and during the nullification crisis of 1832–1833 he edited a newspaper which gave free rein to his views. After serving as a second lieutenant in one of the frequent Seminole wars, he emigrated to the Republic of Texas in 1838 and two years later was elected a district judge. Hemphill was adjutant general of the ill-fated Mier expedition into Mexico in 1842 and in 1846 was elected chief justice of the Texas Supreme Court, a position he occupied for twelve years. The Texas legislature elected him to the United States Senate in 1858 as a states' rights Democrat; he served from March 4, 1859, until he was expelled by a resolution of July 11, 1861, having never resigned and being already a member of the Provisional Confederate Congress.

As a congressman his interest and attention went toward adapting the old United States statutes to meet the Confederacy's needs, particularly those on patents, pensions, tariff duties, and courts of equity. In regard to other legislation he was conservative only on new economic programs, voting against the produce loan, federal control over cotton exportation, and against any delay in settling state claims against the central government. In November, 1861, he lost a close race to Williamson S. Oldham (*q.v.*) for a senate seat in the First Regular Congress. Prior to the expiration of the Provisional Congress, Hemphill died in Richmond on January 7, 1862. His body was taken to Austin, Texas, for burial in the State Cemetery.

GUSTAVUS ADOLPHUS HENRY (Tennessee), senator of Tennessee during the life of the Confederacy, was born October 8, 1804, in Scott County, Kentucky. He graduated from Transylvania University in Lexington in 1825, studied law, and hung out his shingle in Georgetown. From 1831 to 1833 he was a member of the Kentucky legislature, after which he moved to Clarksville, Tennessee. In this state he became one of the leaders of the Whig party and gained great reputation as the "eagle orator of Tennessee" in a day when a premium was placed on high-flown phrases. He was in the Tennessee legislature in 1851, was four times a presidential elector on the Whig ticket, and in 1860 was a supporter of Bell and Everett at the Baltimore convention. Meanwhile, he had twice been defeated (1853 and 1855) for governor of Tennessee by Andrew Johnson.

In October, 1861, the Tennessee legislature on the thirty-second ballot elected Henry as its old Whig choice to the Confederate Senate. In the Senate Henry argued that the conduct of the war should be left to the executive, and that Congress had the constitutional power to provide whatever was needed. A review of the bills which he introduced exhibits his ultra nationalism. At various times he proposed to let commissioners arbitrarily fix impressment prices, to appropriate a half-million dollars for a government ironworks, to let the president detail soldiers and impress slaves, to draft all men between sixteen and sixty, and to repudiate two-thirds of the currency. In addition Henry often wrote Davis and the various commanding generals, urging the repossession of Tennessee and Kentucky. As late as November, 1864, he urged that the war be carried to the enemy and deplored all talk of peace. Although all this caused him to be regarded as an administration stalwart, in early 1865 he voted to put Robert E. Lee in command of all armies and was scolded by Mrs. Davis upon the occasion of his next social visit to the Confederate White House. Henry never again regained his former prestige, nor did he seek office after the close of the war. He lived quietly in Clarksville until his death on September 10, 1880. He was buried in Greenwood Cemetery there.[1]

[1] The Montgomery County (Tenn.) Public Library is the authority for Henry's place of burial.

CALEB CLAIBORNE HERBERT (Texas) was born, according to the 1850 federal census of Colorado County, Texas, in Virginia, probably in Goochland County, about the year 1814. His parents migrated at different times from Virginia to Georgia to Alabama, where Herbert was married. Later he lived in both Tennessee and Mississippi before settling permanently near Columbus, Texas, on a farm, where he soon amassed a large fortune for the day and time, being worth some sixty thousand dollars at the age of thirty-six. He was a member of the Texas Senate in 1857–1858, and again in 1858–1859, and he voted for calling the secession convention in 1861.

In November, 1861, Herbert won a seat in the Regular Confederate Congress over strong opposition, and in 1863 he was reelected primarily on the charge that the exemption laws were class legislation. He was the most radical states' righter of all western congressmen, ceaselessly advocating the protection of the Texas frontier, the adequate financing of the Trans-Mississippi Department, and the inviolability of Texas cotton from restriction, taxation, or impressment. By the same token he failed to support a single measure advanced by the central government and in 1862 warned that Texas might secede from the Confederacy if the draft were extended. In 1863 he was chairman of a committee to investigate the treatment of Federal prisoners in Castle Thunder; when the majority exonerated the prison management, Herbert submitted a minority report condemning it for inhumanity. On the other hand, he never opposed the president in the field of foreign affairs and at no time condoned negotiations for peace. He was elected to both the Thirty-ninth and Fortieth United States congresses after the war ended but was denied his seat on both occasions. On July 5, 1867, in an apparent case of mistaken identity, he was shot to death outside of a saloon in Columbus. He was buried on his plantation at Reel's Bend, twelve miles southeast of Columbus, on the Colorado River. According to a descendant, the family burial ground was later plowed over, and all trace of it has disappeared.[1]

[1] This information was provided by Lee Nesbitt, Columbus, Tex.

BENJAMIN HARVEY HILL (Georgia), who made a career of trimming his sails to the prevailing political breeze, was born in Jasper County, Georgia, September 14, 1823. First an uncompromising Unionist Whig, he became a prominent secessionist and supporter of Jefferson Davis. After the war ended, he was for a time a leading Conservative and opponent of congressional Reconstruction, but he then defected to the Radicals. Still later, when circumstances dictated, he returned to the Conservative fold. He was successively a Whig, a Know-Nothing, a Constitutional Unionist, a Democrat, a Republican, and again a Democrat, and in the words of E. A. Pollard, editor of the Richmond *Examiner* "was the very picture of a smooth and plausible mediocrity."

Hill's parents were not comfortably situated and the boy's early education was scant. By dint of sacrifice he attended the University of Georgia; afterwards he read law and was admitted to the bar. In this profession he achieved marked success and large financial returns; he owned in 1860 fifty-seven Negroes and an estate of one hundred thousand dollars. Prior to the Civil War, Hill's only successful political campaign had been in 1851 for a seat in the Georgia House of Representatives. He was defeated for Congress in 1855 and for governor two years later. He campaigned for Bell and Everett in 1860 and went to the Milledgeville convention in January, 1861, as an avowed opponent of secession, but he wound up signing the ordinance. He was forthwith elected a delegate to the Provisional Congress, and in November the Georgia legislature chose him a senator on the first ballot.

In Congress, Hill soon became recognized as a champion of strong government. As chairman of the Committee on the Judiciary he worked to establish a supreme court and a powerful court of claims. He consistently refused to interfere with the prerogatives of the commander-in-chief and was one of two senators opposing the creation of the office of general-in-chief for Robert E. Lee. Hill soon was typecast as one of the president's "pets," but he accurately claimed that he had disagreed with Davis on many issues. He accepted administration leadership for the most part, but he also had an overriding conviction that it was the function of Congress to divide available manpower between "fighters and producers." His chief initiative, as a result, was to see that such decisions were made judiciously, and he often disagreed with the War Department. But—as was his lifelong practice—when a decision was made over which he had no further control, he would abide by it. He opposed conscription on principle but later went before the Georgia legislature to defend it. Davis relied heavily on Hill, despite the latter's complex posture.

At the end of the war Hill was arrested by the Federal authorities and spent three months in Fort Lafayette before being paroled by President Johnson, upon which he returned to his home in La Grange. From 1867 until 1870 Hill strenuously opposed the congressional Reconstruction acts which virtually reduced the South to a conquered province, but in the latter year he abruptly switched sides and advocated acceptance as a *fait accompli*. This resulted in his political ostracism for five years, after which he was elected to Congress from the Atlanta area against strong opposition from the Conservative Democrats. But upon arrival he soon became known as a champion of southern rights, vigorously defending Davis and the Confederacy on any and all occasions. Hill was elected to the Senate early in 1877, but did not live out his term, dying in ofce from cancer on August 16, 1882, at his home in Atlanta. He was buried in Oakland Cemetery.

ROBERT BENJAMIN HILTON (SMITH) (Florida) was born "somewhere in Virginia" in 1821 of needy parents. After attending public school he began working for a local printer, later securing the same type of work in Richmond. In the mid-1840s he moved to Savannah, Georgia, where he worked for a local newspaper performing a variety of duties. Apparently he also studied law in his spare time.[1] Around 1848 he moved to Florida and in 1849 he had the legislature change his name from Smith to Hilton, a name taken from his mother's side of the family. Hilton settled in Tallahassee where he became editor of the prominent Democratic newspaper, the *Floridian*. He also began the practice of law by entering a partnership with D. W. Gwynn. But in 1851 Hilton returned to Savannah, this time as proprietor and associate editor of the *Georgian*. He informed his readers of his absolute commitment to states' rights and confessed to having advocated secession in 1850. He warned that secession might still be necessary if the South's rights in slavery were not respected. In less than a year, however, Hilton returned to

Tallahassee and this time confined himself to his law practice. In 1855 he returned once more to Savannah where, with money borrowed from his father-in-law, he bought the Savannah *Journal* and the *Georgian*; he also served as editor of both. When his wife became fatally ill in 1857, Hilton returned to Tallahassee, his law practice, and the *Floridian*.[2] Strangely, he is listed in the census of 1860 as having virtually no property.

In October, 1860, Hilton was elected to the United States House of Representatives, but he never took his seat.[3] He had advocated immediate secession when news of Lincoln's election reached Florida, and when Florida left the Union he raised the First Florida Infantry and was elected its captain. After several months of service, mainly at Pensacola, Hilton was elected in November to the Confederate House. Two years later he won reelection over several rivals.

Hilton was Florida's most effective representative, being active on the floor and in a wide variety of subjects. From his place on the Military Committee he was able to voice Florida's concern for its coastal defenses. Except for his constant efforts to keep Florida conscripts at home, however, Hilton was a dependable friend of the War Department. In December, 1863, he proposed to draft all men whose substitutes had become liable to military service. Hilton was also a strong advocate of extensive control of the Confederacy's economic resources. In March, 1862, he proposed a strict limitation on cotton acreage.

After the war Hilton resumed his law practice and his editorship. In 1867 he served briefly as judge of the Leon County criminal court.[4] In 1876 he was a Democratic candidate for a Tilden electorship and was one of the lawyers representing George F. Drew in the disputed gubernatorial race.[5] Hilton died on January 10, 1894, in Tallahassee and is buried in St. John's Episcopal Cemetery.[6]

[1] This information was provided by Elizabeth Alexander, P. K. Yonge Library, University of Florida, Gainesville.

[2] This information was provided by Lilla M. Hawes, Georgia Historical Society, Savannah.

[3] This information was provided by Patty Paul, Division of State Library Services, Tallahassee, Fla.

[4] *Ibid.*

[5] John Wallace, *Carpet-bag Rule in Florida* (Facsimile reprint; Gainesville, Fla., 1964), *passim.*

[6] Information on Hilton's date of death and place of interment was provided by Mrs. Ronald Melton, St. John's Episcopal Church, Tallahassee, Fla.

BENJAMIN LEWIS HODGE (Louisiana) was born, according to the federal censuses of 1850 and 1860, in Tennessee about the year 1824.

Despite the existence of at least one living descendant, and despite the fact that Hodge was one of the wealthiest men in north Louisiana at the outbreak of the Civil War, almost nothing seems to be known of his early life or education. The earliest record of his career which can be found is the 1850 census of Caddo Parish, which lists Hodge as a lawyer, twenty-six years old, possessing real estate worth one thousand dollars. Ten years later he admitted to the ownership of real estate and personal property in excess of one hundred thousand dollars, and by all accounts he was one of the most successful lawyers in the state. Two steamboats named after him plied the Mississippi and Red rivers; he had built and owned business buildings and the finest residence in Shreveport; and he also had interests in land and slaves, his wife's stepfather being one of the prominent planters of the parish.

Not an extreme proslavery advocate, Hodge was a presidential elector for Bell and Everett in 1860, but when the die was cast he was a signer of the Louisiana secession ordinance. Previous to that time he had served several terms in the legislature. However, in November, 1861, he was an unsuccessful candidate for the Confederate Senate. The same month he was elected colonel of the Nineteenth Louisiana Infantry, but after a good deal of sick leave he resigned his commission on May 29, 1862, and went home. The following year he won an uncontested seat in the House of Representatives, where he was in attendance for less than one full session. Colonel Hodge died August 12, 1864, probably at Wildwood, the plantation home of his wife's stepfather, near Shreveport. While in Congress he proposed no bills and voted so seldom that only his advocacy of higher taxes and more stringent regulation of foreign commerce can be inferred. He lies buried in an unmarked grave in Oakland Cemetery in Shreveport, according to a list of names of "soldiers killed during the Civil War" in the possession of the cemetery authorities.[1]

[1] Information about Hodge's place of burial was provided by Malcolm G. Parker, Librarian, Louisiana State University in Shreveport.

GEORGE BAIRD HODGE (Kentucky) was born in Fleming County, Kentucky, April 8, 1828. At the age of seventeen he was graduated from the United States Naval Academy, but he resigned his commission of passed midshipman (acting lieutenant) five years later in order to study law. Hodge was in due course admitted to the bar and in 1852 was an unsuccessful candidate for Congress. In 1859 he was a member of the Kentucky legislature, and in the portentous election of 1860 he was a Breckinridge elector.

After enlisting in the Confederate army as a private, Hodge was appointed by the secessionist government of Kentucky as a representative to the Provisional Congress and in January, 1862, he was elected to the First Regular Congress from the Eighth District. However, he attended neither congress with any degree of regularity; he preferred service on Breckinridge's staff and was promoted successively from captain to colonel. He took little initiative in legislation and was mainly interested in strengthening the army. In the Provisional Congress he approved recruiting single volunteers from the border states and organizing them into militia units. In the First Congress he worked to enlarge the army and to keep it adequately supplied. Later Hodge commanded a brigade of cavalry under Major General Joe Wheeler, and in the closing months of the war he was in command of the district of southwest Mississippi and east Louisiana.

It appears from the records that Hodge began to have second thoughts about the wisdom of secession as early as the spring of 1863; this, plus the fact that he was still technically a member of Congress, twice caused the Senate to reject his nomination to the grade of brigadier general to which the president had appointed him, the last occasion being on February 8, 1865. He was, however, paroled as a brigadier general at Meridian, Mississippi, on May 10, 1865, after which he returned to his home in Newport, Kentucky, across the river from Cincinnati, to resume his law practice. He was a presidential elector for Horace Greeley in 1872, and from 1873 to 1877 he was a member of the Kentucky Senate. In 1877 Hodge moved to Longwood in Orange County, Florida. He died there on August 1, 1892, and was buried in Newport.[1]

[1] Hodge is the subject of a brief sketch in *Appleton's Cyclopedia of American Biography*; however, the above information was taken mainly from Warner, *Generals in Gray*, 138–39, and the findings of W. B. Yearns relative to Hodge's congressional career.

JAMES PHILEMON HOLCOMBE (Virginia) was born on September 20, 1820, in Powhatan County to a family which had been intellectually prominent in Virginia for generations. After being tutored at home he enrolled at Yale in 1837 and at the University of Virginia in 1838, although he received a degree from neither institution. For a while Holcombe practiced law at Fincastle, but about 1844 he moved to Cincinnati. While there he published several volumes on legal subjects, particularly those concerning business and commercial law. He then moved to Alexandria, Virginia, in order to use the Library of Congress. In 1851 Holcombe joined the University of Virginia law faculty. Though he shunned active politics he was a strong Democrat. During the 1850s he became a leading pamphleteer in the defense of slavery and state's rights. Holcombe resigned his professorship to attend the convention of 1861, where his brilliant oratory made him one of the prominent spokesmen of immediate secession. In November he won a close race for a seat in the Confederate House of Representatives.

In Congress Holcombe argued that violations of state's rights would break the public spirit, but generally he avoided dogmatic adherence to principle. He was one of Virginia's few advocates of high taxes, and he wanted punitive taxation on speculators and on those who refused to accept Treasury notes for personal debts. In a similar vein he approved numerous laws giving the president and the War Department whatever control they needed over production and transportation. Holcombe's chief concern, however, was to safeguard private property against arbitrary laws, and most of his suggestions in session aimed to equalize the tax laws and to establish a court to investigate claims against the Confederacy. Holcombe showed similar discretion on army matters, for he eventually agreed to extend the draft age limits to seventeen and fifty-five, though he had opposed conscription originally as being unconstitutional.

Holcombe declined to seek reelection, and in February, 1864, President Davis sent him to Nova Scotia to defend two Confederates who had become privateers without proper authorization. Afterward he cooperated with C. C. Clay (*q.v.*) and other Confederates in Canada to harass the United States in any way possible. On his return to the Confederacy in November Holcombe advised Secretary of State Benjamin to spare no expense in fomenting disaffection in the North and the separation of the Northwest from the United States. After the war Holcombe resided on a large farm in Bedford County which he had bought in 1863. There he edited *Literature in Letters*, prepared a volume of selections which was published in 1866, and opened a private school. The school flourished briefly but declined when Holcombe's health began to fail. He died at Capon Springs, West Virginia, on August 22, 1873, and is interred in the Presbyterian Church cemetery in Lynchburg.

WILLIAM DUNBAR HOLDER (Mississippi) was born March 6, 1824, in Franklin County, Tennessee, to which state his family had moved from Virginia via Kentucky. His grandfather had been an associate of Daniel Boone on his westward trek. When W. D. Holder was about fourteen, his father moved again, this time to Mississippi. Upon his father's death in 1842, Holder took up residence in Pontotoc, Mississippi, where he was subsequently appointed United States district clerk and later a deputy United States marshal. In 1853 he was elected to the lower house of the Mississippi legislature, serving one term and not seeking reelection.

In May, 1861, Holder entered Confederate service as captain of Company C, Seventeenth Mississippi Infantry, with which he fought at First Manassas. When Holder was at Malvern Hill the following year as colonel of the regiment, his left thigh was broken by a rifle ball. Partially recovered from this wound, he led his command at Chancellorsville and Gettysburg. At the latter battle Colonel Holder was shot through the abdomen, a wound which resulted in permanent disability. In November, 1863, he was elected to the Second Congress to succeed Reuben Davis (*q.v.*), the last month of whose term he also served after Davis withdrew.

At the outset of his congressional career Holder was opposed to all of the emergency measures then under discussion; however, the deteriorating military situation forced him to modify his position. He eventually conceded the obvious necessity for higher taxes, arming Negroes, and controls over commerce and railroads. However, his lack of faith in Jefferson Davis impelled him to seek for Congress an equal voice in the selection of cabinet officers and army commanders. His principal contribution as a congressman was the introduction of several bills ameliorating the lot of the enlisted man. Apparently in either disgust or despair Colonel Holder abandoned his seat a month before Congress adjourned for the last time. After the war he engaged in farming, and from 1886 until his death he was employed in the office of the auditor of public accounts. He died in Jackson, Mississippi, on April 26, 1900, and was buried in Greenwood Cemetery.

FREDERICK WILLIAM MACKEY HOLLIDAY (Virginia) was born in Winchester, Virginia, on February 22, 1828. He graduated from Yale College in 1847; then he studied law at home and for one session at the University of Virginia. He began practicing in Winchester in 1848, and in 1849 he was elected commonwealth attorney for Winchester and for Frederick County, a position he held until 1861. By that time Holliday was a leading secessionist in his district, and at the outbreak of war he formed a company and eventually attained the rank of colonel. As commander of the Thirty-third Virginia Infantry in the Stonewall Brigade, Holliday participated in several battles and at Cedar Run lost his right arm. He then contested A. R. Boteler's (*q.v.*) bid for reelection to the Confederate Congress and won a majority of both the army and the civilian vote.

Once in Congress Holliday continued his interest in army matters. Most of his resolutions pertained to army compensation and organization; his bills and amendments generally aimed to improve the latter. He was especially interested in finding uses for disabled soldiers and in seeing that they received the same benefits as men still in service. Holliday also favored placing all able-bodied men in the army despite the need for labor at home, and he allowed the president and the general-in-chief the broadest use of this manpower. He was equally ready to give the central government emergency use of the Confederacy's other resources. Holliday persistently opposed even discussing peace negotiations. In the last resolution in the House, he urged his colleagues to continue working for "our great cause and the prosecution of the war to a successful issue."

After the war Holliday resumed his law practice and commenced farming. In 1876 he was a Democratic elector-at-large and also commissioner for Virginia at the Philadelphia Centennial Exposition. The next year he won the governorship on the Conservative ticket, and his administration was mainly concerned with whether to repudiate part or all of the state debt incurred under the Confederacy. Until he left office Holliday's vetoes foiled the efforts of the repudiationist Readjuster party even though he realized payment in full would seriously damage the new public school system. To his credit, he tried to borrow from the Richmond banks the $200,000 needed to pay teachers' back salaries, but without success. Holliday spent his last years farming and in world travel. He died at Winchester on May 20, 1899, and was interred there in the family plot in Mount Hebron Cemetery.[1]

[1] Information on Holliday's interment was furnished by Mrs. R. O. LaFollette, Winchester, Va.

HINES HOLT (Georgia) was born near Milledgeville, Georgia, on April 27, 1805. He obtained his academic education near home, graduated from the University of Georgia in 1824, and then studied law. After obtaining his license to practice he opened his first law office in Columbus. He was successful from the first and within a decade had also acquired large holdings in land and slaves. Holt took an early interest in public affairs. In 1835 he was one of the leaders in arranging a meeting at Milledgeville for the purpose of asking the whole South to unite against the antislavery movement.[1] In 1841 he was elected as a Whig to Congress to fill the two remaining months of his cousin's term. By the mid-1850s Holt had become a Know-Nothing, and in the election of 1857 he ably stumped the state against the best Democratic speakers in Georgia. In 1859 he was elected to the state senate for one term and was involved in the recodification of the state's laws. Though a strong Unionist, Holt went with his state when it seceded.

In the fall of 1861 Holt used his old party ties to win a seat in the Confederate House of Representatives.[2] In Congress he had no patience with halfway measures. His first proposal was that the Confederacy buy all cotton at four cents a pound and hold it from the market until England broke the blockade. Later he urged "naked, unqualified, unrestricted"[3] conscription and the end of all military exemptions. Generally Holt wanted Congress to meet briefly, give the president what legislation he requested, and leave the conduct of the war to the generals. He once suggested that Congress confine itself to financial matters and those related directly to the war. In October, 1863, Holt lost his race for reelection to M. H. Blandford (q.v.) in a battle of personalities and resigned shortly afterward.

After the war Holt was elected a member of the convention to revise the state constitution, but he died suddenly on November 4, 1865, while attending the convention. He is buried in Linwood Cemetery, Columbus.

[1] Northen (ed.), *Men of Mark in Georgia*, III, 94–96.

[2] Holt later wrote that he sought a place in the Confederate Congress hoping to reunite the nation and that he resigned when he saw that reunion was hopeless. The statement was made by Holt in his petition for amnesty after the war and is included in Thomas B. Alexander and Richard E. Beringer, *The Anatomy of the Confederate Congress* (Nashville, 1972), 41. Holt's record in Congress, however, does not bear out this explanation.

[3] *Southern Historical Society Papers*, XLVI, 166.

JOHN FORD HOUSE (Tennessee) was born near Franklin, Tennessee, January 9, 1827. He attended the local academy and then Transylvania University at Lexington, although he did not graduate. He was, however, graduated from the Lebanon Law School in 1850; he was admitted to practice and hung out his shingle in Franklin. He moved soon after to Clarksville, in Montgomery County, where he attained great distinction in his profession.

House served in the legislature in 1853; in 1860, a staunch Union Whig, he was a Bell and Everett elector. He did not become a secessionist until Lincoln's call for volunteers, after which he was a leader in taking Tennessee out of the Union. He was then elected Eighth District delegate to the Provisional Confederate Congress. Now that war had begun, he gave the central government whatever it needed in matters directly related to the war itself. He did not extend this latitude, however, to the economy, for he refused to sanction the produce loan or to postpone auditing state claims against the Confederacy. As a member of the Committee on Finance, House concentrated on army supply problems and chaired a committee to investigate abuses in the purchase of provisions. He declined to run for election to the Regular Congress; instead, he entered the army and served during a large part of the war on the staff of General George Maney. He was ultimately paroled at Columbus, Mississippi, in June, 1865.

In 1868 House was a delegate to the Democratic national convention and two years later was a member of the state constitutional convention. From 1875 to 1883 he served four consecutive terms as congressman from Tennessee, not being a candidate for renomination in 1882. Thereafter House continued the practice of law in Clarksville. When he died there on June 18, 1904, he was representative of men of the Old South, mannered, courtly, possessed of great legal wisdom, a former Confederate and United States legislator, and a former Confederate officer, and he was the personification of both the virtues and the vices of an age rapidly passing into history. He was buried in Greenwood Cemetery, Clarksville.

ROBERT MERCER TALIAFERRO HUNTER (Virginia), descendant of a number of Virginia's foremost families, was born April 21, 1809, at Mount Pleasant, one of the estates of his maternal ancestors in Essex County, Virginia. He received his primary education from tutors at home and then attended the University of Virginia, following which he studied law in Winchester under the ardent exponent of states' rights, Judge Henry St. George Tucker.

Hunter was admitted to the bar in 1830. He early demonstrated his lifetime political ambivalence by at first refusing to join any party, and from 1834 to 1837 he served in the General Assembly as an independent. He then was elected to Congress as a states' rights Whig and became Speaker of the House in 1839 in only his second term; but he was not reelected as speaker, although he continued to be returned by his constituents until 1843. Having now become a dedicated follower of John C. Calhoun and a states' rights Democrat, he was defeated for reelection in that year but was again successful two years later; before his term expired he was chosen as United States senator and took his seat on March 4, 1847. From that time until the outbreak of the Civil War Hunter wavered in his political convictions, sometimes appearing in the guise of a staunch Unionist, at others not seeming averse to separation of North and South. His voting record was sometimes inconsistent and marked by both a prosouthern bias and a conciliatory policy toward Republicans and Abolitionists.

At the Democratic conventions of 1860 in Charleston and Baltimore, where he was a favorite-son candidate, Hunter waited until all hope of compromise was gone before advising his followers to support John C. Breckinridge. But he still looked to some sort of accommodation; he remained in Washington and continued to confer with President Buchanan until after Lincoln's inauguration. Before the secession of his state Hunter withdrew from the Senate and in April, 1861, took his seat in the Provisional Confederate Congress. After the resignation of Robert Toombs he occupied the post of secretary of state in the Confederate cabinet from July, 1861, to February of the following year. He was then elected to the Senate, where he served until the dissolution of the government. During the Provisional Congress the administration had few, if any, stronger friends; however, Hunter's ingrained weather-vane tendencies resulted in many shifts in his policy. He urged strong enforcement of the tax program but opposed higher taxes; approved drafting old men and youths but favored liberal exemptions; urged stringent inflation control but at the same time assisted in emasculating funding of Treasury notes; sanctioned the suspension of the writ of habeas corpus but concurrently denied the president's unlimited right to execute it. He also sanctioned vigorous impressment laws and opposed arming slaves. Few individuals with so much inherent prestige did less to advance the cause of an expiring nation. In January, 1865, Hunter was one of the delegates who met with Lincoln at Hampton Roads in a fruitless conference already doomed to failure by Davis' *sine qua non* insistence on southern independence. After the war Hunter spent some months as a prisoner of war in Fort Pulaski, in Savannah harbor, during which time the Federal General Ben Butler systematically destroyed his estate. After 1874 Hunter was treasurer of Virginia for six years and then collector of the port of Tappahannock, meanwhile becoming embroiled in a controversy with Davis occasioned by the publication of Hunter's articles in the *Southern Historical Society Papers*. Hunter died at his residence in Essex County on July 18, 1887, and was buried in an old family burial ground near Loretto, Virginia.

PORTER INGRAM[1] (Georgia) was born near the village of Marlborough, Vermont, on April 2, 1810. Though his parents were poor farmers, they were able to send him to Williamson College[2] and to see that he graduated from Yale in 1831. He taught school in New York state for the next five years and then moved to Hamilton, Georgia. His landlord there supported him while he read law, and he soon was admitted to the bar. For a short while Ingram practiced in Hamilton, but in 1853 he moved to Columbus and entered a partnership with Martin J. Crawford (*q.v.*). He was also a successful planter. Ingram attended every session of the Harris County Superior Court from the time of his admission to the bar until his death, 113 times altogether. For almost two decades he was judge of the city court of Columbus, and he retired at his own request. Ingram never sought political office, though in 1858 he was chosen to represent his county in the state Democratic convention. He opposed secession but went with his adopted state when it left the Union. While he was too old to enlist in the army, he had one taste of combat in April, 1865, when his home guard unit attempted to defend Columbus against General Wilson's cavalry.

When Hines Holt (*q.v.*) resigned his place in the Confederate House, Ingram was elected to complete the term. He took his seat on January 12, 1864. Holt's successor had already been elected, so Ingram's total service in Congress was five weeks. He attended sessions regularly, but did not identify himself with a particular issue. During this critical session he supported all major programs to revitalize the war effort, though he showed his sympathy for agriculture by preferring money taxes to taxation in kind.

After the war Ingram practiced law in Columbus until he died at home on December 3, 1893, the oldest member of the Georgia bar. He is buried in Linwood Cemetery.[3]

[1] Northen (ed.), *Men of Mark in Georgia*, III, 178–79.
[2] This information was taken from Ingram's obituary and provided by Jeanne Hollis, Bradley Memorial Library, Columbus, Ga.
[3] *Ibid.*

ROBERT JEMISON,[1] JR.[2] (Alabama) was born into a wealthy planter family of Lincoln County, Georgia, on September 17, 1802. He was educated at Mount Zion Academy in Hancock County and at the University of Georgia. He then read law in Eatonton, but soon found that his talents lay in business. About 1826 the family moved to Pickens County, Alabama, where Robert entered planting with his father. In 1836 Jemison moved to Tuscaloosa, where he continued planting and also developed mills, stagecoach lines, and manufactories.[3] By 1860 he owned six plantations totaling over ten thousand acres, in addition to his other interests. His large home, completed in 1862, has been restored and is now the Friedman Memorial Library. In Tuscaloosa Jemison soon entered politics as a Whig. From 1837 to 1863 he was almost continuously in either the house or the senate of the state legislature and was recognized as an expert in banking and public finance.

In 1847 he was chairman of the Committee on Ways and Means when the entire Alabama revenue system was reorganized.[4] Jemison was also instrumental in establishing an asylum for the insane near Tuscaloosa and in projecting several railroads.

As a delegate to the secession convention of 1861 Jemison was the chief spokesman of the Unionists, and he argued that Yancey's (q.v.) rash demand of immediate separation would lead to a second Reign of Terror. Nevertheless upon Yancey's death in 1863 the legislature elected Jemison to fill the unfinished term in the Confederate Senate.

In his parting speech to the Alabama Senate Jemison brought suspicion upon his loyalty by promising to seek an honorable peace, and his career in Congress did little to redeem him in more dedicated circles. While he seldom offered bill, amendment, or comment, his voting record indicated that he would make few concessions to emergency. It is true that he wished to extend the draft age from sixteen to sixty and to reduce exemptions to a minimum. But he insisted that most new recruits remain under state control for local defense service. In addition Jemison opposed all further demands upon income and property or controls over transportation and production. He remained home after June, 1864, to salvage what he could of his varied interests.

After the war Jemison became a Democrat, but he held no further public office. From 1865 to 1869 he was president of the Northeast and Southwest Railroad. Jemison died in Tuscaloosa on October 16, 1871, and is buried in the family cemetery in Northport, just across the river from Tuscaloosa.[5]

[1] Owen, *History of Alabama*, III, 902.
[2] Jemison added "Jr." to his name to distinguish himself from an uncle with the same name. Garrett, *Public Men in Alabama*, 402.
[3] This information was provided by Marvin L. Harper, Tuscaloosa County Preservation Society, Tuscaloosa, Ala.
[4] Garrett, *Public Men in Alabama*, 402.
[5] This information was provided by Marvin L. Harper.

ALBERT GALLATIN JENKINS (Virginia) was born on November 10, 1830, on his father's large estate, Green Bottom, in Cabell County, Virginia (now West Virginia). He graduated from Jefferson College in Pennsylvania in 1848 and, two years later, from Harvard Law School. He then settled in Charleston, where he practiced law and engaged in planting. Within a decade he had abandoned his law practice and was devoting himself entirely to his plantation. Jenkins was a delegate to the Democratic national convention of 1856, and from 1857 to 1861 he served in the United States House of Representatives. Though he was not an original secessionist, in January of 1861 he and other moderates in Congress wrote an open letter warning President-elect Lincoln not to use force against those states which had already seceded. After Virginia seceded Jenkins recruited a company of cavalry from his district and prepared himself for leadership by mastering Hardee's *Tactics*. He rose to be colonel of the Eighth Virginia Infantry, with which he participated in a number of demoralizing raids, and won considerable renown as an independent leader. In November, 1861, the soldiers and refugees from his district elected him their representative to the Confederate Congress.

In Congress Jenkins drew dull committee assignments, chafed at inactivity, and resigned after one session. In his brief stay his primary concern was to give the Confederacy a large and efficient army. He even wished to draft men whom state governors declared indispensable at home. Jenkins had no patience with those who carped at the president's direction of the war, and he drew peals of laughter by comparing Henry S. Foote (*q.v.*) with the philosopher-fool who proved logically that Hannibal had been incompetent. Jenkins was quite willing to rest the Confederacy's fate with the army, however, and saw no need for the economic reforms which the administration also desired.

On August 5, 1862, Jenkins was appointed brigadier general. Now free from the confines of Congress he led his command on a five-hundred-mile raid into West Virginia and Ohio. Severely wounded at Gettysburg, he returned to his mountain command in the autumn of 1863. On May 9, 1864, Jenkins was wounded and captured in an attempt to rally his regiment near Dublin, Virginia. He failed to survive the amputation of his arm and died on May 21. Twice previously interred, he is now buried in Spring Hill Cemetery, Huntington, West Virginia.

HERSCHEL VESPASIAN JOHNSON (Georgia) was born in Burke County, Georgia, on September 18, 1812. After graduating from the University of Georgia in 1834, he studied law in Augusta and was admitted to the bar in 1835. In 1839 he moved to Jefferson County, bought a large plantation, and divided his time between planting and the law. In 1843 the Democrats in his district nominated Johnson for Congress, but this was a Whig year in Georgia. In ensuing years he served his party so well that in 1847 he was appointed United States senator to fill two years of an unexpired term. In 1849 he was elected judge of the Ocmulgee District. During the sectional crisis of 1850 Johnson took an extreme prosouthern position, and he accepted only reluctantly the compromise ultimately worked out in Congress. Between 1853 and 1857 Johnson served two terms as governor. During these years he grew more moderate, even though he did support the Kansas-Nebraska Act of 1854, and during the tragic "bleeding Kansas" events he deplored the excessess on both sides. Johnson's work in 1860 to preserve the Democratic party so enhanced his reputation as a moderate that he was selected as vice-president on the ticket with Stephen A. Douglas. He continued to work for compromise until the end, proposing in the Georgia secession convention a meeting of the slave states to consider joint action. In November, 1862, the Georgia legislature sent Johnson to the Confederate Senate to fill the vacancy caused by Toombs's (*q.v.*) nonacceptance. This was a two year senatorship, and the next November Johnson won reelection over Toombs on the third ballot.

Johnson reached the Senate on January 19, 1863, and shortly afterward his proposal of a constitutional amendment permitting nullification and secession announced the presence of an extremist. He confessed in his autobiography that he disliked most of the administration's programs, and his record shows his reluctance to compromise even for the emergency. Johnson wanted higher taxes, but he would accept them only on income. He saw the need for impressment, but his bill on February 5, 1863, proposed impossible restrictions on its operation. He worked sincerely to improve the army, but opposed conscription as ineffective and degrading. He particularly abhorred policies that smacked of despotism, such as inflation control, arming the slaves, and suspending the writ of habeas corpus. Johnson had hardly reached Congress before he began plotting for an honorable peace. By 1865 he was working for Reconstruction with only the guarantee that slavery would be recognized.

Johnson was president of the Georgia constitutional convention of October, 1865. The next year he was elected to the United States Senate but was denied his seat. In 1873 he was appointed judge of the Middle Circuit; he held this position until his death at his home near Louisville, Georgia, on August 16, 1880. He is buried in the Louisville Cemetery.

ROBERT WARD JOHNSON (Arkansas), whose family virtually controlled Arkansas politics for more than two decades, was born in Scott County, Kentucky, July 22, 1814. He was the nephew of Richard Mentor Johnson, a man with two unique distinctions: he was the only man ever elected vice-president of the United States by the Senate, and he was reputed to have killed the celebrated Shawnee chieftain Tecumseh at the Battle of the Thames in 1813. Two of his other Johnson uncles were

United States congressmen, and his father sat on the state bench of Kentucky and the federal bench of Arkansas for thirty-eight years. His sister was the wife of Ambrose H. Sevier, Arkansas' first U.S. Senator, and a niece was the wife of T. J. Churchill, postmaster of Little Rock, Confederate major general, and postbellum governor. Altogether, the array of his connections was impressive.

R. W. Johnson was educated at the Choctaw Academy which had been established on land donated by his uncle, Richard Mentor, and at St. Joseph's College in Bardstown, Kentucky. He opened a law office in Little Rock in 1835 and in 1840 became prosecuting attorney for what amounted to the entire state of Arkansas. In 1846 he was elected to Congress and was twice reelected, declining renomination in 1852. However, in 1853 he went to the Senate by appointment of the governor to fill a vacancy and by reelection served until March 3, 1861. During his Washington career his views largely reflected those of his constituents and friends, the slave-owner aristocracy, but he supported the Kansas-Nebraska bill and the homestead bill, and was a leading proponent of the grant of federal lands for railroad construction. Not a candidate to succeed himself in 1860, Johnson, both from Washington and in the newspaper *True Democrat*, urged immediate secession after Lincoln's election. The secession convention elected him to the Provisional Confederate Congress on the first ballot. In 1861 and again in 1862 he won senatorial races and served until the end of the war. On both occasions the main issue was the "Johnson family dynasty." Johnson was chairman of the Committee on Indian Affairs in both regular congresses and pursued, for the day, an enlightened policy which guaranteed protection of the Indians when they came under state jurisdiction, and better supervision of Indian agents. He was also in the forefront of those who wished to keep western troops at home and to make the Trans-Mississippi Department a virtually independent entity. Aside from impressment and the pleas for foreign recognition, he strongly supported the Davis administration. One of his novel suggestions was to require the renomination of department heads every two years, which he explained as not an attack on the government but a means to prevent complacency in the executive branch.

Johnson did not attend the last session of Congress. Fearing reprisals when the Confederacy collapsed, he first planned to seek refuge in Mexico, but he was dissuaded and induced to go to Washington and seek a pardon; it was granted by President Johnson, an old acquaintance. His Arkansas property swept away by creditors, he returned to Washington to form a law partnership with General Albert Pike, late C.S.A., an endeavor in which he does not seem to have been notably successful. After his political disabilities were removed by act of Congress, Johnson sought reelection to the Senate in 1878 but was defeated. The following year, July 26, 1879, he died at his residence in Little Rock and was buried in Mount Holly Cemetery.

THOMAS JOHNSON (Kentucky) was born July 4, 1812, in Montgomery County, Kentucky, son of a father who was a native of Maryland. He received as good an education as the time afforded and quite early in life became a farmer and livestock trader, a business which he conducted over much of the South and in which he amassed over the years a considerable fortune. He also took a great deal of interest in military affairs and rose to the rank of major general in the state militia.

After the secession of Kentucky, the state's pro-Confederate provisional government appointed Johnson to the Provisional Confederate Congress, and he took his seat on December 18, 1861. He attended only a few days, but during his brief tenure he voted without exception to give the central government control over the new nation's manpower and resources. He did not stand for election to the Regular Congress; instead he returned to Montgomery County and late in 1862 raised a regiment of cavalry denominated the Second Kentucky Mounted Rifles. He was commissioned colonel of this command and with it "served throughout the War with various commands, a portion of the time being with General Morgan."[1] Another source states that he "participated in the battles of Dalton, Georgia, Missionary Ridge, and was engaged in Bragg's defeat, and many less important engagements."[2] In any case he seems to have acquitted himself honorably, and at the close of the war he again returned home.

At the age of fifty-nine, Colonel Johnson, a bachelor, was regarded as being quite a catch by the young ladies of Mount Sterling, since he was affluent and thought to be too old to live long. He took as his bride one of these young ladies, aged twenty-six, by whom he fathered six children, the youngest when he was seventy-two. In 1876–1877 Colonel Johnson represented his district in the lower house of the state legislature, and from 1878 to 1882 in the state senate. Colonel Johnson was ninety-three years and nine months old when he died on his farm near Mount Sterling on April 7, 1906. He was buried in Machpelah Cemetery in Mount Sterling.[3]

[1] John M. Prewitt, "The Civil War in Montgomery County," Mount Sterling *Advocate*, June 29, 1961.
[2] *Biographical Encyclopedia of Kentucky*, 450–51.

[3] Biographical and background data on Colonel Johnson was provided by Mrs. Carl Boyd, Mount Sterling, Ky.

WALDO PORTER JOHNSON (Missouri) was born September 16, 1817, in Bridgeport, Harrison County, Virginia (now West Virginia), where his parents and grandparents had emigrated from New York state. He was a nephew of Joseph Johnson, the seven-term congressman from Virginia and governor of the state from 1852 to 1856. The younger Johnson was graduated from Rector College in nearby Pruntytown, studied law, and was admitted to the bar in 1841. After a year of practice in Harrison County, he moved to Osceolo, Missouri, which would be his home for the rest of his life. In 1846 he enlisted as a private for Mexican War duty and while on the plains was honorably discharged so that he could occupy the seat in the legislature to which he had been elected. He was subsequently circuit attorney and judge of his judicial district, resigning the latter post in 1852 to resume law practice.

In 1861 Johnson was a member of the Washington Peace Convention, and the same year he was elected as a Democrat to the United States Senate, serving from March 17, 1861, to January 10, 1862, when he was expelled, having in the meantime joined the Confederate army. He took part in the Battle of Pea Ridge, where he was twice wounded, as lieutenant colonel of the Fourth Missouri Infantry, and he later engaged in recruiting for the forces of Major General Sterling Price. Upon the death of Senator R. L. Y. Peyton in 1863, Governor Reynolds appointed Johnson to fill the vacancy, and he took his seat in time to serve throughout the Second Regular Congress. As a senator, Johnson always favored taking the war to the enemy and advocated the strongest kind of legislation, including a 50 percent tax on all property. On the other hand, and despite the fact that his appointment derived partially from his friendship with Jefferson Davis, he soon became highly critical of the way Confederate affairs were being managed, regarding the secretaries of state and the treasury, Benjamin and Memminger, as particularly incompetent. He supported every effort made in Congress to reform the cabinet and in 1865 joined the scheme to force Davis to turn the prosecution of the war over to Lee, Joe Johnston, and Beauregard. For much of his term he was also Missouri's leading critic of western commanding officers and was a sort of spokesman for Governor Reynolds against alleged neglect of western interests. Johnson fled to Canada after the war and remained until April, 1866, when he returned to Osceola. He then resumed his law practice and in 1875 served as president of the state constitutional

135

convention. He died in Osceola on August 14, 1885, and was buried in Forest Hill Cemetery, Kansas City.

ROBERT JOHNSTON (Virginia) was born October 14, 1818, in Rockbridge County, Virginia. He attended Washington College in Lexington in 1839–1840; he studied law there under John W. Brockenbrough (*q.v.*) and under another well-known lawyer in Staunton. After being admitted to the bar he commenced practice in Harrison County, in what is now West Virginia. Johnston represented several transmontane counties in the General Assembly, and was also for several years first auditor of the state, resigning from this post to resume his law practice in Clarksburg.

In 1861 Johnston was appointed by the Virginia convention as a representative to the Confederate Provisional Congress from the Fifteenth Congressional District, an area which soon became a part of the newly formed state of West Virginia. However, the soldier and refugee vote returned him to a seat in the First and Second Regular congresses, and he served until the end. He was a member of a number of minor committees and seldom participated in debate; however, his voting record made unmistakable his willingness to subordinate all other considerations to victory and independence, although he had some reservations at the outset. Among the many sacrificial measures which he supported were a law denying redress for property illegally impressed, the repudiation of redundant currency, the enrolling of all able-bodied men, and his own resolution instructing the Ways and Means Committee to prepare a comprehensive tax bill which would raise fifty million dollars annually. Johnston was also in favor of permitting the president to organize the army as he saw best and to impress the slave population for any purposes he deemed necessary. Besides this he thought suspension of the writ of habeas corpus at the president's discretion entirely justifiable. In all of this he doubtless reflected the views of those who had elected him. After the war Johnston settled in Harrisonburg, Virginia, and again resumed his law practice. From 1880 until his death on November 6, 1885, he was judge of Rockingham County. He is buried in Woodbine Cemetery, Harrisonburg.

GEORGE WASHINGTON JONES (Tennessee) was a native of Virginia, born in King and Queen County, March 15, 1806, but he moved with his parents to Fayetteville, Tennessee, at an early age. Here, after obtaining a rudimentary education in the local schools, he was apprenticed to a saddler, a trade which he later followed for a time. He served as a justice of the peace from 1832–1835, was a member of the state house of representatives from 1835–1839 and of the state senate from 1839–1841, and was clerk of the Lincoln County Court from 1840–1843. At this point, the veritable prototype of the frontier politician, Jones was elected as a Democrat to the first of eight consecutive terms in the U.S. Congress, serving until 1859.

When war threatened in 1861, Jones was elected a delegate to the peace Conference held in Washington but did not attend. Instead, he devoted his efforts to the cause of secession and in November, 1861, was elected from the Seventh District to the First Regular Confederate Congress, succeeding T. M. Jones (*q.v.*), where he was an unsuccessful candidate for the speakership of the House of Representatives. As chairman of the Committee on Rules and Officers of the House he devoted much of his attention to keeping its affairs running smoothly. This involved him in such matters as rules, salaries, House officials, publication of documents, and the like. On the major body of legislation Jones's agrarian attitudes made him probably Tennessee's strongest states' righter in Congress. He was willing to grant the president almost a free hand in diplomacy and the selection of cabinet officers, but he tried to keep the economy and the army as much under state and local control as possible. He did not stand for reelection. In 1870 he was a delegate to the state constitutional convention, and in 1871 and 1877 he was appointed and reappointed to the board of trustees of the Tennessee Hospital for the Insane. Jones died on November 14, 1884, in Fayetteville and was buried there in Rose Hill Cemetery.

HENRY COX JONES (Alabama) was born on his father's plantation near Russellville, Alabama, January 23, 1821. On his mother's side he was a lineal descendant of John Rolfe and Pocohontas. He received his primary education in the Russellville school and was graduated from LaGrange College in 1840. After studying law, Jones was admitted to the bar in Franklin County in 1841 and the same year was elected probate judge. He was elected to the state legislature in 1842, reelected in 1844, and sent to the state senate in 1853. Three years laters Jones moved to Florence, where he continued his law practice. In 1860 he was a presidential elector on the Douglas–H. V. Johnson (*q. v.*) ticket. The following year Jones represented Lauderdale County in the secession convention and refused to vote for or sign Alabama's secession ordinance. Despite this, when D. P. Lewis (*q.v.*) resigned his seat in the Provisional Confederate Congress Jones was chosen by the Alabama convention as his successor. He took his seat on April 19, 1861, the day the second session convened in Montgomery. Although it was in that session that war actually began, Jones would only rarely make concessions to the emergency by assigning new powers to the central government. He opposed new taxes, new loans, new executive powers, new uses of the militia, and virtually everything smacking of novelty. He made only three suggestions from the floor: one to exempt carriages from taxation, and two to settle claims against the Confederacy. In November he was narrowly defeated in a bid for election to the Regular Congress. Thereafter, during the war, he was engaged in the manufacture of cotton and woolens under a contract for the Confederate government. After the war he resumed his law practice and at one time was associated with Josiah Patterson Campbell (*q.v.*), a former Confederate colonel and member of Congress from Alabama. During the Reconstruction era Jones was chairman of the Democratic Central Committee for five years, and in 1876 he was a Tilden elector. The same year he was elected solicitor for his district; he was twice reelected and held the office for eighteen years. Well into his ninety-third year, Jones died at his residence in Florence on June 20, 1913, and was buried in Florence Cemetery.

ROBERT McDONALD JONES,[1] a delegate from the Choctaw and Chickasaw nations, was born somewhere in the Choctaw territory in what is now southern Mississippi on October 1, 1808. He was well educated at the Choctaw Academy in Kentucky and migrated with his tribe to the Indian Territory in 1832, settling in the neighborhood of Fort Towson. Here he began to demonstrate marked business ability, establishing a chain of general stores which he operated with great success at various points in the Choctaw Nation. The profits from the stores were invested in land and slaves along Red River, until by 1860 he owned six plantations and was said to be the master of five hundred Negroes[2] and worth a million dollars.

Jones naturally sided with the Confederacy and in July, 1861, served as the principal commissioner of the Choctaws to negotiate a treaty with General Albert Pike, acting for the Confederate states. The Choctaw General Council then elected him as the nonvoting representative in the Confederate Congress of the Choctaw and Chickasaw Nations for a two-year term. The terms of the treaties concluded with these nations provided that the congressman should be elected alternately from each nation; however, upon the expiration of Jones's term, the Chickasaws had returned their allegiance to the United States, and there was no member of their nation to sit in the Congress. Accordingly Jones was the two tribes' sole representative in the First and Second congresses. He spent much of 1862, however, enlisting and equipping at his own expense a battalion of Choctaws, and he did not take his seat in Congress until January 17, 1863. His only significant proposal was that two hundred extra copies of the report of the Commissioner of Indian Affairs be printed and distributed to the Indian nations. Following the war, in 1866 he was chairman of a delegation of Choctaws sent to Washington to reestablish relations with the United States. His fortunes largely swept away by the results of the war, Colonel Jones continued to reside at his once-magnificent estate, Rose Hill, near Hugo, Oklahoma, until his death on February 22, 1872. He is buried in the family graveyard at Rose Hill.

[1] There is some question as to Jones's middle name. By his third (white) wife he had five children. According to a document on file in the Oklahoma Historical Society Library, either written or amended by a great-grandson, two of the sons were named Robert Jefferson and James McDonald (Jones). On the other hand, another paper from the same society, written by a deceased professor at Southeastern State Teachers' College in Durant, Okla., refers several times to one of the sons of the third marriage as "Robert McDonald Jones, Jr." and "Robert M. Jones, Jr."

[2] The 1860 census of Indian Territory reveals that Jones admitted owning 227 slaves. Underestimating property by as much as fifty percent for census purposes was not unusual, since few interviewees were convinced that the information supplied would not be available to the tax collector.

THOMAS McKISSICK JONES (Tennessee) was born in Person County on the northern border of North Carolina, December 16, 1816. He was no relation to George Washington Jones (*q.v.*), whom he preceded in the Confederate Congress from the same Tennessee congressional district. After attending the local schools of his native county, he attended, successively, Wertenburg Academy in Pulaski, Tennessee; the University of Alabama; and the University of Virginia. Upon leaving Virginia in 1835 he read law in Pulaski, and after serving in the Seminole War of 1836 in Company A, First Tennessee Mounted Volunteers, he opened a law office there. He was soon one of the prominent men of the town: mayor for many terms, representative and senator in the legislature, director and president of the Nashville and Decatur Railroad, director of the Planters Bank for eighteen years, director of the National Bank of Pulaski for twelve years, delegate to the Democratic national conventions of 1856 and 1860, and a regular delegate to the state conventions for many years.

Soon after Tennessee seceded, Jones was elected to the Provisional Congress from the Seventh District. As a congressman he took initiative only in matters relating to army pay, furloughs, and promotions. Here he placed the soldiers' interests foremost, while on other army matters he worked to preserve state control over the organization and use of volunteers. In contrast, Jones delegated to the central government much emergency use of the nation's economy. He did not stand for reelection to the Regular Congress. Having three sons in the Confederate army, Jones, after his congressional term, became something of a camp follower, remaining with the army until the close of the war. In 1870 Jones was a delegate to the Tennessee constitutional convention, and in 1872–1873 he was a judge of the criminal court. In later years he served as special judge on the state's supreme court on a number of occasions. Judge Jones was also for almost fifty years a member of the Masonic Order, becoming successively Master Mason, Royal Arch Mason, and Knight Templar. He died in Pulaski on March 13, 1892, and was buried in Maplewood Cemetery.[1]

[1] Biographical data on Jones was provided by the Tennessee State Library and Archives.

EDWIN AUGUSTUS KEEBLE (Tennessee), who served in both the Tennessee legislature and the Confederate Congress during the war years, was born February 14, 1807, in Cumberland County, Virginia. He graduated from the University of North Carolina at Chapel Hill with a B.A. degree, then read law and was admitted to the bar. By 1834 he was living in Murfreesboro, Tennessee, where he published and edited the *Central Monitor*, later called simply the *Monitor*. He also practiced law at Murfreesboro, and was mayor of the town from 1838 to 1855. Meanwhile, he was one of the organizers and incorporators of the Murfreesboro Savings Institute, founded in 1850. In 1856 Keeble was a presidential elector on the ticket of Buchanan and Breckinridge, and in 1861 he was elected to the Thirty-fourth (Confederate) General Assembly of Tennessee, representing Rutherford County.

In June, 1863, the Confederate leaders of Tennessee, now largely overrun by Union forces, met at Winchester and nominated Keeble as their candidate for Sixth District congressman. He was elected, as might have been expected, by a comparative handful of voters, and in due course he took his seat in Richmond on May 2, 1864. During his ten months in Congress, Keeble seldom spoke, but he apparently was willing to put states' rights in abeyance. He withheld from the central government few new powers or extensions of old programs that might revitalize the war effort. Like most border-state congressmen whose districts were occupied by Federal armies, his main concern was reconquest. Keeble's principal contribution to the Confederate legislative machinery was a bill to let the president requisition from the state governors all deserters and absentees from their commands, and to assign troops to the governors for this purpose. Keeble did not long survive the war—he died in Murfreesboro on August 26, 1868, and was buried at Old Jefferson, Rutherford County. His third wife was a daughter of John Bell, nominee of the Constitutional Union party in 1860, which secured the electoral votes of Tennessee, Kentucky, and Virginia.[1]

[1] Much of the biographical data here was provided by the Tennessee State Library and Archives.

LAWRENCE MASSILLON KEITT (South Carolina) was born October 4, 1824, in Orangeburg District, South Carolina. He was graduated from South Carolina College (now the University of South Carolina) in 1843, studied law, and was admitted to the bar in 1845. Three years later he entered the South Carolina legislature as an extreme proslavery advocate, and when the Nashville convention of 1850 failed to recommend secession, Keitt urged the secession of South Carolina by herself. In 1852 he was elected to Congress and, with one brief intermission, served until ten days before South Carolina seceded from the Union. In 1856, having acted to aid and abet the murderous attack of Representative Preston Brooks upon Senator Charles Sumner, he was in effect censured by the House and promptly resigned, but he was as promptly reelected by his constituents and resumed his seat only twenty days later.

Keitt did not formally resign his seat in Congress, but he did not occupy it after December 10, 1860. The same month, the secession convention elected Keitt a delegate to the proposed Montgomery convention, which would become the Provisional Congress. He preferred Howell Cobb for president and soon pronounced "Jeff Davis a failure, and his cabinet a farce." However, he was a conscientious nation-maker and withheld from the new government only the right to preempt from the states the appointment of militia officers. Keitt was one of the earliest to advocate the strategic use of cotton. In July he suggested an embargo on all cotton, tobacco, and naval stores; he also hoped that the government would buy all cotton and use it for credit and for leverage in diplomatic matters. He did not seek election to the Regular Congress but instead recruited the Twentieth South Carolina Infantry and was elected its colonel. Until May, 1864, the regiment served in the Charleston area, most of the time on Sullivan's Island, and saw little

141

action. Late in May it was ordered to Virginia to join Lee's army of northern Virginia, and the inexperienced Keitt, by virtue of seniority, assumed command of Kershaw's old brigade of the First Corps, now under the command of Lieutenant General Richard H. Anderson, a fellow South Carolinian. When Anderson attacked at Cold Harbor early on the morning of June 1, Keitt, in his first battle, rode recklessly forward on horseback. His regiment broke and, in an effort to rally it, he fell mortally wounded.[1] He died the next day in a field hospital and was buried in the family cemetery near St. Matthews, South Carolina.

[1] See Douglas Southall Freeman, *Lee's Lieutenants: A Study in Command* (3 vols.; New York, 1942–44), III, 506. For some reason, the *Biographical Directory of the American Congress* records Keitt's fatal injury as occuring on June 3 and his date of death as June 4. See also *DAB*.

AUGUSTUS HOLMES KENAN (Georgia) was born at Montpelier, Baldwin County, Georgia, April 21, 1805. He was educated in Orange, New York, on the Hudson River, studied law and was admitted to the bar, and settled in Milledgeville, then the capital of Georgia. He soon became known as one of the ablest lawyers in the state. Kenan represented Baldwin County six times in the house of representatives of the General Assembly and three times in the state senate between 1834 and 1858. During this period he also served as captain of a company in the Seminole disturbances of 1835 in Florida. Kenan was an old-line Whig and a dedicated opponent of disunion. Elected a member of the Georgia convention called to consider secession, he voted "Nay" on the motion to introduce the ordinance but finally went along with his colleagues and signed the document, reputedly throwing away the pen with which he signed it.[1] He was forthwith elected one of the ten original delegates to the Montgomery convention, two being elected at large and one each from the state's eight congressional districts. His selection was influenced by a desire to add a moderate tone to the Georgia delegation. In November he won election to the Regular Congress over Howell Cobb (*q.v.*), something of a feat in its own right. As one of Jefferson Davis' closest friends, Kenan was always in basic sympathy with the administration. At first, however, he wanted the economy to remain in local hands and opposed innovations like the produce loan and grants for railroad construction. In November, 1861, he proposed to repeal all tariff laws, but the course of the war compelled Kenan to reassess his position, and he soon showed a set determination to enact almost any law necessary for victory. When Davis sent him to reconcile Georgia's Governor Brown to conscription,

Kenan argued that "states Rights will be easily adjusted when we establish the right to have states."[2] He based his campaign for reelection in 1863 on this position and lost decisively to Clifford Anderson of Macon (*q.v.*). On May 23. 1865, he received a presidential pardon at the hands of Andrew Johnson, but he lived to enjoy it scarcely three weeks—he died in Milledgeville on June 16, 1865. He is buried there in the Old Cemetery in an unmarked grave. He was a cousin of Representative Owen R. Kenan of North Carolina (*q.v.*).

[1] Much of the biographical material on Kenan is derived from Alvaretta Kenan Register (comp.), *The Kenan Family and Some Allied Families* (Statesboro, Ga., 1967). See also Lucian Lamar Knight, *Georgia's Bi-Centennial Memoirs and Memories* (N.p., 1932), II, 282–83.

[2] Savannah *Republican*, May 15, 1862.

OWEN RAND KENAN[1] (North Carolina) was born on March 4, 1804,[2] in Kenansville, North Carolina, into a comfortably well-off cotton-and-tobacco-plantation family. He studied medicine briefly but soon decided to read law. He began practicing in Kenansville and later took up planting, which seems to have gradually become his main interest. Kenan served in the North Carolina House of Commons as a Democrat from 1834 to 1838 but thereafter abstained from active politics for a number of years. During this time his splendid home, Liberty Hall, became one of the main centers of Duplin County social affairs. After Lincoln's election Kenan became a strong secessionist, and in the fall of 1861 he campaigned for a seat in the Confederate House of Representatives on the promise to cooperate fully with the Confederacy. He won easily over two more conservative opponents.

In Richmond Kenan was faithful to his campaign pledge, for under the permanent Constitution he and Lander were North Carolina's only strong supporters of vigorous wartime legislation. Kenan himself spoke seldom and proposed neither bill or amendment, but the Davis administration could almost always rely on his vote to counteract the strong state's rights element in Congress. It was only on certain financial measures which Kenan felt would oppress his productive agricultural district, in particular the forced funding of Treasury notes and the tax in kind on farm products, that he placed local over Confederate preferences. At the end of his service in Congress Kenan stated that there was not enough discontent in North Carolina to merit concern and he did not seek reelection.

After the Civil War Kenan devoted himself entirely to his law practice and his planting. He died at Liberty Hall on March 3, 1887, and is buried in the Graham Cemetery near Kenansville. He was a cousin of A. H. Kenan (*q.v.*).

[1] Zebulon V. Walser Papers, Southern Historical Collection, University of North Carolina, Chapel Hill.
[2] Information on Kenan's birth date, date of death, and place of interment was taken from Register (comp.), *The Kenan Family*, 21–23.

DUNCAN FARRAR KENNER (Louisiana), not the least of whose distinctions was membership in all three Confederate congresses, was born to a well-to-do New Orleans family on February 11, 1813. He was educated by private tutors and in the New Orleans public schools before attending Miami University of Oxford, Ohio, the alma mater of many southerners, including several Confederate congressmen-to-be. After graduation in 1831 Kenner traveled abroad for four years and returned to study law in the office of John Slidell. He never practiced, however; instead he took up planting on a property near Donaldsonville in Ascension Parish. Here his fortunes flourished in the fields of both agriculture and horse breeding (his studs became widely known throughout the country, with consistent winners at Saratoga as well as in the South). Like many of his class he regarded politics as an obligation; he was elected to the Louisiana legislature as early as 1836 and served a number of terms in both house and senate. He was a member of both the state constitutional conventions of 1844 and 1852, and he was president of the latter.

In 1861 the secession convention sent Kenner to the Provisional Confederate Congress and he won reelection to both Regular congresses without opposition. In the Provisional Congress Kenner was in the forefront of those seeking a sound economic program for the Confederacy; he was responsible for the clause in the Provisional Congress which made a protective tariff possible; he promoted Federal aid to railroad construction, stringent confiscation and sequestration laws, and higher taxes, maintaining that necessity rather than public approval should govern the course of Congress. In the Regular congresses, where he was chairman of the Ways and Means Committee, he was much less innovative, apparently because of committee work and his increasing involvement in diplomatic affairs. Kenner increasingly felt that the independence of the Confederacy could only be attained by European recognition—which, in turn, was only attainable through the abolition of slavery. Accordingly he urged President Davis and Secretary of State Benjamin to make an offer to England and France to abolish slavery in exchange for recognition. Davis reluctantly appointed Kenner a minister plenipotentiary to treat on the subject. He went to New York in disguise and sailed for Europe but arrived after all confidence in the Confederacy's ultimate success had evaporated.

At the end of the war Kenner returned to the ruins of his plantation, Ashland, and began life anew. He was almost immediately elected to the Louisiana senate, serving from 1866–1867, and again in 1877 after the state had been reclaimed from the Republican Radicals, a movement in which he took a prominent part. Meantime he rebuilt his property and restored his fortune to a size greater than it had been at the beginning of the war, a task accomplished by hard work, know-how, and the introduction of novel methods to the production of cane sugar. He also rebuilt his racing establishment and was president of the Louisiana Jockey Club from its formation until his death. The loser in a contest for a seat in the United States Senate in 1878, he was appointed a member of the United States Tariff Commission by President Arthur in 1882. He also served for years on the Louisiana Levee Board and headed the building committee for the New Orleans Cotton Exposition of 1884–1885. Kenner died at his New Orleans residence on July 3, 1887, and was buried in the family tomb at Donaldsonville.

JOHN TILLMAN LAMKIN (Mississippi) was a native of Georgia, born in Augusta on July 17, 1811. After a common-school education he studied law and was admitted to the bar in 1833. Following two years of practice he determined to go to Texas but, finding that the Republic did not live up to his expectations, came back to New Orleans, where he remained for nearly three years training himself in accountancy. In 1838 he located in Mississippi and, after admission to the bar there, commenced practice, first in Marion County and in 1840 at Holmesville in Pike County. The following year he was elected district attorney; he served for four years, after which he devoted himself exclusively to his practice.

Lamkin had opposed secession from the outset but, like many of his countrymen, cast his lot with his state after the fact. In 1861 he ran for the First Regular Congress but was defeated by John Jones McRae (*q.v.*). He then raised a company of the Thirty-third Mississippi Infantry, which he led as its captain until 1863. By this time the piney-woods vote, disenchanted with the war, gave Lamkin the victory over the proadministration McRae. In the Second Congress Lamkin belonged to a relatively small group who had lost all hope of victory and considered further sacrifice useless. He quietly opposed every new administration proposal and any further grant of power to the executive. Meanwhile he tried to soften the impact of war on the civilian front, urging an increase in military exemptions, immediate payment for property illegally impressed, and repeal of the law authorizing the destruction of private property liable to capture. He also voted for every peace resolution introduced and finally abandoned his seat a month before Congress adjourned for the last time.

Lamkin came home to find his fortunes greatly reduced but resumed his profession with energy, although he survived the war by only five years; he died in Holmesville on May 19, 1870. First buried there, his remains were later moved to Woodlawn Cemetery in Summit, Mississippi.

WILLIAM LANDER[1] (North Carolina) was born in County Tipperary, Ireland, on May 8, 1817. The family immigrated to America the next year, first settling in Salisbury, North Carolina, but moving to Lincolnton about 1826. The father became a coachmaker and also acted as a lay Methodist minister. After attending Lincolnton Academy and Cokesbury College in South Carolina, William read law in Lincolnton under James R. Dodge. He was admitted to the bar in 1839. Lander's oratory and legal brilliance soon earned him a lucrative practice. He later acquired and operated a small farm. He served briefly as county solicitor and became district solicitor in 1853, holding this position until 1862. He was also elected to the legislature in 1852 for one term. But Lander made his political reputation during the secession crisis. At the Charleston Democratic convention of 1860 he labored to keep the party together; but when the convention reconvened at Baltimore and nominated Stephen A. Douglas, Lander was the spokesman for the North Carolinians who withdrew from the hall. Later, in a highly publicized debate with Zebulon B. Vance, he castigated the antisouthern position of the Bell-Everett ticket. By early 1861 Lander advocated secession and in the May convention he voted for immediate disunion. In November he won a seat in the Confederate House of Representatives.

In Congress Lander was a constant, though unassertive, administration stalwart. During the debates on conscription his only concession to state interests was his support of an unsuccessful amendment requiring the president to make the first call for conscripts on states which had thus far furnished the least manpower. Lander also supported most proposals giving the central government whatever controls it wished over individuals and the economy. Only in his belief that repudiation of old Treasury notes was a violation of contract did Lander reflect the disaffection of his state. In 1863 he lost his race for reelection to a peace candidate.

At the end of his term in Congress Lander resumed his law practice in Lincolnton. He died on January 8, 1868, and was buried in the Methodist Church graveyard.

[1] William L. Sherrill, *Annals of Lincoln County, North Carolina* (Charlotte, N.C., 1937), *passim*.

JAMES MADISON LEACH (North Carolina) was born on January 17, 1815, at his family plantation, Lansdowne, in Randolph County, North Carolina. He attended the local schools and Caldwell Institute in Greensboro and graduated from the United States Military Academy in 1838. He then studied law, and after obtaining his license in 1842 he practiced in Lexington for the remainder of his life. Leach served in the General Assembly as a Whig from 1848 to 1858 and in Congress from 1859 to 1861. In 1856 he was a presidential elector on the American party ticket. During the winter of 1860–1861 he opposed secession bitterly and was stumping his district for reelection to Congress on a Unionist platform when news arrived of Lincoln's call for volunteers to quell the southern rebellion. Leach immediately returned home and raised a company of volunteers.[1] He saw considerable action in Virginia and rose to a lieutenant colonelcy. When congressman-elect Samuel H. Christian died in March, 1864, Leach resigned his commission and in April easily won the seat on a peace-with-independence campaign.

An analysis of Leach's record in the Second Congress reveals a complete catalog of efforts made there to halt the tide of wartime legislation. He fought all administration programs. He voted to override every presidential veto and approved resolutions declaring Secretaries Benjamin, Memminger (*q.v.*), and Regan (*q.v.*) incompetent. He tried to compel President Davis to open peace negotiations and by April, 1865, he was urging North Carolina to begin separate state negotiations. Leach's own bills aimed to improve the care of patients in military hospitals, to exempt as many soldiers as possible, and to commit Congress against further suspension of the writ of habeas corpus. At home, a North Carolina captain wrote that Leach "has thrown more obstacles in the way of my arresting deserters . . . than any ten men in this County."[2]

Leach was almost bankrupt at the end of the war, but his popularity as an advocate quickly enabled him to recoup his fortunes. He served four more terms in the North Carolina Senate, where his chief interest was the promotion of internal improvement projects. In 1880 he was chairman of the legislative committee selected to sell the Western North Carolina Railroad to the Richmond and Danville management in the hope that the former line could be completed.[3] From 1871 to 1875 Leach represented the Conservative party in the United States House of Representatives, but he declined to be a candidate for a third term. In 1876 and 1880 he was elector-at-large on the Democratic ticket. Leach died in Lexington on June 1, 1891, and was buried in Hopewell Cemetery near Trinity. He was a cousin of James Thomas Leach (*q.v.*).

[1] Jerome Dowd, *Sketches of Prominent Living North Carolinians* (Raleigh, 1888), 314.

[2] Jesse Hargrave to Zebulon B. Vance, October 15, 1864, in Zebulon B. Vance Papers, North Carolina Department of Archives and History, Raleigh.

[3] *Journal of the General Assembly of the State of North Carolina at Its Special Session, 1880,* 23.

JAMES THOMAS LEACH[1] (North Carolina) was born "in a snow storm" in 1805 on the family plantation, Leachburg, in Johnston County, North Carolina. The community of Leachburg which later developed there was named in honor of this prominent family. After an academic education Leach, who was a cousin of James M. Leach (*q.v.*), studied law briefly at Rutgers and probably in London. But his admiration for his grandfather, who had been a surgeon in the Revolution, caused him to switch to medicine and he earned his diploma from Jefferson Medical College in Philadelphia. Leach then began a practice in Johnston County that lasted over fifty years. He also owned and managed a large plantation, but attempted to acquire only those slaves who wished to earn their freedom. Dr. Leach soon became the leading citizen of his community. In addition to his medical practice and to occasional legal work he opened the sixteen-room home on his large plantation to orphans, ran a free school there and later built several schoolhouses nearby and instructed local farmers in better farm practices. He wanted the plantations in his district to become as self-sufficient as possible. Leach was an Old Line Whig and in 1858 was elected to one term in the legislature. In the early months of 1861 he spoke vigorously against secession, and because of these convictions he failed to win reelection to the legislature.

In 1863 Leach campaigned fiercely against three Confederate enthusiasts for a place in the Confederate House of Representatives. He pledged to seek "a just, honorable and lasting peace" and won easily. In Congress Leach's unbridled antagonism toward the "reckless legislation . . . endorsed by the President and the mighty strides now making toward a military despotism"[2] placed him in the forefront of the malcontents. He was supersensitive to imagined insults to his state and to any further demands upon its people. He voted to override every veto, to impugn the competence of every cabinet member so charged, to exempt everyone possible, and to block any new economic program. When Richmond editors criticized his position Leach wanted them "Dead, Dead, Dead!"[3] When the president refused to open peace negotiations Leach urged separate state action for the best terms available.

After the war Dr. Leach continued his old habits of involvement. He became a strong Prohibitionist and in 1875 resigned his place on the board of county commissioners rather than certify anyone as a "qualified" barroom operator. He was also a director of the state insane asylum for a number of years. Dr. Leach died at home on March 28, 1883, and is buried in the family cemetery near Mount Zion Church.[4]

[1] Biographical information was provided by Nancy McCullers Ferguson of Raleigh, N.C., a direct descendant of Leach.

[2] Raleigh *Weekly Standard*, January 13, 1864.

[3] Richmond *Daily Examiner*, November 23, 1864.

[4] Dr. Leach ordered in his will that no gravestone mark his burial place. Mrs. Ferguson recently placed a gravestone there, nevertheless, but explained to the author that she was unable to find the date of his birth and that the part of the family Bible containing this information had been destroyed.

GEORGE NELSON LESTER[1] (Georgia) was born in Abbeville District, South Carolina, on March 13, 1824. When he was four his parents moved to Gwinnett County, Georgia, and bought a small farm. Farm work came first for this small family and young Lester was forced to be virtually self-educated. Nevertheless he read law in Lawrenceville for a year and was admitted to practice in 1843 at the age of eighteen by special act of the legislature. Lester opened his first office in Cumming and developed a moderate practice, but in the early 1850s he moved to Marietta. In 1855 Lester was appointed supreme court reporter and held the position until his election in 1858 as a Democrat to the state house of representatives. He was reelected in 1860 and was chairman of the judiciary committee which began proceedings that eventually took Georgia out of the Union.

When war began Lester organized a company which became part of the Forty-first Georgia Regiment. In the fall of 1862 he was in the thickest fighting at Perryville, Kentucky, and lost an arm. As soon as he had recuperated he joined the Georgia state reserves. While serving in this capacity he won an easy victory as representative to the Confederate Congress.

Lester reached Richmond convinced that the Confederacy must earn its independence with existing forces. He refused to weaken the army by interfering with its command or with the laws providing for its

149

supply. On the other hand he would not ask the home front for further sacrifices. Most of his bills aimed to exempt labor which he considered vital to production, and he opposed further controls over persons or property. His tax proposal of December 24, 1864, did little but continue the moderate existing laws for one year. Meanwhile he worked quietly for peace, and his last day in Congress was February 3, 1865, the day of the Hampton Roads Peace Conference failure.

After the war Lester continued his law practice in Marietta. For a brief time he was commissioner of the Home Department in the newly appointed Bureau of Immigration, but he resigned under constant Republican criticism and when he saw that the bureau was accomplishing little. Lester then served for many years as judge of the Blue Ridge Circuit. In 1888 he was a Democratic presidential elector. In 1890 he was elected attorney general, but before taking office he suffered a paralytic stroke. He never recovered, and he died on March 30, 1892. He is buried in Citizen's Cemetery, Marietta.[2]

[1] Northen (ed.), *Men of Mark in Georgia*, III, 493–94.
[2] Information on Lester's death and interment was provided by JoAnne P. Stratton, Cobb County Public Library System, Marietta, Ga.

DAVID PETER LEWIS (Alabama), chiefly noted for being one of Alabama's most notorious Scalawags during the Reconstruction period, was born about the year 1820[1] in Charlotte County, Virginia, but was brought to Madison County, Alabama, in childhood. He grew up there, received a college education, studied law in Huntsville, and, after admission to the bar, established his practice in Lawrence County. He represented Lawrence County in the state constitutional convention (secession convention) of 1861 and voted against secession but signed the ordinance which took Alabama out of the Union. Presumably on the strength of this act, he was elected to the Provisional Congress, but he attended only a few days after taking his seat on February 8, 1861. He resigned after the first session, offering as a reason that it would not be "convenient" for him to attend any longer. In 1863 Lewis was appointed judge of the circuit court of Alabama by Governor John G. Shorter (*q.v.*), but he held the office only a few months, defecting from the Confederacy and making his way through the lines to Nashville, where he remained until the end of the war. He returned to Alabama in 1865 to make his residence in Huntsville and resume his law practice. Lewis thereupon allied himself with the Republican-Negro-Carpetbagger faction and in 1872, during the throes of Reconstruction, was elected governor of the state. During his term of office he doubled the taxes of an already impoverished people, recognized a body of Republicans claiming to have been legally elected and since known as the "courthouse legislature," and appealed to the military authorities to uphold his position. The matter was finally referred to the attorney general of the United States, who decided against him. In 1874 he was swept out of office as the Democrats regained control of the state and restored white rule. Lewis then returned to Huntsville and resumed his law practice, a man virtually without a family (he had never married), friends, or political associates. He died in Huntsville, July 3, 1884, and was buried in Maple Hill Cemetery there.

[1] The month and day of Lewis' birth cannot be ascertained. His grave marker recites only that he died "aged 65 years." Owen's *History of Alabama* gives the year of his birth as 1820. The 1860 census, however, records his age as thirty-seven.

DAVID WILLIAM LEWIS [1] (Georgia) was born in Hancock County, Georgia, on October 24, 1815, the descendant of two prominent families. After attending schools in Sparta, he studied at the University of North Carolina and then at the University of Georgia, from which he graduated in 1837. Lewis' first position was as private secretary to Governor George R. Gilmer. When that ended he studied law and was admitted to the bar in 1843. He began his practice in Sparta. In 1845 Lewis was elected to the legislature as a Whig and served there for the next ten years, winning his last two elections without opposition. In the meantime he acquired considerable property and became more interested in agriculture than the law. He was one of the founders of the Georgia State Agricultural Society, serving as its third president and afterwards as secretary for many years. After Lincoln's election Lewis became an avowed secessionist. In November, 1861, he was elected a representative to the Confederate Congress on a pledge of complete support to his new government.

In Congress Lewis quickly proved himself to be the strongest Confederate nationalist in the Georgia delegation. He supported unreservedly, both in principle and in detail, every significant law designed to strengthen the government at home and abroad. The only possible exceptions to this course were two resolutions which he introduced requesting committees to see that the rights of planters were protected from possible abuse by army agents. Otherwise he left the initiative in legislation to others. In his bid for reelection, Lewis ran a poor third in a three-man race.

Lewis' last work was with the North Georgia Agricultural College in Dahlonega. He was its first president and was known affectionately by

151

his students as "the old Colonel." He held the office from 1873 until his death on December 28, 1885. He was buried in the Dahlonega City Cemetery and reinterred on the college campus in 1891 when a monument was placed there in his honor.[2]

[1] Northen (ed.), *Men of Mark in Georgia*, III, 528–30.
[2] Information on Lewis' two interments was provided by Larry Mitchell, North Georgia College, Dahlonega.

JOHN WOOD LEWIS[1] (Georgia) was born February 1, 1801, on a small plantation in Spartanburg District, South Carolina. Though he was orphaned at an early age, his mother saw that he received a good education. He attended Cedar Springs Academy near home, then studied medicine under Dr. Richard Harris of Greenville and began practicing in Spartanburg. He also served in the legislature in 1830 and 1831. But Lewis became caught up in the revival of religion sweeping the state and in 1832 became an ordained Baptist minister. For some years Lewis preached near Greenville, then about 1839 or 1840 he accepted a call to Canton, Georgia. Western Georgia at that time was almost a wilderness, and Lewis found a variety of opportunities. In addition to his church in Canton he organized several churches in nearby communities. He also bought land, erected several iron furnaces and a mill, and built roads at his own expense to make his holdings more valuable. In 1845 the Democrats elected Lewis to the state senate for one term.

Lewis' next enterprise was a railroad management. While studying law, Joseph E. Brown lived in the Lewis home and tutored the numerous Lewis children. Brown then borrowed money from Lewis to attend the Yale Law School. While he was governor, Brown in 1858 appointed Lewis superintendent of the state-owned Western and Atlantic Railroad, then in dire financial straits. Lewis put it on a paying basis by exercising such economy that he was said to have ordered engineers to blow their whistles only when necessary.[2] He held this position until 1861. When Robert Toombs (*q.v.*) refused to accept his election to the Confederate Senate, Brown appointed Lewis to serve until the next meeting of the legislature. He took his seat on April 7, 1862. In September Lewis submitted a resolution pledging Congress' total commitment to victory, but his record indicated that he and Brown were cut from the same cloth. Lewis seldom deviated from a hard state's rights position, quietly opposing programs ranging from conscription to the establishment of a supreme court. Most of his own suggestions came in the form of resolutions questioning the army's efficiency in railroad management. Lewis did not seek reelection to the Senate, as at that time he had already agreed to manage Georgia's interest in the great wells of Saltville, Virginia. He died at home on July 11, 1865, and is buried in Canton's Riverview Cemetery.[3]

[1] *History of the Baptist Denomination in Georgia* (Atlanta, 1881), 332–33.
[2] Sarah Blackwell Gober Temple, *The First Hundred Years: A Short History of Cobb County, in Georgia* (Atlanta, 1935), 79.
[3] Information on Lewis' interment was provided by Louise J. Chandler, R. T. Jones Memorial Library, Canton, Ga.

GEORGE WASHINGTON LOGAN[1] (North Carolina) was born near the quaintly named community of Pools of Hickory Nut Falls in Rutherford County, North Carolina, on February 22, 1815. After receiving a fair education from the local academies and from tutoring at home, he opened a tavern nearby. Logan moved to Rutherfordton, however, when he was elected clerk of his county court in 1841. He held this position until 1849, when he began studying law under Richmond M. Pearson. Logan began practicing law in Rutherfordton in the early 1850s and served as county solicitor from 1855 to 1856. During the late 1840s and much of the 1850s he was a member of the state militia, eventually earning a brigadier generalship. Politically Logan was an Old Line Whig and an ardent admirer of Henry Clay. During the winter of 1860–1861 he opposed secession energetically and seems never to have accepted the Confederacy. In 1863 a peace convention in his district nominated him to contest A. T. Davidson's bid for reelection to the Confederate House of Representatives. The vote of the "disaffected and disloyal men" gave Logan a decisive majority.

The Second Congress had hardly begun when Logan introduced a bill "to protect citizens . . . from unjust and illegal impressments." A week later he proposed to repeal the tax-in-kind. Thereafter he worked closely with the other North Carolina "Holden men" to reverse the growth of Confederate authority. Logan's convictions here were so strong that he seemed willing to protect local interests regardless of the consequences. He proposed to exempt a tanner, a blacksmith, a shoemaker, and a miller for each eight square miles of land; he would restrict the right to impress slaves to once a year; and he wished to exempt families of live or deceased soldiers from the tax-in-kind. Logan's record shows him to be one of the four strongest administration opponents, and he worked for peace on the basis of Reconstruction.

Logan was a member of the state constitutional convention of 1865 and of the House of Commons from 1866 to 1868. By this time he had

153

turned Republican and was rewarded with an appointment as Ninth District superior court judge. Democrats considered him so hostile to them and partial to Negroes that thirty-two lawyers petitioned for his removal on the grounds of unfairness and incompetence. When Logan retained the position the Ku Klux Klan became so active in his district that he had to obtain military protection in order to hold court in Shelby. When his term ended in 1874 he retired to private life. His main interest now was real estate and he acquired large tracts of land, among them the Chimney Rock area where he lived for several years before his death. He died there on October 18, 1889, and is buried in St. Francis Episcopal Cemetery, Rutherfordton.[2]

[1] Most of the biographical information here was taken from a sketch of Logan by his son which is located in the Zebulon V. Walser Papers, Southern Historical Collection, University of North Carolina Library, Chapel Hill.

[2] Information on Logan's place of interment was provided by Mr. C. F. W. Coker, Department of Archives and History, Raleigh, N.C.

FRANCIS STROTHER LYON (Alabama) was born on a large tobacco plantation in Stokes County, North Carolina, on February 25, 1800. After attending the local schools, at the age of seventeen he went to live with his uncle, who was an Indian agent at St. Stephens, Alabama. His neat and legible handwriting won him positions as a bank clerk and then as clerk of court. Lyon read law after working hours and was admitted to the bar in 1821. He then began practicing in Demopolis. In 1822 he became secretary of the state senate, holding the position for eight years. In 1833 Lyon was elected to the Alabama Senate, and in 1835 he won a seat as Whig representative to Congress. After two terms there he returned to his law practice. Lyon soon became one of the most successful attorneys in Alabama, noted for his skill in cross-examination. He also invested heavily in land and by 1860 was one of the largest planters in his district. In 1846 Lyon was made commissioner and trustee to liquidate the bank of the state of Alabama, whose affairs had become hopelessly muddled through years of mismanagement. His vigorous and brilliant efforts over the next seven years saved the state and many creditors millions of dollars and won Lyon a wide reputation in public finance.

By 1860 Lyon had moved into the Yancey (q.v.) wing of the Democratic party. He was chairman of the state party in 1860 and a delegate to the Charleston national convention. Upon Lincoln's election he demanded immediate secession. He was elected to the state legislature in 1861, but in December of that year he won a sweeping victory as a representative to the Confederate Congress. Two years later he won reelection without opposition.

154

In Congress Lyon's wealth and experience earned him a place on the Committee of Ways and Means, and in the Second Congress he was its chairman. Few members showed as much awareness of the Confederacy's needs. Besides sponsoring the moderate administration financial program, Lyon himself proposed to double all taxes, to repudiate all old Treasury notes, to raise the export duty on cotton to five cents a pound in specie, and to impress all needed railroad equipment. His private solution to inflation was an immediate tax to raise $500,000,000, but he saw the futility of proposing such a drastic remedy. Lyon was as much a Confederate nationalist on all other programs before Congress. He differed significantly only in his belief that men over forty-five were needed more in production than in the army.

Most of Lyon's fortune had been lost through heavy subscription to the Confederate cotton loan, and after the war he devoted himself to his practice. But he took part in the constitutional convention of 1875 and made the draft which returned Alabama to conservative hands. He was elected to the state senate in 1876 for one term. He died at Demopolis on December 31, 1882, and is interred in the Old Glover Vault.

JAMES LYONS (Virginia) was born in Hanover County, Virginia, on October 12, 1801. He entered William and Mary College in 1818 for one year's study, then read law and began practicing in Richmond. He developed a large and varied practice, and for ten years he was district attorney.[1] Lyons also served the city in numerous capacities, and contemporary accounts show him to have been a perennial civic leader. At the age of twenty-three he went to New York to arrange LaFayette's visit to Virginia. He also helped develop Richmond as a railroad terminal. Lyons entered politics as a state's rights Whig. He wrote the Whig address of 1840, known as "The Gray Book," pledging the party against a national bank and a protective tariff. In the next decade he served two terms in the state senate and one in the house. In 1850 he was a member of the state convention which wrote a new constitution, and he was also a delegate to the Nashville secession convention of that year.[2] In 1852, however, Lyons became a Democrat.[3] In 1859 he was president of the local Southern Rights Association organized after John Brown's raid on Harper's Ferry, and as early as 1856 he had advised secession if a Republican became president.[4]

In November, 1861, Lyons ran behind John Tyler and W. H. MacFarland (q.q.v.) in a contest for the Confederate House of Representatives. When Tyler died, the secessionist vote concentrated behind Lyons and he easily defeated MacFarland in a special election.

In Congress Lyons was chairman of the Committee on Public Build-

155

ings and of a special committee on sequestration. He was a close friend of President Davis and soon emerged as a pillar of the administration. Lyons supported the most demanding legislation on army and financial matters, and he resented concessions to local interests. Lyons himself introduced several bills giving Davis and his generals emergency powers in appointments, impressment, and habeas corpus suspension. On October 1, 1862, he proposed to respond to the Emancipation Proclamation by ordering officers to take no prisoners and to reward Negroes for killing enemy soldiers. Undoubtedly the House chose wisely when it delegated him to ask the president to explain his ideas on peace, but Davis still declined. Lyons' defeat by W. C. Wickham in 1863 was considered a "rebuke to the administration."[5]

After the war Lyons continued practicing in Richmond. In 1867 he was a signer of Jefferson Davis' bond and was defense counsel at the trial.[6] In 1872 he was chairman of the convention of Straight-out Democrats which met in St. Louis and nominated Charles O'Conor for president.[7] Lyons died at home on December 18, 1882, and is buried in Hollywood Cemetery in Richmond.[8]

[1] This information was provided by Milton C. Russell, Virginia State Library, Richmond.
[2] W. Asbury Christian, *Richmond: Her Past and Present* (Richmond, 1912), 136, 152, 157–59, 167, 171.
[3] According to Milton C. Russell, Virginia State Library, Richmond.
[4] Christian, *Richmond*, 203.
[5] Richmond *Daily Enquirer*, May 28, 1863.
[6] Christian, *Richmond*, 284–88.
[7] According to Milton C. Russell, Virginia State Library, Richmond.
[8] Information provided by Waverly K. Winfree, Virginia Historical Society, Richmond.

JAMES McCALLUM (Tennessee) was born in Robeson County, North Carolina, October 3, 1806. It is not known where he received his academic education, nor where he studied law and was admitted to the bar; however, as early as 1828 he became a Master Mason in Pulaski, Giles County, Tennessee, which would be his home for the rest of his life. In later years he advanced through all the Masonic degrees, eventually becoming Grand Master of the Grand Lodge of Tennessee. McCallum was successively clerk and master of chancery court in the nineteen-year period between 1842 and 1861. The 1860 federal census shows that he was both a lawyer and an agriculturist, and that he owned property worth nearly fifty thousand dollars, including twenty-five Negroes.

Originally a Whig in politics, McCallum became a Democrat at the beginning of the Civil War, and in 1861 was elected to the Thirty-fourth (Confederate) General Assembly, serving until 1863. In June, 1863, he was nominated by a convention of prominent Tennesseans at Winchester as Seventh District representative to the Confederate Congress, to which he was elected with little opposition, the state being largely overrun at this time by Federal troops. In Congress he was most interested in making the best possible use of the Confederacy's resources. To this end he supported a wide variety of measures giving the government control over much of the economy. On January 11, 1865, McCallum advised taking over the entire railway system, and six weeks later he proposed to double all taxes and to impress all gold. The only major war powers that he wished to withhold from the central government were the right to suspend the writ of habeas corpus and the right to use Negroes as soldiers.

After the war McCallum continued to practice law at Pulaski, was a director of the Pulaski Savings Bank from 1870, a ruling elder of the Presbyterian church, and the author of a charming reminiscence, *A Brief Sketch of the Settlement and Early History of Giles County*. He served also as teacher of a Bible class, and as superintendent of the Sunday school. He died at Pulaski on September 16, 1889, and is buried in Maplewood Cemetery there.[1]

[1] Information about McCallum's place of burial and day of birth was obtained from the 1860 census of Giles County, Tennessee State Library and Archives, and from Mrs. Urban Smith, Pulaski, Tenn. Other sources record McCallum's birth date as October 2.

THOMAS DAVID SMITH McDOWELL (North Carolina), who rarely used his third given name,[1] was born on a plantation in Bladen County, North Carolina, on January 4, 1823, the son of an Irish-born doctor who emigrated to the United States in early manhood. Thomas McDowell might have served as the prototype of the antebellum southern planter. He was educated at the Donaldson Academy and at the University of North Carolina in Chapel Hill, from which he graduated in 1843. He served in the lower house of the legislature from 1846 to 1850 and in the senate in 1854 and 1858. He was also a trustee of the university from 1858 to 1860.

In the secession convention McDowell won a close contest as delegate to the Provisional Congress, and in October he was elected to the First Regular Congress without opposition. In Congress he was always alert to secure the best possible coastal defenses for North Carolina, but his only other suggestion was the somewhat novel one that all Negroes captured from Union armies be sold and the proceeds distrib-

157

uted among the troops capturing them. During 1861 McDowell's voting record indicated a willingness to allow the central government the necessary basic war powers. However, during the next two years his conviction that this early legislation was sufficient gradually hardened. He made no serious effort to repeal existing programs, but he resisted most efforts to amplify or extend them. When new issues arose, such as suspending the writ of habeas corpus or repudiating inflated currency, McDowell opposed them adamantly. He did not run for reelection in 1863.

McDowell seems to have taken no part in politics in the postwar years; he continued to live on the same 320-acre plantation on which he was born—and on which, before the war, he had employed fifty-seven slaves. He died there on May 1, 1898, and was buried in the family cemetery three miles north of Elizabethtown, North Carolina.[2]

[1] McDowell was named for his maternal grandfather, Thomas David Smith; he is listed in the alumni directory of the University of North Carolina in this manner. In the Raleigh *Register*, October 28, 1845, the notice of his marriage refers to him as Thomas S. D. McDowell [*sic*]. However, his grave marker records his name as Thomas D. McDowell; he signed his will "Thomas D. McDowell," and the entry in the McDowell Family Bible refers to him as Thomas David McDowell. In the records of the Confederate Congress he is also listed as Thomas D. McDowell.

[2] All sources but one, including his grave marker, record McDowell's date of death as May 1. The entry in the McDowell Family Bible, however, for some reason has May 5.

WILLIAM HAMILTON MacFARLAND (Virginia), one of only eleven Confederate congressmen to be born in the eighteenth century, was born in Lunenburg County, Virginia, on February 9, 1799. He was educated at Hampden-Sydney College and at the College of William and Mary, and he obtained his legal training at the Litchfield Law School in Litchfield, Connecticut. He began practice in Lunenburg County in 1820, and two years later he was elected from that county to the House of Delegates, where he served until 1824. He then moved to Petersburg and represented the town in the house during the 1830–1831 session. Sometime before 1836 MacFarland made Richmond his permanent residence, and in the years which followed he became a prominent man in the business and social life of the city as president of the Richmond and Petersburg Railroad, president of the Farmers' Bank of Richmond, vestryman of St. Paul's Church, and a vice-president of the Virginia Historical Society. Although he was held in high esteem by many, others found him pompous and overbearing, and he was once characterized as "the curly-headed poodle . . . nearly overcome with dignity and fat."[1]

MacFarland was elected to the Virginia state convention of 1861 as a

Unionist and voted against secession on April 4 but voted for it on April 17. The convention sent him to the Provisional Congress where he served on the Committee on Commercial Affairs. His principal activity was as a guardian of parochial interests at the expense of Confederate nationalism; he favored a tax program which would exempt large areas of personal and corporate wealth. He was the most diligent of all congressmen in safeguarding private interests from the effects of confiscation and sequestration laws enacted by Congress. Paradoxically, he was one of the readiest to concede to the central government full jurisdiction over commerce and transportation. In November, 1861, he was defeated by former president John Tyler (*q.v.*) in a run-off. MacFarland then retired to his private business affairs, and continued as president of the Farmers' Bank until it was forced to close its doors with the collapse of the Confederacy. He took no part in the Reconstruction era. He died at his summer home, Glencoe, in Greenbrier County, West Virginia, on January 10, 1872, and was buried in Hollywood Cemetery, Richmond.

[1] William H. Gaines, *Biographical Register of Members, Virginia State Convention of 1861, First Session* (Richmond, 1969).

WILLIS BENSON MACHEN (Kentucky) was born in that part of Caldwell County which is now Lyon County, Kentucky, on April 10, 1810. He obtained his education in the neighborhood schools and at Cumberland College, Princeton, Kentucky, after which he engaged in farming near Eddyville. Machen was a delegate to the state constitutional convention of 1849, and was once a member of the state senate and twice a member of the state house of representatives in the 1850s. In January, 1862, the voters of the First District elected Machen their representative in the First Regular Confederate Congress, and two years later the soldiers and refugees reelected him. In the Second Congress he was chairman of the Committee on the Quartermaster's and Commissary Departments.

Machen was a strong legislator and was unwilling to truckle to malcontents and state supreme courts. He did not believe that the war necessitated the destruction of property by retreating armies, the impressment of supplies without immediate compensation, or the nationalization of railroads or specie under any circumstance. But he supported without reservation the other emergency legislation proposed by the administration. While he had no use for General Braxton Bragg, he highly esteemed President Davis, Bragg's chief admirer, and supported most of his appointees. For instance, in 1862 he proposed to

159

let the secretary of war exempt whatever skilled labor he wished and to let impressment officers seize war material without specific orders.

With the collapse of the Confederacy Machen returned to his farm at Eddyville. Upon the death of United States Senator Garrett Davis he was appointed to fill the vacancy and served from September 27, 1872, to March 3, 1873. His appointment demonstrated the swing of sentiment in Kentucky back to the old Democratic leaders, many of whom had supported the Confederacy. When his term expired, Machen again resumed his farming interests. He died in Hopkinsville, Kentucky, September 29, 1893, and was buried in Riverview Cemetery, Eddyville.

JAMES ROBERT McLEAN[1] (North Carolina) was born at Enfield, North Carolina, on September 21, 1823. Though orphaned at an early age he obtained a good education with the support of his relatives. He attended the Bingham School at Hillsboro and the Caldwell Institute at Greensboro. He then read law for two years under John A. Gilmer (*q.v.*) in Greensboro and became licensed to practice in 1844. McLean practiced law in and around Greensboro for a few months, but before the year had ended he moved his practice to Rockford, then the county seat of Surry. During the session of 1850–1851 he represented Surry as a Democrat in the General Assembly. Afterward he moved his practice back to Greensboro and soon was well established there. Within the next few years he also bought a small plantation. During the critical winter of 1860–1861 McLean was an active secessionist, and as the Confederacy was popular in North Carolina in November, 1861, he won a seat in the Confederate House of Representatives over two more moderate rivals.

During his two years in Congress McLean generally left the initiative in lawmaking to others, asserting himself primarily to defend North Carolina's loyalty and to bait Henry S. Foote (*q.v.*) during Military Committee meetings. McLean's votes indicated that he approved all reasonable delegation of powers to the central government, and he differed only occasionally with the administration leadership on how to manage the Confederacy's finances. McLean preferred to curb inflation by heavier taxes rather than by the forced funding of Treasury notes; he desired a steeply graduated income tax; and he believed that the payment of market prices for impressed goods would produce far more supplies without causing serious inflation. McLean announced in August, 1863, that poor health would prevent him from seeking reelection.

In November, 1864, McLean was elected major of the Alamance

160

County "senior reserves," the Seventy-seventh North Carolina Regiment. In December President Davis nominated him to be a commandant of a camp of instruction with the rank of major, but the Senate rejected the nomination. For a while the Seventy-seventh was stationed in Wilmington, but when that port fell in January, 1865, the regiment was sent to South Carolina to impede Sherman's northward progress. The regiment's final engagement was in the Battle of Bentonville.

After the war McLean devoted his energies to recouping his fortunes at home. He was just beginning to recover financially when he died in Greensboro on April 15, 1870.[2] He is buried in "old" First Presbyterian Church Cemetery.[3]

[1] Connor *et al.*, *North Carolina Biography*, VI, 116–17.
[2] The information on McLean after his service in Congress was taken from his biographical folder in the Walser Papers.
[3] Information on McLean's place of interment was provided by C. F. W. Coker, Department of Archives and History, Raleigh, N.C.

LaFAYETTE McMULLEN (Virginia) was born in Bedford County, Virginia, on May 18, 1805. Shortly afterward the family moved to Scott County in southwest Virginia.[1] McMullen attended private schools but had no university education, an omission which was often used against him in his political career. His father operated a wagon train and coach line service in Scott County, and Fayette (as he was called) followed in his footsteps somewhat by becoming state driver and teamster. A Democrat most of his life, he served in the General Assembly almost continuously from 1832 to 1847[2] and in the United States House of Representatives from 1849 to 1857. He was a delegate to the Democratic national conventions in 1852 and 1856. In 1857 President Buchanan appointed McMullen governor of Washington Territory. He served there for a year[3] and then returned to Marion, Virginia, and commenced farming.

McMullen was an early secessionist who predicted in 1856 that the election of a Republican president would dissolve the Union. In the fall of 1861 he lost his first race for a seat in the Confederate House of Representatives to the incumbent, Walter Preston. In 1863 McMullen won a close decision over Preston; his majority of three hundred army votes was the deciding factor.

In the Second Congress McMullen was chairman of the Committee on Public Buildings. Ordinarily he allowed the president and the War Department whatever powers they needed, even the most extreme. On December 2, 1864, he himself asked Congress to consider advising the states to fix price ceilings, a suggestion that Congress rejected. But whenever possible McMullen tried to ease the lot of the small farmer. He wished to focus taxation on money and corporations rather than on land and produce. He proposed to equalize the tithe on produce and then to let the farmers commute it into money, at much profit to themselves. He also suggested exempting all farmers and artisans from army service. By the end of 1864 McMullen was convinced that the war was "unholy and uncivilized" and suggested a peace commission to the North. He was no submissionist, however, and on the last day he proposed to arrest all members absent without leave.

After the war McMullen continued farming and also was one of the founders of the Bank of Marion. In 1878 he ran for governor as a Conservative-Independent-Greenbacker and advocated the construction by the federal government of the Cumberland Gap railroad, but he lost badly. McMullen was killed in Wytheville in a train accident on November 8, 1880, and is interred in Round Hill Cemetery, Marion.

[1] The *Biographical Directory of the American Congress* states that McMullen was born in Estellville (now Gate City), Va. The late E. Frank Hilton, a Scott County historian, researched this matter and established that McMullen was born in Bedford County before the family moved to Scott County. The next edition of the *Biographical Directory* will include this correction. This information was provided by Kenneth E. Crouch, Bedford, Va.

[2] The *Journals* of the Virginia General Assembly show that McMullen served in the House of Delegates in 1832, 1833, and 1835; and in the senate from 1836 to 1847. The *Biographical Directory of the American Congress* states only that he served in the Virginia Senate from 1839 to 1849.

[3] The *Biographical Directory of the American Congress* states that McMullen was governor of Washington Territory until 1861. The territorial records show that he held this position only until July, 1858. This information was provided by Kenneth E. Crouch, Bedford, Va.

JOHN McQUEEN (South Carolina) was born in Queensdale, Roberson County, North Carolina, on February 9, 1804. After being prepared by private tutors, he entered the University of North Carolina. After graduation[1] he studied law and was admitted to the bar in 1828, beginning his practice in Bennettsville, South Carolina. From 1833 to 1837 McQueen served in the state militia, attaining the rank of major general. In 1844 he was an unsuccessful candidate for Congress on the Democratic ticket. In 1849, however, he was appointed to the House of Representatives to fill an unexpired term and served there uninterruptedly until 1860. McQueen was an early state's rights extremist. As early as 1856 he joined other radicals in dire predictions of what would result if Kansas became a free state. Four years later he stated that South Carolina would be degraded if she refused to secede in case Lincoln were elected. On December 21 he resigned his seat in Congress with his delegation. A year later he was unopposed in his campaign as representative to the Confederate Congress.

In Congress McQueen was chairman of the Committee on Accounts. He was an unassertive representative and the records reveal little but his voting pattern. Few members, however, were so opposed to taxation and conscription. He refused even to sanction a national tax-collection system, nor was he willing to relinquish state controls over soldiers and their officers. Otherwise the central government had few more consistent supporters. McQueen wished Congress to make full use of the Confederacy's physical resources, to permit frequent suspensions of the habeas corpus, to give the president free rein in appointments and diplomacy, and to abstain from all peace talks. Perhaps he was politically motivated, for he supported the administration on less sensitive issues, but despite a fierce and emotional campaign he was defeated in his race for reelection by J. W. Witherspoon.

After the war McQueen moved his family and his practice to Society Hill. He died there on August 30, 1867, and is interred in the Episcopal Cemetery in Society Hill.

[1] The statement that McQueen graduated from the University of North Carolina is taken from the *Biographical Directory of the American Congress*. The records of that university and those of the University of South Carolina do not mention his attendance.

COLIN JOHN McRAE (Alabama) was born October 22, 1812, in what is now McFarlan, North Carolina (then called Sneedsboro). When he was five, his father determined to move his large and growing family to the Mississippi frontier, where he became a prosperous trader and commission merchant. He eventually settled at the mouth of the Pascagoula River in Jackson County, where Colin grew to manhood. He was educated at the best schools the county afforded and attended a small Jesuit college in Biloxi for a year. In 1835, when his father died, Colin assumed responsibility for his mother and ten brothers and sisters—one of whom, John J. McRae (*q.v.*), later became governor of Mississippi and United States senator and was also a member of the Confederate Congress.

Colin McRae greatly expanded his father's mercantile business and within a few years came to be known as one of the shrewdest and most successful entrepreneurs on the Gulf Coast. He was one of the founders of Mississippi City, a large operator of coastal trading vessels, and the owner of thousands of acres of land. In 1838 he served a term in the Mississippi legislature. Two years later he moved the headquarters of his commercial operations to Mobile, and subsequently came to be identified with the state of Alabama. During the decade preceding the

Civil War he continued to expand his factoring and commission business, was an active railroad promotor, and speculated in land and Negroes.

In January, 1861, McRae was one of the original seven Alabama representatives to the Provisional Confederate Congress, being, as might be supposed, a strong Democrat and a zealous states' rights supporter. As a congressman he was so concerned about the defense of Mobile that he opposed most efforts to extend Confederate authority over Alabama's local defense troops. Otherwise he supported the moderate program of 1861 to place the Confederacy on a sound wartime basis. His major contribution to legislation was to introduce a bill proposing a volunteer navy of privately owned vessels to engage in privateering. Such a bill, however, was not approved until more than a year later.

McRae did not seek election to the Regular Congress but interested himself in establishing an arsenal at Selma, Alabama, for the manufacture of munitions. In 1863 he became chief financial agent of the Confederate states in Europe, and as such he entered into the Erlanger cotton loan, one of the Confederacy's ruinous ventures into international finance, by virtue of which the government pledged itself to pay a principal amount of five million pounds sterling at a discount of some 40 percent. The terms were exorbitant, and when the price of the bonds fell the situation was worsened by authorization for the Erlangers to buy back bonds to support the market. McRae attempted, without great success, to coordinate Confederate finance abroad and probably did as good a job of maintaining the struggling nation's credit under impossible circumstances as anyone could have. His was a losing cause, further complicated by his involvement, at the request of Secretary of State Benjamin, in a scheme to recruit Polish exiles. The loss of the port of Wilmington in February, 1865, virtually terminated Confederate shipping as well as McRae's official functions. Sued for nonexistent Confederate balances in England and the Continent, McRae was fully acquitted and in the autumn of 1867 left England for Belize, British Honduras, where he acquired property. He never returned to the United States and died in Belize sometime during the month of February, 1877, and was buried there.[1]

[1] Extensive correspondence has revealed neither the day of McRae's death (not recorded in the family Bible), nor the cemetery in which he lies buried with his brother John, who died in Belize while visiting Colin on May 31, 1868.

JOHN JONES McRAE (Mississippi) was born in what is now McFarlan (then Sneedsboro), North Carolina, January 10, 1815. He was a younger brother of Colin John McRae (*q.v.*). When John J. was two, the family moved to Wayne County, Mississippi. After a local primary education he graduated from Miami University of Ohio in 1834. He then studied law in Pearlington, Mississippi, was admitted to the bar, and commenced practice. Before serving in the state house of representatives from 1848 to 1850, and as its speaker in 1850, he took time to found a newspaper at Paulding, Mississippi. He was appointed to the United States Senate in 1851 to fill the vacancy left when Jefferson Davis resigned to run for governor.

From 1854 to 1858 McRae was governor of Mississippi himself, and when his term expired he was elected to the lower house of Congress, where he served until his withdrawal, with the rest of the Mississippi delegation, in January, 1861. From the floor of Congress McRae vowed that he would never tolerate a Republican president, and upon the election of Lincoln he urged immediate secession. Running for a seat in the First Regular Confederate Congress in the fall of 1861, he won easily over John T. Lamkin (*q.v.*). As a congressman McRae was totally committed to the programs of the Davis administration. In fact, he significantly deviated from this allegiance only twice: in his advocacy of free trade and of the exemption of postal employees from conscription. His particular interest lay in making all military laws as comprehensive as possible, and on February 12, 1863, he introduced a bill which would repeal all exemption statutes and give the secretary of war sole power over exemption and detailing, a proposal which never was reported from committee. In 1863, owing to disenchantment with the war in his constituency, he lost his seat to Lamkin. McRae did not long survive the war. Already ill, he and his sister sought to join their brother Colin in British Honduras, where the latter had established himself in business. John Jones McRae died in Belize on May 31, 1868, and was buried there.

MARCUS H. MACWILLIE, delegate from the Confederate territory of Arizona, possesses an excellent claim to being the most anonymous figure in American legislative annals. Although the surname Macwillie (or McWillie) is so unusual as to be almost unrecorded in a telephone directory, it has proved impossible to locate a person or a document which casts any light on the career of Marcus Macwillie before 1860 or after 1865. Although he was a practicing lawyer and prominent citizen of Mesilla, New Mexico, in 1860, he seems to have evaded the census taker, and does not appear in the federal census of that year for any New Mexico county (which then included all of present-day Arizona).

Macwillie was a leader in the insignificant group which attempted to

165

ally the southern half of New Mexico Territory with the Confederacy, and he had made strongly secessionist speeches in mining camps of the area. He had also been designated attorney general of the proposed new territory when John R. Baylor (*q.v.*) took over as military governor in August, 1861. There seems to have been a bond between Baylor and Macwillie, but whether it derived from a former time or arose after the "occupation" is not known. In any event, subsequent to the election of Oury (*q.v.*) as a delegate to the Provisional Congress, Baylor precipitously called for the election of a delegate to the Regular Congress, strongly endorsing the candidacy of Macwillie, who was elected. Many of Oury's friends abstained from voting, contending that due notice of the election was not given. In any event, Macwillie made his way to Richmond and, upon his arrival there, submitted his suggestions for territorial officers, which President Davis adopted instead of the list submitted by the provisional delegate, "Grant" Oury.

Macwillie's only recorded action in Congress was to present two claims for impressed property, neither of which was reported by the Committee on Claims. Beyond this Macwillie remained Baylor's staunch supporter, defending him in particular on Baylor's avowed policy of exterminating hostile Apaches. With the collapse of the Confederacy in the spring of 1865, Macwillie vanished much as if he had never existed. Nothing has been found bearing upon his postbellum life, not even so much as a mention in a newspaper. Where he went—and where and when he died—remains one of the unresolved enigmas of the Civil War period.

HENRY MARSHALL (Louisiana), a cousin of Brigadier General Maxcy Gregg, C.S.A., was born in Darlington District, South Carolina, December 28, 1805. He attended Union College at Schenectady, New York, and, while an underclassman there, walked from Philadelphia to his home at Society Hill, South Carolina, a trip about which he left a most interesting diary. In the middle 1830s, spurred by the promise of new and cheap land in the West, Marshall moved to Louisiana, finally settling in what is now De Soto Parish. By 1860 he owned eight thousand acres of land and 201 Negroes, and was worth in excess of $200,000, a very large sum for the place and time. He was at the same time a member of the Louisiana Senate and, in January, 1861, of the secession convention which took the state out of the Union by a vote of 113 to 17. He was then elected to the Montgomery convention which became the Provisional Congress, defeating Benjamin L. Hodge (*q.v.*) by a vote of sixty-two to fifty-four, and in November he won a close

166

race for reelection to the First Regular Congress. Meantime, he is said to have equipped a South Carolina regiment for his cousin, General (then Colonel) Gregg.

In the Provisional Congress, Marshall was chairman of the Committee on Public Lands. Unlike other Louisiana congressmen, who tended to give Davis and his advisors free rein, Marshall unequivocally refused to temper his extreme states' rights convictions. He opposed direct taxation; proposed to man the army through state levies; wanted the states to determine the appointment of officers as well as exemptions from service; opposed federal control over commerce and transportation; and was reluctant to accord the president any new powers. He chose not to run for reelection in 1863, perhaps because his beliefs did not fit the realities of a beleaguered Confederacy. He died at his plantation, Land's End, in the De Soto Parish on July 13, 1864, and was buried in Trinity Cemetery near Gloster, Louisiana.

HUMPHREY MARSHALL (Kentucky), whose father was a collateral descendant of Chief Justice John Marshall, and whose mother was a sister of the antislavery leader James G. Birney, was born at Frankfort, Kentucky, on January 13, 1812. At the age of sixteen he was appointed to the Military Academy, from which he was graduated in 1832, forty-second in a class of forty-five members. He resigned from the army, after less than a year of service, to study law. There is some evidence that he practiced briefly in Franklin, Tennessee, his wife's home, and served as the town's mayor, before moving to Frankfort and in 1834 to Louisville.[1] He was a member of the city council there in 1836 and the following year was an unsuccessful candidate for state representative. Marshall was an active member of the state militia, progressing from captain to lieutenant colonel, and upon the outbreak of war with Mexico he raised the First Kentucky Cavalry and was commissioned its colonel. With his regiment he took a prominent part in the Battle of Buena Vista. Marshall was elected to Congress in 1848 as a Whig, and was reelected in 1850. He resigned from Congress in 1852 to accept the post of minister to China. In 1854 he was again elected to Congress on the Know-Nothing ticket, and he was reelected in 1856 but declined the unanimous renomination which was given him in 1858.

Marshall was a Breckinridge supporter in the campaign of 1860 and as such endeavored to maintain the border states in a posture of neutrality. When this program failed he accepted a commission as brigadier general in the Confederate army on October 30, 1861. His military service was not remarkable, his most important success being a minor affair at Princeton, (West) Virginia. Marshall resigned for some reason on June 16, 1862, but was reappointed brigadier general to date from his first appointment; however, the records of the Confederate Senate do not reveal that the second appointment was submitted for confirmation. After participating in Bragg's Kentucky invasion in the fall of 1862, he saw no further important service and resigned a second time on June 17, 1863, after which he practiced law in Richmond. In February, 1864, Marshall was elected by the soldier and refugee vote to represent Kentucky's Eighth District in the Second Congress, where his aggressive parliamentary ability soon made him a force. He had the utmost faith in President Davis, and on more than one occasion it was suspected that he desired a dictatorship. Marshall was particularly interested in army matters and had no reservations about policy: the president should take every able-bodied man and either detail him or grasp him "by the nape of the neck and put [him] in the army."[2] On February 5, 1865, he suggested that the army take over all means of transportation, and two weeks later, as the sands of the Confederacy were running out, he proposed to let Davis draft and arm slaves at will. Nevertheless, paradoxically, he opposed heavier taxes and suspension of the writ of habeas corpus. When the war was over he fled to Texas and in November, 1865, obtained permission to go to New Orleans, where he lived until his civil disabilities were removed by President Johnson on December 18, 1867. Marshall then returned to Louisville and practiced law until his death on March 28, 1872. He was buried in the State Cemetery in Frankfort.

[1] Campbell H. Brown (Williamson County historian, Franklin, Tenn.) to Ezra J. Warner, March 9, 22, 1967.
[2] Richmond *Daily Enquirer*, January 18, 1865.

JOHN MARSHALL MARTIN[1] (Florida) was born on a large plantation in Edgefield District, South Carolina, on March 18, 1832.[2] He studied at home under private tutors for a number of years and finished his education at The Citadel. For the next several years Martin traveled, studied, and, finally, began planting near home in 1854. Two years later he moved to Ocala, Florida, and soon became one of the leading planters in the district. During the election of 1860 he was an active Breckinridge supporter, and when Lincoln was elected president Martin advocated immediate secession. When war began he organized the Marion Light Artillery and was elected its captain. He was wounded in the Battle of Richmond, Kentucky, and was forced to take a long furlough. Soon after his return to active duty he was elected in January, 1863, to fill the vacancy in the Confederate House of Representatives caused by the resignation of J. B. Dawkins (*q.v.*). Martin took his seat on March 25.

Martin appears to have been little interested in lawmaking; he generally abstained from discussions and submitted only one bill, a proposal to establish a post route from Waldo to Micanopy in his home county. He strongly supported measures to man and supply the army, but he obviously believed that Congress should interfere very little with the economy. He opposed high taxes, inflation controls, and even the prohibition on the importation of luxuries. Near the end of his term Martin publicly stated that he greatly preferred army life and would decline to seek reelection to Congress. He returned to the army as lieutenant colonel of the Sixth Florida Infantry and served until the end of the war.

After the war Martin resumed planting in Marion County. In 1874 he switched to orange production and eventually became one of the largest shippers and dealers of that fruit in Florida. His groves were located near Martin, a community near Ocala named in his honor. His only postwar public office was as postmaster of Ocala during Grover Cleveland's second administration. Martin died at home on August 10, 1921, and is buried in Greenwood Cemetery, Ocala.[3]

[1] Rerrick, *Memoirs of Florida*, II, 620–21.
[2] Information on Martin's birth date was provided by Elizabeth C. Moore, Central Florida Regional Library, Ocala.
[3] Information on Martin's date of death and place of interment was provided by Elizabeth C. Moore.

JAMES MURRAY MASON (Virginia), grandson of George Mason of revolutionary renown, was born November 3, 1798, in Georgetown, D.C., according to his daughter. Other sources record his birthplace as Analostan (or Mason's) Island on the Virginia side of the Potomac, then in Fairfax County,[1] Virginia. He received his early education in the Georgetown schools and from private tutors, after which he was graduated in 1818 from the University of Pennsylvania. He studied law at William and Mary. Mason practiced for a short time in Richmond but then moved to the Valley of Virginia, establishing himself at Winchester in 1820.

From 1826 until the collapse of the Confederacy Mason was almost constantly in political office, beginning with his election to the House of Delegates. In 1832 he was a Jackson elector, but he subsequently became an intimate and follower of John C. Calhoun, and a leading exponent of southern rights. In 1837 he was elected to the house of

169

representatives; ten years later he was elected to the senate, where he sat when Virginia seceded. Mason's service in the Provisional Confederate Congress was so nominal that his sketch in *Dictionary of American Biography* omits any mention thereof; however, although not one of the original five members chosen by the Virginia convention, he served from July 4 until August 30. Then a variety of factors, including a decade of service as chairman of the Committee on Foreign Affairs of the Senate, impelled Jefferson Davis to choose Mason and John Slidell of Louisiana as diplomatic representatives to England and France. The resulting imbroglio, in which both men were forcibly removed from the British mail-steamer *Trent* by Captain Wilkes of the United States Navy, brought England and the United States to the brink of war. It also engendered considerable goodwill toward the Confederacy in the British Isles. After two months of confinement in Fort Warren in the harbor of Boston, Mason was released and proceeded to his post. Although his reception in England was that of a social lion, the diplomatic courtesies extended to him were meager. He was politely ignored in official circles, and although he assiduously wooed representatives of the upper classes who were his friends, his conviction that England would be forced to recognize the Confederacy because of a shortage of cotton to fuel its mills was not realized. In point of fact, a surplus of cotton in 1861, added to the risk of losing its merchant marine, and an enormously profitable trade with both the United States and the Confederacy precluded such recognition.

In 1866 Mason made his way to Canada, where he lived for two years until returning to Virginia. His home near Winchester having been burned by Sheridan in 1864, he lived near Alexandria until his death on April 28, 1871. He was buried in St. Paul's Cemetery in Alexandria.

[1] See *DAB*, which cites Virginia Mason, *The Pub. Life and Diplomatic Correspondence of James M. Mason, with Some Personal History by His Daughter* (Roanoke, Va., 1903). Also see the *Biographical Directory of the American Congress* and Appleton's *Cyclopedia of American Biography*.

AUGUSTUS EMMETT MAXWELL (Florida) was born in Elberton, Georgia, on September 21, 1820. In 1822 the family moved to Greene County, Alabama, where Maxwell attended private schools. After studying at the University of Virginia from 1837 to 1840, he read law at home and was admitted to the bar in 1843. He practiced in Eutaw for two years, after which he moved to Tallahassee, Florida. Maxwell entered politics as a Democrat and spent much of his remaining years in public office. He was attorney general in 1846 and 1847, secretary of state in 1848 and 1849, and a legislator in 1847, 1849, and 1850. His work on legislative committees earned him a wide reputation, and from 1853 to 1857 he was in the United States House of Representatives. He left Congress after two undistinguished terms and for the next four years divided his time between his law practice and the post of naval agent at Pensacola. Maxwell's stand on secession has evaded historians, although the voting pattern of the balloting in the Florida legislature for the Confederate senatorships strongly suggests that he was a secessionist. In November, 1861, the legislature elected him a senator on the forty-seventh ballot.

In the Senate, Maxwell was chairman of the Committee on Patents and of a special committee to investigate the Navy Department, headed by one of his best friends, Stephen R. Mallory. Needless to say, Mallory fared well by this investigation. Maxwell was an exceptionally practical congressman. Florida's main contributions to the Confederacy were food and manufactured goods, and Maxwell opposed several tax, impressment, and conscription laws which in his opinion would damage production there. On March 9, 1863, he proposed to ask the president to warn people against planting anything other than food crops. Otherwise Maxwell had few qualms about any type of legislation needed for victory and was one of the strongest supporters of flexible executive powers and aggressive army policy. On December 14, 1863, he proposed to conscript all speculators.

After the war Maxwell was appointed an associate justice of the Florida Supreme Court, but in 1866 he resigned and formed a law partnership with his old friend Mallory. When the Democrats regained control of Florida in 1877 Maxwell was appointed judge of the first judicial circuit and served until his resignation in 1885. In that year he was a member of the state constitutional convention called to replace the so-called Carpetbag Constitution of 1868. Between 1887 and 1891, Maxwell was chief justice and then associate justice of the Florida Supreme Court. He then retired to private practice, and in 1896 he retired from active life. He moved to Chipley, Florida, in 1902 and died there on May 5, 1902. He is buried in the graveyard of Christ Episcopal Church in Pensacola.

CHRISTOPHER GUSTAVUS MEMMINGER (South Carolina), one of the only four foreign-born members of the Confederate Congress, was a native of the duchy of Wurtemberg, Germany, and was born January 9, 1803, the son of the officer in the duke's army who was killed when Christopher was an infant. Some years later his mother emigrated to

Charleston, South Carolina, where she soon died; the boy was placed in an orphanage when he was four years old. At the age of eleven he was adopted by Governor Thomas Bennett and was soon sent to South Carolina College, where he was graduated at the age of sixteen. Memminger then returned to Charleston, studied law, and, after admission to the bar, rapidly became prominent in the several fields of law, politics, finance, and education.

For thirty years Memminger was a school commissioner for Charleston, and for thirty-two years he was a member of the board of South Carolina College (now the University of South Carolina). Meanwhile, he served a number of terms in the legislature, where he acquired considerable reputation as a money manager while chairman of the committee on finance. Always convinced of the righteousness of slavery, he was an opponent of disunion until after John Brown's raid on Harper's Ferry and the North's subsequent veneration of Brown as a martyr. He took an active part in the South Carolina secession convention in December, 1860, signed the ordinance, and was immediately elected as one of the state's eight delegates to the Provisional Congress, where he served as chairman of the Committee on Commercial Affairs. At the suggestion of Robert Barnwell (*q.v.*), Jefferson Davis appointed Memminger secretary of the treasury and, since cabinet officers were under Confederate law allowed to attend and participate in sessions of congress, Memminger operated in a sort of dual capacity. He actively engaged in writing both constitutions; in establishing financial policy; and in organizing courts, marine hospitals, and a variety of other programs. His only opposition to the line laid down by the administration was his unwillingness to have the proposed supreme court (which never materialized, anyway) exercise appellate jurisdiction over state courts. In the Treasury Department Memminger had assumed responsibilities which would have taxed a magician. The entire Confederate economic program from the outset was unsound, patched together, and the victim of tinkering by Congress. When the export of cotton was embargoed in a visionary effort to force recognition of the Confederacy by European nations, the basis of credit collapsed, and the huge expenditures for war were financed by an ever-increasing output of printing-press money. Perhaps no man could have successfully operated at the helm of the Confederate Treasury Department; in any case, Memminger, although wholly cognizant of the causes of disaster, seemed unable to remedy the situation. Despite the fact that his recommendations went mostly unheeded by Congress, when the inevitable collapse of Confederate credit took place, he was assigned the blame. Memminger resigned on June 15, 1864, and retired to his

172

country home at Flat Rock, North Carolina. In 1867 he obtained a presidential pardon and returned to Charleston, again taking up the practice of law. In the years after the war he was foremost in advocating schools for both the white and black races. Memminger died in Charleston at the age of eighty-five on March 7, 1888, and was buried at St. John's of the Wilderness First Mission of the Episcopal Church in Flat Rock.

THOMAS MENEES (Tennessee) was born June 26, 1823, near Nashville, Tennessee. After obtaining an academic education, he was graduated in medicine from Transylvania University, Lexington, Kentucky, in 1846. He practiced his profession in Springfield, Tennessee, and in surrounding Robertson County, of which Springfield was the seat. He also engaged in agricultural pursuits, and by 1860 he owned eighteen slaves and an estate worth more than sixty thousand dollars, according to the United States census of that year. In 1857 he was a member of the state senate.

In November, 1861, Dr. Menees was elected to the First Regular Congress by the voters of the Eighth Congressional District, and two years later he easily won reelection. During his service as congressman he worked quietly to put the Confederacy on a sound basis for war. He accepted the need for a large army and at least temporary control by the central government over the Confederacy's resources. On October 1, 1862, he made his only significant suggestion during debate, an amendment to end the exemption of workers whose employer made more than 25 percent profit. Menees, however, was reluctant to let the army strip the states of their manpower too rapidly. While approving the draft, he wanted the men called out gradually, and even then he tried to retain considerable state control over their officers and organization. In 1864 he became an opponent of the suspension of the writ of habeas corpus when suspension threatened to prevent state employees from challenging their liability to conscription.

After the war Dr. Menees made his home in Nashville, where he continued his medical practice. In 1874 he was chosen professor of materia medica and therapeutics at the University of Nashville, and the following year he was elected to the chair of obstetrics. He was elected to the same chair at Vanderbilt University in 1875 and subsequently became dean of its medical department. In addition to his practice and teaching duties, he wrote prolifically for medical journals of the day. Dr. Menees died in Nashville on September 6, 1905, and was buried there in Mount Olive Cemetery.

WILLIAM PORCHER MILES (South Carolina) was born at Walterboro, South Carolina, July 4, 1822. He spent one year at Willington Academy in Abbeville County before enrolling at the College of Charleston, from which he was graduated with highest honors in 1842. After this he studied law for a time but abandoned these studies to become a teacher; from 1843 to 1855 he was assistant professor of mathematics at his alma mater. During this period he won a host of friends, and in 1855 he was elected mayor of Charleston.

In 1857 Miles was elected to Congress and served until he withdrew on December 13, 1860. He was at all times a champion of slavery and of secession, and he joined other southern congressmen in signing a manifesto that the organization of the Confederacy was a necessity. He was chairman of the Committee on Foreign Relations of the South Carolina secession convention and signed the ordinance of secession. Miles was also one of three commissioners appointed by General Beauregard to arrange the terms of surrender of Fort Sumter. Before this Miles was sent to the Provisional Congress and was elected without opposition to both Regular Congresses. As chairman of the Committee on Military Affairs he was probably the most powerful member of the House of Representatives, and he demonstrated prodigious industry. The amount of military legislation alone was staggering. During sessions Miles corresponded voluminously with the various commanding generals, and between sessions he visited them in the field. He also had crosses to bear, including his close friendship with the unpopular and inefficient Quartermaster General Abraham C. Myers, and with Beauregard, who never ceased begging for additional means to defend Charleston. In matters directly related to army maintenance Miles grew so ultra that by 1864 Richmond newspapers were wont to refer to him as the president's "mouthpiece," when he proposed to end all exemptions and give the secretary of war complete power of detail. He was more moderate on subjects less directly concerned with the war, even taking issue with the administration on such matters as penalties on speculators, railroad grants, a strong Supreme Court, and, in the Second Congress, the suspension of habeas corpus. Nevertheless his colleagues, as well as the public, always considered him one of Davis' strongest friends.

In 1863 Miles had married the daughter of a wealthy Virginia and Louisiana planter who retained his land holdings despite the war, and for the rest of his life Miles was in comfortable circumstances. From 1865 until 1880 he lived in Nelson County, Virginia. He then served two years as the first president of the reorganized University of South Carolina. After that he managed his father-in-law's sugar plantation in

Ascension Parish, Louisiana, and became one of the largest planters in the state. Miles took no further part in public life. He died May 11, 1899, at his estate, Houmas House, near Burnside, Louisiana. He was buried in Union Cemetery in Union, West Virginia, the ancestral home of his wife.

SAMUEL AUGUSTINE MILLER[1] (Virginia) was born in Shenandoah County, Virginia, on October 16, 1819. He attended Gettysburg College, Pennsylvania, from 1835 to 1839 but did not graduate.[2] After working for a year as assistant to the local "Cattle King," Beale Steenberger, he traveled in Europe and then returned to study law under Judge Summers in Kanawha (now in West Virginia). Miller became partners with the judge and soon became a leader of the bar with a special reputation as a land lawyer. At the same time he became president of the Kanawha Salt Company. Miller was a leading secessionist in his area, and when Virginia left the Union he became a major in the Commissary Department with the Twenty-second Virginia Regiment. When A. G. Jenkins (q.v.) resigned his position in the Confederate House of Representatives Miller won the position in a special election[3] and took his seat on February 24, 1863. He won reelection that fall, the soldier and refugee vote giving him a narrow victory over his rivals in both elections.

When Miller reached Richmond his district was entirely in enemy hands, and there were few emergency laws before Congress with which he took issue. While enlarging the army by any means possible was foremost in his thinking, his own experience steered him to problems of army maintenance and supply, and most of his suggestions were on such matters. In the Second Congress he was chairman of a special committee on army pay and clothing, which reported that soldiers refused to take old Treasury notes and that much more legislation was needed to supply the army.[4] Miller also supported a wide variety of laws giving the government control over the economy and even over personal rights. He was less inclined than most strong Confederate nationalists, however, to abdicate congressional powers. He tended to withhold discretionary powers from the president; he joined those seeking to reform the cabinet; and he voted to let Robert E. Lee as general-in-chief encroach on the president's authority as commander-in-chief.

After the war Miller took his family home to Kanawha County and found their house stripped bare. When Lincoln was assassinated, Miller fled to Canada to escape possible recrimination. He returned once again late in 1865 after receiving a pardon from the United States government. But he and other former Confederate lawyers were disbarred by an act of the new state, and it was not until the passage of the "Flick Amendment" to the West Virginia constitution in 1870 that he was permitted to practice again. He served one term in the legislature in 1874. He died in Parkersburg on November 19, 1890, and is buried in Spring Hill Cemetery in Charleston.

[1] Most of the biographical information on Miller was provided by Jane Brand, Department of Archives and History, Charleston, W. Va.

[2] Details of Miller's attendance at college were provided by Richard E. Walker, Director of Alumni Relations, Gettysburg College, Gettysburg, Pa.

[3] This was the first resignation submitted to the permanent Congress, and the Committee on Elections reported that under the Constitution the state laws should determine all elections unless Congress chose to make its own recommendations. The committee then decided that no legislation on the part of Congress was necessary.

[4] *Report of the Special Committee on Pay and Clothing of the Army. House, February 11, 1865. By Mr. Miller* (Richmond, 1865).

CHARLES BURTON MITCHEL (Arkansas), whose principal claim to immortality seems to have been his election to the U.S. Senate by the Arkansas legislature immediately after being defeated for a seat in the House of Representatives, was born September 19, 1815, in Gallatin, Tennessee. After attending the local schools, he received a degree at the University of Nashville in 1833, and in 1836 he was graduated from the Jefferson Medical College in Philadelphia. He then went to Washington, Hempstead County, Arkansas, where he practiced medicine for twenty-five years. In 1848 Mitchel was a member of the state legislature, and from 1853 to 1856 he was receiver of public moneys.

In the campaign of 1860 Mitchel ran for a house seat, was narrowly defeated, and was immediately elected to a six-year term in the senate by the General Assembly. He took his seat there on March 4, 1861, but went south early in May and was expelled by a resolution on July 11. In November the General Assembly elected Mitchel to the Confederate Senate, where he continued to serve until his death. He was chairman of the Committee on Accounts in the First Congress, and of the Committee on Post Offices in the second. Mitchel allowed others to hammer out the major pieces of legislation; he gave almost all his attention to the needs of his region. He wanted Congress to increase the number of gunboats on western waters, to place guards along the Mississippi to preserve communications, and to see that the Trans-Mississippi Department was properly financed and protected—little of which he was able to accomplish. On matters of a more general nature he usually supported the administration's war efforts, although he harbored the usual western distrust of fiscal reform, fearing that it would devalue the small amount of currency then circulating in the West. Mitchel died in Little Rock, between sessions of Congress, on September 20, 1864, and was buried in the Presbyterian Cemetery at Washington.

THOMAS BELL MONROE (Kentucky), one of the oldest members of the Confederate Congress, was born October 7, 1791, in Albemarle County, Virginia. He was a distant cousin of President James Monroe. His parents located in Scott County, Kentucky, as early as 1793, and he acquired the meager education available on the frontier at the time. Upon reaching manhood he settled in Barren County and in 1816 was elected to the Kentucky legislature. In 1819, having suffered some financial reverses, he determined to become a lawyer and hung out his shingle to practice while at the same time reading law, a procedure which could have obtained only in that day and time.

In 1821 Monroe moved to Frankfort and graduated from the law department of Transylvania University. He was a man of prodigious industry, serving as secretary of state of Kentucky for one year; reporter of the decisions of the court of appeals; publisher of *Moore's Kentucky Reports* in seven volumes; United States district attorney in 1833–1834; United States district judge by appointment of Andrew Jackson from 1834 until he resigned at the outbreak of the Civil War in 1861; professor of law at the University of Louisiana (now Tulane) in New Orleans, where he spent his winters for some years; and professor of law at Transylvania and at the Western Military Academy at Drennon Springs, Kentucky. On top of all this, he conducted a law class at his magnificent estate, Montrose, overlooking Frankfort and the Kentucky River. He was the recipient of three honorary law degrees, among them one from Harvard.

In 1861, after his five sons had all declared for the Confederacy, Judge Monroe fled to the South and took the oath of allegiance. In December he was appointed a delegate to the Provisional Congress, where his prewar reputation won him important committee assignments. He was most active in protecting the rights of border-state citizens. He worked diligently preparing laws governing sequestration, retaliation, and territorial judicial organization, and on the sections of treaties with the Indians defining their judicial rights. On other matters Monroe strongly supported centralizing the powers of government in the hands of the executive, at least for the duration of the war.

Monroe did not stand for election to the Regular Congress but retired to private life, refugeeing at various points in the fast-shrinking Confederacy: Canton, Mississippi; Marietta, Georgia; Richmond; Abbeville, South Carolina; and, after the surrender of Lee at Appomattox, Pass Christian, Mississippi. Here Judge Monroe died on December 24, 1865, never again to see his beautiful home in Kentucky. He was buried in Pass Christian.

ROBERT LATANE MONTAGUE[1] (Virginia) was born at Ellaslee in Jamaica, Middlesex County, Virginia, on May 23, 1819. After attending Fleetwood Academy he studied law in Fredericksburg and then attended William and Mary College for two years, receiving his law degree in 1842. He began practicing near home in Saluda, acquired a large plantation nearby, and built there his home, Inglewood. Montague entered politics as a Democrat and in 1850 was elected to the House of Delegates for one term. He served several times as a Democratic elector. In 1852 Montague became commonwealth attorney for Middlesex County and held the position until 1860. In that year he was chosen lieutenant governor, leading his ticket by five thousand votes. Upon Lincoln's election Montague demanded immediate secession and was president of the convention of 1861. After Virginia seceded, Governor John Letcher appointed him to an executive committee to prepare Virginia for war. In 1863 Montague won a decisive victory over M. R. H. Garnett (*q.v.*) as a representative to the Confederate Congress.

In sharp contrast to Garnett, Montague gave the central government his full support. He wished so strongly to enlarge the army that he tried to prevent men from legally testing their liability to conscription. He saw no reason to embarrass the Treasury by ordering immediate payment for property illegally impressed, and he even consented to the impressment of state-owned railroad equipment. Montague showed particular respect for executive privilege. In habeas corpus and army matters he tended to grant the president and the generals wide latitude in applying laws. He even consented to the Treasury Department's adding "certificates of indebtedness" to the already inflated currency. Montague limited most of his own suggestions to remedying minor injustices in financial legislation and seeing that prisoners of war and hospitalized soldiers received proper compensation for their confinement.

After the war Montague continued his law practice. He was elected as a Conservative to the House of Delegates in 1872, and in 1875 he was elected judge of the Eighth Judicial District, a position he held until his death. For many years he was moderator of the Virginia Baptist General Association. Montague died at home on March 2, 1880, of erysipelas infection. He was buried at Inglewood, but his remains were later removed to the Christ Church Graveyard, Middlesex County.[2]

[1] Lyon G. Tyler (ed.), *Encyclopedia of Virginia Biography* (5 vols., New York, 1915), III, 42.
[2] This information was provided by R. L. Montague, Urbanna, Va.

JAMES WILLIAM MOORE (Kentucky) was a lifelong resident of Montgomery County, Kentucky, where he was born on February 12, 1818. After receiving an education in the neighborhood schools, he studied law and was admitted to the bar. Moore was a quiet, sturdy, diligent lawyer who plodded steadily ahead in his profession, acquiring along the way an extensive practice and the lasting confidence of his clients. He was elected circuit judge of his district in 1851; in 1858, while serving his second term in the office, he was nominated for Congress by the Whig party in what was deemed a safe Whig district. His opponent on the Know-Nothing ticket was a suave, handsome young lawyer. Moore, perhaps regarding it as inappropriate to campaign for Congress while sitting on the bench, and perhaps also regarding his election as a settled thing, resigned his judgeship prior to the election. To the consternation of the local politicians, and no doubt to Moore himself, he was defeated.

In January, 1862, the voters of the same (tenth) district elected Moore to the Confederate Congress, and in 1864 he was returned by the soldiers and refugees. During his years in Congress Moore's primary interest was to create as strong an army as possible. In 1863 he asked Congress to end the exemption of men who had hired substitutes, and a year later he asked the Military Committee to consider letting the president use all Negroes in whatever ways would best serve the army. He was a staunch opponent of Secretary of War Judah P. Benjamin, and his resolution of March 4, 1862, that Benjamin "has not the confidence of the people . . . nor of the Army" was part of the attack which caused the secretary's dismissal (although Davis, with characteristic disputatiousness immediately appointed Benjamin secretary of state). Moore supported just as earnestly legislation to mobilize the home front, although he apparently believed that the arbitrary controls over coin and currency desired by the administration were ill advised. After the collapse of the Confederacy, Moore returned to his home in Mount Sterling, Kentucky, where he continued to practice law until his death there on September 17, 1877. A lifelong bachelor, he left no descendants. He was buried in Machpelah Cemetery in Mount Sterling.

179

JOHN MOTLEY MOREHEAD (North Carolina) was born July 4, 1796, in Pittsylvania County, Virginia, the son of John Morehead and his wife Obedience. The Morehead family had been in Virginia since 1630, but John Morehead moved to Rockingham County, North Carolina, in 1798. His son attended the "log college" of David Caldwell, a noted Presbyterian divine, and was graduated from the University of North Carolina at the age of twenty-one. After reading law, he began practice in Wentworth and represented Rockingham County in the legislature in 1821. After subsequently moving to Greensboro, he represented Guilford County in 1826 and 1827. Prior to 1835 Morehead had been a Jacksonian Democrat, but in that year he became a Whig, and in 1840 he was elected governor of North Carolina. He was reelected in 1842. During his two terms of office he was able to accomplish few of his aims, in particular public improvements, because of a Democratic majority in the legislature.

Always a proponent of railroads, and of state aid to them, Morehead became one of the leading businessmen of his state. He was either president or promoter of a number of lines projected to furnish North Carolina with a transportation system from the Alleghenies to the Atlantic Ocean. He was also connected with cotton mills and a variety of mercantile businesses. When the secession crisis became acute, Morehead remained a staunch advocate of adherence to the Union, and after separation had become an accomplished fact he was elected to the Provisional Congress by a caucus of former Unionists in the secession convention. In Montgomery and Richmond his business background made him one of the new government's strongest friends. He supported every major centralist program before Congress, even that subjecting his own corporation to the war tax. His most prized coup was approval of an appropriation measure authorizing an extension of the Richmond and Danville Railroad to his home town of Greensboro. Morehead did not stand for reelection to the Regular Congress but instead devoted himself to his commercial interests in the few years that were left to him. He died while vacationing in Rockbridge Alum Springs, Virginia, on August 27, 1866, and was buried in the yard of the First Presbyterian Church in Greensboro.

SIMPSON HARRIS MORGAN (Texas) was born in Rutherford County, Tennessee, about the year 1821. The descendants of his only daughter, the late Mrs. Albert B. Fall, do not know his exact birth date. He eimgrated to Red River County, Texas, in 1844 and was admitted to law practice in "the various courts of this Republic."[1] Morgan rapidly became one of the most prominent citizens of Clarksville and its vicinity, and he acquired land in several counties. He was one of the promoters of the Memphis, El Paso, and Pacific Railway, which later became a part of the Texas and Pacific, and served as its president for a time. Morgan married into the Garland family of Lafayette County, Arkansas, to which belonged Augustus H. Garland and his brother, Rufus K. Garland (*q.q.v.*), both subsequently members of the Confederate Congress. In November, 1863, Morgan won a seat of his own in the Second Regular Confederate Congress, defeating William B. Wright (*q.v.*) in a race which was evidently based upon personalities rather than issues. During the one session which he attended he seldom participated in the discussions. Except for his adamant stand against special taxes on agriculture, he consistently supported measures designed to give the central government a stronger hand in war-making. En route to the second session of the Second Congress, which had convened on November 7, 1864, Morgan contracted pneumonia and died at Monticello, Arkansas, December 15, 1864. His body was returned to Clarkesville for burial in the family cemetery on his property, which is now the Simpson H. Morgan Memorial Park. The burial area is enclosed by a pipe fence, and there are no markers identifying the separate graves. Curiously enough, despite the national prominence of Morgan's son-in-law, the *Handbook of Texas* observed that "No biographical material could be located concerning Simpson H. Morgan."[2]

[1] Information about Morgan's career was supplied by his great-grandchildren, Mrs. Tom Jones, Ruidoso, N.M., and Mahlon Everhart, Hachita, N.M., and by R. C. Garland, Las Cruces, N.M.

[2] *Handbook of Texas* (Austin, 1952), 152.

JACKSON MORTON (Florida), usually known as "Billy" Morton, was born August 10, 1794, near Fredericksburg, Virginia. After attending the common schools of his native Spotsylvania County, he was graduated from Washington College (now Washington and Lee) in 1814 and from William and Mary the following year. In 1820 Morton moved to Pensacola, Florida, and engaged in the lumber business. In the next forty years he was markedly successful as a lumberman, merchant, and planter, and by 1860 he was the owner of 159 Negroes and an estate worth $200,000. He was a member of the Florida legislative council in 1836–1837 and its president in 1837; a delegate to the Florida constitutional convention of 1838; U.S. Navy agent at Pensacola from 1841 to 1845; and a presidential elector on the ticket of Taylor and Fillmore in 1848. The same year Morton was elected to the U.S. Senate, serving from 1849 to 1855. He was not a candidate for reelection and returned to his business interests.

Although a lifelong Whig and an opponent of secession, Morton accepted an appointment to the Provisional Confederate Congress at the hands of Governor Madison Perry, as one of Florida's original three delegates after the state seceded in January, 1861. Morton served as chairman of the Committee on Indian Affairs in that body, although his chief activity was in securing special-interest legislation for his then isolated state. For the most part he supported the central government and its war preparations, but he developed an early hostility to Jefferson Davis, who had appointed Stephen R. Mallory of Key West to be secretary of the navy without consulting the Florida congressional delegation. Morton led the fight to prevent the confirmation of his old political foe and subsequently attempted to limit the appointment power itself. In November he was a candidate for the senate, but he withdrew when the legislature was deadlocked after forty-three ballots. Morton thereupon returned to his estate, Mortonia, near Milton, Florida, and seems to have taken no further part in public affairs.[1] He died at Mortonia on November 20, 1874, and was buried in the family cemetery there. His brother, Jeremiah, was a member of the U.S. Congress from Virginia and a member of the Virginia secession convention.

[1] The *Biographical Directory of the American Congress* errs in stating that Jackson Morton was a "member of the Confederate Congress [from] 1862–1865." He was a member of the Provisional Congress only.

CHARLES JAMES MUNNERLYN[1] (Georgia) was born in Georgetown, South Carolina, on February 14, 1822. The family moved to Gadsden County, Florida, in 1833 but found conditions too primitive there and in 1837 moved near Bainbridge in Decatur County, Georgia, where the senior Munnerlyn became a successful planter. Charles was educated at Emory College, and then studied law under its president, Judge A. B. Longstreet, the uncle of Lieutenant General James Longstreet, C.S.A. He was admitted to the bar but never practiced, having inherited his father's large property holdings at an early age. Munnerlyn's first public office was as a member of the secession convention in January, 1861, where he voted for immediate secession. When war began he volunteered as a private in the First Georgia Volunteers and saw service at Pensacola and in West Virginia. His health, however, forced him to give up his commission. In November, 1861, he was elected by a comfortable majority over two opponents to represent his district in the Confederate Congress.

In Congress Munnerlyn was Georgia's silent member, abstaining from debate, proposing no bill or amendment, and only occasionally offering a petition or a resolution relating to some local-interest group in Georgia. But Munnerlyn was one of the government's strongest backers. A survey of his voting record shows his consistent support of every major program before Congress to mobilize the Confederacy for war. He campaigned in 1863 for reelection on this faithful record—particularly his advocacy of conscription—and ran a poor third in a field of four.

After his defeat, Munnerlyn reenlisted in the army, this time as a private in the cavalry. But when President Davis heard this he had Munnerlyn commissioned as a major and ordered him to Florida to organize a regiment of reserves there. The special duty of these reserves was to collect and forward supplies to the armies in Virginia. Munnerlyn performed his duties so successfully that he shipped one hundred thousand head of cattle northward and was made lieutenant colonel for his efforts.

After the war Munnerlyn remained in Florida for several months helping Confederates flee the country; Judah P. Benjamin was one of his refugees. He then returned home to rebuild his fortune. Though Munnerlyn had lost over two hundred slaves, he was able to retain most of his land and successfully make the transition to free labor. He realized the value of railroads to the New South and was instrumental in building the Savannah, Florida, and Western Railroad. In 1884 he was elected ordinary of Decatur County, which necessitated his living in Bainbridge. Munnerlyn died on May 17, 1898, and is buried in the family cemetery near his old home, Refuge, outside Bainbridge.

[1] Northen (ed.), *Men of Mark in Georgia*, III, 385–88.

JOHN PORRY MURRAY (Tennessee) lived all his life in or near Gainesboro, Jackson County, Tennessee. He was born there July 14, 1830. After obtaining a common-school education in the local institutions of learning, he studied law and was admitted to the bar in 1852. He rose to be one of the ablest lawyers in the state, meanwhile exerting considerable influence in politics and in his home community. In 1857 Murray was appointed judge of the sixth judicial circuit by Governor Isham P. Harris. When the Civil War broke out, he enlisted as a private in an infantry company recruited locally; by promotion he soon became colonel of the Twenty-eighth Tennessee Infantry, at the head of which he took part in a number of engagements, particularly the Battle of Shiloh, where he was badly wounded.

In June, 1863, a number of prominent Tennesseans serving as an *ad hoc* nominating convention met at Winchester and put Murray's name on the ballot for the Second Confederate Congress from the Fourth District, and he won without difficulty. In Congress Murray recognized the country's absolute dependence on an effective army and seldom denied it anything or interfered with its administration. On five occasions he introduced bills intended to ease the lot of the soldiers. But on economic matters, even those relating to army maintenance, he made few concessions to the emergency. His speech of May 27, 1864, against the "imaginary dangers" that caused suspensions of the writ of habeas corpus was so excellent that the Richmond *Daily Enquirer* published it in its entirety. It may also be remarked that Murray's stake in the cause of slavery in 1860 amounted to a single Negro, who was probably the family cook.[1]

Following the war Murray resumed his practice in Gainesboro, where he lived for another thirty years. He died there on December 21, 1895, and was buried in the family burial ground on his estate.

[1] 1860 Census, Jackson County, Tenn.

EUGENIUS ARISTIDES NISBET (Georgia), whose family name was originally Nesbitt, was born December 7, 1803, in Greene County, Georgia, near the village of Union Point. After preparatory studies in the local school, he attended successively Powellton Academy in Hancock County, Georgia; the University of South Carolina; and the University of Georgia, from which he was graduated in 1821. He then studied law, was admitted to the bar by special act of the Georgia legislature, being under the age of twenty-one; and commenced practice in Madison, Georgia. He was a member of the state house of representatives from 1827 to 1830 and of the state senate from 1830 to 1837, when he moved to Macon, Georgia. As a Whig he ran unsuccessfully for Congress in 1836 but was elected two years later and was reelected in 1840. He resigned prior to the expiration of his second term because of financial obligations incurred by his law firm during the absence in Washington.

In 1845 when the Georgia Supreme Court was established, Nisbet was elected one of its three justices by the General Assembly. In 1853 he retired from the bench to resume his law practice and, along with Benjamin H. Hill (*q.v.*), became a leader of the Know-Nothings in Georgia. Three years later, however, he supported Buchanan for president, and in 1860 he supported Stephen A. Douglas. When he was elected to the Georgia secession convention in 1861, he was regarded as an unconditional Unionist, but he soon shifted his ground and pro-

184

posed a resolution to the effect that it was the right and duty of the state to secede. As chairman of a committee appointed to draft an ordinance to that effect, he wrote and presented the measure which took Georgia out of the Union, and was then selected as a delegate to the Provisional Confederate Congress. During the writing of the permanent Constitution Nisbet suggested the election of congressmen by general ticket and also an eight-year term for the president, both of which proposals failed. He is also credited with suggesting the name of Alexander H. Stephens (*q.v.*) for vice-president. Except for a quite typical reluctance to relinquish state control over militia volunteers, Nisbet was in complete sympathy with his new government. He was particularly convinced that the Confederacy's treasury should depend primarily on the export duty on cotton, and that cotton should be the key to Confederate diplomacy. During July, 1861, Nisbet toured Georgia to encourage subscriptions to the Produce Loan. He resigned early in December because of ill health.[1] Nisbet's activities during the last decade of his life are obscure. One source says he practiced law until his death, another that he was a writer and lecturer. He died in Macon on March 18, 1871, and was buried there in Rose Hill Cemetery.

[1] Although Nisbet's connection with the Provisional Confederate Congress is well established, the author of his sketch in *DAB* (XIII, 528), states that Nisbet "declined in election" to that body, and the summary of his career in the *Biographical Directory of the American Congress* does not mention the Confederate Congress, although it records that Nisbet was a member of the Georgia secession convention and the author of its ordinance of secession. *Appleton's Cyclopedia of American Biography*, on the other hand, recounts his membership in both the Milledgeville convention and the Provisional Congress.

NIMROD LINDSAY NORTON (Missouri) was born April 18, 1830, in Nicholas County, Kentucky. Like so many other members of the Confederate Congress, he was descended from forebears on both sides who had sacrificed everything, even their lives, to gain and hold American independence in 1776 and 1812. Nimrod Norton "took the log school house course near the old home"[1] and later attended Fredonia Academy in western New York, and the Kentucky Military Institute. After his marriage in 1853 he moved to Callaway County, Missouri, and established a farm in the rich Missouri River bottoms which were a slavery stronghold at the time. Although opposed to secession, he was even more strongly opposed to coercion, opted for the Confederacy, and organized one of the first infantry companies raised north of the river. Subsequently he served, with the rank of colonel, on the staff of Major General Sterling Price, who characterized him as "infinite in resource."

185

In the spring of 1864 Norton became the self-proclaimed guardian of "morality and sobriety" in opposition to the reelection bid of Thomas A. Harris, a *bon vivant* of the first chop, and it is an entertaining commentary on the times that 80 percent of the soldier and refugee vote, in what was essentially a popularity contest, was cast for the prim and proper candidate. Norton took his seat on November 21, but on February 11, 1865, illness forced him to take permanent leave of absence. Colonel Norton was less willing than most Missouri congressmen to sacrifice home-front affairs for the sake of the army. He wanted the military exemption lists to include necessary state employees, artisans, and overseers; and he opposed removing slaves from the field to the army. Otherwise during his brief service he supported the emergency legislation proposed in the last session.

Norton emigrated to Texas during the Reconstruction period and established a home on the Lavaca River in the southern part of the state. Later he moved to Austin, where he was one of the two state capitol building commissioners and assisted in locating and surveying the three million acres of land allotted by the constitution of 1876 to defray the cost of construction. In the later years of his life he had farming interests near Austin, where he died September 28, 1903, and where he is buried in Oakwood Cemetery.

[1] John Henry Brown, *Indian Wars and Pioneers of Texas* (Austin, n.d.), 697.

WILLIAM BECK OCHILTREE (Texas) was born in Fayetteville, North Carolina, October 18, 1811. His parents migrated first to Florida and after 1820 to Alabama, where Ochiltree began the practice of law. In 1839 he moved to Nacogdoches, Texas, and rapidly became prominent in public life. During the life of the Republic he served as judge of the Fifth Judicial District, secretary of the treasury, and adjutant general. After the admission of Texas as a state, Ochiltree was a representative in the 1855 legislature and a delegate to the Texas convention in 1861. He had by now become a confirmed secessionist, and the convention sent him to the Provisional Congress. In that body he was the most single-minded guardian of the best interests of his state. He had Sabine Pass made a port of entry and urged the War Department to build a fort there. He opposed any type of legislation that would permit the president to draft militia away from local defense service. He voted for every railroad construction bill that might tie Texas to the East, and he opposed the law prohibiting planters from selling their cotton wherever there was a market. In June, 1861, he announced that he would not seek election to the Regular Congress lest it lead to political bickering, but

186

he kept his seat in the Provisional Congress until the end of his term, February 17, 1862. He then returned to Texas to recruit a regiment for the war but was compelled to resign in 1863 because of ill health. He resided in Jefferson, Texas, until his death there on December 27, 1867. Judge Ochiltree was buried in Oakwood Cemetery, Jefferson.

WILLIAMSON SIMPSON OLDHAM (Texas) was a native of Franklin County, Tennessee, where he was born on July 19, 1813. Largely self-taught himself, he essayed teaching school for a time and then studied law and was admitted to the Tennessee bar in 1836. Soon after, Oldham moved to Arkansas, where in Fayetteville he became a prosperous lawyer and public figure. He was elected to the General Assembly in 1838, was speaker of the state house of representatives in 1842, and the same year was appointed an associate justice of the Arkansas Supreme Court. However, his ambition for national office was thwarted by his defeat in a bid for Congress in 1846 and for the Senate two years later. Seeking to recoup his political fortunes, and suffering from a mild case of tuberculosis, he moved to Austin, Texas, in 1849. His successes here were not much greater—he was defeated in his races for state representative in 1853 and for Congress in 1859. Meanwhile, he served as one of the editors of the *State Gazette*, the Texas Democratic house organ.

Oldham moved to Brenham, Texas, in 1859, and in January, 1861, was a member of the secession convention, which elected him to the Provisional Congress. The following November the legislature chose him senator in the Regular Congress, an office which he occupied until the end of the war. Oldham was chairman of the Committee on Post Offices in both Regular Congresses, and of the Committee on Commerce in the second. He labored under a constant fear that the "battering ram of executive influence" and the claim of "military necessity" would destroy the fundamental principles of the Confederacy. However, when there was no question of national jurisdiction, Oldham advocated quite vigorous legislation, including high taxes, extremist devices to counter inflation, and the arming of slaves. On the other hand his states' rights convictions placed him in opposition to administration programs for the establishment of a navy, for drafting and reorganizing troops, and for regimenting the economy. He was especially hostile to measures that might violate personal or property rights. In the local area, much of his time was spent in protesting inadequate defense of the Texas frontier and arbitrary actions of the Cotton Bureau.

After the collapse of the Confederacy, Oldham fled to Mexico and then made his way to Canada. In 1866, however, he returned to Texas and took up residence in Houston. Unrepentant, unpardoned, and unreconstructed, Oldham died there of typhoid fever on May 8, 1868, and is buried in Brookside Memorial Park, to which his remains were removed in 1938 from Episcopal Cemetery. Oldham County in the Panhandle was named after him, and his "Memoirs of a Confederate Senator"[1] constitutes a good source of data for the period.

[1] Williamson Simpson Oldham, "Memoirs of a Confederate Senator, 1861–1865" (MS in University of Texas Library, Austin).

JAMES LAWRENCE ORR (South Carolina), a brother of Jehu A. Orr (*q.v.*), was born at Craytonville, a hamlet in Anderson County, South Carolina, May 12, 1822. In his early years he attended the local schools and clerked in his father's store. He then entered the University of Virginia, where he began the study of law, and completed his course with a local South Carolina attorney. He was admitted to the bar at the age of twenty-one. He edited the weekly *Anderson Gazette* for two years, but then gave up journalism for politics and the law. At twenty-two he was a member of the legislature, where he served for six years, and in 1848 he was elected to Congress. Here he remained until 1859; in the Thirty-fifth Congress he was Speaker of the House, an office which he owed to his support of the policies of Stephen A. Douglas and his opposition to Know-Nothingism, both of which attitudes had made him popular in the North.

Although originally a moderate on the question of secession, Orr staunchly upheld slavery and eventually veered with the sentiment in his state, signing the ordinance of secession and going to Washington as one of three South Carolina commissioners to treat for possession of the forts in Charleston Harbor. He saw some brief military service as commander of Orr's Rifles, a unit which he had organized, and then was appointed to fill the place in the Provisional Congress from which T. J. Withers had resigned in June, 1861. He attended on only the last day of the Congress, but he had in the meantime been elected to the Senate of the Regular Congress, where he remained until the collapse of the Confederacy, and in which he was chairman of the Foreign Affairs and Rules committes. At first Orr allowed the central government relatively broad powers except when the individual states' rights were threatened. Eventually, however, the increasing centralization made necessary by the prosecution of the war drove him into an exaggerated posture of defense of state and local interests. By 1863 he had

188

added to his early and entrenched opposition to conscription and habeas corpus suspension almost the entire administration war program. He himself proposed that the army must pay market prices for impressed merchandise, that the state should have more control over vessels in foreign commerce, and that the Senate should play a much stronger role in foreign policy. He was also publicly and privately inimical to some of Davis' pets, including General Braxton Bragg and Commissary General Lucius Northrop, and by 1865 he was the recognized leader of the peace movement in the Senate, realizing that victory was impossible.

After the surrender Orr trimmed his sails to the prevailing breeze and, accommodating himself to President Johnson's Reconstruction policies, was elected governor of South Carolina. When congressional Reconstruction replaced the moderate Johnson policy, Orr again changed course and joined the Radicals. For this he was rewarded by a circuit court judgeship and, in 1872, the post of U.S. minister to Russia. After less than four months in St. Petersburg, he died of pneumonia on May 5, 1873, and was buried in the Presbyterian Cemetery in Anderson, South Carolina.

JEHU AMAZIAH ORR (Mississippi), the next-to-last survivor of the Confederate Congress, and a brother of James Lawrence Orr (*q.v.*), was born in Anderson County, South Carolina, on April 10, 1828. He attended Erskine College in his native state and the College of New Jersey, now Princeton University, and at the age of twenty-one he opened a law office in Houston, Mississippi. The same year he was chosen secretary of the state senate. In 1852 Orr was elected to a term in the legislature and then served as United States attorney for the northern district of Mississippi. He was a delegate to the Democratic national conventions of 1856 and 1860, and in the latter he was a staunch Unionist and supporter of Stephen A. Douglas. Subsequent events, however, convinced him that war was inevitable, and as a member of the Mississippi constitutional convention he voted for secession.

When William Sydney Wilson (*q.v.*) resigned from the Provisional Congress, Orr was named as his replacement, taking his seat on April 29, 1861. That fall he lost reelection to the First Regular Congress to J. W. Clapp (*q.v.*), but two years later he defeated Clapp decisively. In both the Provisional and Second congresses Orr worked diligently to strengthen both the army and the southern economy. He introduced bills to end exemptions, to punish speculators, and to repudiate old

Treasury notes and make new issues legal tender. However, he totally lacked confidence in Jefferson Davis and voted against most of his nominees, new presidential appointive powers, army promotions on the basis of merit, and any executive discretion in suspending the writ of habeas corpus. He was prominent in the Confederate peace movement; blamed the failure of the Hampton Roads conference on Davis' stubborn insistence on independence; and spent the last month of the war in Mississippi arraigning the administration.

Like his brother, Jehu A. Orr believed in the philosophy of accommodation to the stronger party. After the surrender he advised enfranchisement of Negroes on a limited basis—which was anathema to his former constituents—and other policies tending to ameliorate the hardships of congressional reconstruction. He accepted a circuit judgeship in 1870 and served for six years, but he also took part in the movement that rescued Mississippi from the Carpetbag regime. For more than thirty years he was a trustee of the University of Mississippi, and for fifty years he was a Presbyterian Church elder. He practiced law almost until the time of his death, which occurred at his home in Columbus, Mississippi, in his ninety-third year, on March 9, 1921. He was buried in Friendship Cemetery there.

GRANVILLE HENDERSON OURY (Arizona Territory), who was the third earliest American pioneer in the present state of Arizona,[1] was born March 12, 1825, in Abingdon, Virginia, but moved to Missouri with his parents when he was eleven years old. There he worked on his father's farm and attended a county school in Bowling Green. At the age of twenty-three Oury was admitted to the Missouri bar, and the same year he went to Texas. In 1849 he joined the gold rush and took up residence in Marysville, California. Seven years later he moved to Tucson, in what was then New Mexico Territory, a tiny village in an Indian-infested desert wilderness.

In August, 1861, a convention of sixty-eight voters met in Tucson and chose Oury a delegate to the Provisional Confederate Congress. He hurried to Richmond and asked President Davis to recommend in his next message the early organization of a territorial government for the southern half of the territory, which then comprised the present states of both Arizona and New Mexico. Davis ignored the request, but John H. Reagan (*q.v.*) introduced such a bill, and it became law on January 18, 1862, with Oury recognized as the nonvoting delegate of the Arizona Territory. Meanwhile, however, in faraway Mesilla, New Mexico, Military Governor John R. Baylor (*q.v.*) had called an election for a delegate to the permanent Congress, recommending Marcus H. Macwillie (*q.v.*) over Oury. Oury's friends in the territory largely abstained from voting, with the result that Macwillie was elected. During the remainder of the war Oury served on the staff of General H. H. Sibley, with the rank of colonel. In 1866 he was elected to the legislature of the recently erected United States Territory of Arizona, and he was again elected in 1873 and 1875. Meanwhile, he served as district attorney of Pinal County in 1879 and then was twice elected a delegate to the United States Congress, serving from 1881 to 1885. He was again district attorney of Pinal County when he succumbed to cancer of the throat in Tucson, Arizona, January 11, 1891. He was buried in Florence.

[1] Phoenix *Herald*, January 15, 1891.

JAMES BYERAM OWENS (Florida) was born about the year 1816, near Winnsboro in what is now Fairfield County, South Carolina.[1] He was educated for the Baptist ministry at Edgefield Academy (now Furman University) at Greenville, South Carolina. He is said to have preached in Alabama before moving to Holmes County, Mississippi, in the late 1840s. Some years later, because of his health, he gave up the active ministry and followed his two brothers to Marion County, Florida, where he established a cotton and citrus plantation, Plainfield, near Sparr. By 1860 Dr. Owens owned eighty-nine Negroes and an estate of $118,000.[2] He is also credited with growing and naming the first "pineapple orange" and being the originator of that industry.

Owens was a delegate to the 1860 Democratic convention in Baltimore, was a member of the Florida secession convention, signed the ordinance of secession, and was appointed by Governor Perry as one of Florida's original three delegates to the Montgomery convention which resolved itself into the Provisional Confederate Congress. In this body he was chairman of the Committee on Accounts. While he was a singularly passive congressman in most respects, Owens' voting record reveals that he was the only doctrinaire states' righter in his delegation. His colleagues granted the central government considerable emergency powers if only because of Florida's exposed position. Owens, however, wanted free trade, and voted against emergency appointment powers for the president, the export duty on cotton, and any aid to railroad construction. He did not seek election to the Regular Congress.

Dr. Owens returned to his eighteen-hundred-acre plantation in Marion County after the war was over. According to his grandson,

191

former ex-Governor John W. Martin of Florida, Owens studied medicine and practiced in the Ocala area,[3] besides devoting himself to agricultural pursuits. Reconstruction in Florida was not the problem it was in other southern states; the area was never overrun by Federal armies; and because of its relative isolation and small population the freedmen had no place to go and were usually content to work for their former masters. Consequently, Dr. Owens was able to more or less continue his old way of life on his plantation until his death on August 1, 1889. He was buried in Evergreen Cemetery, Ocala.

[1] John A. Kehoe to Ezra J. Warner, December 4, 1970.
[2] United States Census of 1860, Marion County, Fla.
[3] This information was provided by John A. Kehoe, Atlanta, whose wife is a great-grandniece of James B. Owens. Her uncle, John W. Martin, was governor of Florida in the 1920s.

JOHN PERKINS, JR. (Louisiana) was a native of Mississippi, born in Natchez on July 1, 1819. He obtained his primary education from private tutors and then graduated from Yale in 1840 and from Harvard Law School two years later. He was admitted to the bar in 1843 and began practice in New Orleans. He also interested himself in cotton planting. Perkins had inherited the means to enjoy leisure, and at this period of his life he traveled extensively in Europe. In 1851 he was appointed a circuit judge, and in 1853 he took his seat in Congress as a representative from the Louisiana district which embraced his plantation, Ashwood, in Madison Parish. He was not a candidate for renomination the following year.

Perkins was chairman of the Louisiana secession convention, was a delegate to the Provisional Congress, and twice won reelection to the Regular Congresses with little opposition. In the Second Congress he was chairman of the Rules Committee. An indefatigable worker, he was the only congressman to be individually thanked by a resolution of his own state legislature. Although President Davis' chief critic termed him "a special devotee and confidant of Mr. Davis,"[1] Perkins was actually rather independent in his thinking: he believed conscription unconstitutional, arming the slaves degrading, favorable terms of peace a possibility, and some of the president's chief advisors utterly incompetent. His principal interest was in economic planning. He induced Congress to pass a bill establishing a bureau of foreign supplies; when Davis vetoed it, Perkins tried to persuade the government to buy up all cotton and tobacco as a basis for foreign credit. To combat inflation he successively urged making Treasury notes legal tender, repudiating them entirely, and establishing a 50 percent profit tax. To stimulate industry he advocated free trade during the war and a discriminatory tariff against the United States after it was over. Upon the collapse of the Confederacy Perkins made his way to Mexico and then to Europe; he did not return to the United States until 1878. He spent the remaining years of his life in Louisiana and Canada, and he died in Baltimore, Maryland, November 28, 1885. He was buried in Natchez Cemetery.

[1] Henry S. Foote, *Casket of Reminiscences* (Washington, D.C., 1874), 294.

ROBERT LUDWELL YATES PEYTON (Missouri) scion of an old Virginia family, was born in Loudoun County on February 8, 1822, but in early boyhood was taken by his parents to Oxford, Ohio. There he grew up and graduated from Miami University in 1841. Two years later he received a bachelor of laws degree from the University of Virginia and almost immediately moved to Harrisonville, in western Missouri, to establish practice.

Peyton ran for several public offices with no particular success (provided opposition manifested itself), and was described by a contemporary as doing nothing today that could be put off until tomorrow. However, in 1858, unopposed, he won a seat in the state senate from a district comprising the counties of Bates, Cass, and Jackson. In the fall of 1861, his reputation as a spread-eagle orator was such that the rump Neosho legislature chose him as one of Missouri's two senators.[1] He took his seat on January 21, 1862, in time to attend the fifth and last session of the Provisional Congress. Meanwhile as colonel of the Third Missouri Cavalry, Eighth Division, Missouri State Guard, Peyton participated in a number of engagements unimportant in themselves but of great significance in firmly attaching Missouri to the Union cause: Carthage, Springfield, Big Dry Wood, and Lexington. Once in Congress, his diffidence in addressing that body was in marked contrast to his reputation and made him almost a silent member. He generally supported vigorous legislation on military matters, but otherwise he was rather conservative, preferring to requisition rather than draft, and to exempt local defense units in active service. He conceded the central government emergency control over the South's resources and commerce, but opposed curbs on inflation and staple crop production (cotton and tobacco). On matters not directly affecting the war effort, Peyton was willing to make few concessions to the administration, despite the fact that his elder half-sister was the (first) wife of General Joseph R. Davis, the president's nephew.

The circumstances surrounding Peyton's death are obscure. It must

193

be assumed that he died at Bladon Springs, Alabama, on September 3, 1863, but whether his death resulted from malaria contracted while he was aiding in the defense of Vicksburg,[2] or he died "while attempting to make his way to a portion of the constituents"[3] cannot be determined. He died between sessions of the First Regular Congress; so it is possible that he was present with the forces involved in the defense of Vicksburg and after the surrender was en route to Texas at the time of his death. Although he is said to have been engaged to the only daughter of General Sterling Price when he died, exhaustive research has failed to identify his place of burial.[4]

[1] See the above sketch of C. W. Bell for Missouri's method of choosing delegates to the Confederate Congress.

[2] "Sketch of Hon. Robert L. Y. Peyton of Missouri, 1825–1863," J. Lewis Peyton, *Magazine of American History* XVI (July–December, 1886), 394–98.

[3] Address of Caspar W. Bell in *Proceedings and Speeches on the Announcement of the Death of Hon. R. L. Y. Peyton of Missouri, etc.* (Richmond, 1864).

[4] According to H. E. Hayden, *Virginia Genealogies* (N.p., 1931). But Hazel Price of Glasgow, Mo., Price's granddaughter, says that in all the family discussions she listened to as a child, she never heard Peyton's name mentioned. (Hazel Price to Ezra J. Warner, November 11, 1972.)

JAMES PHELAN (Mississippi), the son of New Jersey parents, was born October 11, 1821, in Huntsville, Alabama. At the age of fourteen he was apprenticed as a printer to the Huntsville *Democrat*, which his older brother edited. Subsequently he edited a paper of his own, the *Flag of the Union*, a Democratic organ, and he was later rewarded by being appointed state printer in 1843. Phelan then turned his attention to the law, was admitted to the Alabama bar in 1846, and in 1849 moved to Aberdeen, Mississippi, where he was soon a prominent and eminently successful attorney. He was elected to the Mississippi state senate in 1860. In the fall of 1861 he was chosen senator to the First Regular Confederate Congress but drew only a two-year term. Although he held no important committee chairmanship, his extreme Confederate nationalism made him one of the more controversial senators. Oldham of Texas (*q.v.*) once complained that Phelan "had no use for state governments."[1] As early as 1862 he proposed to give the central government control over all commerce and to drastically restrict cotton production. In 1863 he rocked the conservative establishment on its foundations by introducing a bill to impress all the cotton in the South, to pay for it in Confederate bonds with the purpose of using it for foreign credit, and to punish all violators by death. In like manner he supported a variety of radical legislation introduced by others. He was also strongly opposed to anything he deemed class legislation,

194

such as the use of military substitutes and the exemption of plantation overseers. Having been burned in effigy by some of his constituents after his introduction of the cotton impressment bill, he was defeated for reelection in 1863 by John W. C. Watson (*q.v.*), who had been his opponent two years before. Phelan then served as judge-advocate until the end of the war, after which he took up residence in Memphis. He practiced law there until his death, May 17, 1873. He is buried in Elmwood Cemetery.

[1] *Southern Historical Society Papers*, XLIV, 165.

WALTER PRESTON (Virginia) was born at Abingdon, Virginia, in July, 1819. He is often understandably confused with his second cousin, Walter Eugene Preston—they were born and died a few months apart; both were from Washington County, Virginia; and both were lawyers. The Preston clan was a large one, with members in several states, and its relationships are made more puzzling by several "cousin marriages." Walter Preston enjoyed an excellent primary education, after which he entered Princeton in his junior year and graduated in 1839. Three years later he graduated from Harvard Law School and returned to Abingdon to practice. In 1857 he ran for attorney general of Virginia as a Whig and was defeated by the Democratic candidate John Randolph Tucker. In June, 1861, the Virginia convention appointed Preston to the Provisional Congress and in November he won election to the First Regular Congress from southwest Virginia over LaFayette McMullen (*q.v.*), who in turn defeated him in a close race in 1863.

Preston was neither strong nor inspired as a member of Congress, despite the fact that he was a member of several important committees—including that on foreign affairs—and of the Quartermaster's and Commissary departments. Although there was no question of his loyalty, he seemed to favor only halfway measures for the Confederacy's survival, frequently voting to enlarge the already long list of classes exempt from military service. He approved all major tax bills, but again he favored more than the usual number of exemptions. Conceding the necessity of suspending the writ of habeas corpus in certain situations, he nevertheless worked to include numerous exceptions. In the matter of runaway inflation caused by the enormous issues of paper money, he opposed repudiation, believing that making Treasury notes legal tender would suffice. So far as foreign affairs, commerce, and army affairs were concerned, he was generally to be found on the side of the administration.

Following his defeat in 1863, Preston returned home but lived only a short time; he died at Abingdon in November, 1867. The exact day is not known, nor is his place of burial; his estate was probated in January, 1868. He was a distant cousin of William B. Preston (*q.v.*), who was also his wife's cousin.

WILLIAM BALLARD PRESTON (Virginia), who was a first cousin of Walter Preston's stepmother as well as a first cousin twice removed of his wife, was born at Smithfield, Montgomery County, Virginia, on November 25, 1805. He was graduated from Hampden-Sydney College in 1824 and then studied law at the University of Virginia; he was admitted to the bar in 1826. His father, James Patton Preston, who had been governor of the state from 1816 to 1819, was a prominent planter in Montgomery County, and the son soon became prominent in both politics and the legal profession, serving a number of terms in both houses of the legislature in the 1830s and 1840s. In 1846 Preston was elected to Congress as an antislavery Whig, and in 1849 he supported the admission of California as a free state. That same year President Zachary Taylor appointed him Secretary of the Navy, a post he occupied until the cabinet was reorganized upon the accession of Millard Fillmore.

As a member of the Virginia convention in 1861 Preston opposed the secession of his state even after the states of the lower South had left the Union, despite the fact that he believed in secession as an abstract right inherent in the United States Constitution. Nevertheless, on the day Lincoln called for seventy-five thousand volunteers Preston presented to the convention the ordinance of secession; he was presumably selected because of his known previous opposition to the step. He was then sent to the Provisional Congress, and on January 23, 1862, the General Assembly chose him as its western senator. He was a member of both the Committee on Military Affairs and the Committee on Foreign Affairs during his brief legislative career. He was also one of the stronger supporters of states' rights and local autonomy, conceding only minimum war powers to the central government. While approving conscription, he sought extensive exemptions to support the local economy. He was also at odds with the administration over the reorganization and officering of state militia units and the use of irregulars for guerrilla service, a practice he felt would weaken local defense. Preston also seemed to deny the central government's authority over the Confederate economy, voting against the moderate tax program of 1861, the issuance of currency, the destruction of property to prevent its capture, the regulation of local commerce and transportation, and even a resolution urging farmers and planters to emphasize food production as against staple crops. He died at his birthplace in Montgomery County, November 16, 1862, and was buried in the family cemetery on the estate.[1]

[1] The *Biographical Directory of the American Congress*, in its sketch of Preston, has confused the village of Smithfield, in Isle of Wight County, with the estate Smithfield in Montgomery County. This confusion, of course, leads to the erroneous statement that Preston is buried "probably in the cemetery of the Old Brick Church, near Smithfield, Isle of Wight County, Virginia." The estate of Smithfield is near Blacksburg, Va., and is maintained by the Society for the Preservation of Virginia Antiquities.

ROGER ATKINSON PRYOR (Virginia), a secession firebrand who had much to do with inciting the firing on Fort Sumter, was born near Petersburg, Virginia, on July 19, 1828. He grew up, however, in Nottoway County, where he attended the local schools. Later he attended the Classical Academy in Petersburg, and was graduated as class valedictorian from Hampden-Sydney College in 1845, having already attained considerable reputation as a stump orator. In later years it would be said of him that he could convert the political views of an entire community with a single speech. Following two years of law study at the University of Virginia, Pryor was admitted to the bar in 1849 and practiced for a short time, but he was chiefly known antebellum for his connection with a number of newspapers in Petersburg, Richmond, and Washington. In Washington in 1857 he founded *The South*, an ultra states' rights organ, which he ran while he also served on the staff of the Washington *States*. He was elected to Congress in 1859 to fill a vacancy, and he was reelected in 1860 but resigned on March 3, 1861.

Pryor's southern views were so extreme and his public and private utterances so violent, that he was involved in a number of duels. In one of them, his opponent named bowie knives as the weapons; Pryor's seconds declined to allow him to participate, terming such arms barbarous. He emerged unscathed from all these encounters. In April, 1861, Pryor was a visitor in Charleston and urged the South Carolinians to attack Sumter, asserting "Strike one blow and Virginia will secede in an hour." He is supposed to have been offered the honor of firing the first shot and to have declined in favor of Edmund Ruffin, but if this is so his gallantry was in vain, for the first shot was actually fired by an obscure artillery captain.[1] The Virginia convention elected Pryor to the Provisional Congress, and in November he easily won reelection in the First Regular Congress on the promise to have the constitutional prohibition on plural office holding repealed; when unable to do this he resigned before taking his seat. He then entered the army as colonel of

197

the Third Virginia Infantry and was promoted to brigadier general after the battle of Williamsburg. Pryor's essential interest was in the military, and during his congressional career he was an enthusiastic member of the Committee on Military Affairs. He attended Congress so infrequently that his positions are not very clear, but he worked to create as large an army as possible, to send recruiters into border states, and to repeal the local defense laws—his was the only Virginia vote in favor of the latter. On the other hand, he opposed the administration when it sought new powers over officer selection and army organization. He favored the destruction of cotton exposed to capture.

Pryor led his brigade during the Battle of the Seven Days, at Second Manassas, and at Sharpsburg. In November, 1862, he was transferred to the command of a small brigade which was stationed south of the James River. The following spring, for reasons which do not appear in the records, Pryor's regiments were separately reassigned and he was left without a command. He resigned his brigadier general's commission on August 18, 1863, and served thereafter without rank as a special courier attached to the cavalry. In November, 1864, he was captured and spent some months in Fort Lafayette in Boston Harbor before being made eligible for exchange by Lincoln's personal order.

In September, 1865, General Pryor made his way to New York with the proceeds of his wife's jewels to make a new life. He first became associated with the *Daily News*, writing anonymously, and studying for admission to the New York bar at odd moments. He rose to recognition in both fields and in 1890 was appointed to the court of common pleas. From 1896 until 1899, when he resigned because of age, he was a New York state supreme court justice. For the last seven years of his life he served as a referee for the appellate division of the court. General Pryor died on March 14, 1919, in his ninety-first year, in New York, and was buried in Princeton Cemetery, Princeton, New Jersey, one of the last survivors of the Confederate Congress.

[1] See S. C. Lee in *Southern History Society Papers*, XI, 501–502, for what should be a resolution of this celebrated debate as to who fired the first shot at Fort Sumter.

JAMES LAWRENCE PUGH[1] (Alabama) was born near Waynesboro, Georgia, on December 12, 1820.[2] In 1824 the family moved to Pike County, Alabama, and settled on public land. When his father died in 1830 James moved to Louisville to live with a cousin. For the next few years he attended seven academies in Alabama and Georgia, working at odd jobs much of the time but finally completing this part of his education. He then read law under John Gill Shorter (*q.v.*) of Eufaula and was admitted to the bar in 1841. Pugh practiced law in Eufaula for the next thirty-nine years and also managed the estate which his wife had inherited. During the 1840s Pugh was an active Whig, but in 1850 he turned Democrat. He was a presidential elector in 1848, 1856, and 1876. In 1859 he was elected to Congress, but he had been an early secessionist and resigned when Alabama left the Union. Pugh then enlisted as a private in the Eufaula Rifles, a unit in which he had served during the Indian war of the mid-1830s and which escorted Jefferson Davis at his inauguration as president of the Confederacy.

In December, 1861, Pugh was elected to the Confederate Congress without opposition, but two years later he barely won reelection over three opponents. In both congresses he was a staunch advocate of legislation to strengthen the central government, and he joined none of the forays against the president's leadership. But Pugh's main interest was the economy, and here he sometimes clashed with Secretary of the Treasury Memminger (*q.v.*). Pugh believed that Congress' primary economic goal should be to increase production. He particularly felt that taxes on property depressed the economy. To avoid this he preferred to increase existing rates rather than the diversification requested by Memminger. In a speech in August, 1863, Pugh argued that doubling the tax in kind would solve all the Confederacy's financial problems. The next January he sought to encourage production by reducing the money taxes on industry and agriculture. Pugh also advocated free trade and saw no sense in moving older men from labor to the army.

After the war Pugh returned to his law practice in Eufaula. In 1874 he was president of the state Democratic convention, and the next year he was a member of the Alabama constitutional convention. In 1878 he lost a race for the United States Senate by two votes but was elected to fill the unexpired term when the incumbent died. He was twice reelected to the Senate, where he was chairman of the Judiciary Committee in the Fifty-third and Fifty-fourth congresses. In 1888 President Cleveland offered Pugh a place on the Supreme Court bench, but Pugh declined because of his age. After his retirement from the Senate in 1897 he lived in Washington, D.C., until his death on March 9, 1907. He is buried in Fairview Cemetery in Eufaula.

[1] Owen, *History of Alabama*, IV, 1, 397–98.
[2] The *Biographical Directory of the American Congress* correctly gives Pugh's birth date as December 12, 1820. Owen gives May 3, 1819.

RICHARD CLAUSELLE PURYEAR (North Carolina), at best a reluctant Confederate, was born February 9, 1801, in Mecklenburg County, Virginia, but moved with his parents to Surry County, North Carolina, in childhood. He was probably educated by private tutors; the euphemism employed by the *Biographical Directory of the American Congress* is that he "pursued classical studies." He then engaged in planting near Huntsville at his estate, Shallow Ford, and was colonel of the militia and magistrate of Surry County. In 1838, 1844, and 1846, he served in the state house of commons, or lower branch of the legislature, and in 1852 he was a member of the state senate. The same year Puryear was elected as a Whig to the United States House of Representatives, and he was reelected in 1854. He was defeated for a third term in 1856.

After secession, a caucus of former Unionists, of which Puryear was a prominent member, secured his election as a delegate to the Provisional Confederate Congress. Puryear's heart had never been in the secession movement, although he owned thirty-two Negroes in 1860 and might have been considered to have a substantial stake in the perpetuation of slavery. In Montgomery and Richmond he took so little interest in the proceedings that his positions are often unclear. Certainly he disliked taxation, for he voted both to reduce the already low war tax by half and to add numerous exemptions to the bill. He seems to have supported the other moderate war measures under discussion. He did not seek election to the Regular Congress, possibly because he felt that "it was the great object of the inaugurators of this Revolution to build up a Monarchy upon the remains of our glorious Republic," [1] a sentiment which in a way illustrates the division between Puryear and his Whig colleagues and their fiery Democratic brethren. After the war he was a delegate to the peace congress in Philadelphia. He continued to reside on his plantation, Shallow Ford, in Yadkin County, until his death there on July 30, 1867. He was buried in a family graveyard on his estate.

[1] R. C. Puryear to "My Dear Baby," March 3, 1862, in Clingman-Puryear Papers, Southern Historical Collection, University of North Carolina, Chapel Hill.

JOHN PERKINS RALLS [1] (Alabama) was born in Greensboro, Greene County, Georgia, on January 1, 1812. After attending academies in Greensboro and in Cassville, he entered the Medical College in Augusta, graduating in 1845. After studying for a year in the hospitals of Paris, France, Ralls began practicing medicine in Centre, Alabama. He also accumulated several hundred acres of land and engaged in planting. Ralls was always a strong Methodist and devoted much of his spare time to work in the Alabama prohibition movement and as a circuit rider for his district. While Dr. Ralls was a Democrat, he took no part in politics before 1861, but in January of that year he was elected to the secession convention as an immediate secessionist. The following December he badly defeated his Unionist opponent, Williamson R. W. Cobb, a seven-term member of the U.S. House, in a race for a seat in the Confederate House of Representatives.

Soon after reaching Congress Ralls introduced a resolution, unanimously adopted, declaring that the Confederacy would "*never*, on any terms," reunite with the United States.[2] Thereafter he was one of the many unobtrusive members who were willing to enlarge the powers of the central government at least for the duration of the war. His only significant reservations were his convictions that men under eighteen and over forty-five would be of more use at home than in the army, and that the tax in kind placed an excessive burden on agriculture. Ralls was chairman of a select committee to investigate alleged abuses in the Medical Department. Their only serious indictment of the department was that its system of discharges and furloughs for wounded men was distressingly complicated. In 1863 Ralls lost his race for reelection to Cobb by a wide margin.[3]

After the war Ralls practiced in Gadsden for the remainder of his life, eventually forming a partnership with his son Arthur. Dr. Ralls's last forays into politics were his service in the constitutional convention of 1875 and his election to the legislature in 1878. He died in Gadsden on November 22, 1904, and he is buried there in Forrest Cemetery.[4]

[1] Owen, *History of Alabama*, IV, 1,406.

[2] Wilmington (N.C.) *Daily Journal*, March 5, 1862.

[3] The House of Representatives appointed a committee to inquire into Cobb's loyalty. The committee obtained evidence that Cobb had been seen mingling with the enemy since his election to Congress. It also reported that it had been unable to inform Cobb that he was on trial, because he was known to be behind enemy lines and on friendly terms with the enemy. The House then unanimously declared Cobb's seat to be vacant. In February, 1865, Thomas B. Cooper was elected to the place but never took his seat.

[4] Information on Ralls's place of interment was provided by Margaret C. Rouse, Gadsden Public Library, Gadsden, Ala.

JAMES GRAHAM RAMSAY[1] (North Carolina) was born on March 1, 1823, on a small plantation in Iredell County, North Carolina, where his family had lived since 1766. After attending the local old field schools, he entered Davidson College in 1838 and graduated three years later. After teaching school for a year, Ramsay began studying medicine under his brother-in-law. He next entered the Jefferson Medical College in Philadelphia and graduated in 1848. He began practicing near Cleveland and used part of his fine home, Palermo, as his office. In 1849 he promoted the first medical society in Rowan County and was elected its president. He also farmed on a small scale. Ramsay soon became involved in politics, electioneering for Whig candidates and serving in the state senate from 1856 to 1864. He supported the Bell-Everett ticket in 1860 and even after Lincoln's election spoke frequently in his district against disunion. When Lincoln's call for volunteers in April, 1861, resulted in the secession of North Carolina, Ramsay reluctantly went with his state. In 1863 he campaigned successfully for a seat in the Confederate House of Representatives, attacking the incumbent William Lander's (*q.v.*) strong support of Confederate legislation and promising to work for peace negotiations.

In Congress Ramsay seldom offered suggestions of his own, but he voted so consistently to place individual and state interests over those of the Confederacy that his loyalty was questioned. He tried to lower all taxes except those on corporations; he wished to make broad new grants of exemption from military service, despite the army's thinning ranks; he sought to let farmers commute the productive tax in kind into worthless paper currency; and he considered all impressment laws little but legalized robbery. Ramsay was just as opposed to other administration programs, and by April, 1865, he urged a state convention to return North Carolina to the Union.

After the war Ramsay entered the Republican party. He was a presidential elector in 1872 and in 1883 was elected again to the state senate for one more term. President Hayes offered him a diplomatic post in South America, but Ramsay preferred to continue his medical practice at home. When his wife died in 1895 he lived his remaining days in Salisbury with his son, dying there on January 10, 1903. Ramsay is interred in the cemetery of the Third Creek Presbyterian Church near Cleveland, where he had been a ruling elder for forty-nine years.

[1] Most of the information in Ramsay's biography was provided by his granddaughter, Mrs. Charles L. Putzel of Salisbury, N.C. Information about certain parts of his political career was taken from the James G. Ramsay biographical folder in the Walser Papers.

HENRY ENGLISH READ (Kentucky), a somewhat elusive character, was born in Larue County, Kentucky, on December 25, 1824. According to his obituary in the Louisville *Courier-Journal* on November 10, 1868, he began as a blacksmith but soon became a lawyer, practicing in Hodgenville, Shelbyville, and Elizabethtown. He is supposed to have fought in the Mexican War as an officer in one or another of two different regiments, but neither his name nor that of his two stated commanding officers can be found in Heitman.[1] According to the *Courier-Journal*, he was "the first man to plant the American flag on the heights of Chapultepec, beneath whose walls he fell covered with wounds." He was presented with a sword by the Kentucky legislature (of which he was later a member) and made a brigadier general of militia by the governor for his Mexican War services. He was referred to as "General" Read upon the occasion of his death.

In the special election of June, 1861, Read was the Southern Rights candidate for the United States Congress but was defeated. In January, 1862, he was elected to the First Regular Confederate Congress, and two years later he was returned by the votes of Kentucky soldiers and refugees scattered over that portion of the South still within Confederate lines. While in Congress, Read worked mainly in behalf of the army's enlisted men. At different times he introduced bills providing them with better rations and pay, compensation if they were disabled, exchange if they were captured, transportation if they were on furlough, and transfer to home militia units if they wished. He argued that Kentucky and Missouri volunteers, depressed by their states' occupation, would fight better if grouped with others from home. By 1864 he had become convinced that efforts to stabilize the currency created undue hardships on the people, but on all other vital issues he supported vigorous legislation. After the war he went to Louisville to practice law, an occupation terminated by his suicide on November 9, 1868. Read left a note attributing his act to "pecuniary want [which] at all times [of my life] . . . has been embarrassing." He is buried in Elizabethtown City Cemetery.[2]

[1] Heitman, *Historical Register of the United States Army.*

[2] There are several references to Read in Lewis Collins and Richard H. Collins, *History of Kentucky* (Covington, Ky., 1874), few of which can be verified. The least ephemeral evidences of his career are in the pages of the Louisville *Courier-Journal* and on Read's gravestone in Elizabethtown.

EDWIN GODWIN READE (North Carolina) was born of poor farming parents on November 13, 1812, at Mount Tirzah, North Carolina. As a youth he worked at various menial jobs to help his widowed mother, studying under her tutelage in his spare time. Later he attended two nearby academies and then read law at home in books borrowed from a retired attorney. He was admitted to the bar in 1835 and began practicing in Roxboro, eventually becoming one of the most brilliant speakers and successful advocates in the history of the state. He also engaged in planting on a small holding near town. Reade was a Whig until 1855, when he joined the American party because of its anti-Catholic and antiforeign positions. He was elected to Congress in 1855 but disliked the work and refused to seek reelection. In 1856 he was the only southerner in Congress who voted to censure L. M. Keitt (*q.v.*) for rushing into the Senate to prevent any interference while Preston Brooks caned Charles Sumner. Reade was such a strong Unionist that William H. Seward sounded him out for a place in Lincoln's cabinet, but Reade declined the honor. Even after Lincoln's call for volunteers to quell the southern rebellion Reade was so much the Unionist that he refused to be a candidate for the secession convention. In 1863 he was elected to the superior court, but before his term began Governor Vance appointed him to serve the remaining month of George Davis' (*q.v.*) term as Confederate senator.

Reade took his seat on January 22, 1864, and immediately began to make the most of his brief opportunity. In an interview with President Davis the next day Reade advised him to "trust North Carolina and *let her alone.*"[1] A week later he described to the Senate North Carolina's dissatisfaction with the course of affairs and intimated that she might begin peace negotiations unless the trend toward military rule were halted. Reade supported almost none of the emergency laws then before the Senate. He sought reelection as a peace candidate but his position was too extreme even for North Carolina.

In 1865 Reade was president of the "Johnson" Reconstruction convention, and in the same year he was made associate justice of the state supreme court. He turned Republican in 1868, but was reelected until 1879 with the support of both parties. He voluntarily retired from the bench to become president of a Raleigh bank in which most of his wealth was invested. He was a good businessman and nursed the bank from near bankruptcy back to solvency. During these years he took no part in politics and did not even vote after 1874. He died in Raleigh on October 18, 1894, and is buried in Oakwood Cemetery.

[1] Edwin G. Reade to Zebulon B. Vance, February 10, 1864, in Zebulon B. Vance Papers, Department of Archives and History, Raleigh, N.C.

JOHN HENNINGER REAGAN (Texas) was born in Sevierville, Tennessee, October 8, 1818, and was educated in the local schools and at the academy in Maryville, Tennessee. After acting as overseer of a plantation near Natchez, Mississippi, he moved to Texas in 1839 and joined the army of the Republic for the campaign against the Cherokees. He then worked as a surveyor for three years but subsequently studied law and was admitted to practice. Reagan was a member of the legislature from Henderson County in 1847 and in 1851 moved to Palestine, where he was soon recognized as one of the state's leading lawyers. He was twice elected district judge and in 1856 was elected to Congress, where he was a member until March 3, 1861. During this period he was a moderate on the questions of slavery and states' rights; nevertheless, he accepted a seat in the secession convention, which sent him to the Provisional Confederate Congress. He took his seat on March 2, 1861, but served only four days before being appointed postmaster general, an office which he had already declined twice. He attended few sessions of Congress; his occasional participation (cabinet members under the Confederate constitution occupied ex officio congressional seats) indicates that he advocated quick and thorough preparations for war. A vintage pragmatist, he once startled his colleagues by suggesting that government departments be allowed to trade with the United States at their discretion. At the end of the war Reagan was seized and confined in Fort Warren for several months. During the interval he took occasion to write President Andrew Johnson, appealing as one descendant of poor east Tennesseans to another against harsh measures toward the South. He wrote a second, open letter to his Texas constituents counseling acceptance of the inevitable, including the extinction of slavery and the admission of the Negro to civil status and qualified voting privileges. These attitudes won him no friends among the diehards in a stricken, poverty-ridden economy, and he was almost universally condemned. Ten years later, however, Reagan was elected to Congress, and he was continuously reelected until 1887, when the legislature chose him to be a member of the United States Senate, where he served until 1891. In that year he was persuaded to resign to become chairman of the newly authorized Texas Railroad Commission. He retired to private life in 1903, and died at the age of eighty-six on March 6, 1905, at his home in Palestine. The presence of the entire Texas legislature at his funeral attested to the esteem in which this last survivor of the Confederate cabinet was held by his fellow citizens. Judge Reagan was buried in East Hill Cemetery, Palestine. Reagan County in west Texas was named in his honor.

ROBERT BARNWELL RHETT (South Carolina) was first, last, and always a nullifier, secessionist, and revolutionist, the stormy petrel of southern politics. He was born in Beaufort, South Carolina, on December 21, 1800. Until 1837 the family name had been Smith, at which time—supposedly at the instance of Rhett's brothers—it was changed to the more aristocratic cognomen of an ancestor, despite the fact that their Smith forebears had played a long and honored part in the history of the state and province. Rhett's father was poor, and the boy's education did not extend past his seventeenth year. He studied law, however, and was admitted to practice in 1821. He accumulated property and at one time was said to own 190 slaves on two estates, although the 1860 census reports his possessing only seventy-six Negroes and a total wealth of thirty-four thousand dollars. His material possessions, however, were insignificant by comparison with his total career.

Rhett was the apotheosis of intransigence so far as states' rights were concerned, and he did battle—first as a disciple of Calhoun, and later on his own account—for thirty-five years until he was finally able to foment, as the "father of secession," a southern Confederacy. Meanwhile he served as a member of the legislature; as attorney general of South Carolina; as a United States senator; and as publisher of the ultraradical Charleston *Mercury*, of which his son, equally zealous in the cause of disunion, was editor. As might be supposed, Rhett signed the ordinance of secession and was a delegate to the South Carolina secession convention, where he was temporarily the hero of the hour. After guiding his state out of the Union, Rhett accepted a seat in the Provisional Congress, hoping for a position of leadership. But by now conservatism prevailed and he had to be satisfied with the chairmanship of the Committee on Foreign Affairs. Rhett then tried to preempt leadership by seeking to block the organization of a provisional government lest it lead to Reconstruction. Failing here, he attempted to radicalize the permanent Constitution but achieved limited success. Rhett then tried to set diplomatic policy by proposing tariff favoritism to European nations but was defeated by the Davis forces.

Despite such rebuffs, Rhett supported a surprisingly strong tax and army program and at the same time remained adamantly opposed to the administration on matters less directly related to war preparations. During the balance of the war he joined his son on the *Mercury* to mount a vitriolic attack on Jefferson Davis, his administration, his appointments, his strategy, and even his last-ditch proposal to arm— and free—the slaves in order to achieve independence. Rhett once again offered himself for Congress in 1863 but was defeated by Lewis M. Ayer (*q.v.*). After the war he wrote an unpublished history of the Confederacy which was in essence his apologia, and he remained sublimely self-satisfied and self-righteous until he died at the home of a son-in-law in St. James Parish, Louisiana, on September 14, 1876. He was buried in Magnolia Cemetery in Charleston, South Carolina.

WILLIAM CABELL RIVES (Virginia), who may with propriety be characterized as an elder statesman of the Confederacy, was born May 4, 1793, in Virginia, at his maternal grandfather's estate, Union Hill, in that part of Amherst County which is now Nelson.[1] His long and distinguished legislative and diplomatic antebellum career completely overshadowed his later, not altogether voluntary, adherence to the Confederacy.

Rives was educated at Hampden-Sydney and William and Mary; he was graduated from the latter in 1809. For the next few years he studied law and politics with Thomas Jefferson as his preceptor, and briefly during the War of 1812 he was an aide on the staff of a local commander. A half-century in public service began with his membership in the Virginia constitutional convention of 1816. From 1817 to 1821 he represented Nelson County in the House of Delegates, and later he represented Albermarle County, in which lay the estate of his wife. In 1823 Rives was sent to the United States House of Reepresentatives where he remained until President Andrew Jackson dispatched him as minister to France in 1829. His relations with the court of Louis Philippe were so friendly that Queen Amelie was godmother to his eldest daughter.

In 1832, after his return to the United States, Rives was elected to the Senate by the Virginia legislature upon his avowal of Jacksonian principles, but in subsequent years he veered between support of the Jacksonians and the Whig policy of Henry Clay, resigning and being reelected from time to time over various issues until in 1844 he became a full-blown Whig. He was again minister to France from 1849 to 1853 during the administrations of Taylor and Fillmore, before which time he had begun work on what would be his most enduring monument: the three-volume *History of the Life and Times of James Madison*.

In 1861 Rives was a member of the Virginia convention, having previously been a member of the so-called peace convention in Washington. He was a lukewarm supporter of secession, declaring such a course unjustifiable even if inevitable, and won election to the Provisional Congress by only a single vote over James A. Seddon (*q.v.*). The following January he ran a poor fourth in a contest for Virginia's western senatorial seat. He was again defeated in 1863, but in June he won an uncontested election to the lower house in the Second Regular Congress, where his attendance was spasmodic owing to poor health. While serving on the Committee on Foreign Affairs, he was a vigorous supporter of President Davis, withholding from him only certain extraordinary powers governing the appointment of army officers. Among the administration measures which he approved were the replacement of Treasury notes with "certificates of indebtedness" and the control of state vessels operating in foreign commerce, a euphemism for blockade runners. In 1864, realizing the hopelessness of the Confederate cause, Rives became a rather passive peace advocate. He resigned from Congress on March 1, 1865, and went home to his estate, Castle Hill, near Charlottesville, where he died on April 25, 1868, and where he is buried in a family cemetery.

[1] Published sources differ as to the place and date of Rives's birth. The statistics given above presumably rest upon the authority of Rives's granddaughter, the Princess Troubetzkoy of Castle Hill, who was interviewed by the author of the sketch in the *DAB*.

CORNELIUS ROBINSON (Alabama), a native of North Carolina, was born there at Wadesboro on September 25, 1805. His forebears on both sides went back to early colonial days, and one of his grandfathers was forced to vacate his seat in the state legislature because of his Tory sentiments. Young Cornelius was educated at the University of North Carolina, graduating with a bachelor of laws degree in 1824, although he never practiced. He subsequently moved (at some time prior to 1828) to Alabama, settling in Lowndes County in the central part of the state, where he engaged in planting.

In 1836 Robinson is said to have "served in the Indian War of 1836, as captain of Benton Company of Lowdnes County." This can only refer to the Seminole War of that year which took place in Florida, and which consisted of a number of separate actions in which the regular army took part. He was also a brigadier general of state militia at one time, and it is also claimed that he was a brigadier general during the Mexican War. Prior to the Civil War Robinson engaged in the planting and commission business at Mobile before returning to Lowndes County. When John Gill Shorter (*q.v.*) resigned his seat in the Provisional Confederate Congress to become governor of Alabama, the General Assembly chose Robinson as his replacement. He took his seat on November 30, 1861, but resigned the following January 24, explaining that his health was poor and that he did not want to risk the hazard of going to Richmond for the next session. In his few days in Congress he revealed nothing of his position on the issues of the day. Robinson is then reputed to have been a member of the staff of General Braxton Bragg for a time. In any event, when the war closed, he was living on his estate, Church Hill, near Benton, Lowndes County, Alabama, where he died July 29, 1867. He may be the same Cornelius Robinson who is buried in Mount Gilead (or Trickem) Cemetery, near Benton, under a marker reading "Captain Cornelius Robinson, Robinson Co., Ala. Inf., Creek War," an inscription which is both truncated and misleading.[1]

[1] Owen's *History of Alabama* is the only source for Robinson's career and is rather obscure in its statements. Nothing can be found to substantiate any information about

Robinson's military career save the inscription on his marker, which refers incorrectly to the Seminole War as the Creek War, and may not even refer to the same man. Nothing can be learned from descendants in the neighborhood.

SAMUEL ST. GEORGE ROGERS (Florida) was born on June 30, 1832, in Pulaski, Tennessee.[1] After an academic education there he moved to Columbus, Georgia, to study law. His health being poor, he soon decided to go even further south[2] and in 1851 opened his first law office in Ocala, Florida. Either he was an astonishingly successful young lawyer or his South Carolina–born wife had considerable wealth, for Florida records of 1855 list him as owning seventy-six slaves and a large plantation near Ocala. The census of 1860 shows him to be worth over ninety thousand dollars. For a few months in 1853 Rogers was solicitor for the eastern circuit of Florida and in 1860 he was elected to the state senate for one term as a Democrat. Rogers also accepted less restrictive assignments. In 1857 he was the colonel in command of ten companies of mounted volunteers operating in south Florida during the protracted Third Seminole War.[3] After Lincoln's election Rogers advocated immediate secession, and when war began he became lieutenant colonel of the second regiment of Florida infantry. In May, 1862, he transferred to the Marion Light Artillery under John M. Martin (*q.v.*). When Martin was wounded at the Battle of Richmond (Kentucky) in August, Rogers succeeded to the command. In October he accepted an appointment in the adjutant general's office. The following April he was assigned to the military court for Beauregard's corps with the rank of colonel. When Martin declined to seek reelection to the Confederate House of Representatives Rogers won the race in October of 1863 to replace him.

In Congress Rogers showed unshakable faith in the army. He supported the War Department's efforts to increase its size and efficiency, and in February of 1865 he proposed that the general officers in charge of reserves be made responsible for executing the conscription laws. He even tried to organize Congress into a company to defend Richmond. As late as February, 1865, Rogers expressed confidence in victory and promised that "we will not hesitate to resort to the use of slaves in our armies."[4] Probably this same confidence in the military permitted Rogers to oppose any interference with the personal or property rights of civilians.

After the War Rogers restored both his practice and his plantation to their former prosperity. In 1868 he stumped the state for the Democratic ticket, but thereafter the conditions of Reconstruction politics kept him in private life. During the 1870s his health grew worse and apparently early in 1880 he made an extended visit with his son in Terre

209

Haute, Indiana, in an effort to find relief. He died there on September 11, 1880, and is buried in the family plot of his daughter-in-law in Crown Hill Cemetery, Indianapolis.[5]

[1] This information was provided by H. T. Wood, Crown Hill Cemetery, Indianapolis, Ind.

[2] This information was partly provided by Elizabeth R. Merrill, Vigo County Public Library, Terre Haute, Ind., and partly taken from Rogers' obituary.

[3] This information was provided by Donald N. Denson, Ocala, Fla.

[4] *Mr. Rogers' Minority Report, House, February 15, 1865.*

[5] This information was provided by Elizabeth R. Merrill and by Rogers' obituary.

GRANDISON DELANEY ROYSTON (Arkansas) was a native of Tennessee, born on December 9, 1809, in Carter County, "of unmixed English blood" according to Hallum's *History of Arkansas*. He attended the Presbyterian Academy in Washington County, Tennessee, and then studied law at Jonesboro, being admitted to the bar in 1831. The following year he moved to Arkansas, first to Fayetteville and then to Washington, at the time a thriving county-seat town on the main road from Little Rock to Texarkana, where he settled permanently. In 1833 Royston was elected prosecuting attorney for one of the three territorial judicial circuits, and in 1836 he represented Hempstead County in the constitutional convention preparatory to admission to the Union that year. He also served on the governor's staff with the rank of brigadier general, was elected speaker of the General Assembly in 1837, and in 1841 was appointed U.S. district attorney by President Tyler. In 1858 he was elected a member of the state senate.

Following Lincoln's election Royston signed a petition asking the General Assembly to demand immediate guarantees for slavery in the territories and to secede if Congress refused. By March, 1861, he was urging immediate withdrawal from the Union. In the November election he won a House seat in the First Regular Confederate Congress from the Second District. Within the first month of his service he had asked Congress to consider only bills related to the war, to give the executive what money he needed, and to adjourn and leave the war to the army. Royston always considered any effort to control money and prices as useless, and he advocated a long exemption list to maintain home-front production. Otherwise, he conceded to the central government any powers that it sought. He stood for reelection in 1863 but refused to campaign and lost to Rufus K. Garland (*q.v.*), who held diametrically opposite views. In 1877 Royston was elected to the state constitutional convention and was chosen its presiding officer. He died in Washington, Arkansas, on August 14, 1889, and was buried there in Presbyterian Cemetery.

THOMAS RUFFIN, [1](North Carolina) was born in Louisburg, in what is now Franklin County (then a part of Edgecombe), North Carolina, September 9, 1820. After attending the local schools, he went to the University of North Carolina in Chapel Hill, from whose law department he was graduated in 1841. The same year he was admitted to the bar and began practice in Goldsboro, North Carolina. Some time later, for reasons not disclosed in his records, Ruffin moved to Missouri, where from 1844 to 1848 he served as circuit attorney of the Seventh Judicial District of that state. He did not return to Goldsboro until 1850. Two years later he was elected as a Democrat to the Thirty-third Congress, and he was reelected in 1854, 1856, and 1858, serving until March 3, 1861.

In May the North Carolina secession convention chose Ruffin as a delegate to the Provisional Congress. Here, while he offered no bill or amendment, he apparently disliked the centralist tendencies developing even this early. He voted to repeal the law of May 11 giving the president emergency use of state militia units, and he even refused to let Davis appoint cadets without the consent of Congress. Ruffin opposed a bill prohibiting the restriction of cotton exports and voted to halve the moderate war tax. He was completely against any aid to railroad construction or extension. It is small wonder that he did not seek election to the Regular Congress, but instead he went into the army as an officer of the First North Carolina Cavalry Regiment. He rose in rank with this command until he became its colonel shortly after the Battle of Gettysburg, when Laurence S. Baker was promoted brigadier general. In one of the cavalry fights leading up to the Battle of Bristoe Station, probably on October 11, 1863, Ruffin was mortally wounded. He died, a prisoner of war, at Alexandria, Virginia, October 13, 1863, and was buried in the private cemetery on the Ruffin homestead near Louisburg.[2]

[1] Ruffin was a distant cousin of Chief Justice Thomas Ruffin of Hillsboro, North Carolina.

[2] The *Biographical Directory of the American Congress* states that Ruffin was "mortally wounded at Bristoe Station, near Alexandria, Virginia," without giving a date. However, the battle of Bristoe Station was fought on October 14, the day after Ruffin died. His regiment of Wade Hampton's Brigade was engaged, however, in a series of actions between the tenth and the thirteenth, with the Federal cavalry, which led up to the infantry fight at Bristoe proper. There were no cavalry engaged on the fourteenth.

CHARLES WELLS RUSSELL (Virginia) was born July 22, 1818, in the Ohio River village of Sistersville, in the northwestern portion of what is now West Virginia. He obtained his primary education in the schools of Tyler County and then studied law at Jefferson College (now Washington and Jefferson) in Washington, Pennsylvania, graduating in the class of 1836. After residence in Martinsburg and Staunton in the Shenandoah Valley, he practiced his profession in Wheeling from 1847 to 1860.

The Virginia convention appointed Russell to the Provisional Congress, and he won election to both regular congresses from a congressional district embracing the counties lying contiguous to the southwest corner of Pennsylvania, which were under Federal control almost from the outset of the war. He was in every respect a refugee congressman. Described as "a pillar of the administration" by a colleague, Russell was one of the most active members, serving on the committees on Naval Affairs and Judiciary. At first dubious of replacing a volunteer army with conscription, he later became its vigorous defender and was among the leaders in restricting exempt classes. Although he had early reservations on the question, he ultimately became a prominent high-tax spokesman and in January, 1864, proposed a 20 percent tax-in-kind on agricultural produce. He was also a consistent supporter of suspension of the writ of habeas corpus at the president's discretion. Only in currency matters did he seriously differ with administration policy, opposing a rigorous funding program and advocating the issuance of other forms of fiat money. He firmly supported arming the slaves and was a last ditch opponent of peace negotiations. Following the war Russell went to Baltimore, where he practiced law until his death on November 22, 1867. He is buried there in Woodlawn Cemetery. His novel *Roebuck* was published posthumously.

ALBERT RUST (Arkansas) was born in Virginia, probably in Fauquier County, about 1818—the exact date is unknown to his descendants.[1] Nothing seems to be known about his early education; however, in 1837 he emigrated to the newly admitted state of Arkansas with a government contract to survey land. He settled in Union County, where he laid out the townsite of El Dorado, which was to be his home for a number of years. There he studied law and was admitted to the bar. Rust was a member of the Arkansas General Assembly from 1842 to 1848 and again from 1852 to 1854. In 1854 he was elected to Congress as a Democrat; he was defeated for reelection two years later, but in 1858 he was again elected and served until March 3, 1861.

Rust was a strong Union man, but when Arkansas seceded he accepted a seat in the Provisional Confederate Congress. Shortly afterwards he was instrumental in recruiting the Third Arkansas Infantry and was appointed its colonel. He preferred service in the field and made infrequent appearances in the halls of congress, attending on only about a dozen occasions; he did not seek election to the Regular Congress. At the head of his regiment, he took part in the Cheat Mountain campaign in western Virginia in the autumn of 1861. He served under Stonewall Jackson the following winter and was appointed brigadier general to rank from March 4, 1862. After participating in the Battle of Corinth in Mansfield Lovell's division, he served in the Trans-Mississippi until the close of the war under Generals Hindman and Richard Taylor. In 1858 Rust had moved from El Dorado to a farm he owned on the north side of the Arkansas River near Little Rock. He died there on April 4, 1870 (contrary to his sketch in the *Biographical Directory of the American Congress*, which records his place of death and burial as El Dorado). He was buried in an unmarked grave in Mount Holly Cemetery, Little Rock, according to a contemporary local newspaper.[2]

[1] Georgia Breckinridge Rust Busick (Rust's granddaughter) to John W. Rust, September 30, 1954 (letter in the possession of Mrs. Ezra J. Warner).
[2] Little Rock *Arkansas Gazette*, April 6, 7, 1870. The late Mrs. C. S. Woodward of Little Rock, who served twenty-one years as treasurer of Mount Holly Cemetery Association, was also the authority for the fact that General Rust was buried there, but his grave cannot be found. (Mrs. C. S. Woodward to Ezra J. Warner, October 31, 1952.)

JOHN PEASE SANDERSON (Florida) was one of only four members of the Confederate Congress to be born north of the Mason and Dixon line. He was born November 28, 1816, in Sunderland, Vermont, a hamlet in Bennington County. He prepared for college in Bennington and was graduated from Amherst in the class of 1839, after which he studied law in Arlington, Vermont, for three years. At this point the twenty-six-year-old Vermont Yankee removed to Fernandina, Florida, where he practiced his profession and married into a southern family long established on Amelia Island. Subsequently he moved to Lake City, and finally to Jacksonville, meanwhile accumulating a fortune in land and slaves.[1]

At the same time Sanderson became prominent politically, serving in the Florida House of Representatives in 1843, in the state senate in 1848, and for five years as solicitor of the Eastern Circuit of Florida. In 1852 he was a presidential elector for Franklin Pierce. He also became interested in railroad development in Florida and was an officer of two early-day railroads which later became part of the Southern Railway System. By 1860, despite his northern birth and upbringing, Sanderson had become wholly converted to the southern cause, and the following year, as a member of the Florida secession convention, he voted for and signed the ordinance which took the state out of the Union.

213

When George T. Ward (*q.v.*) resigned his seat in the Provisional Congress, Sanderson was appointed as his replacement[2] and took his seat on February 5, 1862. His thirteen-day tenure is notable primarily for the consistency with which he supported bills to construct connecting railroad lines, readily understandable when it is considered that he was president of the Fernandina, Amelia, and Gulf Coast Railroad and vice-president of the Jacksonville, Pensacola, and Mobile. Since his successor had already been elected, Sanderson had no opportunity to succeed himself in the First Regular Congress. He continued to practice law in Jacksonville until his death. He died in New York City on June 28, 1871, while on a business trip. He was buried in his wife's family cemetery on Amelia Island.[3]

[1] The 1860 census of Duval County records his ownership of eighty-two Negroes and an estate of eighty thousand dollars.

[2] A resolution of the Florida convention provided that vacancies in the Provisional Congress should be filled by the convention's president when the convention was not in session. (*Journal of the Florida Convention*, 123.)

[3] Most of the biographical data on Sanderson derives from the *Biographical Record* of Amherst College, courtesy of archivist J. Richard Phillips, which gives his middle name as Pease. Other sources give "Philip." Once one of its leading citizens, Sanderson is almost unknown in Jacksonville today.

ROBERT EDEN SCOTT (Virginia) was born in Warrenton, Fauquier County, Virginia, on April 23, 1808. After obtaining the rudiments of an education in the local schools, he attended the University of Virginia, graduating in law there. He then practiced in Fauquier and surrounding counties. He was a member of the House of Delegates from 1835 until 1842, and again from 1845 until 1852, and he was a member of the constitutional convention of 1850–1851. Scott was a lifelong Whig and an opponent of secession, but as one of Fauquier's two delegates to the Virginia convention of 1861, having voted against secession on April 4, he voted for it on the seventeenth. Meanwhile, according to family tradition, Lincoln sent William H. Seward to Oakwood, Scott's estate near Warrenton, to offer him the secretaryship of the navy. In any event he was elected in June to the Provisional Confederate Congress, where he adopted a strong states' rights posture, opposing even the modest tax program before Congress at the time. Otherwise he favored implementing the government for both peace and war; opposed free trade; and advocated withholding cotton from Europe and granting the president emergency powers in such matters as officer appointment, border state recruitment, and railroad construction. He announced his candidacy for the Regular Congress, but was defeated by former governor William Smith (*q.v.*). By the time he returned home, his district in northern Virginia had been overrun by the enemy and continued to be the scene of both legitimate military operations and guerrilla warfare until the end of the war. Scott, who had equipped a company of infantry for the Confederate army (of which his son was captain), was active in the home guard and on May 3, 1862, set forth with a party of local civilians to capture a band of Union deserters who had been robbing and otherwise molesting citizens in the area. As they approached a house owned by one B. F. Smith, one of the deserters fired, killing Scott almost instantly. He is buried with his parents and other relatives in the graveyard at Oakwood. His headstone notes that he was "Killed by a Yankee deserter" and bears a quotation from *Julius Caesar*, but it makes no mention of his service in the Confederate Congress.[1]

[1] Family data on Scott was provided by John A. C. Keith of Warrenton, Va., a descendant of Robert E. Scott; Mrs. Richard M. Cutts, The Plains, Va.; Mrs. Robert K. Neilson, Warrenton; and Lemuel C. Shepherd, La Jolla, Calif.

JAMES ALEXANDER SEDDON (Virginia), who is best remembered as the Confederate secretary of war, was born July 13, 1815, in Fredericksburg, Virginia. He obtained all his education from private tutors prior to attending the University of Virginia Law School, from which he was graduated in 1835. He then practiced in Richmond and served two terms in Congress, 1845–1847 and 1849–1851, declining renomination in 1846 and 1850. After his second term he retired to his estate, Sabot Hill, in Goochland County, to live the life of a country squire.

In 1861 Seddon was a member of the unsuccessful Washington Peace Conference and in April of that year, after the secession of his state, he was nominated to the Provisional Congress by the Virginia convention, losing to William C. Rives (*q.v.*) by one vote. He was, however, successful in being appointed in June. During his congressional career Seddon was in the main an enthusiastic Davis supporter, deviating from the administration line only in his support of low taxes and tax exemptions. In the autumn of 1861 he announced that he would not run for election to the Regular Congress, but upon the resignation of Roger Pryor (*q.v.*) from that body in April, 1862, Seddon became a candidate for the vacancy, running third in a three-man race. He was thus a two-time loser at the polls, but when Secretary of War George W. Randolph (a grandson of Thomas Jefferson) resigned in November, Jefferson Davis, with the instinctive combativeness which characterized many of his executive decisions, and seeking a supporter of unquestioning loyalty, "prevailed upon (him) to assume the important and difficult post."[1] It is too much to say that another choice would have

215

won independence for the Confederacy; it is hardly too much to say that the secretary's wholehearted deference to the president's wishes and prejudices certainly did little to prolong its existence. Aside from questions of strategy, on which his counsel was seldom sought, his principal effect was a vast capacity for indecision, a shortcoming possibly attributable to lifelong poor health—his chief clerk observed that he resembled "an exhumed corpse after a month's interment."[2]

The nadir of Seddon's career in public estimation came in July, 1864, when he acquiesced in the president's decision to remove General Joseph E. Johnston from the command of the Army of Tennessee in front of Atlanta. When the Virginia delegation to the Confederate Congress formally demanded cabinet reorganization in January, 1865, Seddon resigned. Davis at the same time denounced Congress for what he deemed unconstitutional interference with his prerogatives and praised his secretary of war. Seddon was imprisoned for a short time at the end of hostilities, and then lived in retirement at Sabot Hill until his death on August 19, 1880. He is buried in Hollywood Cemetery, Richmond.

[1] *DAB*, XVI, 546.
[2] John B. Jones, *A Rebel War Clerk's Diary at the Confederate States Capital*, ed. Howard Swiggett (2 vols.; New York, 1935), I, 380.

THOMAS JENKINS SEMMES (Louisiana), a first cousin of the celebrated Confederate raider Admiral Raphael Semmes, was born in Georgetown, D.C., on December 16, 1824. His early education was obtained wholly in Georgetown, where he graduated from Georgetown College in 1842. He then attended the Harvard Law School, from which he received a degree in 1845. After practicing in Washington Semmes moved in 1850 to New Orleans, where he soon attained prominence and political recognition. He served a term in the legislature and then, by virtue of appointment by President Buchanan as United States District Attorney, was called upon to prosecute the filibusterer, William Walker, for violation of the neutrality laws in connection with the Nicaragua expedition.

In 1861 Semmes was attorney general of Louisiana and a member of the secession convention, and he helped frame the ordinance which took the state out of the Union. Although he was not sent to the Provisional Congress, he served as one of Louisiana's two senators from November, 1861, until the Confederacy ceased to function. He displayed one of the most balanced attitudes of any member of Congress. He preferred excise taxes, but when hunger faced the army late in 1864 he proposed to double the tithe on agricultural products. He supported all draft laws but opposed suspending the writ of habeas corpus, at the same time consenting to the suspension when the need was obvious. He even publicly stated that the government might be forced to seize all private property in order to sustain itself. When a movement developed in the Senate to dictate military appointments to the president, Semmes sprang to Davis' defense with a denunciation of the competence of Joseph Eggleston Johnston. And he would arm and free the slaves to save "part of the cargo." In short, Semmes was essentially a master pragmatist, and in his postbellum career he was even more distinguished in this capacity than he had been heretofore. He appeared as counsel in virtually every prominent civil case in the Louisiana courts; dominated the Louisiana constitutional convention of 1879; taught Civil Law in what is now Tulane University Law School until his death; was for many years president of the New Orleans school board; and in 1886, in an unprecedented accolade, was elected president of the American Bar Association. He died at his home in New Orleans on June 23, 1899, and was buried in Metairie Cemetery.

FRANKLIN BARLOW SEXTON (Texas) was born April 29, 1828, in New Harmony, Indiana, on the banks of the Wabash, but at the age of three he was brought to San Augustine, Texas, by his parents. There he grew up and attended Wesleyan College, graduating in 1846. Two years later, at the age of twenty, he was admitted to the practice of law by special enactment of the legislature. By 1860 he was president of the state Democratic convention; and in November, 1861, he was elected to the First Regular Confederate Congress and reelected in 1863, serving until the close of the war. Sexton highly esteemed President Davis but could not entirely overcome the suspicion entertained by most western congressmen that the Trans-Mississippi was merely "a field from which to draw beef and common soliders." He favored only direct taxation and abhorred the tax in kind on agricultural products. He objected to the army taking slaves from the fields for any purpose, and he opposed permitting the War Department to take local reserve troops outside their respective states.

On the other hand, the administration had few better friends when there appeared to be no discrimination against Texas. Sexton was a leading proponent of conscription and of leaving military strategy to the generals. He also incidentally won the admiration of the Texas press with his concern for the common soldier and for the improvement of the mail service. In 1876 Sexton was a delegate to the Democratic national convention and as such seconded the nomination of Samuel J. Tilden. A prominent Mason for many years, in 1870 he became Grand

Commander of the Knights Templar of Texas. Two years later he moved to Marshall and—upon the death of his wife—to El Paso, where he lived with a daughter and acted as United States Commissioner until his last illness. Judge Sexton died in El Paso on May 15, 1900, and was buried in Marshall.

JOHN TROUP SHEWMAKE [1] (Georgia) was born on January 23, 1828,[2] at the old family plantation in Burke County, Georgia. He studied at home until the age of eighteeen, then entered Princeton College in New Jersey. After a year there, he studied law for another year in Augusta under Judge William T. Gould and was admitted to the bar in 1848. Shewmake quickly established a successful practice in Waynesboro, but he soon moved to Augusta for wider opportunities. Through most of his life he also operated a small plantation midway between Augusta and Waynesboro. Shewmake's first legislative experience occurred in 1861, when he was elected to the Georgia senate for one term.[3] In October, 1863, he won a seat in the Confederate House of Representatives by a small plurality.

As Shewmake represented a district which was constantly threatened and eventually occupied by Union forces, he lent unflinching support to the army. But he obviously considered the government's demands upon the economy of his highly productive district excessive. He adamantly opposed any kind of fiscal experiment or reform, and by means of resolutions requesting committee inquiries he sought various concessions to agriculturalists. On January 25, 1865, Shewmake proposed that the army unequivocally pay market prices for all goods impressed. Three days later he took a leave of Congress and never returned.

After the war, Shewmake resumed his law practice in Augusta, but ill health forced him to retire in 1866. In 1874 he was elected president of the Augusta board of education, a post which he held for five years. In 1879 he was elected to the Georgia senate, but he declined reelection after serving for two terms. He died in Augusta on December 1, 1898, and is buried there in Magnolia Cemetery.

[1] *Memoirs of Georgia* (2 vols.; Atlanta, 1895), II, 808–809.
[2] This is the date inscribed on Shewmake's gravestone. *Memoirs of Georgia* gives the date of his birth as January 22, 1826. The records of the cemetery in which he is buried state that he died of senility at the age of seventy-two, which would make the year of his birth 1826. The census records also give the year of his birth as 1826. There seems to be no definitive record of his birth date.
[3] There is no evidence of Shewmake's politics, but his strong support of H. V. Johnson over Toombs in the Georgia senatorial race of 1862 might indicate that he had been conservative on the issue of secession.

JOHN GILL SHORTER (Alabama) was born on April 23, 1818, in Monticello, Georgia. He graduated from Franklin College (now the University of Georgia) in 1837 and immediately removed to Eufaula, Alabama, where he studied law and was admitted to the bar in 1838. From
1842 until 1845 he was solicitor of his district, being elected to the state
senate in 1845. In 1851 he was elected to the lower house of the legislature, but he gave up his seat to accept an appointment to the circuit
court and in 1852 and 1858 was elected without opposition.

Shorter was a strong secessionist and resigned his judicial post to
accept an appointment as Alabama's commissioner to the Georgia
secession convention. The same month he was elected by the Alabama
secession convention as a delegate to the Provisional Confederate
Congress, where he was named chairman of the Committee on Engrossment. Outside of seeing that certain routine procedures of government were undertaken, he took the initiative in policy-making only
in having Congress acknowledge each state's title to all public land
within its borders. Shorter was an unwavering supporter of President
Davis, differing only in his nonacceptance of the need for taxation until
the third session of Congress. He was elected governor of Alabama in
August, 1861, and resigned his congressional seat.

As governor, Shorter first enjoyed almost unlimited approval while
he strove to bolster the defenses of Mobile, to raise and equip troops,
and to place the state on a war footing. But as the war wore on, the best
men were in the army, and those who were left increasingly resisted the
sacrifices they were called upon to make. In addition to this, Shorter
was staunchly proadministration; he supported conscription and the
collection of the tax in kind, and the central government's increasing
unpopularity affected him directly. When he ran for reelection in 1863,
he was defeated by more than three to one. Upon this defeat, he returned to Eufaula, resumed his law practice, and took no further part in
political life, either during the war or in the Reconstruction period
which followed. He died in Eufaula on May 29, 1872, and was buried in
a family cemetery there.[1]

[1] Information on Shorter's place of burial was provided by the Eufaula Heritage
Association.

WILLIAM ELLIOTT SIMMS (Kentucky)[1] was born near Cynthiana, Kentucky, January 2, 1822, but moved to Bourbon County with his parents
at the age of six. After obtaining a meager education in the local
schools, he commenced reading law in Lexington, later graduating
from the law department of Transylvania University. Soon after he

commenced practice in Paris, the county seat of Bourbon, the Mexican War broke out and Simms raised a company of the Third Kentucky Infantry with which he served under Winfield Scott. In 1849 he went to the Kentucky House of Representatives as a Democrat for one term.

During the ensuing decade Simms practiced law, edited a political news organ, the *Kentucky State Flag*, and in 1858 was elected to Congress. Here he was violently partisan in his feelings and utterances, bitterly assailing the Republicans for virtually every sin common to mankind including the tariff. His southern sympathies were so pronounced that in the special election of June, 1861, he was defeated for reelection by the moderate John J. Crittenden. In September, 1861, Simms served under Humphrey Marshall (*q.v.*) in the Kentucky–West Virginia operations as a colonel, and on November 21 he was appointed one of the commissioners to the Confederacy by the secessionist government of Kentucky. He was then appointed to the Confederate Senate and served for the duration in that body.

Simms was no less outspoken in Richmond than he had been in Washington, hotly accusing Yancey (*q.v.*) of Alabama of posing as the spokesman for states' rights while refusing to recognize the need for total war. In the matter of exemptions he would only excuse state governors and high court judges; he would let the army impress anything so long as market prices were paid; in the spring of 1864 he had the Committee on Finance consider taking over all cotton, tobacco, and naval stores for sale abroad. At first he sustained the president in his capacity of commander-in-chief almost to the letter. In 1862, in fact, he asked the senate to insist that Davis take the field in person. By 1865, however, Simms was so discouraged with the progress of the war that he joined the combination trying to totally reshape the nation's high army command. With the collapse of the Confederacy Simms fled to Canada, not returning to Kentucky until 1866. It would be thirty years before his political disabilities would be totally removed; meantime, he gave over politics for agriculture at his estate, Mount Airy, near Paris. Here he became one of the most affluent men in Bourbon County, and here he died on June 25, 1898. He was buried in Paris Cemetery.

[1] Simms's middle name is given by the *Biographical Directory of the American Congress* as *Emmett*. However, *DAB*, XVII, 171n states that an entry in the Simms family Bible in the holograph of Simms's father records it as *Elliott*.

WILLIAM DUNLAP SIMPSON [1] (South Carolina) was born at Belfast in Laurens District, South Carolina, on October 27, 1823. After studying at Laurens Academy, he graduated from South Carolina College in 1843, the youngest member of his class. He then entered Harvard Law

School, but the climate was too rigorous for him and he returned home after one session to read law. Simpson began practicing in Laurens Court House in 1846, and was for several terms a Democratic member of the General Assembly. During the 1850s he also acquired and operated a small plantation. A strong secessionist, Simpson became an aide to General M. L. Bonham (*q.v.*) and was present at the siege of Fort Sumter. He next became lieutenant colonel of the Fourteenth South Carolina Volunteers and fought in important battles from First Manassas to Antietam. He was wounded at Germantown, and at Cold Harbor the bow of his cravat was shot away. When Bonham resigned his seat in the Confederate Congress, Simpson was elected to the position without his knowledge. He took his seat on February 5, 1863, and that October was reelected without opposition.

In the House of Representatives, Simpson was particularly interested in army matters, but he weighed all his votes most judiciously. Generally he attempted to limit the central government only when bills under discussion threatened to reach arbitrary levels. For instance, he favored reducing the exemption list to a hard core but proposed that the states be permitted to exempt whom they wished; he accepted the forced funding of Treasury notes but disliked repudiating completely those unfunded; he accepted a surprising degree of state socialism but balked at drafting speculators and impressing railroad stock. Whenever logic so dictated, Simpson did not hesitate to give the president a free hand or to vest him with broad powers. He was an outright conservative only in regard to habeas corpus suspension.

After the war, Simpson rebuilt his law practice in Laurens and remained in politics. He was a delegate to the national Democratic convention in 1868 and was also elected to Congress. He was denied his seat, however, as being disqualified under the Fourteenth Amendment. In 1876 Simpson was chosen lieutenant-governor on Wade Hampton's ticket. The Republican majority in the Senate sought to prevent him from presiding over that body on a technicality, but he held his ground and soon engineered a Democratic majority in the Senate. He was reelected in 1878 and became governor when Hampton swapped that position for the United States Senate. Simpson resigned two months before his term ended to become state chief justice. His chief contribution here was the clarification of many points of judicial procedure. He was also instrumental in developing South Carolina College into a university. Simpson died in Columbia on December 26, 1890, and is buried in the Laurens Cemetery.

[1] Emily B. Reynolds and Joan R. Faunt (comps.), *Biographical Directory of the Senate of the State of South Carolina, 1776–1964* (Columbia, S.C., 1964), 308.

OTHO ROBARDS SINGLETON (Mississippi), a representative in both the United States and Confederate congresses from Mississippi, was born in Jessamine County, Kentucky, on October 14, 1814. After a primary education obtained in the common schools, he was graduated from St. Joseph's College at Bardstown, and the law department of Transylvania University at Lexington, Kentucky. After admission to the bar, he moved to Canton, Mississippi, in 1838 and commenced practice there.

Singleton's virtually lifelong political career began with election to the Mississippi House of Representatives in 1846. He was a state senator for three terms after 1848, a presidential elector for Franklin Pierce in 1852, and in the same year he was elected to the first of nine nonconsecutive terms in the Congress of the United States, both ante- and postbellum. With an interregnum of two years, 1855–1857, he served until the withdrawal of the Mississippi delegation in January, 1861. At this point he enlisted as a private in the Confederate army, but while still in service he published a card announcing his candidacy for the First Regular Congress, to which he was easily elected over Josiah A. P. Campbell (*q.v.*). He won reelection in 1863 but attended the Second Congress only briefly, requesting several successive leaves of absence after June 14, 1864, for what reason we do not know, since he was the perfect prototype of the administration standard-bearer.

Singleton chaired the Committee on Indian Affairs, a post more important than it now seems, and until the end of his service retained implicit faith in the president and his cabinet. He consistently voted to limit debate and to adjourn early, and he once argued that if a state withheld munitions from the central government, they should be taken by force. His only significant foray into policy-making was in the fight to end the hiring of substitutes for army service. He continued to live in Canton after the collapse of the Confederacy and took part in redeeming the state from the Carpetbag regime. He served again in Congress from 1875 to 1887, and was not a candidate for reelection in 1886. Singleton died in Washington on January 11, 1889, and was buried in Canton Cemetery in his hometown.

JAMES MILTON SMITH[1] (Georgia) was born on his father's plantation in Twiggs County, Georgia, on October 24, 1823. His parents compelled their children to learn every aspect of farm life and "Milt" became one of the best blacksmiths in the community. In later life he liked to show that he had retained this skill. After attending the local schools, Smith studied at Culloden High School in Monroe County and then read law at home. He was admitted to the bar in 1846 and opened his first office in

Columbus. In 1855 Smith was an unsuccessful candidate for Congress as an independent states' rights Democrat. He was a Unionist during the winter of 1860–1861, but when war came he was mustered into service as a major in the Thirteenth Georgia Infantry. As a result of his valor in action around Richmond, Virginia, Smith was promoted to colonel. He was wounded at Cold Harbor and returned home to be elected in 1863 by an overwhelming majority as a representative to the Confederate Congress.

In Congress Smith was convinced that war legislation had reached its limits. He generally refused to extend existing programs or to attempt such experiments as arming the slaves or impressing specie. Instead, Smith placed sole reliance on the existing army. He supported the search for better commanding generals, opposed new exemptions from military service, and worked to reorganize depleted army units into more effective ones. His only significant bill, however, indicates that by February, 1865, he was resigned to last-ditch local defense. In the bill, Smith advocated the discharge of all men over forty-five and a change from conscription to requisitions on the governors. By this time he had also become a strong peace advocate.

After the war, Smith resumed his practice in Columbus. In one of his most famous cases he, A. H. Stephens, and L. J. Gartrell (*q.v.*) successfully defended the "Columbus prisoners," a group of young men accused of murdering a leading white Republican who had fraternized with Negroes. In 1870 Smith was elected to the legislature and from that podium he denounced Reconstruction so boldly that he was elected Speaker of the House. When Governor Bullock fled the state Smith was elected by the legislature in December, 1871, to complete the term. In 1872 he was elected governor for a four-year term. Smith's governorship is notable for the creation of the state geological survey, a department of agriculture, and a state railroad commission. In 1877 he was an unsuccessful candidate for the United States Senate. Smith was chairman of the Georgia Railroad Commission from 1879 to 1885 and judge of the superior court from 1888 until his death in Columbus on November 26, 1890. He is buried in Alta Vista Cemetery in Gainesville.[2]

[1] Northen (ed.), *Men of Mark in Georgia*, III, 478–82.
[2] Information on Smith's interment was provided by Jeanne Hollis, Bradley Memorial Library, Columbus, Ga.

ROBERT HARDY SMITH (Alabama) was born in Camden County, North Carolina, on March 21, 1813, the grandson of a native of London, England. He received an appointment to West Point in the class of

1835, but did not graduate, and seems to have had difficulty in deciding on a profession—he taught school for a while in various counties of Virginia and Alabama, studied medicine, and finally decided to become a lawyer. The year he would have graduated from West Point he was admitted to the bar and hung out his shingle in Livingston, Alabama, where he had previously taught school.

A lifelong Whig, Smith supported Harrison in 1840 and Clay in 1844 and in 1849 was the only member of his party to be elected to the legislature from Sumter County. In 1851 Smith lost a race for the state senate to a states' rights Democrat by but one vote. In 1853 he moved to Mobile, and until the beginning of the Civil War he was untiring in his efforts to oppose the growing secession sentiment in Alabama, supporting the ticket of Bell and Everett in 1860. But like many others when the die was cast, he loyally supported Alabama's decision and in January, 1861, accepted a seat in the Provisional Confederate Congress as a delegate-at-large. He proved himself to be an industrious member and did much of the detail work in writing the early statutes. He was also the strongest nationalist of the Alabama delegation, suggesting in February several constitutional ideas too centralist for his more moderate colleagues. It was also his suggestion that the term of the provisional government be limited to one year. After Fort Sumter, Smith proposed to let the president accept independent volunteers, and he generally conceded Davis wide latitude in raising troops. Almost his sole stand against the administration program was his rejection of the produce loan, which he felt would be unfair to planters. He refused to seek reelection and instead organized the Thirty-sixth Alabama Infantry, of which he was elected colonel. Smith soon had to resign this position because of poor health; thereafter he practiced law in Mobile until his death, taking no part in the politics of the Reconstruction era. Colonel Smith died in Mobile on March 13, 1878, and was buried in Magnolia Cemetery.

WILLIAM SMITH (Virginia) was born at Marengo in King George County, Virginia, on September 6, 1797. After attending academies in Plainfield, Connecticut, and Hanover County, Virginia, he read law first in Warrenton and then in Baltimore; in 1818 he began practicing in Culpeper.[1] In 1827 Smith began a mail-coach service, and by 1834 he was operating a daily post from Washington, D.C., to Milledgeville, Georgia. From the rapid expansion of this route and the resulting mail payments Smith derived the sobriquet "Extra Billy," which followed him the rest of his life. Between 1836 and 1861 he served as a Democrat for five years in the state senate and for five terms in Congress. He was governor from 1846 to 1849 and saw to it that Virginia participated vigorously in the Mexican War. Smith moved to California in 1849 and would have become its first United States senator had that not entailed giving up his Virginia citizenship. When he returned to Virginia in 1852 he settled in Warrenton. He was in Congress during the secession crisis and worked for compromise until Lincoln's call for troops. When war began Smith became colonel of the Forty-ninth Virginia Infantry and took part in the Battle of First Manassas. In November, 1861, he was elected to the Confederate House of Representatives over the incumbent R. E. Scott (*q.v.*).

In the First Congress Smith was chairman of the Committee on Claims, but he attended for only a total of six months and even then answered few roll calls. When McClellan began his Peninsular Campaign, Smith left Congress for the rest of the year, taking part in several major engagements and being wounded five times. As a congressman he spoke mainly when army affairs were under discussion, and he favored "any bill increasing the army in any way." He also continued the prohibitionist work in which he was always involved by trying to ban all intoxicants from the army. While the evidence is not clear, Smith seemed willing to grant the central government almost anything it needed to prosecute the war.

At the insistence of his old regiment Smith resigned his seat on April 4, 1863, to accept an appointment as brigadier general. He took part in Lee's invasion of Pennsylvania and was promoted to major general on August 12, 1863, but was again elected governor and took office on January 1, 1864, When Richmond was evacuated Smith moved the state government to Danville and did not surrender it until May 9. He spent the remainder of his life farming his small estate, Monterose, near Warrenton. In 1877 he was elected to one term in the Virginia House of Delegates and the next year he came within a few votes of being elected to the United States Senate. He died at home on May 18, 1887, and is buried in Hollywood Cemetery in Richmond.

[1] John W. Bell, *Memoirs of Governor William Smith of Virginia* (New York, 1891), 5, 6.

WILLIAM EPHRAIM SMITH (Georgia) was born in Augusta, Georgia, on March 14, 1829. He was small for his age and after a Frenchman once addressed him as "mon petit" Smith was nicknamed "Tete" for life. After an academic education he read law and was admitted to the bar in 1846 by special act of the legislature. He began practicing in Albany and later acquired a small plantation. Smith served as ordinary of Daugherty County from 1854 to 1858 and then was solicitor of the southwest circuit for two years. He opposed secession, but when war began he entered as first lieutenant of Company E in the Fourth Georgia Volunteer Infantry. He was elected captain in April, 1862. Smith lost his right leg at the Battle of Oak Grove near Richmond, Virginia, on June 25, 1862, and returned home to win a place during the fall of 1863 in the Confederate Congress, defeating the incumbent C. J. Munnerlyn (*q.v.*).

In Congress Smith gave most of his constructive attention to army matters. On May 27, 1864, he instructed the Committee on Military Affairs to consider placing all able-bodied men in the army and detailing all others to civilian duties. He later agreed to arm the slaves. In organizational matters Smith proposed to reassign men in depleted regiments and supported other efforts to improve the use of the thinning ranks. He was far less cooperative on other matters, though his concern was for personal rather than state's rights. He was unusually critical of economic programs, and his chief effort here was to abolish discrimination in the tax and impressment laws.

After the war Smith resumed his old life in Albany. It was during the Reconstruction days that he became known as the lawyer of widows and orphans. In 1874 he declined an appointment as circuit judge of Georgia, but the next year he was elected as a Democrat to the United States House of Representatives. In 1876 he was the only Georgian to vote against establishing an electoral commission to settle the Hayes-Tilden presidential dispute. After two terms he declined to be a candidate for renomination. In 1886 Smith was president of the state Democratic convention, and his last public office was a term in the Georgia senate from 1886 to 1888. He died in Albany on March 11, 1890, and is buried in Oakview Cemetery.

WILLIAM NATHAN HARRELL SMITH (North Carolina), the only North Carolina member of all three Confederate congresses, was born at Murfreesboro, North Carolina, on September 24, 1812. His father was a native of Connecticut and a Yale graduate, and the younger Smith, after a preparatory school education received in New England, was himself graduated from Yale in the class of 1834. He also took his law studies there. Smith began his practice in Murfreesboro and became an active member of the Whig Party. He went to the North Carolina legislature in 1840 and in 1848 was a member of the senate. From 1849 until 1857 he was solicitor of his district. In that year he was nominated for Congress as a Know-Nothing, although he repudiated much of the so-called "American" doctrine. He was defeated, but two years later, after again serving in the legislature, he was elected as a

Democrat to the Thirty-sixth Congress, serving until March 3, 1861.

In the long contest for the speakership which marked the organization of the House in 1859, Smith was actually elected by a single vote, only to be subsequently defeated by a change of heart on the part of certain members of the Pennsylvania delegation. In the secession crisis he was heart and soul for the Union, laboring unceasingly for some sort of an accommodation between the two sections, but Lincoln's call for volunteers to put down rebellion threw him into the arms of his former political opponents. After secession became a *fait accompli*, the former Unionists in the convention secured Smith's election to the Provisional Congress. He won reelection twice with but token opposition, the sole representative from the Tarheel State to do so. In the First and Second Regular congresses he chaired the Committee on Elections, and in the Second Congress he chaired the Committee on Claims. Positive, articulate, and aggressive, Smith was by all odds North Carolina's most effective representative. His talent for detail and precise phraseology involved him in a wide range of subjects, although the economy was his chief concern. He was also regarded as one of the half-dozen most effective guardians of local interests. He conceded the central government broad control over volunteers and the full right to regulate commerce and transportation, but beyond this his latitude ended. His votes and his scores of proposals generally sought to reduce the impact of legislation on states and individuals. He was particularly eager to keep skilled labor out of the army and to provide for the quick settlement of claims against the Confederacy.

When the war ended, Smith was again elected to the North Carolina legislature, supported President Johnson's plan of Reconstruction, and was a leader in organizing the Conservative party to oppose Radical control of the state. In 1870 he made his home in Norfolk, but two years later he moved to Raleigh, and in 1878 he became chief justice of the North Carolina Supreme Court, an ofce which he held until his death. Judge Smith died in Raleigh on November 14, 1889, and was buried in Oakwood Cemetery.

WILLIAM RUSSELL SMITH (Alabama) was born in Russellville, Kentucky, on March 27, 1815. His father soon died and in 1820 the family settled in Tuscaloosa, Alabama. He was orphaned in 1823 and lived with his brother-in-law until he reached maturity. After an academic education Smith entered the University of Alabama in 1831, but he left after three years for financial reasons. He then read law for a year and began practicing in Greensboro in 1835.

For the rest of his life Smith pursued a varied career. In 1836 he raised a company to help quell an Indian uprising, but it was over before they arrived. The company next decided to aid the Texan revolution, but had only reached Mobile when that, too, was over. For six months Smith published a monthly paper in Mobile; he then edited the *Monitor*, a Whig newspaper in Tuscaloosa. He was elected to the legislature in 1841 and 1842, though he opposed much of the Whig program and left the party in 1843. Smith next moved to Fayette, where in 1850 he was elected circuit judge. After one year he was elected to Congress, this time in the American party. In Congress he became known as "the Kossuth-Killer" for his opposition to American entanglement in Central European affairs. Smith was a vice-presidential possibility in 1856, but he lost both the nomination and his place in Congress. In 1860 he supported the Bell-Everett ticket and later was styled the most consistent opponent of secession in the Alabama convention of 1861. Once the Confederacy was formed Smith recruited and became colonel of the Twenty-sixth Alabama Regiment. Before he saw combat he was elected to the Confederate Congress and won reelection in 1863.

In Congress Smith found himself completely at odds with the course of legislation. He refused to bend the Constitution on such controversial issues as conscription, the habeas corpus, and executive appointments. On clearly constitutional matters like taxation, regulation of commerce, and foreign affairs he voted as if an emergency did not exist. Smith himself proposed free trade and a ban on hiring slaves for army labor. He attended the Second Congress irregularly and left for good in February, 1865, when the House refused to receive a resolution condemning the Richmond *Sentinel*'s editorial "Treason! Treason! Treason!" on peace agitation.

After the war, Smith was a candidate for governor in 1865 and ran twice for Congress, but he lost each race. In 1870 he was elected president of the University of Alabama by the Radical board of trustees, but few students enrolled and he resigned after a year. He practiced law in Tuscaloosa until 1879 and then moved to Washington, D.C., where he continued his practice. Since 1833 Smith had published volumes of poetry, plays, essays, legal studies, and Alabama Supreme Court *Reports*; in 1889 he published his *Reminiscences*. In the census of 1860 he was the only Confederate congressman to list "writer" as one of his occupations. He died in Washington on February 26, 1896, and was interred in Tuscaloosa; he was later reinterred in Mount Olivet Cemetery in Washington, D.C.

THOMAS LOWNDES SNEAD (Missouri), a native of Virginia, was born in Henrico County on January 10, 1828. After attending Richmond College, he studied law at the University of Virginia and was admitted to the bar in 1850, but shortly thereafter he moved to St. Louis to practice. Snead successfully combined the practice of law with a newspaper career, and in 1860–1861 he was on the staff of the St. Louis *Bulletin*. In the same year he became aide-de-camp and secretary to Governor Claiborne F. Jackson. As acting adjutant general, with the rank of colonel, of the Missouri State Guard, he took part in the battles of Booneville, Carthage, Wilson's Creek, and Lexington—which, although they were tactical southern victories, nevertheless won Missouri to the Union cause.

After transferring from state to Confederate service, Snead served as chief of staff to General Sterling Price, with the rank of major. In May, 1864, he won an easy victory to succeed the late William Mordecai Cooke (*q.v.*) as representative from the First Congressional District and resigned his army commission. In Congress, despite the statement in the *Dictionary of American Biography*, which paints him as a "faithful supporter of Jefferson Davis," Snead in fact entertained a deep distrust of Davis' administrative ability which compelled him to limit the chief executive's jurisdiction wherever possible. He refused to share Congress' right to decide who should work and who should fight; he voted several times to advise the president what commanding generals to appoint; and he zealously guarded for the states control of their few remaining local defense units. The sole proposal which he initiated was to see that the army consolidation bill under discussion in January, 1865, was as free as possible of executive discretion. On other matters Snead strongly supported the emergency legislation of the Second Congress.

During the Reconstruction era, former Confederate attorneys were virtually put in a straitjacket by the repressive Missouri test oath; Snead accordingly made his home in New York City. Here he became managing editor of the New York *Daily News* and in 1866 was admitted to the New York state bar, after which he devoted his time to the law and to writing. He envisioned a complete history of the war in the Trans-Mississippi, of which the first volume, *The Fight for Missouri*, was published in 1886. He also wrote a series of penetrating and informative articles for that cornerstone of Civil War libraries, *Battles and Leaders of the Civil War*. Snead died at his home in New York City on October 17, 1890, and was buried in Bellefontaine Cemetery in St. Louis.

229

EDWARD SPARROW (Louisiana) was born in Dublin, Ireland, December 29, 1810. His father, a follower of Robert Emmett, had been forced to flee Ireland after the ill-fated uprising of 1803 but had returned on a visit at the time of Edward's birth. Edward was brought up from infancy at his parents' home in Columbus, Ohio, and according to family tradition attended Kenyon College, with which his brother William was long associated; however, the college has no record of Edward's attendance.[1] In any event, he was a well-educated man when, in 1831, he journeyed to Louisiana to seek his fortune. He located first at Vidalia, where he studied law and was admitted to the bar. He was elected the clerk of court of Concordia Parish in 1833 and in 1834 he was elected sheriff, an office he held until 1840. After that, he practiced law until 1852, when he moved to Carroll Parish and established on the shore of Lake Providence a plantation, Arlington, which is still a showplace of the region.

In January, 1861, Sparrow was elected as an immediate secessionist to the convention, which in turn unanimously appointed him to membership in the Provisional Congress. In November he was chosen, along with T. J. Semmes (*q.v.*), as senator, a position he continued to occupy until the end. During the entire war period he was chairman of the powerful Committee on Military Affairs, but unlike his House counterpart he was rather self-effacing and noted for his tact and impartiality. Nevertheless, Sparrow had the strong feeling that Congress possessed unlimited war powers and that the Confederacy's salvation lay in a large and aggressive army headed by a commander-in-chief with unlimited authority. His only contradiction of this belief was his feeling that state exemption laws should be respected. Even his prewar conservatism on the tax question had yielded by 1864 to a conviction that high imposts were an economic necessity.

At war's end Sparrow returned to Arlington, which, fortunately for him, had been spared burning because it had housed some members of Grant's staff during the Vicksburg campaign. Sparrow was in the process of rebuilding his shattered fortunes when he died on July 4, 1882. He is buried in the family cemetery on his plantation.

[1] Archivist, Kenyon College, Gambier, Ohio, to Ezra J. Warner, August 12, 1970. Much of the information on Sparrow was provided by Mrs. Stephen H. Guenard, Lake Providence, La., a great-great-granddaughter of Sparrow, who resides at Arlington, the last of the great antebellum homes in the Lake Providence region.

WALLER REDD STAPLES (Virginia), a cousin of William B. Preston's (*q. v.*) wife, was born in Patrick Court House (now Stuart), Virginia, on February 24, 1826. He entered the University of North Carolina at the

230

age of sixteen and after two years there transferred to William and Mary, where he was graduated in 1846. He then studied law and in 1848 began practice in Christiansburg with his kinsman, Preston.

A Whig by persuasion, he represented Montgomery County in the House of Delegates from 1853–1854, and in 1861 he was a member of the Virginia convention, which sent him as one of the state's first four delegates to the Provisional Confederate Congress. He was subsequently elected to both Regular Congresses with but slight opposition. During his congressional career he served on the committees on Military Affairs, Patents, and Elections, and like many other Confederate legislators he shifted his position as the war progressed. In the beginning he wanted low taxes, coupled with entire cooperation with the war effort and with the president's requests. As conditions worsened, he became convinced that the home front was being ruinously depleted of manpower, and he fought both an extension of the draft age and a reduction in the exempt classes. Ultimately he opposed suspension of the writ of habeas corpus, arbitrary currency management, army reorganization, and impressment of foodstuffs, and he came to regard President Davis as "an autocrat." He voted to dismiss Benjamin and Memminger (*q.v.*) from the cabinet, but at the same time he paradoxically favored the destruction of property to prevent its capture, stringent curbs on speculation, impressment of railroads and staple crops (*i.e.*, cotton and tobacco), and arming slaves. Beyond this he vigorously opposed peace negotiations. After the war Staples resumed his practice in Montgomery County, and in later years he became recognized as one of the state's foremost attorneys. He sat on the Virginia Supreme Court for twelve years between 1870 and 1882, and in 1884 he began a compilation of the state code, a task which he completed three years later. He was also the legal representative of several railroads, president of the state bar association, and the senior member of a leading Richmond law firm. Judge Staples died at his home in Christiansburg on August 20, 1897, and, having never married, was buried next to his brother in Fair View Cemetery in Roanoke, Virginia.

ALEXANDER HAMILTON STEPHENS (Georgia), was called "Little Ellick" since, although he was of average height, his weight never exceeded one hundred pounds. He was born in what is now Taliaferro County (then Wilkes County), Georgia, on February 11, 1812. With the exception of the Reconstruction era in Georgia, he held public office almost continuously from 1836 until his death in 1883; as state legislator, congressman, vice-president of the Confederacy, U.S. representative, and governor of Georgia. After attending public and private schools Stephens was graduated from the University of Georgia at Athens in 1832. Two years later he was admitted to the bar in Crawfordville where he practiced law intermittently for the next half-century; he lived nearby on his estate, Liberty Hall.

Stephens served in Congress from 1843 to 1859, at first as a Whig and later as a Democrat, successively supporting the tickets of Harrison, Clay, Taylor, Pierce, and Buchanan. In 1860 he was a presidential elector on the ticket of Stephen A. Douglas and was elected to the Milledgeville convention of January, 1861, as a quasi supporter of the Union. After the fact of secession he was sent to Montgomery as one of Georgia's ten delegates to what would become the Provisional Confederate Congress. He accepted a seat in that body, however, only after the convention asked that the Confederate constitution be based on the old constitution. He hoped to become the Confederacy's first president but gratefully accepted the vice-presidency when it was offered. This office under the provisional constitution had no stated functions, so for a year he was simply a member of Congress. Stephens was chairman of the committees on Rules and on the Executive Departments. Surprisingly, he seldom asserted his leadership except in the formulation of committees and executive departments. Otherwise he supported with commendable regularity the efforts being made to erect a strong central government and an effective army. His states' rights convictions appeared primarily against economic experimentation, like the export duty on cotton and federal grants for railroad construction. But as the war wore on, Stephens' attitude changed in the face of conscription, suspension of the writ of habeas corpus, and the establishment of military government in some localities, all of which seemed to him outrageous invasions of time-honored civil rights. As presiding officer of the Senate under the permanent Constitution, he was a leader of the anti-Davis group when present (he was away from Richmond at one point for eighteen months); he oscillated between prognostications of doom, appeals for support of the Confederacy, and encouragement of Governor Brown in the latter's resistance to conscription.

On February 3, 1865, Stephens was one of the three Confederate commissioners who met with President Lincoln at Hampton Roads in a peace conference which foundered on the rock of Union versus southern independence. On May 11 he was arrested by Federal troops, taken to Fort Warren in Boston Harbor, and not released until October. Returning to Liberty Hall, Stephens was elected to the Senate in 1866 but was refused his seat. About this time he wrote his *Constitutional View of the Late War Between the States*, a dull and tedious rationalization of slavery and states' rights, which nevertheless earned its author some $35,000 in royalties. In 1872 he was defeated for the Senate by General John B. Gordon, late C.S.A., but the same year he was elected to the House of Representatives, where he remained for ten years. Resigning on November 4, 1882, he was soon elected governor of Georgia but served only a few months. He died in Atlanta on March 4, 1883, and was buried at Liberty Hall.

HARDY STRICKLAND[1] (Georgia) was born on November 24, 1818, on his father's plantation in Jackson County, Georgia. He attended the local schools and was then tutored at home. When he was still a very young man he moved to Forsyth County where he and his brother Henry opened near Cumming what was known for years as the Strickland Old Gold Mine. It was a successful enterprise and they had their gold coined in the United States mint at Dahlonega. During the 1850s Strickland also acquired a modest plantation and operated it most of his life. In 1847 while superintending his mine Strickland was unanimously elected without his knowledge to represent Forsyth County in the legislature. Except for two years he was there continually until 1858. In 1860 Strickland was a Democratic elector on the Breckinridge-Lane ticket and campaigned vigorously over his district. As a member of the Georgia convention of January, 1861, he worked for immediate and separate state secession. When war began Strickland enlisted as a private in the cavalry and served for several months in Howell Cobb's brigade. In November, 1861, he won a place in the Confederate House of Representatives over two rival candidates.

Strickland was a faithful but unassertive congressman, the extent of his suggestions being for a mint at Dahlonega and the general improvement of hospitals. His voting record shows that he generally supported the Confederate government and its wartime policies, provided they did not threaten to impair the economy unnecessarily. It was for this reason that Strickland desired to exempt from military service every laborer possible and that he opposed inflation curbs lest business enterprise be stifled. He declined to seek reelection in 1863 because of his increasingly severe rheumatism, but when his term ended he accepted an appointment as a brigade quartermaster in the state reserves.

By 1870 Strickland's rheumatism had become so bad that he was unable to walk. He died at his home in Acworth[2] on January 24, 1884. He is buried in Liberty Hill Cemetery near Acworth.[3]

[1] Information was obtained from the biographical information folder, Georgia De-

233

partment of Archives and History, Atlanta. Hardy Strickland is not to be confused with his cousin of the same name who ran a ferry nearby.

[2] Acworth became incorporated in 1870 and included Strickland's home. He was a member of its first board of town commissioners. See Temple, *The First Hundred Years*, 410.

[3] *Ibid.*, 782.

WILLIAM GRAHAM SWAN (Tennessee), according to his grave marker in Elmwood Cemetery in Memphis, was born in the year 1821. The only two published sources dealing with his life say the place was "East Tennessee"; however, the 1860 census of Knox County, Tennessee, records his place of birth as Alabama. In any case he graduated from East Tennessee College (now the University of Tennessee) in 1838, studied law, and practiced his profession in Knoxville until the outbreak of the Civil War. Meanwhile, he also became a successful man of affairs and owned considerable real estate in the city, worth seventy thousand dollars by 1860. He did not own a single slave.

In 1851 at the age of thirty he was elected attorney general and reporter of Tennessee, and in 1855–1856 he served as mayor of Knoxville. An ardent southerner, Swan enlisted in the Confederate army as a private, but in November, 1861, he scored a decisive victory over a Unionist opponent as Second District representative to the First Regular Congress.[1] He won reelection easily in 1863 as a friend of the administration. In Richmond Swan concentrated on certain basic reforms in government policy. He proposed to break all ties with Europe and secure recognition by levying a heavy export tax on goods sent to nations refusing recognition. He thought that inflation could be halted by issuing a new class of currency and making it legal tender. Also, by both his votes and the bills he introduced, he showed the most careful discrimination as to whether particular men should be in the army or in productive labor at home. The only major powers that Swan denied the central government were the right to levy taxes and the right to arm slaves. The dominant sentiment of east Tennessee was opposed to secession and when the Confederacy collapsed, a number of lawyers from that section who had actively served the southern cause moved to the more congenial atmosphere of Memphis. Among them was Swan. He continued his law practice there until his death on April 10, 1869, at the rather early age of forty-eight.[2]

[1] In the elections to the Provisional Confederate Congress, Swan was decisively beaten by Horace Maynard, the candidate to the United States Congress from the Second Congressional District. Like J. B. Heiskell (*q.v.*) in the First District, he refused to take his seat.

[2] See John W. Green, *Law and Lawyers* (Jackson, Tenn., 1950), for a sketch of Swan's life.

JAMES HOUSTON THOMAS (Tennessee), whose sketch in the *Biographical Directory of the American Congress* makes no mention of his Confederate affiliation, was born in Iredell County, North Carolina, September 22, 1808. According to the same sketch, he "attended the rural schools; [and] was graduated from Jackson College, Columbia, Tenn., in 1830," but it is not clear in which state he obtained his early education or when he came to Tennessee. He proceeded to study law, was admitted to the bar, and hung out his shingle in Columbia in 1831.

Thomas served as attorney general of Tennessee from 1836 to 1842 and in 1846 was elected as a Democrat to Congress. He served four years (1847–1851) and then was defeated for reelection in 1850; but he was again elected to the Thirty-sixth Congress and served until the inauguration of Abraham Lincoln in March, 1861. At this point Thomas' position became somewhat equivocal. There is no question that he campaigned for and easily won a seat in the Provisional Confederate Congress as the representative of Tennessee's Sixth Congressional District. There is also no question of his service in that body, where he made only a few minor suggestions, but where his voting record indicated that he would give the Confederate government any emergency power it needed except the extended loan of local defense militia units. On the other hand he wanted the army to have every right to recruit men not belonging to any such unit. Perhaps here Thomas may have begun to have reservations as to his course, for he did not seek reelection to the First Regular Congress and from then on disassociated himself from the Confederate cause. It is only stated that thereafter he resumed the practice of law in Columbia; that he died near Fayetteville, Tennessee, August 4, 1876; and that he was buried in St. John's Cemetery at Ashwood. Unlike many former Confederates, he does not appear to have been the recipient of any position of trust after the Reconstruction period.

JOHN J. THOMAS (Kentucky), whose middle name is not known to his descendants,[1] was born in Albemarle County, Virginia, August 8, 1813, and was related on his mother's side to Thomas Jefferson.[2] The same source relates that he was graduated from the University of Virginia, but that institution has no record of his attendance. In any event, he was in Christian County, Kentucky, at an early date. There he was a surveyor and farmer before receiving a clerkship in the post office department at Washington, serving during the administration of James K. Polk.

In 1851 Thomas was elected to the Kentucky legislature, but after one term he resumed farming in Christian County, where he continued until the outbreak of war in 1861. In December of that year the governor and executive council of the Confederate Kentucky government appointed Thomas to the Provisional Congress. During his two months there he worked quietly to exclude from the president's jurisdiction the local defense troops serving in southern Kentucky. Otherwise he was a strong administration supporter, particularly in his votes to construct needed railroad links. He did not stand for election to the Regular Congress but entered the army as an aide to General John Stuart Williams and served with him until the end of the war.

Thomas then embarked on a career as a tobacco broker in Clarksville, Tennessee, until about 1873 when he was employed for some five years as a tobacco inspector in New York City. He then settled in Paducah, Kentucky, where he was a dealer in tobacco for some time. In his old age he obtained the sinecure of city weigher of Paducah and lived with a daughter. Upon her death in 1895 Thomas went to live with another daughter in Camden, Arkansas, where his son-in-law was operating a hotel. There, at the age of eighty-two, Thomas seems to have disappeared. On a lot in Oak Grove Cemetery in Paducah, deeded to Thomas in 1882, there are grave markers for his second wife and for his elder daughter and her husband. There are also two unmarked graves on the lot which family members suppose to be those of Thomas and his son by his second marriage. But in the absence of cemetery or any other records, the place and date of his death are unknown.

[1] Mrs. J. R. Pritchard (Elizabethtown, Ky.) to Ezra J. Warner, October 20, November 10, 1971. Mrs. Thomas T. Quigley (Short Hills, N.J.) to Ezra J. Warner, August 25, 1971. At least one authority is of the opinion that the "J." must have been only an initial. Julia Neal (Director, Kentucky Library and Museum, Western Kentucky University, Bowling Green) to Ezra J. Warner, June 11, 1971.

[2] Battle, Perrin, and Kniffen, *Kentucky.*

HUGH FRENCH THOMASON (Arkansas) was born February 22, 1826, in Smith County, Tennessee, but was taken by his parents at the age of three to Washington County, Arkansas Territory, because his father felt that Tennessee was becoming too populous. He was brought up on a farm in Washington County and received little but a log-cabin-school education. However, he persevered, studied law, and, after teaching school for a year, was admitted to the bar at Fayetteville in 1847. He later moved to Van Buren, Arkansas, which was his residence for the rest of his life. For a number of years, beginning in 1851, Thomason was the prosecuting attorney for a ten-county circuit. Originally a Democrat, he switched to the Know-Nothings upon the passage of the Kansas-Nebraska bill and in 1860 was an elector on the Bell and

Everett ticket. He remained a Unionist until after the firing upon Fort Sumter, but in the May, 1861, convention he signed the ordinance of secession, whereupon he was elected to the Provisional Congress on the first ballot.

Thomason was a diligent worker for the new Confederacy, participating actively in the formulation of tax laws, Indian treaties, and establishment of the judiciary. Except for an inclination to deny the president emergency appointment powers, he cooperated fully to put the new nation on a sound war footing. A novel contribution to this effort was his suggestion that troops be armed with pikes, lances, spears, and shotguns. He sought to be elected to the First Regular Congress but was defeated by Felix I. Batson (*q.v.*) on the grounds that he (Thomason) was not an original secessionist and Batson was. Thomason then took no further part in the war. In 1866, upon the reorganization of the Little Rock and Fort Smith railroad project, he was elected a director and aided in its completion. The same year he won election to the legislature from Crawford County. In 1874 he served in the state's constitutional convention.

Involved in the turbulence of postwar Arkansas politics almost until the end of his life, General Thomason (his honorific derived from antebellum service on the staff of Governor John S. Roane, later a Confederate brigadier) made an unsuccessful race for Congress that same year and was on several occasions a delegate to the various Democratic national conventions of the 1870s and 1880s. In 1880 he was elected to the Arkansas Senate from Crawford and Franklin counties, and in 1886 he was elected to the General Assembly. In 1890 General Thomason was elected judge of a newly erected judicial district, an office he was holding when he died at Van Buren on July 30, 1893. He was buried in Fairview Cemetery there.

WILLIAM HENRY TIBBS (Tennessee) was born June 10, 1816, at Appomattox, Virginia, but was brought by his parents in infancy to Smith County, in central Tennessee. His entire education was received in the common schools of Smith County. At the age of seventeen he began to work as a blacksmith and carpenter. Later he moved to Yazoo City, Mississippi, to engage in merchandising. After a few years there Tibbs returned to Tennessee, this time to Cleveland, an event which occurred some time prior to 1844, a date when he was elected a trustee of Bradley County. He established a merchandising business in Cleveland and engaged in trading; he also served on the board of trustees of the Masonic Female Academy.

Due in large part to his extreme stand in favor of secession, Tibbs was elected to the First Regular Congress from Tennessee's Third Congressional District. In that body he debated seldom, and his only significant suggestion was a resolution instructing the secretary of war to enforce the draft in Tennessee wherever possible. However, Tibbs's voting record reveals him as the strongest nationalist of his delegation. He wished to place men from seventeen to fifty-five in the army; to pare the exemption list to a minimum; and to give the Confederate government extensive control over currency, production, and transportation. He refrained from criticizing cabinet members, and he refused to tie the president's hands in matters of either diplomacy or appointments. He did not seek reelection in 1863.

After this Tibbs seems to have refugeed to Dalton, Georgia, which he made his home for the rest of a long life. In later years, he farmed in the vicinity, and conducted a hotel in the town, a hotel in which General Robert E. Lee is said to have stayed on a visit to Dalton in the postwar years. Tibbs was ninety years old when he died on October 18, 1906. He is buried in West Hill Cemetery, Dalton.

ROBERT AUGUSTUS TOOMBS (Georgia), who did not use his middle name, and was usually known as Bob Toombs, was born July 2, 1810, in Wilkes County, Georgia, the son of an officer in the Revolutionary army. He attended the University of Georgia at Athens for a time but withdrew because of a youthful escapade; he eventually graduated from Union College in Schenectady, New York, in 1828. Two years later he was admitted to the bar and began practice in his hometown of Washington, Georgia, a practice frequently interrupted, like that of his lifelong friend Alexander H. Stephens (*q.v.*), by public service.

Toombs soon became not only politically prominent but also wealthy, investing the earnings from his vocation in land and slaves in southwestern Georgia. He served six terms in the Georgia General Assembly between 1837 and 1843, and the next year he was elected to Congress as a conservative Whig. He supported the Compromise of 1850, and along with Stephens and Howell Cobb (*q.v.*) he stumped the state to secure its ratification. In 1852 Toombs was elected to the United States Senate and remained there until February 4, 1861, when he withdrew. Meanwhile, following the failure of the Crittenden Compromise, he became an active secessionist, was chosen a member of the Georgia secession convention, and was chosen by that body a member of the Provisional Confederate Congress.

Toombs was a strong candidate for the presidency and upon the election of Jefferson Davis was offered the State Department, which he accepted but soon tired of; he resigned on July 24, 1861. For the next seven months he divided his time between Congress and the army, since he had been appointed a brigadier general on July 19. While in Congress Toombs generally strove to put the Confederacy on sound bases. As chairman of the Committee on Finance he sponsored Memminger's tax suggestions, and it was his thought to guarantee the first Confederate bonds by pledging the entire export duty on cotton to their redemption. He was willing to give the central government wide latitude in creating an effective army. Otherwise, Toombs saw no reason to interfere with personal or property rights. He had been responsible for the constitutional ban on appropriations for internal improvements, for example; so he opposed all aid to railroad construction.

In November, 1861, the Georgia legislature elected Toombs a Confederate senator, but not until the fifth ballot, and he indignantly declined. A year later he lost such an election, this time to Herschel V. Johnson (*q.v.*) on the third ballot. Toombs's career in the army exhibited some capability, but he was forever at odds with his superiors over what he deemed the dilatory tactics of the old regular army, once remarking that the epitaph of the Confederate army should be: "Died of West Point." He took part in the Peninsular Campaign, led his brigade during the campaign of Second Manassas, and was positively distinguished in the defense of Burnside's bridge at Sharpsburg where he was wounded. He felt he was entitled to promotion and, failing to receive it, resigned on March 4, 1863. He spent the balance of the war castigating the administration for its sins of omission and commission, although he saw some further military service as a divisional adjutant and inspector general in the ragtag Georgia militia during the Atlanta campaign.

Toombs fled abroad in 1865 to escape arrest and resided in London until he returned to Georgia in 1867. He soon regained his old public prominence as a champion of the downtrodden South but refused to apply for a pardon as a means of regaining his citizenship; consequently, he never again held public office. His last years were darkened by alcoholism and general decrepitude after the loss of his wife. Toombs died in Washington on December 15, 1885, and is buried there in Rest Haven Cemetery.

GEORGE WASHINGTON TRIPLETT (Kentucky) was born in Franklin County, Kentucky, on February 18, 1809. His father and four uncles were officers of the Revolutionary Line, and his grandfather held a commission as a surveyor under George III in Virginia. George Triplett, after acquiring an education in the local county schools, began teaching, himself, in 1827. He was subsequently deputy county surveyor for some years. He then moved to Davis County in 1833, engaged in surveying and farming, and was county surveyor for seventeen years. Meanwhile, he was elected to the legislature in 1840 and to the state senate in 1848, remaining there until 1852. Triplett joined the Confederate army in 1861 as a captain in the First Kentucky Cavalry. Afterwards he was promoted to major in the Quartermaster Corps and served successively on the staffs of Generals Helm, Hanson, Van Dorn, and Forrest, and as chief quartermaster under Major General John C. Breckinridge. It is stated that during three years of army service he was never absent for a day.

In February, 1864, the Kentucky soldiers and refugees chose Major Triplett as their Second District congressman. Triplett seldom balked at programs to supply, equip, and enlarge the army, but he rejected other centralizing tendencies that were developing. He advocated doubling the tithe on agriculture to feed the army, but not the destruction of property to prevent its capture; he wished to draft all remaining state militia, but not farmers and mechanics; and he zealously guarded Congress' right to share in the selection of officers and officials. Such conservatism put him out of step with the more nationalist Kentucky delegation. On his return home in 1865 Major Triplett found his house burned and his property destroyed. Beginning anew, he in large measure restored his former prosperity and was elected judge of Daviess County, an office to which he was returned regularly until his death at the advanced age of eighty-five. He died in Owensboro on June 25, 1894, and was buried there in Elmwood Cemetery.[1]

[1] *The Biographical Encyclopedia of Kentucky* (Cincinnati, 1878); "History of the Triplett Family" (photostatic copy of a typescript in possession of the Filson Club); Triplett monument, Elmwood Cemetery, Owensboro, Ky.

ROBERT PLEASANT TRIPPE[1] (Georgia) was born in Jasper County, Georgia, on December 21, 1819. His father soon took the family to Monroe County and bought a small plantation near Culloden. Robert attended Randolph-Macon College in Virginia and the University of Georgia, graduating from the latter with first honors in 1839. After reading law in Athens, Trippe was admitted to the bar in 1840 and began practicing in Forsyth. He preferred civil cases, where his broad learning and scrupulous honesty—he would not even accept a railroad pass—earned him a wide reputation for dependability. He also engaged in farming on a small scale. Trippe served in the Georgia legislature from 1849 to 1853. After one unsuccessful attempt he was elected in 1855 as a Whig to the United States House of Representatives. He was not a candidate for reelection but returned to the state senate during 1858 and 1859, this time as a Democrat. But by 1860 the mounting sectional discord had driven Trippe into the Constitutional Union party. He attended its national convention in Baltimore in 1860 and worked energetically for its compromise ticket. As a member of the Georgia secession convention of January, 1861, he voted against disunion. Nevertheless when war began Trippe refused a commission and enlisted in the army as a private. In November, 1861, he defeated his company commander, Judge E. C. Cabaniss, in a race for the Confederate House of Representatives.

Trippe introduced himself to Congress by a resolution demanding a vigorous offensive and defensive war effort. But he differed with the majority on how to muster the necessary army. He always preferred requisitions on the states to conscription, and he advocated liberal exemptions, proposing that men pay heavily for their exemptions. Trippe's only other special effort was to propose several minor bills improving tax-collection procedures. His general support of the central government over the states on most other matters won him little favor at home, and he withdrew his bid for reelection to avoid a possibly disruptive campaign. At the end of his term in Congress Trippe reenlisted in the army, again as a private.

After the war Trippe resumed his law practice in Forsyth. In 1873 he was appointed associate justice of the Georgia Supreme Court for a twenty-year term, the longest appointment ever made for this position. He resigned in 1875, however, and moved his law practice to Atlanta. He died there on July 22, 1900. He is buried in the Forsyth city cemetery.

[1] Northen (ed.), *Men of Mark in Georgia*, III, 197–200.

JOSIAH TURNER (North Carolina) was born on December 27, 1821, in Hillsboro, North Carolina. After graduating from the University of North Carolina he studied law and was admitted to the bar in 1845. He then opened a law office in Hillsboro and soon had a fair practice, though as late as 1860 he owned property worth only five thousand dollars and was in debt to his father-in-law.[1] Between 1852 and 1860 Turner served four years as a Whig in the General Assembly. During the secession movement he fought bitterly the disruption of the Union, and in the convention of May, 1861, he cast one of the three votes against secession. After disunion, however, Turner enlisted in the army and rose to a captaincy in the cavalry. In November, 1861, he campaigned briefly for a place in the Confederate Congress but lost to A. H. Arrington (*q.v.*). Turner was wounded badly after the battle of New Bern and resigned his commission in November, 1862. The following October he ran for Congress again as a peace advocate and as an opponent of the Confederacy's wartime legislation and easily defeated Arrington.

In Congress Turner followed through on his campaign promises. Every bill and resolution that he introduced attacked some existing Confederate program. His votes showed him as basically hostile to every major administration policy. He considered forced funding of inflated currency "false in its general principles and ruinous in its details";[2] he argued that the plan to draft slave labor made Jefferson Davis an "abolition president."[3] On December 16, 1864, Turner introduced a resolution asking Davis to open peace negotiations. His letters to his wife indicate that he attended the last two months of Congress primarily in the hope of securing peace terms short of unconditional Reconstruction.

In 1865 Turner was elected to Congress and in 1868 to the legislature, but he was denied both positions because of his Confederate record. Between those dates he served two years as president of the North Carolina Railroad but found the work unrewarding. In 1868 Turner bought the Democratic Raleigh *Sentinel*. From this podium his unrelenting and vitriolic attacks upon Republican government made him the leading figure in the eventual overthrow of Reconstruction government in North Carolina. His arrest and imprisonment because of these attacks was the dramatic highlight of his life and one of the charges for the impeachment of Governor W. W. Holden. But the Democratic party considered Turner too erratic for high office. It denied him the nomination for Congress in 1874 and saw to his defeat as an independent candidate in 1878 and as a Republican in 1884. Turner served in the constitutional convention of 1875 and in the legislature of 1879, though he was so disorderly in the latter that he was expelled. He lost his newspaper in 1876 through poor financial management. Turner died at home near Hillsboro on October 26, 1901, and was interred in the family plot in St. Matthew's Episcopal churchyard.[4]

[1] Martha B. Clauset, "Josiah Turner, Jr.: Portrait of a North Carolina Whig, 1821–1865" (M.A. thesis, Wake Forest University, 1967), 41–42.

[2] Richmond *Daily Examiner*, December 15, 1864.

[3] Richmond *Daily Enquirer,* January 28, 1965.

[4] Ashe *et al.* (eds.), *Biographical History of North Carolina*, III, 426.

JOHN TYLER (Virginia), state legislator, congressman, governor, United States senator, tenth president of the United States, and rather incidentally a member of the Provisional Confederate Congress, was born at his father's estate, Greenway, in Charles City County, Virginia, on March 29, 1790. With the exception of Thomas Fearn (*q.v.*), Tyler was the oldest member of the Confederate Congress. Although much has been written by historians to depreciate Tyler's career as a statesman, he had the singular virtue of consistency. Political parties might shift their ground, factions coalesce and fall away, and politicians bow to expediency, but Tyler's principles and convictions remained unaltered, based as they were upon a strict construction of the United States Constitution as it was drawn up and signed by the founders of the country. At one point such constancy left him standing alone as a president without a cabinet and virtually without a party.

After a brief attendance at a local academy, Tyler was sent to the College of William and Mary at the age of twelve. He completed his academic course there at age seventeen, and then studied law under his father, also named John Tyler, who had been a prominent Revolutionary patriot, governor of Virginia, and federal district judge. At the age of twenty-one the son was elected to the Virginia House of Delegates. He was a congressman from 1817–1821, again a member of the House of Delegates from 1823–1825, governor of Virginia from 1825–1827, and United States senator for the next nine years. He served yet another term in the House of Delegates in 1839 and in 1840 was elected vice-president of the United States. The death of William Henry Harrison a month later made him president, the first to succeed to the office owing to the demise of his superior.

During all this time Tyler bore any number of party labels, ranging from National Republican to Whig to Democrat, but he always maintained his convictions—once he even resigned from the senate in protest when the Virginia legislature attempted to dictate his vote on a measure. The great crisis of his presidential administration turned on the bank question; Tyler deemed it unconstitutional for Congress to establish a national bank with branches in the states without the states' prior consent and vetoed several bills passed by the supporters of Henry Clay. The resulting contest saw the resignations of every cabinet member save that of Daniel Webster, vacancies which Tyler promptly filled by choices as promptly confirmed by the Senate. The achievements of the administration were the Webster-Ashburton treaty which settled the long disputed Canadian-American boundary, and the annexation of Texas.

After his term of office the former president retired to his estate, Sherwood Forest, on the James River, five miles from Greenway, which he also owned. When civil war threatened, Tyler emerged from retirement to chair the Washington Peace Conference held in February, 1861. When all compromise measures failed, Tyler, a strict constructionist to the end, became a member of the Virginia convention and voted for separation. The convention appointed him to the Provisional Congress, and he was subsequently elected to the First Regular Congress over two opponents, securing a clear majority of the votes cast, but he did not live to take his seat. The former president attended legislative sessions infrequently and seldom took part in debates. He did go on record against granting Davis emergency military powers, but he otherwise approved the president's policies, and he early recognized the need for an adequate tax program. Tyler died in Richmond on January 18, 1862, and was buried in Hollywood Cemetery there.

ABRAHAM WATKINS VENABLE (North Carolina) was a native of Virginia, born in Prince Edward County on October 17, 1799. He was graduated from Hampden-Sydney, in the same county, in 1816, and then studied medicine for two years. In 1819 he was graduated from Princeton and began the study of law. He was admitted to the bar in 1821 and pursued the vocation of law until his death. After practicing for a time in Prince Edward and Mecklenburg counties, he moved to North Carolina in the year 1829 and settled in Granville County in the now defunct town of Brownsville.

Venable was a presidential elector on the ticket of Jackson and Van Buren in 1832, and on that of Van Buren and Johnson in 1836; in 1846 he was elected to the first of three consecutive congressional terms and served until March 3, 1853. He had been defeated for renomination in 1852. In 1860 Venable was again a presidential elector, this time on the extreme Southern Rights ticket of Breckinridge and Lane. After the ordinance of secession had been adopted on May 20, 1861, the Democrats in the state convention secured Venable's election as a delegate to the Provisional Confederate Congress. As a congressman he was a good friend of the common soldier, introducing several bills and resolutions for their health and comfort. His strong states' rights convictions forced him to oppose practically all taxation and executive interference in the election of company officers, one of the unmitigated evils of the Confederate military system which frequently resulted in the accession to command not of the best qualified but of the most popular. Otherwise he accepted the necessity of giving the central government whatever powers the administration requested. Venable announced for reelection to the First Regular Congress, but he refused to campaign.

244

His district chose to replace him with Archibald H. Arrington (*q.v.*). At this juncture Venable retired from public life and soon from active law practice. He took no part in the recovery of the state from the Carpetbag regime, but he lived to see its successful completion. He died in Oxford, North Carolina, on February 24, 1876, and was buried in Shiloh Presbyterian Churchyard in Granville Cemetery.

GEORGE GRAHAM VEST (Missouri) was born December 6, 1830, in Frankfort, Kentucky. He graduated from Centre College at Danville in 1848 and from the law department of Transylvania University at Lexington in 1853. The next year he migrated to Missouri where in 1856 he established a permanent residence in Boonville. In 1860 he was both a Douglas elector and a member of the Missouri House of Representatives—needless to say, he was of the secessionist persuasion. By the same rump wing of the legislature which convened at Neosho he was appointed to the Confederate Congress, where he arrived to take part in the deliberations of the provisional body.[1] In May, 1864, he easily won reelection as an administration supporter by the votes of soldiers and refugees, and for this reason he was elevated to the senate by Governor Thomas C. Reynolds to succeed John Bullock Clark (*q.v.*), whose private life was deemed suspect by Missouri's chief executive.

It might be remarked here that Vest later enjoyed the distinction of having been the sole member of Congress to be publicly horsewhipped. One affiant stated, for publication,[2] that Vest's assailant was outraged by his introduction of a resolution calling for the ages of government clerks; however, a colleague privately wrote his wife that the horsewhipper took possession of the speaker's rostrum to declaim that Vest had "traduced her character and caused her husband to leave her by saying she had been on intimate and criminal terms with him."[3] Be that as it may, Vest was one of the most effective members of Congress. In the winter of 1861–1862, when he fully expected that Missouri would be redeemed by Confederate forces, he tried to keep as many troops as possible under the governor's jurisdiction. But, as this hope dimmed, for the next three years he supported every program that might strengthen the arm of the central government for the reconquest.

By 1865, however, Vest had lost faith in the Confederacy's leadership. He joined the cabal led by Bocock (*q.v.*) of Virginia which aimed to reform the cabinet, force the president to reshuffle his high command, and establish a general-in-chief with sweeping powers. Unlike most members of this group, however, Vest continued to support the most aggressive type of emergency legislation and never considered peace. At the end of the war Vest submitted to Missouri's oppressive test oath and resumed the practice of law. In 1877 he moved to Kansas City, then just coming into its own as a metropolis, and in 1879 he was elected to the United States Senate, where he served for twenty-four years. His postbellum career was mainly distinguished by his resistance to anything new and by his celebrated oration, "Tribute to a Dog," which he delivered in the course of a jury case, and which has come to be considered a sentimental gem of the first magnitude, worldwide. As late as 1900 the Chicago *Journal*, a Republican paper, acknowledged him to be "half the brains of the Democratic side of the Senate."[4] Senator Vest died in Sweet Springs, Saline County, Missouri, on August 9, 1904, and was buried in Bellefontaine Cemetery in St. Louis.

[1] See the above sketch of C. W. Bell for Missouri's method of choosing delegates to the Confederate Congress.

[2] Jones, *A Rebel War Clerk's Diary*, II, 347.

[3] Josiah Turner, Jr., to his wife, December 5, 1864, in Turner Papers, Duke University Library, Durham, N.C.

[4] Boonville *Weekly Advertiser*, February 24, 1900.

CHARLES JACQUES VILLERÉ (Louisiana), whose sister was the wife of General Pierre G. T. Beauregard, was born on his father's plantation, which occupied a part of the site of the Battle of New Orleans, in St. Bernard Parish, Louisiana, probably in 1828. The only clue to the exact date of his birth, which even his descendants do not know, is the statement that he had passed his seventieth birthday at the time of his death on January 7, 1899.[1] Villeré was educated at St. Mary's College in Baltimore, graduating with high honors. He then returned to New Orleans to study law, being admitted to the bar in 1849. However, he preferred planting to the legal profession and settled on his estate in Plaquemines Parish.

Villeré was elected to the constitutional convention of 1852 and the same year was appointed district attorney of Plaquemines. In 1854 he was elected to the legislature and served two terms. He was a presidential elector for James Buchanan in 1856 and lost a close race for the U.S. Congress in 1860. When Louisiana seceded the following year, Villeré organized a company of cavalry, but before it got into the field he was elected to the First Regular Confederate Congress, and was reelected in 1863, both times by scant majorities. Before his reelection he was commissioned colonel, C.S.A., by Governor Henry W. Allen, a title by which he was afterwards known. During his congressional

246

career Villeré emerged as a strong nationalist, supporting all major programs designed to strengthen the central government. However, his relationship to Beauregard colored his attitude toward President Davis. When Davis removed the Creole Napoleon as commander of the Army of Tennessee, Villeré quickly resorted to publication of a pamphlet which defended his brother-in-law at the expense of Davis. He also voted no confidence in General Bragg and in secretarys Mallory and Memminger (*q.v.*), all trusted administration advisors. After the war he led a life of almost complete retirement, emerging only to succeed Beauregard as a supervisor of the Louisiana lottery after the general's death in 1893. Colonel Villeré died at his home in Jefferson Parish, near New Orleans, and was buried in the tomb of the Army of Tennessee in Metairie Cemetery.

[1] B. L. Layton to Ezra J. Warner, January 15, 1971, quoting Sidney L. Villeré. See also New Orleans *Times-Picayune*, January 8, 1899.

RICHARD WILDE WALKER (Alabama), whose father was Alabama's first senator, and whose elder brother was L. Pope Walker, Confederate secretary of war, was born in Huntsville, Alabama, February 16, 1823. He was educated at Spring Hill College, Mobile, the University of Virginia, and Princeton, where he graduated in 1841. After graduation he returned to Huntsville, read law, and was admitted to the bar in 1844. He moved to Florence where he served from 1845 to 1848 as district solicitor. Walker was elected to the legislature from Lauderdale County in 1851 and again in 1855 when he was chosen speaker. In 1859 he was appointed to fill an unexpired term on the supreme court, and he was later elected to a full term. While still serving, he was chosen by the secession convention as a delegate at large to the Provisional Congress. He did not seek election to the First Regular Congress, but when the senatorial election of 1863 reached a stalemate in the legislature, Walker's name was introduced as a compromise and he won on the next ballot.

In the Provisional Congress Walker administered the oath of office to Jefferson Davis, served on both constitution committees, and approved the entire administration program except the produce loan. However, when he returned as senator in 1864 he was obviously distressed by the course legislation had taken. He proposed to ban the destruction of property subject to capture, to pay market prices for impressed goods, and to let the states trade with the enemy. His voting record placed him strongly against any further increase of central authority. But Walker was never a defeatist. He refused to hamper the army's procurement of men and supplies, and on February 2, 1865, he proposed to double the tithe on agriculture. While he favored initiating peace negotiations, after the failure of the Hampton Roads conference he voted to arm and then free the slaves, preferring this to a dishonorable peace. When the war ended, Walker located again in Huntsville, resumed his law practice, and took no further part in politics. He died in Huntsville on June 16, 1874.[1] He is presumably buried in Maple Hill Cemetery there, where the rest of his family is buried, but the Huntsville Library's Heritage Room has no record of his burial, nor can a stone be found on any of the several Walker lots.

[1] Wright, *General Officers of the Confederate Army*, 157.

GEORGE TALIAFERRO WARD (Florida) was born in Fayette County, Kentucky. According to the 1850 and 1860 censuses of Leon County, Florida, the year of his birth was 1810; however, this information hardly comports with the fact that he was graduated from Transylvania University in Lexington, Kentucky, with an A.B. degree in 1824. In any case, in 1825 his father, George Washington Ward, was appointed register of the U.S. Land Office in Tallahassee, Florida, and the family moved there. The younger man worked as a clerk in the land office for a time and may have briefly practiced law; however, his primary interest was in agriculture, in which he became eminently successful.

By 1860, by virtue of his own efforts and his marriage to the daughter of Benjamin Chaires—who was said to have been at the time of his death Florida's only millionaire—Ward owned three plantations in Leon County with a total of 4,200 acres, 2,500 of which were under cultivation; 170 Negroes; and an estate in excess of $200,000. He was a member of the Territorial Legislative Council in 1833 and 1834, a principal stockholder in the Union Bank, chairman of the Committee on the State of the Territory which recommended adoption of a state government, and a delegate to the Florida constitutional convention of 1838–1839. However, he was defeated in his bid for territorial delegate to Congress in 1841 and, after the admission of Florida as a state, he lost a seat in the U.S. Senate to Jackson Morton (*q.v.*) in 1848.

In 1852 Ward lost a close race for governor by only 212 votes. In 1861 he was a delegate to the secession convention and, as a lifelong Whig, was a leader of the so-called "cooperationists" who opposed immediate secession, and advocated popular ratification of the step, if it were taken. Failing in this, he reluctantly signed the ordinance. When J. Patton Anderson (*q.v.*) resigned from the Provisional Congress to enter the army, Ward was chosen his successor and took his seat May

2, 1861, although he cared little for lawmaking. Between sessions he hurried to his command in the field—the Second Florida Infantry—of which he had been elected the colonel, and which he took to Virginia. His only legislative proposals were for the construction of two military roads in Florida. Generally he supported the modest efforts being made to put the Confederacy on a war basis, the major exception being his typical reluctance to commit state troops to distant service.

In November Ward was an unsuccessful candidate for the Confederate Senate. His resignation from Congress was accepted on February 5, 1862. Exactly three months later Ward was shot dead at the head of his regiment at the battle of Williamsburg. In the course of the Confederate retreat his body was left on the doorstep of a house in the town whose occupant, a former friend and classmate of Ward's, buried him in the Episcopal Cemetery.[1]

[1] The author is indebted to Dorothy Dodd, retired Florida state librarian, for information on Ward. See also Francis P. Fleming, *Memoir of Capt. C. Seton Fleming of the Second Florida Infantry* (Jacksonville, 1884), and Clifton Paisley, *From Cotton to Quail* (Gainesville, Fla., 1968). Ward's remains apparently still lie in an unmarked grave in Williamsburg since, according to Paisley, there is not even a marker of any nature in the family cemetery at Southwood, Ward's principal plantation.

WILLIAM WIRT WATKINS (Arkansas) was born in Jefferson County, Tennessee, April, 1, 1826. However, he lived in Carroll County and neighboring Boone County, Arkansas, almost all his life. Educated as a lawyer, he was the most prominent man of the region both before and after the Civil War and seems to have been highly esteemed by all who knew him. Watkins was three times elected to the Arkansas senate, in 1856, 1858, and 1860. In the convention of March, 1861, Watkins fought secession and proposed that Arkansas send a delegation to the border state convention scheduled to meet in Kentucky. He is a perfect example of the swing of sentiment which resulted from Lincoln's call for volunteers after the bombardment of Sumter. Union candidates to the convention from Carroll County—who numbered Watkins and another man—overwhelmed the secessionist opposition 1,464 to 36. But when the same body reconvened in May, its members (including Watkins) voted almost unanimously to ally the state with the new Confederacy. Watkins was elected one of five delegates to the Provisional Congress. In that body he was almost a silent member. His voting record, however, exhibits a distrust of centralized authority. For the prosecution of the war he conceded the Confederacy control over commerce and military affairs, but he disliked any form of taxation and consistently opposed aid to railroad construction. Watkins did not seek election to the Regular Congress and seems to have taken no further active part in the war. In 1866 he was again elected to the state senate. After the demise of the Carpetbag regime Judge Watkins, as he had come to be known, was twice more sent to the senate by the voters of his district, in 1878 and in 1880. He moved from Carroll County to Boone County after the war and died in Harrison, the county seat of Boone County, on January 15, 1898. He was buried in the local cemetery.

JOHN WILLIAM CLARK WATSON (Mississippi) was born February 27, 1808, in Albemarle County, Virginia. He obtained his early education in the local schools, after which he attended the University of Virginia Law School, from which he graduated in 1830. From 1831 to 1845 Watson practiced in Abingdon, Virginia. In 1845 he moved to Holly Springs, Mississippi, where he formed a partnership with Jeremiah W. Clapp (*q.v.*). Watson had been a lifelong Whig and continued his affiliation with that party until it dissolved. He opposed secession and during the 1860 presidential campaign established a newspaper in Holly Springs with the intention of fighting the rising tide of disunion sentiment. Because of this stand, he was defeated for election to the Mississippi constitutional convention of 1861 which took the state out of the Union. However, when the die was cast he resigned himself, and in 1863 he won a senatorial seat in the Second Congress from James Phelan (*q.v.*). As long as there was any hope of Confederate success, Watson labored diligently to see that existing programs were better administered; he insisted, for example, that the laws in force governing conscription would provide enough soldiers if properly applied. He accepted the need for impressment but demanded that fair market values be paid and claims settled promptly. He also felt that both the cabinet and the army command system needed to be restructured. By 1865 Watson was an advocate of peace negotiations, but at the same time he was willing to suspend habeas corpus and arm the slaves, which would seem to deny any Reconstructionist tendencies. Following the war, however, he reasoned, like his colleague Orr (*q.v.*), that the victorious party should not be antagonized, going so far as to disavow Jefferson Davis. Nevertheless, he took an active part in restoring the state to white rule and, after the ouster of Governor Adelbert Ames, was appointed a judge of the circuit court by acting Governor John M. Stone. Here he was said to have been a "terror to evil doers." After his six-year term ended in 1882, Judge Watson returned to his law practice. In 1885 he represented the state of Mississippi in a celebrated case before the United States Supreme Court in which the constitutionality of the state railroad commission was upheld. He was reputed to be "the smartest man who ever lived in Holly Springs";[1] he was also one of the pioneer prohibitionists in the state and financed Frances E. Willard's statewide temperance crusade in 1882. Judge Watson died in Holly Springs on September 24, 1890, and was buried in Hill Crest Cemetery in an unmarked grave.[2]

[1] Mrs. Fred Swaney (Holly Springs, Miss.) to Ezra J. Warner, January 26, 1971.
[2] Holograph manuscript of Maud Craig Mathews, Holly Springs Public Library. Mrs. Matthews was the daughter of Dr. [?] Craig, the minister of the Presbyterian Church in Holly Springs in the 1880s and 1890s.

THOMAS NEVILLE WAUL (Texas) was born on January 5, 1813, in Sumter District, South Carolina. He attended South Carolina College (now the University of South Carolina) until his junior year. He then taught school for a time in Florence, Alabama, after which he studied law and was admitted to the bar in Vicksburg, Mississippi. Waul moved to Gonzales County, Texas, in 1836, where he established a plantation and also practiced his profession. He was an unsuccessful candidate for Congress in 1859, and after the election of Lincoln in 1860 he worked diligently to take Texas out of the Union. In January, 1861, the Texas secession convention chose him to be a delegate to the Provisional Congress. In that body he showed great talent for detail and precise phraseology in lawmaking. He favored a broad spectrum of emergency legislation and introduced the controversial bill to provide for local defense and special service. He sought to place in the permanent Constitution the right to import slaves from any place except Africa. Waul was conservative only on commercial affairs, preferring free trade and opposing any regulation whatsoever on the cotton trade. In November, 1861, he lost his bid for a seat in the Confederate Senate. The following spring he recruited Waul's Texas Legion and was commissioned its colonel on May 17. He and his command were surrendered at Vicksburg in July, 1863, and after his exchange he was promoted brigadier general to rank from September 18, 1863. In the Red River campaign of 1864 Waul commanded a brigade of John G. Walker's division at the battles of Mansfield and Pleasant Hill. Later he was transferred to Arkansas to oppose the Federal General Steele, and he fought at the Battle of Jenkins' Ferry. Immediately following the close of hostilities in 1865 General Waul was elected to the first Texas Reconstruction convention. Thereafter he practiced law in Galveston, and in later life he retired to a farm in Hunt County, near Greenville, some fifty miles northeast of Dallas. He died there in his ninety-first year, on July 28, 1903, leaving no blood relatives, the last of his line. He was buried in Fort Worth.[1]

[1] Waul, by virtue of his Confederate army rank, was the subject of a sketch in Warner's *Generals in Gray*. See also *Confederate Veteran Magazine*, III, 380; the University of South Carolina *Annual*, 1902; and the Dallas *Morning News*, July 29, 1903.

ISRAEL VICTOR WELCH (Mississippi), whose name is frequently and incorrectly spelled *Welsh*, was born at Old St. Stephens, Alabama, on January 20, 1822.[1] At the age of twelve he moved with his parents to Mississippi, first to Wahalak in Kemper County, and later to Noxubee County, where for years he resided in Macon. The sources of his early education and legal training are obscure, but he was known as a brilliant lawyer when he was elected to the Mississippi legislature in 1858. He was an ardent secessionist, and in the Mississippi convention of 1861 he voted against any delay in leaving the Union. After secession he enlisted as a private in a company of the Eleventh Mississippi Infantry known as the Noxubee Rifles, which was one of two companies of that regiment to take part in the Battle of First Manassas.

While in service Welch was elected to the First Regular Congress from a district embracing seven counties in east central Mississippi lying along the Alabama line, and he won reelection in 1863. Although Welch was a constant exponent of requisitioning manpower through the individual states, once the draft became an established policy he made the execution of it his primary concern. He wished to exempt only those so specified by separate state action. On August 23, 1862, he proposed to repeal all laws allowing the hiring of substitutes and played a leading part in the congressional struggle to enact this reform. Subsequently he urged the drafting of one hundred thousand slaves from menial army labor into the fighting forces. In a few matters of relative unimportance Welch adhered to his states' rights convictions, but in all major policy matters he was in the vanguard of supporters of the administration. After the war he returned to Macon and resumed his law practice; but he died only a few years later on May 18, 1869. His headstone in Odd Fellows Cemetery there is inscribed "Israel V. Welch, Company F, 11th Mississippi Infantry, Confederate States of America." There is no mention of his congressional service.

[1] An historical site location near the present village of St. Stephens in Washington County, Ala.

DANIEL PRICE WHITE (Kentucky) was born November 16, 1814, in Green County, Kentucky. His father, like many Kentuckians, had migrated from Virginia and settled in Green County about 1790. White was prepared for college in the local schools, attended Centre College, and then studied medicine in Lexington and in Cincinnati. He established a practice in his native county and conducted it for many years. Meanwhile, he was several times elected to the legislature and from 1857 to 1859 served as its speaker. White was a delegate to the Charleston convention of 1860 and that autumn was a Douglas elector-at-large for the state. After the election of Lincoln he declared his allegiance to the southern cause and, when war came, transported his slave property to Yell County, Arkansas. He then returned to Camp Boone and in an unofficial capacity rendered medical service to the Kentucky volunteers who were assembling there.

In December, 1861, the Kentucky Confederate government appointed White as a delegate to the Provisional Congress, but he occupied his seat for only six weeks. He tried to reserve to Governor George W. Johnson the appointment of most officers in Kentucky volunteer militia units, but in other matters he accepted the need for more central control. Most important, he did not join the large clique' of border state congressmen who would keep the president from using local defense troops. He did not stand for election to the Regular Congress. During the balance of the war Dr. White was intermittently on duty as a volunteer surgeon with troops in the field, being present at a number of battles, including Shiloh, Prairie Grove, Poison Spring, and Jenkins' Ferry; his son was a member of the Second Arkansas Cavalry. After the war he came back to Kentucky and gave over the practice of his profession to engage in the tobacco business in Louisville, Kentucky. By the time of his death there on April 12, 1890, he had accumulated a considerable estate. Dr. White was buried in Greensburg, Kentucky.[1]

[1] White's service in the field, although unofficial, led to his inclusion in Thompson's *History of the Orphan Brigade*, which contains the best sketch of him. Information on White's place of burial was obtained from the Louisville *Commercial*, April 13, 1890.

ROBERT HENRY WHITFIELD (Virginia) was born on the Nansemond County plantation of his grandfather on September 14, 1814. After attending Randolph-Macon College[1] he studied for a year at the University of Virginia, receiving his bachelor of law degree in 1839.[2] He then began practicing law in Smithfield and was soon recognized as a leading member of the bar. In 1849 Whitfield married Rebecca Ann Peebles[3] and built the handsome brick home now known as the Sinclair-Langhorne house.[4] In 1851 he was an unsuccessful independent candidate for the United States House of Representatives. The next year he became commonwealth attorney for Isle of Wight County, holding the position until 1860. During these same years he acquired and operated a small plantation near Smithfield.[5] Whitfield was elected to the Virginia convention of 1861 as a Unionist,[6] but while there he proposed that Virginia secede if the Washington Peace Convention of February failed to satisfy southern demands. On April 4 he voted against secession, but he reversed himself on April 17 after Lincoln's call for volunteers.[7] When a force of Union soldiers invaded Smithfield in 1862 Whitfield refused to take the oath of allegiance to the United States and was threatened with imprisonment at Fort Monroe. Upon the arrival of a senior officer, however, he was released.[8] In 1863 Whitfield won a seat in the Confederate House of Representatives, defeating William Mahone and two others.

Whitfield attended the Second Congress erratically—and not at all after December, 1864. He resigned on March 7, 1865. His sketchy record indicates that even this late he refused to concede the central government new controls over currency or commerce. His suggestions during debate generally aimed to relieve those whom he considered overtaxed. In contrast, Whitfield never tried to restrict either the army or the executive, and he never condoned peace negotiations.

After the war Whitfield lived at home quietly, his estate "very much reduced by the casualties" of the past conflict. He died at Smithfield on October 5, 1868, and was buried in the family cemetery. His and his family's bodies were later moved to the cemetery at St. Luke's Church just outside the town.[9]

[1] This information was provided by Milton C. Russell, Virginia State Library, Richmond. Records of the University of Virginia and other sources give Whitfield's birthplace as Isle of Wight County. The discrepancy might be explained if his mother followed a common practice of the day by going to her mother's for her lying-in.

[2] This information was provided by Hope M. Cinquegrana, University of Virginia Library, Charlottesville.

[3] According to David Wyatt, Winston-Salem, N.C.

[4] According to Mrs. Harry G. Dashiell, Smithfield, Va.

[5] Alexander and Beringer, *The Anatomy of the Confederate Congress*, 388,389.

[6] This information was provided by Milton C. Russell, Virginia State Library, Richmond.

[7] George H. Reese (ed.), *Proceedings of the Virginia State Convention of 1861* (4 vols.; Richmond, 1965), I, 162; III, 137–44; IV, 144.

[8] According to Mrs. Harry G. Dashiell, Smithfield, Va.

[9] *Ibid.*

WILLIAMS CARTER WICKHAM[1] (Virginia) was born in Richmond, Virginia, on September 21, 1820, into a family which had been prominent for generations. In 1827 the family moved to Hickory Hill, their new home in Hanover County. Williams attended private schools in Alexandria and Fredericksburg, then enrolled in the university for the academic year 1837–1838.[2] He read law in Richmond under James Lyons (*q.v.*) and was admitted to the bar in 1842. He soon abandoned the law, however, for the life of a planter. In 1849 Wickham was elected to the House of Delegates as a Whig, and in 1859 he was elected to the state senate. Meanwhile he was for many years the presiding justice of the Hanover County court.

Wickham was one of the foremost Unionists in the secession convention of 1861, but after Virginia's break with the Union he took into Confederate service his militia company "the Hanover Dragoons." His army career was connected uninterruptedly with Stuart's Cavalry Corps. He attained the rank of brigadier general, participated in numerous major battles and campaigns, and was wounded twice. In May, 1862, he received a severe sabre wound at Williamsburg and was then captured. Upon his exchange, he returned to active service. In May, 1863, Wickham contested Lyons' bid for reelection to the Confederate House of Representatives in a campaign that became a test of the popularity of secessionism. Wickham won by a wide margin, including a majority of the army vote—undoubtedly provoked at Lyons' opposition to increasing the pay of soldiers. Wickham remained with the army during the first session of the Second Congress, his last active service being with Early in the Shenandoah Valley.

When Wickham reached Congress on November 7, 1864, he had so little hope of victory that he refused to demand further sacrifices of person or property. He considered it useless to enact new emergency laws or to extend existing ones. He particularly opposed giving any new authority to the president and never supported one of his vetoes. Most of Wickham's numerous bills were to settle claims against the Confederacy, to relieve hardship areas from taxation, to exchange prisoners, and to exempt more men from army service. In January, 1865, he wrote that "the house of cards maintained by Davis & Co. crumbles,"[3] and in Congress he worked for peace at any price.

After the war Wickham espoused the Republican party, and from 1871 to his death he was chairman of the board of supervisors of Hanover County. In 1865 he was elected president of the Virginia Central Railroad, and in 1868 he was made president of the Chesapeake and Ohio. He resigned the latter position after a year but continued to be the receiver or vice-president of the railroad until his death. In 1880 Wickham declined the secretaryship of the navy offered him by President Hayes, and the following year he refused the Republican nomination for governor. For the last five years of his life he was a member of the state senate. Wickham died in Richmond on July 23, 1888, and is buried in the family cemetery at Hickory Hill.

[1] Most of the information for this sketch was provided by Mrs. Williams C. Wickham, Jr., of Hanover, Va.

[2] Wickham's study at the university was researched by Michael F. Plunkett, University of Virginia Library, Charlottesville.

[3] W. C. Wickham to A. H. H. Stuart, January 20, 1865, in Stuart Papers, Library of Congress, Washington, D.C.

LOUIS TREZEVANT WIGFALL (Texas), one of the most partisan of southern sectionalists, was born, appropriately, in South Carolina, near Edgefield, on April 21, 1816. He was educated at the University of Virginia and at South Carolina College (now the University of South Carolina), from which he graduated in 1837. Two years later he was admitted to the bar. Almost at once he became involved in political feuds, killing one man in a duel and severely wounding another. As early as 1844 he advocated the secession of South Carolina in protest against the protective tariff and the defeat of the Texas annexation treaty.

In 1848 Wigfall emigrated to Marshall, Texas, and in the next decade he served in both houses of the Texas legislature, which in 1859 elected him to the United States Senate. Here his intransigence was displayed before a national audience; he hurled defiance in the face of his northern adversaries. In January, 1861, along with five other Democrats, he refrained from voting, enabling the Republicans to kill the Crittenden Compromise, a measure which might have forestalled the Civil War. He was ultimately expelled from the Senate, where he had occupied his seat for three weeks after Lincoln's inauguration, in July. Meanwhile, Wigfall had been present at the bombardment of Sumter, serving as an aide to General Beauregard, and had visited the fort to demand its surrender.

The Texas secession convention chose Wigfall as a delegate to the Provisional Congress on the first ballot; however, on August 28, 1861, he was appointed colonel of the First Texas Infantry, and on October 21 Davis gave him a brigadier's commission. He neglected his congressional duties, preferring action with his brigade or as the president's aide, but in November he accepted a senatorship in the Regular Congress from the legislature; he resigned from the army on February 18, 1862. In the Confederate Senate he was chairman of the Committee on Territories and, for the last month of the war, the Committee on Military Affairs. His friendship with Jefferson Davis diminished in direct proportion to the latter's unwillingness to share decision-making

256

with the Senate, and soon he was corresponding with disgruntled officers—Joseph E. Johnston in particular—regarding Davis' shortcomings. In 1864 he publicly branded Davis as an incompetent, and shortly before the Confederacy's collapse he asked the Senate to seek the president's resignation and supersede him with R. M. T. Hunter.

As a lawmaker Wigfall was primarily interested in military matters, a field in which he performed yeoman's service. Making few concessions in the areas of personal rights, property, use of slaves, and finance, he nevertheless was a strong proponent of army reorganization, conscription, and the best possible equipment and supplies for troops in the field. Having worked unceasingly to undermine the president's executive powers, General Wigfall was largely responsible for the bill which made Robert E. Lee general-in-chief of the armies of the Confederacy in the closing weeks of the war. Wigfall then escaped to England, but he returned to the United States in 1872, taking up residence with his daughter in Baltimore. Two years later he went to Galveston, Texas, where he died on February 18, 1874, and where he is buried in the Episcopal Cemetery.

JOHN ALLEN WILCOX (Texas), brother of Major General Cadmus M. Wilcox, C.S.A., was born April 18, 1819, in Greene County, North Carolina. His early life is somewhat obscure, but he seems to have been brought up and educated in Tipton County, Tennessee.[1] By 1850 he was living in Aberdeen, Mississippi, was a Union Whig and a lawyer, and had been a member of the Mississippi legislature and lieutenant colonel of the Second Mississippi in the Mexican War. That same year he was elected to Congress, where his record apparently did not impress his constituents, for he failed to win reelection in 1852.[2]

Upon the expiration of his congressional term Wilcox, seeking greener pastures, moved to San Antonio, Texas. There he continued the practice of his profession and reentered politics as a member of the American, or Know-Nothing, party, which named him as a presidential elector for the state at large in 1856. By 1858 he was back in the Democratic fold, pledging his allegiance in the course of the party convention of that year. As a delegate to the secession convention of 1861 Wilcox was a member of the committee which prepared the ordinance of secession. In November he won a sweeping victory as congressman from the First District to the First Regular Congress, where he served as chairman of the Committee on Territories and Public Lands.

Wilcox was one of the most loyal of the administration's friends,

257

routinely endorsing measure after measure requested by the president and his department heads, because he believed that during the war Congress should bow to the executive's will. He himself introduced only administration-approved measures and heeded Texas' special interests only to the extent of advocating free trade. Curiously enough, he easily won reelection on this record, perhaps because he served as a volunteer aide to General John B. Magruder between sessions. Prior to the convening of the Second Congress, Wilcox died suddenly in Richmond on February 7, 1864, of what was described as "apoplexy." His funeral and interment in Hollywood Cemetery were attended by Congress in a body. To his wife and two small children in San Antonio, he left a fractional interest in some land and town lots and a law library valued at $275.[3]

[1] Dunbar Rowland (ed.), *Encyclopedia of Mississippi History* (4 vols.; Atlanta, 1907), II, 962. Wilcox's middle name was found on a Mexican War service bounty land application by Louis Carr Henry, Washington, D.C., and appears nowhere else.

[2] Wilcox defeated W. S. Featherston (later a Confederate brigadier) in 1850, and was in turn defeated in 1852 by William T. S. Barry (*q.v.*) subsequently a member of the Provisional Confederate Congress from Mississippi.

[3] Probate records, Bexar County, Tex. General Wilcox, however, made a home for his widowed sister-in-law and her children in Washington after the war. His niece, John A. Wilcox's daughter, Mrs. Moncure Burke, was living there as late as 1944. See Freeman, *Lee's Lieutenants*, I, 744.

PETER SINGLETON WILKES (Missouri), according to the record of his enlistment as a private in the Third Missouri (Confederate) Cavalry, was born in Maury County, Tennessee. His grave marker in Rural Cemetery, Stockton, California, states that the year of his birth was 1827. Almost nothing reliable or verifiable has been written about his antebellum career. According to an obituary in the Jefferson City, Missouri, *State Tribune*, he was graduated from college in Missouri in 1852, and a week afterward was elected to the state legislature. The second statement is demonstrably false, and the first cannot be verified. He is usually described as a "Springfield lawyer"; however, his name cannot be found in the 1860 census of Greene County, Missouri, nor in any of the surrounding counties. He gave his occupation as "lawyer" when he enlisted in the Third Missouri on January 20, 1862. According to his obituary in the Stockton, California, *Record*, he served in the commissary department and somehow acquired the honorific of "Colonel," by which he was known in later life. Presumably while still serving in the army, he was elected by the soldier and refugee vote to the Second Regular Confederate Congress in May, 1864,[1] and took his seat on November 8.

Wilkes greatly admired President Davis and in the last desperate months of the Confederacy centered his attention on giving him every power that a commander-in-chief might need. His sole reservation was his unexplained refusal to draft and arm slaves. The rigid Missouri "test oath" drove him from the state at the end of the war, and he made his way to California, some say by way of Mazatlan, Mexico, where he may have tarried for some years. Upon his arrival in Stockton, California, which was to be his permanent home, Wilkes formed a law partnership with the celebrated former chief justice David S. Terry of the California Supreme Court. Like Wilkes, Terry was a former Confederate; his exploits included killing a United States senator and some years later being killed himself by the bodyguard of United States Supreme Court Justice Stephen J. Field, whom he had threatened with violence. Wilkes died in Stockton on January 2, 1900, and was buried there.

[1] His opponent was Thomas W. Freeman (q.v.).

WILLIAM SYDNEY WILSON (Mississippi) was born November 7, 1816, in Snow Hill, Maryland, a state whose loyalties were sharply divided by the Civil War. He may have attended Jefferson College (now Washington and Jefferson) in Pennsylvania, which was the alma mater of his brother Ephraim, a United States senator from Maryland from 1885 until his death in 1891. Their father, also named Ephraim, was a member of the House of Representatives from 1827 to 1831. William Sydney Wilson became a lawyer and, perceiving the opportunities for advancement in the state of Mississippi and having relatives in Natchez, settled in Port Gibson and quickly built up a lucrative practice. He represented Claiborne County in the state legislature during the years 1858–1859 and 1860–1861.

In a special session of the legislature held in November, 1860, Wilson was selected on a committee appointed to draw up the bill which would bring into being the state secession convention. The latter in turn chose him as a delegate to the Provisional Confederate Congress at Montgomery; however, he attended only a few days and resigned in March, 1861. About all that is known of his activities while a member is that he opposed the action of the original convention resolving itself into a provisional congress. Upon his resignation he immediately set about recruiting the Claiborne Volunteers, an infantry company of which he was elected captain and which became Company F of the Second Mississippi Battalion. Wilson soon became its major and with it fought at the Battle of Seven Pines on the peninsula, and in the subsequent campaign in northern Virginia. At the bloody Battle of Sharpsburg on September 17, 1862, Wilson's command was a part of Featherston's brigade of R. H. Anderson's division. Here he was wounded, presumably mortally, for he died on November 3. His body was brought back to Snow Hill for burial in Makemie Memorial Presbyterian Churchyard, where it lies under a stone with the simple inscription "In memory of our beloved brother William Sydney Wilson of the State of Mississippi."

THOMAS JEFFERSON WITHERS (South Carolina) was born at Ebenezer, near Rock Hill, South Carolina, in the year 1804.[1] He was the eldest of nine children, and it is said that when he and his brothers were put to work in the garden, Thomas, by mutual consent, would sit on the fence and regale the others with numerous stories while they did the grubbing.[2] He attended school at Ebenezer and was graduated from South Carolina College (now the state university) in 1825. Three years later he assumed the editorship of the *Telescope*, then an influential newspaper in Columbia, where he remained two years. After marrying the sister-in-law of Governor Stephen Decatur Miller, Withers moved to Camden and commenced the practice of law, having been admitted to the bar in 1828. In 1832 he was elected circuit solicitor and was reelected several times; in 1846 he was elected one of the common-law judges, an office which he held until his death.

During the secession agitation which rent South Carolina for decades, Withers was a moderate, but he was a member of the secession convention, signed the ordinance, and was one of the six delegates from South Carolina to the Montgomery convention which became the Provisional Congress. Here he shocked some people by refusing to kiss the Bible on being sworn in.[3] Considering his grievance against President Davis for a supposed affront years earlier,[4] Withers agreed to surprisingly strong military and financial programs. However, his main interest was in safeguarding the rights of the states. In constitution-writing he proposed to omit "We, the people," to make the powers of Congress "delegated" rather than "granted," and to prevent a state's being sued by a foreign citizen. He was the only congressman to attack the parliamentary features added by Stephens and others. In lawmaking Withers wished to specify state ownership of all former United States property, to let state laws govern river navigation, and to let states administer sequestered property. Finally, and mainly because of a suggestion that the proposed Supreme Court be given appellate jurisdiction over state courts, he resigned in June, 1861.[5] Withers then returned to Camden and resumed his judicial duties. Possessed of more than $100,000 in property in 1860, Judge Withers died almost penniless on November 7, 1865, at his home. He was buried in Quaker Cemetery in Camden.

[1] His only surviving great-granddaughter, Mrs. John Whitaker of Camden, does not know the month and year of Withers' birth, nor is it recorded on his grave marker.

[2] John Amasa May and Joan Reynolds Faunt, *South Carolina Secedes* (Columbia, S.C., 1960), 229.

[3] Howell Cobb to his wife, February 9, 1861, in A. L. Hull, "Correspondence of Thomas Reade Rootes Cobb, 1860–1862," *Southern History Association Publication*, XI, 169.

[4] Chesnut, *A Diary from Dixie*, 9.

[5] T. J. Withers to C. C. Clay, April 18, 1863, in Clay Papers, Duke University, Durham, N.C.

JAMES HERVEY WITHERSPOON [1] (South Carolina) was born at Rock Spring on March 23, 1810, in the Waxhaws of Lancaster District, South Carolina. After a preparatory education, he entered South Carolina College in 1829 and received his bachelor's degree in December, 1831. He then began a long and successful career as a planter. In 1837 Governor Pierce M. Butler appointed him commissioner in equity for Lancaster District, which position he held by successive elections for twenty-seven years. He was also district ordinary for sixteen years. Witherspoon, a lifelong Democrat, apparently did not take an active part in the secession of South Carolina. But when war began he entered the army as a fifty-one-year-old private in the Lancaster Greys commanded by his son-in-law. In August, 1862, he was commissioned colonel of the Eighth Regiment of Reserves, and a year later he became colonel of the Fourth South Carolina Regiment. In October, 1863, while at Camp Witherspoon (named in his honor), he was elected to the Confederate House of Representatives.

In Congress Witherspoon seldom sought to promote his own ideas except to secure tax relief for agriculture. His voting generally indicates acceptance, at least during the war, of Confederate authority over all but the most local matters. He wished Congress rather than the executive departments, however, to make the major decisions about army manpower and taxation. But Witherspoon also saw that the swift course of war required that the president and his subordinates have considerable latitude on other matters. This would explain why he accepted the destruction of property to prevent its capture, Confederate control over the cargo space of state-owned vessels, and wide impressment rights. Only on the questions of habeas corpus and arming the slaves did he reject federal jurisdiction completely.

Witherspoon died at Lancaster Court House on October 3, 1865. It was thought that his death was the result of his constantly holding an unlighted cigar in his mouth, which caused an ulcer on his lip and which eventually undermined his health. He is buried in the Old Presbyterian Churchyard, Lancaster.[2]

[1] Joseph G. Wardlaw (comp.), *Genealogy of the Witherspoon Family* (Yorkville, S.C., 1910), 133.
[2] Information on Witherspoon's interment was provided by Joseph H. Croxton, Lancaster, S.C.

AUGUSTUS ROMALDUS WRIGHT (Georgia) was a native of Georgia, born June 16, 1813, in Wrightsboro, a long-dead village in what is now McDufe (then Columbia) County.[1] He obtained his early education in the school at Appling, the county seat, and then attended the University of Georgia at Athens. Wright studied law at the Litchfield, Connecticut, Law School, was admitted to the bar in 1835, and began practice in Crawfordville, Georgia. The following year he moved to Cassville, where he served as judge of the superior courts of the circuit from 1842 until 1849 when he resigned to resume his law practice. In 1855 he moved to Rome, Georgia, from where he was elected to Congress as a Democrat in 1856 and served one term.

Wright was an antisecession delegate to the Milledgeville convention in January, 1861, but when the die was cast he signed the ordinance along with his colleagues. The same month he was sent to the Montgomery convention (which became the Provisional Congress) as a representative from Georgia's Fifth Congressional District, and in November he was elected over two opponents to the Regular Congress from the new Tenth District. At first he was one of the stronger Confederate nationalists, sometimes voting the central government even broader powers than the administration had requested. His most advanced suggestion, which was enacted, was a bill to let the president bypass the state governors and call directly into service for special duty as many as one hundred thousand volunteers. However, Wright increasingly objected to much of the emergency legislation presented to Congress during 1862 and 1863. He still worked for a larger and better army, but only of volunteers. And he now became a vigilant guardian of personal and property rights. As early as February, 1864, he proposed resolutions asking the president to open peace negotiations, thereupon withdrawing his candidacy for reelection to avoid open controversy.

During the time he served in Congress, Wright organized and equipped Wright's Legion, a command which became a part of the Thirty-eighth Georgia Infantry. According to his sketch in the *Biographical Directory of the American Congress*, he was offered the provisional governorship of Georgia by Abraham Lincoln, perhaps in an effort to revive Union sentiment in the state after Federal troops had invaded it, a post which he declined. When the war ended, Wright resumed his law practice in Rome, and in 1877 he was a member of the Georgia constitutional convention. He died at his estate, Glenwood, near Rome, on March 31, 1891, and was buried in Myrtle Hill Cemetery.

[1] George Raffalovich (comp.), *Dead Towns of Georgia* (Atlanta, 1938), courtesy of Carroll Hart, Director, Georgia Department of Archives and History, Atlanta.

JOHN VINES WRIGHT (Tennessee) was born June 28, 1828, in Purdy, Tennessee, a now defunct village in McNairy County which had the misfortune to be located four miles east of the future right-of-way of the Mobile and Ohio Railroad. After completing preparatory studies, he took courses in both medicine and law at what is now the University of Tennessee in Knoxville, graduating in the latter. He commenced legal practice in Purdy and at once involved himself in politics. At the age of twenty-six Wright was elected to the Thirty-fourth Congress as a Democrat; he was reelected to the two succeeding congresses, serving from March 4, 1855, to March 3, 1861.

With the coming of the Civil War, Wright entered the Confederate army as colonel of the Thirteenth Tennessee Infantry, of which he had recruited a company from McNairy County known as the Wright Boys.[1] In November, 1861, however, he was elected Tenth District representative to the First Regular Confederate Congress, and he was reelected in 1863 by the soldier and refugee vote from his then-occupied district. Wright was absent during much of the First Congress and most of the Second, often due to illness in his refugee family. He seldom participated in debate, but none of this should imply divided loyalty. His voting record indicates that except for an aversion to suspending the writ of habeas corpus, he would confer upon the central government wide jurisdiction over the Confederacy's manpower and resources. Historians are indebted to his article in Volume IV of the *Publications* of the Southern History Association describing discussions in hotel rooms on the advisability of a Confederate Supreme Court.

Wright's career in the years after the war was no less distinguished; he was judge of the circuit court of Tennessee, chancellor and judge of the state supreme court, and in 1880 the candidate of the Anti-Republican Democrats for the office of governor. In 1886 he was chairman of the Northwest Indian Commission and a member of the commission to treat with the Dakota Sioux. The following year President Cleveland appointed Judge Wright to the law division of the General

Land Office, a post which he continued to occupy until his death in Washington on June 11, 1908. He was buried in Rock Creek Cemetery there.

[1] Marcus J. Wright, *Tennessee in the War, 1861–1865* (New York, 1908), Pt. 1, p. 201.

WILLIAM BACON WRIGHT (Texas) was born July 4, 1830, in Columbus, Georgia. According to his obituary in the San Antonio *Daily Express*, he graduated from Princeton at the age of seventeen; however, the university has no record of his attendance. He is also said to have been admitted to law practice in the state of Georgia at the age of nineteen; shortly thereafter, he moved to Eufaula, Alabama. In 1854 Wright moved to Paris, Texas, where he both practiced his profession and engaged in politics. In 1860 he was elected a delegate to the Democratic national convention in Charleston but did not attend. In October, 1861, he campaigned vigorously for a seat in the Confederate Congress and won decisively over three opponents.

In Richmond, Wright was a businesslike congressman who believed that long discussions profited no one. He made only two significant amendments to bills before Congress: to exempt from the draft all militia units engaged in frontier defense, and to exempt from impressment all slaves employed exclusively in raising grain. He disliked any taxes except the tax-in-kind but otherwise was willing to grant the administration whatever it requested. He lost his seat to Simpson H. Morgan (*q.v.*) in 1863. During the last year of the war he served on President Davis' personal staff with the rank of major. Upon the conclusion of hostilities Wright practiced law in Clarksville, Texas, for a time, but he returned to Paris in 1873. Over the years he is said to have defended ninety-two murderers without, according to one source, losing a case.

In 1888, having married a second time, he moved to San Antonio and was for some time engaged in the banking business. He died there August 10, 1895, and was buried in Dignowity Cemetery. He was a great-grandson of George Walton, a signer of the Declaration of Independence.

WILLIAM LOWNDES YANCEY (Alabama) was born on August 10, 1814, in Warren County, Georgia. His father soon died and when his mother remarried in 1822 the family moved to Troy, New York. Yancey attended Williams College from 1830 to 1833 but left before graduation and read law in Greenville, South Carolina, under the antinullificationist Benjamin F. Perry. After practicing law and editing a Unionist

264

newspaper in Greenville for about a year, Yancey moved to Dallas County, Alabama, in 1836. There he began a newspaper and operated a rented plantation, but he was forced back into law when his slaves were decimated by poisoning. In 1841 and 1843 Yancey was elected to the state legislature, and in 1844 he went to Congress. His first debate in Congress led to his second duel, this time with Thomas L. Clingman, who later became a Confederate brigadier. Though neither was injured, Yancey resigned and held no public office for some years; he now lived in Montgomery.

Nevertheless Yancey soon emerged as the strongest and most single-minded defender of southern rights. His Alabama platform of 1848 in answer to the Wilmot Proviso was a complete statement of principles from which he never varied. He delivered hundreds of addresses to spellbound audiences, and his "Scarlet Letter," published in 1858, suggested a southern Confederacy. In the Charleston Democratic convention of 1860 he formulated the "Yancey platform" around which radical state's righters rallied. When it was rejected he led the schism which nominated John C. Breckinridge and endorsed the Yancey platform. In the Alabama secession convention Yancey was the recognized leader of disunion and penned the ordinance of secession. Too radical to be president of the Confederacy, Yancey was sent to Europe to seek recognition for the new nation. Discouraged by his lack of success, he wrote from London that he would accept a senatorship if elected and was duly honored.

As a senator, Yancey saw the presidency as a major threat to constitutional liberty. He wrangled with Davis over appointments, and when denied a commission for his son he accused Davis of "personal enmity."[1] His attacks on Davis as "an irresponsible military dictator"[2] won him wide notoriety—probably more than he deserved.[3] While Yancey used state's rights rhetoric lavishly, he supported most of Memminger's (q.v.) economic programs and voted for conscription and a quite modest list of exemptions. He was far less flexible, however, when executive authority was involved. He demanded that army agents pay market prices for produce impressed; he proposed a quota system of brigadier generals for the states and numerous other devices to reduce Davis' powers of appointment; and he constantly tried to tie the president's hands in foreign affairs. Yancey died at home on July 23, 1863, and is buried in Oakwood Cemetery.

[1] William L. Yancey to Jefferson Davis, May 6, 1863, in William L. Yancey Papers, Department of Archives and History, Montgomery, Ala.

[2] Southern Historical Society Papers, XLVI, 99.

[3] Yancey said "A crew may not like their captain, but if they are mad enough to mutiny while a storm is raging, all hands are bound to go to the bottom." Chesnut, A Diary from Dixie, 207.

APPENDIX I

SESSIONS OF THE
CONFEDERATE CONGRESS

PROVISIONAL CONGRESS

First Session, at Montgomery, Alabama, February 4, 1861, to March 16, 1861

Second Session, at Montgomery, April 29, 1861, to May 21, 1861

Third Session, at Richmond, Virginia, July 20, 1861, to August 31, 1861

Fourth Session, at Richmond, September 3, 1861 (one day only)

Fifth Session, at Richmond, November 18, 1861, to February 17, 1862

FIRST CONGRESS

First Session, at Richmond, February 18, 1862, to April 21, 1862

Second Session, at Richmond, August 18, 1862, to October 13, 1862

Third Session, at Richmond, January 12, 1863, to May 1, 1863

Fourth Session, at Richmond, December 7, 1863, to February 17, 1864

SECOND CONGRESS

First Session, at Richmond, May 2, 1864, to June 14, 1864

Second Session, at Richmond, November 7, 1864, to March 18, 1865

APPENDIX II

STANDING COMMITTEES OF THE CONFEDERATE CONGRESSES

* Temporary appointment.
** No record of an appointment *to* this committee, but recorded in the *Journal of the Confederate Congress* as reporting a bill *from* this committee. Apparently a secretarial error.
# Corresponding member.

The permanent Constitution provided for larger delegations than had existed under the United States, so the Confederate states were forced to redistrict themselves. The numbers below, therefore, designate only the districts represented in the First and Second congresses.

CONGRESSMEN AND REPRESENTATIVE'S DISTRICT	PROVISIONAL CONGRESS	FIRST CONGRESS	SECOND CONGRESS
Akin, Warren Georgia (10)			Claims
Anderson, Clifford Georgia (4)			Ways & Means
Anderson, J. P. Florida	Military Affairs, Public Lands		
Arrington, A. H. North Carolina (5)		Indian Affairs	
Ashe, T. S. North Carolina (7)		Judiciary	

268

CONGRESSMEN AND REPRESENTATIVE'S DISTRICT	PROVISIONAL CONGRESS	FIRST CONGRESS	SECOND CONGRESS
Atkins, J. D. C. Tennessee (9)	Military Affairs	Post Offices & Post Roads	Commerce, Foreign Affairs, Ordnance & Ordnance Stores
Avery, W. W. North Carolina	Military Affairs		
Ayer, L. M. South Carolina (3)		Quartermaster's & Commissary departments, Ordnance & Ordnance Stores	Commerce, Ordnance & Ordnance Stores
Baker, J. M. Florida		Claims, Commerce, Engrossment & Enrollment, Buildings, Naval Affairs, Post Offices & Post Roads, Public Lands	Claims, Naval Affairs, Post Offices & Post Roads, Public Buildings, Public Lands
Baldwin, J. B. Virginia (11)		Ways & Means	Ways & Means
Barksdale, Ethelbert Mississippi (6)		Foreign Affairs, Printing	Ordnance & Ordnance Stores, Ways & Means
Barnwell, R. W. South Carolina	Finance	Finance	Finance, Territories
Barry, W. T. S. Mississippi	Finance		
Bartow, F. S. Georgia	Engrossment, Flag & Seal, Military Affairs		
Bass, Nathan Georgia	None		
Batson, F. I. Arkansas (1)		Military Affairs, Territories & Public Lands	Judiciary

269

CONGRESSMEN AND REPRESENTATIVE'S DISTRICT	PROVISIONAL CONGRESS	FIRST CONGRESS	SECOND CONGRESS
Baylor, J. R. Texas (5)			Indian Affairs, Patents
Bell, C. W. Missouri (3)	Public Lands, Territories	Medical Department, Military Affairs, Patents	
Bell, H. P. Georgia (9)			Elections, Patents, Post Offices & Post Roads
Blandford, M. H. Georgia (3)			Judiciary, *Pay & Mileage
Bocock, T. S. Virginia (5)	None	None	None
Bonham, M. L. South Carolina (4)		Ways & Means	
Boteler, A. R. Virginia (10)	Buildings, Flag & Seal, Indian Affairs, Printing	Flag & Seal, Ordnance & Ordnance Stores, Rules & Officers	
Boudinot, E. C. Cherokee Nation		#Indian Affairs	#Indian Affairs
Boyce, W. W. South Carolina (6)	Executive Departments, Postal Affairs	Naval Affairs, Ways & Means	Naval Affairs
Bradford, A. B. Mississippi	Public Lands		
Bradley, B. F. Kentucky (11)			Ordnance & Ordnance Stores Post Offices & Post Roads
Branch, A. M. Texas (3)			Elections, Military Affairs, Territories & Public Lands
Breckinridge, R. J. Kentucky (11)		Foreign Affairs	

270

CONGRESSMEN AND REPRESENTATIVE'S DISTRICT	PROVISIONAL CONGRESS	FIRST CONGRESS	SECOND CONGRESS
Bridgers, R. R. North Carolina (2)		Military Affairs, Pay & Mileage	Military Affairs
Brockenbrough, J. W. Virginia	Judiciary		
Brooke, Walter Mississippi	Executive Departments, Patents		
Brown, A. G. Mississippi		Naval Affairs, Territories	Naval Affairs
Bruce, E. M. Kentucky (9)		Military Affairs	Ways & Means
Bruce, H. W. Kentucky (7)		Commerce, Enrolled Bills	Foreign Affairs, Patents
Burnett, H. C. Kentucky	None	Buildings, Claims, Commerce, Judiciary, Military Affairs, *Naval Affairs, Pay & Mileage	Claims, Engrossment & Enrollment
Burnett, T. L. Kentucky (6)	None	Claims, Pay & Mileage	Commerce, Pay & Mileage
Callahan, S. B. Creek & Seminole Nations			None
Campbell, J. A. P. Mississippi	Accounts, Pay & Mileage, Territories		
Caperton, A. T. Virginia	Territories	Accounts, Engrossment & Enrollment, Judiciary	Accounts, Engrossment & Enrollment, Foreign Relations, Indian Affairs, Post Offices & Post Roads
Carroll, D. W. Arkansas (3)			Commerce
Caruthers, R. L. Tennessee	Judiciary		

CONGRESSMEN AND REPRESENTATIVE'S DISTRICT	PROVISIONAL CONGRESS	FIRST CONGRESS	SECOND CONGRESS
Chambers, H. C. Mississippi (4)		Commerce, Enrolled Bills, Military Affairs	Flag & Seal, Military Affairs
Chambliss, J. R. Virginia (2)		Naval Affairs	
Chesnut, James South Carolina	Naval Affairs, Territories		
Chilton, W. P. Alabama (6)	Buildings, Postal Affairs, Printing	Patents, Post Offices & Post Roads, Quartermaster's & Commissary departments	Flag & Seal, Judiciary, Patents, Rules & Officers
Chrisman, J. S. Kentucky (5)		Medical Department	Elections, Indian Affairs, Territories & Public Lands
Clapp, J. W. Mississippi (1)		Claims, Elections, Ordnance & Ordnance Stores	
Clark, J. B. Missouri (3)	Foreign Affairs, Indian Affairs	Foreign Affairs, Indian Affairs, Post Offices & Post Roads, Printing, Public Lands, Territories	Elections, Military Affairs
Clark, W. W. Georgia (6)		**Medical Department, Post Offices & Post Roads, Quartermaster's & Commissary departments	
Clay, C. C. Alabama		Commerce, Indian Affairs, Military Affairs	
Clayton, A. M. Mississippi	Judiciary		

272

CONGRESSMEN AND REPRESENTATIVE'S DISTRICT	PROVISIONAL CONGRESS	FIRST CONGRESS	SECOND CONGRESS
Clopton, David Alabama (7)		Claims, Naval Affairs, Ordnance & Ordnance Stores	Medical Department, Naval Affairs
Cluskey, M. W. Tennessee (11)			Naval Affairs
Cobb, Howell Georgia	None		
Cobb, T. R. R. Georgia	Judiciary, Printing		
Collier, C. F. Virginia (4)		Commerce, Naval Affairs	
Colyar, A. S. Tennessee (3)			Ways & Means
Conrad, C. M. Louisiana (2)	Executive Departments, Naval Affairs	Naval Affairs, Ordnance & Ordnance Stores	Public Buildings, Ways & Means
Conrow, A. H. Missouri (4)	Finance	Post Offices & Post Roads	Public Buildings, Quartermaster's & Commissary departments
Cooke, W. M. Missouri (1)	Accounts, Commerce, Naval Affairs	Commerce, Ordnance & Ordnance Stores	
Craige, Burton North Carolina	None		
Crawford, M. J. Georgia	Accounts, Commercial Affairs		
Crockett, J. W. Kentucky (2)		Elections	
Cruikshank, M. H. Alabama (4)			Enrolled Bills, Ordnance & Ordnance Stores, Printing

CONGRESSMEN AND REPRESENTATIVE'S DISTRICT	PROVISIONAL CONGRESS	FIRST CONGRESS	SECOND CONGRESS
Currin, D. M. Tennessee (1)	Commercial Affairs, Naval Affairs	Buildings, Naval Affairs	
Curry, J. L. M. Alabama (4)	Commercial Affairs, Flag & Seal, Postal Affairs	Commerce, Elections	
Darden, S. H. Texas (1)			Naval Affairs
Dargan, E. S. Alabama (9)		Judiciary	
Davidson, A. T. North Carolina (10)	None	Post Offices & Post Roads, Quartermaster's & Commissary departments	
Davis, George North Carolina	None	Buildings, Claims, Finance, *Naval Affairs	
Davis, Nicholas Alabama	Pay & Mileage, Public Lands, Territories		
Davis, Reuben Mississippi (2)		Military Affairs	
Dawkins, J. B. Florida (1)		Elections, Naval Affairs, Quartermaster's & Commissary departments	
De Clouet, Alexandre Louisiana	Accounts, Commercial Affairs		
De Jarnette, D. C. Virginia (8)		Foreign Affairs	Foreign Affairs, Medical Department
DeWitt, W. H. Tennessee	Printing, Territories		
Dickinson, J. S. Alabama (9)			Claims, Commerce

CONGRESSMEN AND REPRESENTATIVE'S DISTRICT	PROVISIONAL CONGRESS	FIRST CONGRESS	SECOND CONGRESS
Dortch, W. T. North Carolina		Accounts, Commerce, Engrossment & Enrollment, Naval Affairs	Accounts, Commerce, Engossment & Enrollment
Dupré, L. J. Louisiana (4)		Indian Affairs, Printing	Judiciary, Printing
Echols, J. H. Georgia (6)			Indian Affairs, Medical Department, Pay & Mileage
Elliott, J. M. Kentucky (12)	None	Enrolled Bills, Indian Affairs	Indian Affairs, Post Offices & Post Roads
Ewing, G. W. Kentucky (4)	None	Territories & Public Lands	Claims, Territories & Public Lands
Farrow, James South Carolina (5)		Claims, Medical Department	Accounts, Claims, Commerce, Medical Department
Fearn, Thomas Alabama	Public Lands, Territories		
Foote, H. S. Tennessee (5)		Foreign Affairs, Quartermaster's & Commissary departments	Foreign Affairs, Quartermaster's & Commissary departments
Ford, S. H. Kentucky	None		
Forman, T. M. Georgia	None		
Foster, T. J. Alabama (1)		Accounts, Territories & Public Lands	Indian Affairs, Post Offices & Post Roads, Territories & Public Lands
Freeman, T. W. Missouri (6)	Postal Affairs	Enrolled Bills, Naval Affairs, Territories & Public Lands	

275

CONGRESSMEN AND REPRESENTATIVE'S DISTRICT	PROVISIONAL CONGRESS	FIRST CONGRESS	SECOND CONGRESS
Fuller, T. C. North Carolina (4)			Commerce, Enrolled Bills, Patents
Funsten, David Virginia (9)		Printing	*Flag & Seal, Naval Affairs
Gaither, B. S. North Carolina (9)		Naval Affairs	Judiciary
Gardenhire, E. L. Tennessee (4)		Claims, Elections, **Enrolled Bills	
Garland, A. H. Arkansas (3)	**Judiciary, Public Lands	Enrolled Bills, Judiciary, Medical Department	Judiciary (House), *Military Affairs (Senate), Post Offices & Post Roads (Senate), Territories & Public Lands (House)
Garland, R. K. Arkansas (2)			Ways & Means
Garnett, M. R. H. Virginia (1)		Military Affairs, Ways & Means	
Gartrell, L. J. Georgia (8)		Judiciary	
Gentry, M. P. Tennessee (6)		None	
Gholson, T. S. Virginia (4)			Judiciary
Gilmer, J. A. North Carolina (6)			Elections, Ways & Means
Goode, John Virginia (6)		*Enrolled Bills, Indian Affairs, Medical Department	Commerce, Printing
Graham, M. D. Texas (5)		Ways & Means	
Graham, W. A. North Carolina			Finance, Naval Affairs

CONGRESSMEN AND REPRESENTATIVE'S DISTRICT	PROVISIONAL CONGRESS	FIRST CONGRESS	SECOND CONGRESS
Gray, Henry Louisiana (5)			Judiciary
Gray, P. W. Texas (3)		Flag & Seal, Judiciary	
Gregg, John Texas	Accounts, Claims, Military Affairs		
Hale, S. F. Alabama	Indian Affairs, Judiciary, Military Affairs		
Hanly, T. B. Arkansas (4)		Accounts, **Claims, Enrolled Bills, Indian Affairs, Post Offices & Post Roads, *Quartermaster's & Commissary departments	Indian Affairs, Military Affairs, Pay & Mileage
Harris, T. A. Missouri (2)	Military Affairs	Military Affairs	
Harris, W. P. Mississippi	Judiciary, Military Affairs, Public Lands		
Harrison, J. T. Mississippi	Flag & Seal, Postal Affairs, Printing		
Hartridge, Julian Georgia (1)		Commerce, Ordnance & Ordnance Stores, *Ways & Means	Commerce
Hatcher, R. A. Missouri (7)			*Enrolled Bills, Ordnance & Ordnance Stores
Haynes, L. C. Tennessee		Judiciary, Patents, Post Offices & Post Roads, Printing	Commerce, Judiciary, Patents, Post Offices & Post Roads, Printing

277

CONGRESSMEN AND REPRESENTATIVE'S DISTRICT	PROVISIONAL CONGRESS	FIRST CONGRESS	SECOND CONGRESS
Heiskell, J. B. Tennessee (1)		Judiciary	Claims, Elections, Patents
Hemphill, John Texas	**Finance, Judiciary		
Henry, G. A. Tennessee		Finance, Military Affairs, Pay & Mileage	Military Affairs, Public Lands
Herbert, C. C. Texas (2)		Ordnance & Ordnance Stores, Post Offices & Post Roads	Claims, Commerce
Hill, B. H. Georgia	Claims, Patents, Postal Affairs	Judiciary, *Naval Affairs, Patents, Printing	Judiciary, Patents
Hilton, R. B. Florida (2)		Military Affairs, Patents, Post Offices & Post Roads	Elections, Military Affairs, Territories & Public Lands
Hodge, B. L. Louisiana (5)			None
Hodge, G. B. Kentucky (8)	None	Naval Affairs, Ordnance & Ordnance Stores	
Holcombe, J. P. Virginia (7)		Judiciary	
Holder, W. D. Mississippi (2)		None	Elections, Medical Department, Naval Affairs, Public Buildings
Holliday, F. W. M. Virginia (10)			Claims, Quartermaster's & Commissary departments
Holt, Hines, Georgia (3)		Ways & Means	

278

CONGRESSMEN AND REPRESENTATIVE'S DISTRICT	PROVISIONAL CONGRESS	FIRST CONGRESS	SECOND CONGRESS
House, J. F. Tennessee	Finance		
Hunter, R. M. . M. T. Virginia	Finance	Finance, Foreign Affairs	Finance
Ingram, Porter Georgia (3)		*Medical Department	
Jemison, Robert Alabama		*Claims, *Finance, Naval Affairs	Finance, Post Offices & Post Roads
Jenkins, A. G. Virginia (14)		Printing, Territories & Public Lands	
Johnson, H. V. Georgia		Finance, Foreign Affairs, Naval Affairs, *Post Offices & Post Roads	Naval Affairs
Johnson, R. W. Arkansas	Indian Affairs, **Military Affairs	*Accounts, Indian Affairs, Military Affairs, Naval Affairs	Indian Affairs, Military Affairs, Public Lands, Rules
Johnson, Thomas Kentucky	Military Affairs		
Johnson, W. P. Missouri		Claims	Claims, Engrossment & Enrollment, Foreign Relations, Indian Affairs
Johnston, Robert Virginia (15)	None	Post Offices & Post Roads	Accounts, Quartermaster's & Commissary departments
Jones, G. W. Tennessee (7)		Rules & Officers, Ways & Means	
Jones, H. C. Alabama	Claims, Indian Affairs, Patents, Pay & Mileage		

279

CONGRESSMEN AND REPRESENTATIVE'S DISTRICT	PROVISIONAL CONGRESS	FIRST CONGRESS	SECOND CONGRESS
Jones, R. M. Choctaw Nation		None	
Jones, T. M. Tennessee	Flag & Seal, Naval Affairs		
Keeble, E. A. Tennessee (6)			Judiciary
Keitt, L. M. South Carolina	Foreign Affairs, Indian Affairs		
Kenan, A. H. Georgia (4)	Engrossment, Military Affairs	Military Affairs	
Kenan, O. R. North Carolina (3)		Accounts	
Kenner, D. F. Louisiana (3)	Finance, Patents	Ways & Means	Ways & Means
Lamkin, J. T. Mississippi (7)			Commerce, Patents, Post Offices & Post Roads
Lander, William North Carolina (8)		Patents, Quartermaster's & Commissary departments	
Leach, J. M. North Carolina (7)			Quartermaster's & Commissary departments
Leach, J. T. North Carolina (3)			Post Offices & Post Roads, Territories & Public Lands
Lester, G. N. Georgia (8)			Quartermaster's & Commissary departments, Rules & Officers
Lewis, D. P. Alabama	Indian Affairs, Patents		
Lewis, D. W. Georgia (5)		*Printing, Rules & Officers, Territories & Public Lands	

CONGRESSMEN AND REPRESENTATIVE'S DISTRICT	PROVISIONAL CONGRESS	FIRST CONGRESS	SECOND CONGRESS
Lewis, J. W. Georgia		Finance, Post Offices & Post Roads	
Logan, G. W. North Carolina (10)			Ordnance & Ordnance Stores, Printing
Lyon, F. S. Alabama (5)		Ways & Means	Ways & Means
Lyons, James Virginia (3)		Commerce, Public Buildings	
McCallum, James Tennessee (7)			Accounts, Medical Department, Post Offices & Post Roads
McDowell, T. D. S. North Carolina (4)	None	Commerce	
MacFarland, W. H. Virginia	*Commercial Affairs		
Machen, W. B. Kentucky (1)		Accounts, Ways & Means	Quartermaster's & Commissary departments
McLean, J. R. North Carolina (6)		Claims, Foreign Affairs	
McMullen, LaFayette Virginia (13)			Post Offices & Post Roads, Public Buildings, Territories & Public Lands
McQueen, John South Carolina (1)		Accounts, Foreign Affairs	
McRae, C. J. Alabama	Buildings, Engrossment, Finance, Naval Affairs		
McRae, J. J. Mississippi (7)			Quartermaster's & Commissary departments, Ways & Means

CONGRESSMEN AND REPRESENTATIVE'S DISTRICT	PROVISIONAL CONGRESS	FIRST CONGRESS	SECOND CONGRESS
Macwillie, M. H. Arizona Territory		None	None
Marshall, Henry Louisiana (5)	Claims, Public Lands, Territories	Patents, Quartermaster's & Commissary departments, Territories & Public Lands	
Marshall, Humphrey Kentucky (8)			Military Affairs
Martin, J. M. Florida (1)		Naval Affairs	
Mason, J. M. Virginia	**Foreign Affairs		
Maxwell, A. E. Florida		Commerce, Engrossment & Enrollment, Foreign Affairs, Naval Affairs, Patents	Commerce, Engrossment & Enrollment, Indian Affairs, Patents
Memminger, C. G. South Carolina	Commercial Affairs		
Menees, Thomas Tennessee (8)		Medical Department, Printing, Territories & Public Lands	Medical Department, Territories & Public Lands
Miles, W. P. South Carolina (2)	Commercial Affairs, Flag & Seal, Military Affairs, Printing	Military Affairs	Military Affairs
Miller, S. A. Virginia (14)		Territories & Public Lands	Elections, Indian Affairs
Mitchel, C. B. Arkansas		Accounts, Engrossment & Enrollment, Post Offices & Post Roads	Post Offices & Post Roads, Territories

282

CONGRESSMEN AND REPRESENTATIVE'S DISTRICT	PROVISIONAL CONGRESS	FIRST CONGRESS	SECOND CONGRESS
Monroe, T. B. Kentucky	Foreign Affairs, Judiciary, **Military Affairs		
Montague, R. L. Virginia (1)			Ordnance & Ordnance Stores, Rules & Officers
Moore, J. W. Kentucky (10)		Judiciary	Judiciary
Morehead, J. M. North Carolina	None		
Morgan, S. H. Texas (6)			Judiciary
Morton, Jackson Florida	Commercial Affairs, Flag & Seal, Indian Affairs		
Munnerlyn, C. J. Georgia (2)		Claims, *Naval Affairs	
Murray, J. P. Tennessee (4)			Indian Affairs, Ordnance & Ordnance Stores
Nisbet, E. A. Georgia	Foreign Affairs, Territories		
Norton, N. L. Missouri (2)			Claims, Territories & Public Lands
Ochiltree, W. B. Texas	Military Affairs, Pay & Mileage, Postal Affairs, Territories		
Oldham, W. S. Texas	**Engrossment, Judiciary, Naval Affairs, Territories	Commerce, Indian Affairs, Naval Affairs, Post Offices & Post Roads	Claims, Commerce, *Finance, Indian Affairs, *Judiciary, Post Offices & Post Roads

283

CONGRESSMEN AND REPRESENTATIVE'S DISTRICT	PROVISIONAL CONGRESS	FIRST CONGRESS	SECOND CONGRESS
Orr, James L. South Carolina	None	Commerce, Flag & Seal, Foreign Affairs, Pay & Mileage	*Finance, Foreign Relations, Printing, Rules
Orr, Jehu A. Mississippi (1)	Claims, Engrossment, Patents		Foreign Affairs, Quartermaster's & Commissary departments
Oury, G. H. Arizona Territory	None		
Owens, J. B. Florida	Accounts, Naval Affairs		
Perkins, John Louisiana (6)	Foreign Affairs, **Military Affairs, Printing	Foreign Affairs, Rules & Officers, Ways & Means	Commerce, Foreign Affairs, Rules & Officers
Peyton, R. L. Y. Missouri	None	Claims, Commerce, Engrossment & Enrollment, Indian Affairs, Post Offices & Post Roads	
Phelan, James Mississippi		Engrossment & Enrollment, Indian Affairs, Judiciary, Printing	
Preston, Walter Virginia (13)	None	Foreign Affairs, Quartermaster's & Commissary departments	
Preston, William B. Virginia	**Military Affairs	Flag & Seal, Foreign Affairs, Military Affairs	
Pryor, R. A. Virginia (4)	Military Affairs	Military Affairs	
Pugh, J. L. Alabama (8)		Military Affairs, Public Buildings	Military Affairs, Public Buildings
Puryear, R. C. North Carolina	**Naval Affairs		

284

CONGRESSMEN AND REPRESENTATIVE'S DISTRICT	PROVISIONAL CONGRESS	FIRST CONGRESS	SECOND CONGRESS
Ralls, J. P. Alabama (3)		Indian Affairs, Medical Department	
Ramsay, J. G. North Carolina (8)			Medical Department, Naval Affairs
Read, H. E. Kentucky (3)		Patents	Medical Department, Quartermaster's & Commissary departments
Reade, E. G. North Carolina		Finance	
Reagan, J. H. Texas	None		
Rhett, R. B. South Carolina	Foreign Affairs		
Rives, W. C. Virginia (7)	Foreign Affairs		Flag & Seal, Foreign Affairs
Robinson, Cornelius Alabama	Postal Affairs		
Rogers, S. S. Florida (1)			Enrolled Bills, Indian Affairs, Naval Affairs
Royston, G. D. Arkansas (2)		Medical Department, Post Offices & Post Roads, Quartermaster's & Commissary departments	
Ruffin, Thomas North Carolina	None		
Russell, C. W. Virginia (16)	None	Judiciary, **Naval Affairs	Judiciary
Rust, Albert Arkansas	Postal Affairs		
Sanderson, J. P. Florida	Claims, Military Affairs, Public Lands		

285

CONGRESSMEN AND REPRESENTATIVE'S DISTRICT	PROVISIONAL CONGRESS	FIRST CONGRESS	SECOND CONGRESS
Smith, W. N. H. North Carolina (1)	None	Elections, Medical Department, Rules & Officers	Claims, Rules & Officers
Smith, W. R. Alabama (2)		Flag & Seal, Foreign Affairs, *Printing	Foreign Affairs
Snead, T. L. Missouri (1)			Foreign Affairs
Sparrow, Edward Louisiana	Flag & Seal, Indian Affairs, Military Affairs	Military Affairs	Military Affairs
Staples, W. R. Virginia (12)	Military Affairs	Elections, Patents	Military Affairs
Stephens, A. H. Georgia	Executive Departments		
Strickland, Hardy Georgia (9)		Accounts, Patents	
Swan, W. G. Tennessee (2)		Military Affairs	Military Affairs, Printing
Thomas, J. H. Tennessee	Foreign Affairs		
Thomas, J. J. Kentucky	None		
Thomason, H. F. Arkansas	Territories		
Tibbs, W. H. Tennessee (3)		Enrolled Bills, Indian Affairs	
Toombs, R. A. Georgia	Finance		
Triplett, G. W. Kentucky (2)			Claims
Trippe, R. P. Georgia (7)		Commerce, Elections, Quartermaster's & Commissary departments	
Turner, Josiah North Carolina (5)			Foreign Affairs, Indian Affairs

CONGRESSMEN AND REPRESENTATIVE'S DISTRICT	PROVISIONAL CONGRESS	FIRST CONGRESS	SECOND CONGRESS
Tyler, John Virginia	None		
Venable, A W. North Carolina	**Foreign Affairs, Naval Affairs		
Vest, G. G. Missouri (5)	Judiciary	Elections	Judiciary (House), None (Senate)
Villeré, C. J. Louisiana (1)		Claims, Commerce, Military Affairs	Military Affairs
Walker, R. W. Alabama	Foreign Affairs		Commerce, Engrossment & Enrollment, Judiciary, Post Offices & Post Roads, Public Buildings
Ward, G. T. Florida	Claims, Military Affairs, Public Lands		
Watkins, W. W. Arkansas	Commerce		
Watson, J. W. C. Mississippi			Claims, Engrossment & Enrollment, Judiciary, Printing
Waul, T. N. Texas	Commercial Affairs, Indian Affairs		
Welch, Israel Mississippi (3)		Pay & Mileage, Post Offices & Post Roads, Quartermaster's & Commissary departments	Accounts, Claims
White, D. P. Kentucky	None		
Whitfield, R. H. Virginia (2)			Naval Affairs, Patents

CONGRESSMEN AND REPRESENTATIVE'S DISTRICT	PROVISIONAL CONGRESS	FIRST CONGRESS	SECOND CONGRESS
Wickham, W. C. Virginia (3)			Military Affairs
Wigfall, L. T. Texas	Foreign Affairs	Flag & Seal, Foreign Affairs, Military Affairs, Territories	Foreign Relations, Military Affairs, Territories
Wilcox, J. A. Texas (1)		Enrolled Bills, Military Affairs, Territories & Public Lands	
Wilkes, P. S. Missouri (6)			Indian Affairs, Post Offices & Post Roads
Wilson, W. S. Mississippi	Engrossment, Patents		
Withers, T. J. South Carolina	Judiciary		
Witherspoon, J. H. South Carolina (1)			Foreign Affairs, Ordnance & Ordnance Stores, Post Offices & Post Roads
Wright, A. R. Georgia (10)	Naval Affairs, Public Lands	Medical Department, Naval Affairs, Pay & Mileage, Printing	
Wright, J. V. Tennessee (10)		Ordnance & Ordnance Stores	Naval Affairs
Wright, W. B. Texas (6)		Claims, Enrolled Bills, Indian Affairs, Patents	
Yancey, W. L. Alabama		Foreign Affairs, Naval Affairs, Public Lands, Territories	

APPENDIX III

MEMBERSHIP OF THE CONGRESSES

PROVISIONAL CONGRESS

February 4, 1861, to February 17, 1862

First Session: February 4, 1861, to March 16, 1861

Second Session: April 29, 1861, to May 21, 1861

Third Session: July 20, 1861, to August 31, 1861

Fourth Session (called): September 3, 1861

Fifth Session: November 18, 1861, to February 17, 1862

President of Congress: Howell Cobb
Secretary of Congress: Johnson J. Hooper, Alabama

ALABAMA

William P. Chilton
Jabez L. M. Curry
Thomas Fearn[1]
Nicholas Davis[2]
Stephen F. Hale
David P. Lewis[3]

Henry C. Jones[4]
Colin J. McRae
John G. Shorter[5]
Cornelius Robinson[6]
Robert H. Smith
Richard W. Walker

[1] Resigned after first session.
[2] Elected to fill vacancy caused by resignation of Thomas Fearn; took his seat on April 29, 1861.
[3] Resigned after first session.
[4] Elected to fill vacancy caused by resignation of David Lewis; took his seat on April 29, 1861.
[5] Resigned in November, 1861, to become governor of Alabama.
[6] Elected to fill vacancy caused by resignation of John G. Shorter; took his seat on November 30, 1861. Resigned January 24, 1862.

ARKANSAS

Augustus H. Garland
Robert W. Johnson
Albert Rust

Hugh F. Thomason
W. W. Watkins

FLORIDA

James P. Anderson[7]
George T. Ward[8]
John P. Sanderson[9]

Jackson Morton
James B. Owens

GEORGIA

Francis S. Bartow[10]
Thomas M. Forman[11]
Howell Cobb
Thomas R. R. Cobb
Martin J. Crawford
Benjamin H. Hill

Augustus H. Kenan
Eugenius A. Nisbet[12]
Nathan Bass[13]
Alexander H. Stephens
Robert Toombs
Augustus R. Wright

KENTUCKY

Henry C. Burnett
Theodore L. Burnett
John M. Elliott
George W. Ewing
Samuel H. Ford

George B. Hodge
Thomas Johnson
Thomas B. Monroe
John J. Thomas
Daniel P. White

LOUISIANA

Charles M. Conrad
Alexandre de Clouet
Duncan F. Kenner

Henry Marshall
John Perkins
Edward Sparrow

MISSISSIPPI

William T. S. Barry
Walker Brooke

Wiley P. Harris
James T. Harrison

[7] Resigned April 8, 1861.

[8] Elected to fill vacancy caused by resignation of James P. Anderson; took his seat on May 2, 1861. Resigned February 5, 1862.

[9] Appointed to fill vacancy caused by resignation of George T. Ward; took his seat on February 5, 1862.

[10] Killed at First Manassas on July 21, 1861.

[11] Appointed to fill vacancy caused by death of Francis S. Bartow; took his seat on August 7, 1861.

[12] Resigned in December, 1861.

[13] Appointed to fill vacancy caused by resignation of Eugenius A. Nisbet; took his seat on January 14, 1862.

Josiah A. P. Campbell
Alexander M. Clayton[14]
Alexander B. Bradford[15]

William S. Wilson[16]
Jehu A. Orr[17]

MISSOURI

Caspar W. Bell
John B. Clark
Aaron H. Conrow
William M. Cooke

Thomas W. Freeman
Thomas A. Harris
Robert L. Y. Peyton
George G. Vest

NORTH CAROLINA

Francis B. Craige
Allen T. Davidson
George Davis
Thomas D. S. McDowell
John M. Morehead

Richard C. Puryear
Thomas Ruffin
William N. H. Smith
Abraham W. Venable

SOUTH CAROLINA

Robert W. Barnwell
William W. Boyce
James Chesnut
Lawrence M. Keitt
Christopher G. Memminger

William P. Miles
Robert B Rhett
Thomas J. Withers[18]
James L. Orr[19]

TENNESSEE

John D. C. Atkins
Robert L. Caruthers
David M. Currin
William H. DeWitt

John F. House
Thomas M. Jones
James H. Thomas

TEXAS

John Gregg
John Hemphill[20]
William B. Ochiltree
Williamson S. Oldham

John H. Reagan
Thomas N. Waul
Louis T. Wigfall

[14] Resigned May 11, 1861.
[15] Elected to fill vacancy caused by resignation of Alexander M. Clayton; took his seat on December 5, 1861.
[16] Resigned after first session.
[17] Elected to fill vacancy caused by resignation of William S. Wilson; took his seat on April 29, 1861.
[18] Resigned after second session.
[19] Appointed to fill vacancy caused by resignation of Thomas J. Withers; took his seat on February 17, 1862.
[20] Died January 4, 1862.

292

VIRGINIA

Thomas S. Bocock	William B. Preston
Alexander R. Boteler	Roger A. Pryor
John W. Brockenbrough	William C. Rives
Robert M. T. Hunter	Charles W. Russell
Robert Johnston	Robert E. Scott
William H. MacFarland	James A. Seddon
James M. Mason	Waller R. Staples
Walter Preston	John Tyler[21]

ARIZONA TERRITORY

Granville Oury

FIRST CONGRESS

February 18, 1862, to February 17, 1864

First Session: February 18, 1862, to April 21, 1862

Second Session: August 18, 1862, to October 13, 1862

Third Session: January 12, 1863, to May 1, 1863

Fourth Session: December 7, 1863, to February 17, 1864

Vice-President: Alexander H. Stephens, Georgia

President of the Senate Pro Tempore: Robert M. T. Hunter

Secretary of the Senate: James H. Nash, South Carolina

Speaker of the House: Thomas S. Bocock

Clerks of the House: Robert E. Dixon, Georgia; Albert R. Lamar,[22] Georgia

ALABAMA

Senators

Clement C. Clay	Robert Jemison[24]
William L. Yancey[23]	

[21] Died January 18, 1862.
[22] Elected April 25, 1865.
[23] Died July 23, 1863.
[24] Elected to fill vacancy caused by death of William L. Yancey; took his seat on December 28, 1863.

293

Representatives

William P. Chilton
David Clopton
Jabez L. M. Curry
Edmund S. Dargan
Thomas J. Foster

Francis S. Lyon
James L. Pugh
John P. Ralls
William R. Smith

ARKANSAS

Senators

Robert W. Johnson

Charles B. Mitchel

Representatives

Felix I. Batson
Augustus H. Garland[25]

Thomas B. Hanly
Grandison D. Royston

FLORIDA

Senators

James M. Baker

Augustus E. Maxwell

Representatives

James B. Dawkins[26]
James M. Martin[27]

Robert B. Hilton

GEORGIA

Senators

Benjamin H. Hill
John W. Lewis[28]

Herschel V. Johnson[29]

Representatives

William W. Clark
Lucius J. Gartrell
Julian Hartridge
Hines Holt[30]

David W. Lewis
Charles J. Munnerlyn
Hardy Strickland
Robert P. Trippe

[25] Election unsuccessfully contested by Jilson P. Johnson.

[26] Resigned December 8, 1862.

[27] Elected to fill vacancy caused by resignation of James B. Dawkins; took his seat on March 25, 1863.

[28] When Robert Toombs refused to accept his election to the Confederate Senate, Lewis was appointed to the position to serve until the place could be filled. He took his seat on April 7, 1862.

[29] Elected to fill vacancy caused by Robert Toombs's nonacceptance of the position; took his seat on January 19, 1863.

[30] Resigned after third session.

Porter Ingram[31]   Augustus R. Wright
Augustus H. Kenan

Senators

Henry C. Burnett   William E. Simms

Representatives

Robert J. Breckinridge   John M. Elliott
Eli M. Bruce   George W. Ewing
Horatio W. Bruce   George B. Hodge
Theodore L. Burnett   Willis B. Machen
James S. Chrisman   James W. Moore
John W. Crockett   Henry E. Read

LOUISIANA

Senators

Thomas J. Semmes   Edward Sparrow

Representatives

Charles M. Conrad   Henry Marshall
Lucius J. Dupré   John Perkins
Duncan F. Kenner   Charles J. Villeré

MISSISSIPPI

Senators

Albert G. Brown   James Phelan

Representatives

Ethelbert Barksdale   William D. Holder[33]
Henry C. Chambers   John J. McRae
Jeremiah W. Clapp   Otho R. Singleton
Reuben Davis[32]   Israel Welsh

MISSOURI[34]

[31] Elected to fill vacancy caused by resignation of Hines Holt; took his seat on January 12, 1864.

[32] Resigned after third session.

[33] Elected to fill vacancy caused by resignation of Reuben Davis; took his seat on January 21, 1864.

[34] Representative-elect Hyer never took his seat and the seventh district was unrepresented for the entire First Congress.

295

Senators

John B. Clark   Waldo P. Johnson[36]
Robert L. Y. Peyton[35]

Representatives

Caspar W. Bell   Thomas W. Freeman
Aaron H. Conrow   Thomas A. Harris
William M. Cooke[37]   George G. Vest

NORTH CAROLINA

Senators

George Davis[38]   William T. Dortch
Edwin G. Reade[39]

Representatives

Archibald H. Arrington   Owen R. Kenan
Thomas S. Ashe   William Lander
Robert R. Bridgers   Thomas D. S. McDowell
Allen T. Davidson   James R. McLean
Burgess S. Gaither   William N. H. Smith

SOUTH CAROLINA

Senators

Robert W. Barnwell   James L. Orr

Representatives

Lewis M. Ayer   James Farrow
Milledge L. Bonham[40]   John McQueen
William D. Simpson[41]   William P. Miles
William W. Boyce

TENNESSEE

Senators

Gustavus A. Henry   Landon C. Haynes

[35] Died September 3, 1863.

[36] Appointed to fill vacancy caused by death of Robert L. Y. Peyton; took his seat on December 24, 1863.

[37] Died April 14, 1863.

[38] Resigned in January, 1864, to become Confederate attorney general.

[39] Appointed to fill vacancy caused by resignation of George Davis; took his seat on January 22, 1864.

[40] Resigned after second session to become governor of South Carolina.

[41] Elected to fill vacancy caused by resignation of Milledge L. Bonham; took his seat on February 5, 1863.

Representatives

John D. C. Atkins

David M. Currin

Henry S. Foote

E. L. Gardenhire

Meredith P. Gentry

Joseph B. Heiskell[42]

George W. Jones

Thomas Menees

William G. Swan

William H. Tibbs

John V. Wright

TEXAS

Senators

Williamson S. Oldham

Louis T. Wigfall

Representatives

Malcolm D. Graham

Peter W. Gray

Caleb C. Herbert

Franklin B. Sexton

John A. Wilcox

William B. Wright

VIRGINIA

Senators

Robert M. T. Hunter

William B. Preston[43]

Allen T. Caperton[44]

Representatives

John B. Baldwin

Thomas S. Bocock

Alexander R. Boteler

John R. Chambliss

Daniel C. De Jarnette

Muscoe R. H. Garnett

John Goode

James P. Holcombe

Albert G. Jenkins[45]

Samuel A. Miller[46]

Robert Johnston

James Lyons

Walter Preston

Roger A. Pryor[47]

Charles F. Collier[48]

Charles W. Russell

William Smith[49]

David Funsten[50]

Waller R. Staples

[42] Resigned February 6, 1864.

[43] Died November 16, 1862.

[44] Elected to fill vacancy caused by death of William B. Preston; took his seat on January 26, 1863.

[45] Resigned after first session.

[46] Elected to fill vacancy caused by resignation of Albert G. Jenkins; took his seat on February 24, 1863.

[47] Resigned April 5, 1862.

[48] Elected to fill vacancy caused by resignation of Roger A. Pryor; took his seat on August 18, 1862.

[49] Resigned April 4, 1863.

[50] Elected to fill vacancy caused by resignation of William Smith; took his seat on December 7, 1863.

Malcolm H. Macwillie

CHEROKEE NATION

Elias C. Boudinot

CHOCTAW NATION

Robert M. Jones

SECOND CONGRESS

May 2, 1864, to March 18, 1865

First Session: May 2, 1864, to June 14, 1864

Second Session: November 7, 1864, to March 18, 1865

Vice President: Alexander H. Stephens, Georgia

President of the Senate Pro Tempore: Robert M. T. Hunter

Secretary of the Senate: James H. Nash, South Carolina

Speaker of the House: Thomas S. Bocock

Clerk of the House: Albert R. Lamar, Georgia

ALABAMA[51]

Senators

Robert Jemison   Richard W. Walker

Representatives

William P. Chilton	Thomas J. Foster
David Clopton	Francis S. Lyon
Marcus H. Cruikshank	James L. Pugh
James S. Dickinson	William R. Smith

---

[51] Congress refused to seat Representative-elect W. R. R. Cobb, an avowed Unionist, and the third district of Alabama was not represented in the Second Congress.

ARKANSAS

Senators

Robert W. Johnson

Charles B. Mitchel[52]

Augustus H. Garland[53]

Representatives

Felix I. Batson

Augustus H. Garland

David W. Carroll[54]

Rufus K. Garland

Thomas B. Hanly

FLORIDA

Senators

James M. Baker

Augustus E. Maxwell

Representatives

Robert B. Hilton

Samuel S. Rogers

GEORGIA

Senators

Benjamin H. Hill

Herschel V. Johnson

Representatives

Warren Akin

Clifford Anderson

Hiram P. Bell

Mark H. Blandford

Joseph H. Echols

Julian Hartridge

George N. Lester

John T. Shewmake

James M. Smith

William E. Smith

KENTUCKY

Senators

Henry C. Burnett

William E. Simms

Representatives

Benjamin F. Bradley

Eli M. Bruce

George W. Ewing

Willis B. Machen

---

[52] Died September 20, 1864.

[53] Appointed to the Senate to fill vacancy caused by the death of Charles B. Mitchel; took his seat on November 8, 1864.

[54] Appointed to fill vacancy caused by appointment of Augustus H. Garland to the Senate; took his seat on January 11, 1865.

299

Horatio W. Bruce
Theodore L. Burnett
James S. Chrisman
John M. Elliott

Humphrey Marshall
James W. Moore
Henry E. Read
George W. Triplett

LOUISIANA

Senators

Edward Sparrow

Thomas J. Semmes

Representatives

Charles M. Conrad
Lucius J. Dupré
Duncan F. Kenner
Benjamin L. Hodge[55]

Henry Gray[56]
John Perkins
Charles J. Villeré

MISSISSIPPI

Senators

Albert G. Brown

John W. C. Watson

Representatives

Ethelbert Barksdale
Henry C. Chambers
William D. Holder
John T. Lamkin

Jehu A. Orr
Otho R. Singleton
Israel Welch

MISSOURI

Senators

Waldo P. Johnson

George G. Vest[57]

Representatives

John B. Clark
Aaron H. Conrow
Robert A. Hatcher
Nimrod L. Norton

Thomas L. Snead
George G. Vest
Peter S. Wilkes

---

[55] Died August 12, 1864.

[56] Elected to fill vacancy caused by death of Benjamin L. Hodge; took his seat on December 28, 1864.

[57] Appointed to the Senate to fill vacancy caused by the inability of the Missouri legislature to meet and elect a senator. Resigned his seat in the House on January 12, 1865; took his seat in the Senate on the same day.

NORTH CAROLINA

Senators

William T. Dortch   William A. Graham

Representatives

Robert R. Bridgers   James T. Leach
Thomas C. Fuller   George W. Logan
Burgess S. Gaither   James G. Ramsay
John A. Gilmer   William N. H. Smith
James M. Leach   Josiah Turner

SOUTH CAROLINA

Senators

Robert W. Barnwell   James L. Orr

Representatives

Lewis M. Ayer   William P. Miles
William W. Boyce   William D. Simpson
James Farrow   James H. Witherspoon

TENNESSEE

Senators

Gustavus A. Henry   Landon C. Haynes

Representatives

John D. C. Atkins   James McCallum
Michael W. Cluskey   Thomas Menees
Arthur S. Colyar   John P. Murray
Henry S. Foote   William G. Swan
Joseph B. Heiskell   John V. Wright
Edwin A. Keeble

TEXAS

Senators

Williamson S. Oldham   Louis T. Wigfall

Representatives

John R. Baylor   Caleb C. Herbert
Anthony M. Branch   Simpson H. Morgan[58]
Stephen H. Darden   Franklin B. Sexton

[58] Died December 15, 1864.

Senators

Allen T. Caperton   Robert M. T. Hunter

Representatives

John B. Baldwin   LaFayette McMullen
Thomas S. Bocock   Samuel A. Miller
Daniel C. De Jarnette   Robert L. Montague
David Funsten   William C. Rives[59]
Thomas S. Gholson   Charles W. Russell
John Goode   Waller R. Staples
Frederick W. M. Holliday   Robert H. Whitfield[60]
Robert Johnston   Williams C. Wickham

ARIZONA TERRITORY

Malcolm H. Macwillie

CHEROKEE NATION

Elias C. Boudinot

CREEK AND SEMINOLE NATIONS

Samuel B. Callahan

---

[59] Resigned March 2, 1865.
[60] Resigned March 7, 1865.

APPENDIX IV

MAPS OF OCCUPIED CONFEDERATE TERRITORY
1861–1864

Shaded area denotes the Confederate territory lost at the end of each year.

Territory lost at the end of 1861.

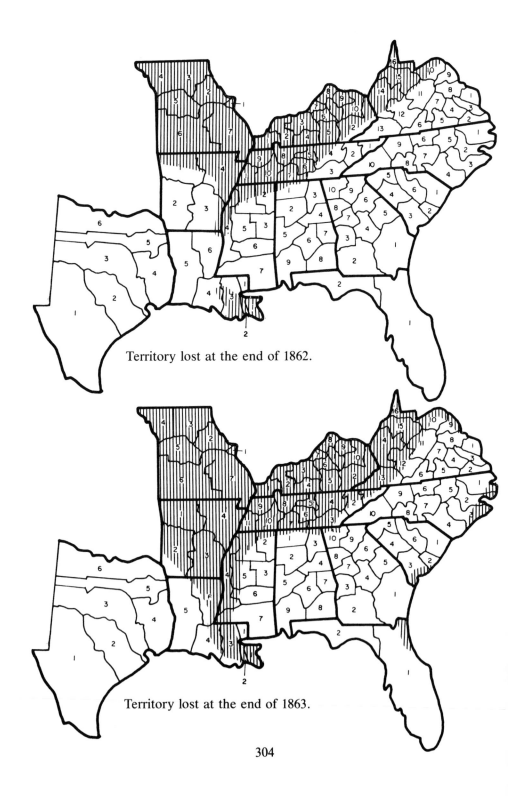

Territory lost at the end of 1862.

Territory lost at the end of 1863.

304

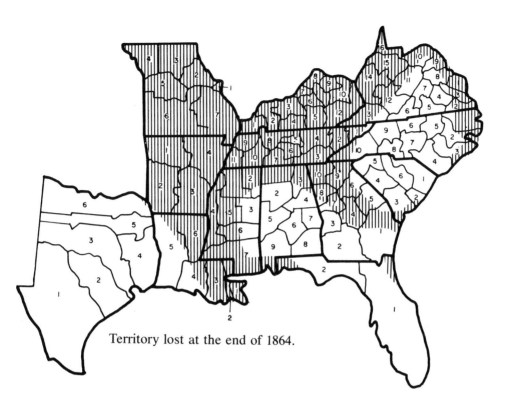

Territory lost at the end of 1864.

BIBLIOGRAPHY

THOUGH THE WORK of the Confederate Congress occupies an important place in many volumes of Confederate history and biography, the literature on the Congress itself is surprisingly scanty. Both Edward Pollard and John Goode published articles entitled "The Confederate Congress," but they wrote from a participant's viewpoint and their judgments are self-serving. The first analysis of the Congress by a trained historian was Enock Walter Sikes's twenty-nine-page pamphlet *Confederate States Congress*, and it was not until more than a decade later that Robert Cleland published his study of the Congress in the *Southwestern Historical Quarterly*. Both men suffered from adulation of Jefferson Davis, but they were acutely aware of the difficult position of a legislative body in wartime.

The first monograph on the subject was W. B. Yearns's *The Confederate Congress* (1960), which emphasized chiefly the formulation of the legislation of Congress. Four years later John Brawner Robbins added a thorough analysis of congressional politics and elections. Richard E. Beringer's "Political Factionalism in the Confederate Congress" is an early study by roll-call analysis. Beringer and Thomas B. Alexander later published *The Anatomy of the Confederate Congress*, an exhaustive roll-call analysis of the congressmen's votes correlated with their politics, wealth, district locations, and other variables.

Mention should also be made of the splendid collection "Proceedings of the . . . Confederate Congress," taken mainly from the Richmond *Examiner*. The authors of this volume, however, advise against total dependence on these "Proceedings" for congressional debate. Other Richmond newspapers reported the debates almost as extensively and often included different material. In addition, newspapers from other states often kept observers in Congress for long stretches, and they naturally paid the greatest attention to their own delegations. The files of the Wilmington (N.C.) *Daily*

Journal and the Charleston (S.C.) *Mercury* are particularly replete with debate nowhere else recorded.

The criterion for who was properly a member of one of the three Confederate congresses rests in the *Executive and Congressional Directory of the Confederate States*, compiled from the *Official Records* and published under the imprimatur of the Record and Pension Office of the War Department in 1899. The compilation was probably made by Brigadier General Marcus J. Wright, late C.S.A., who had been for years the department's agent for the collection of Confederate records. However, this work, a sixteen-page pamphlet, contains several misspellings, does not contain the names of all persons elsewhere listed as members, and does not in every case agree with Wright's own privately printed *General Officers of the Confederate Army*, which as an afterthought also contains a list of the executive and legislative branches of the Confederate government. However, the present volume does include every man who, according to our research in the *Journal of the Congress of the Confederate States of America, 1861–1865,* actually took his seat in that body during its brief existence. There is a gray area, admittedly—the Confederate government was not only insurrectionary but extemporized; elections were not infrequently travesties; and records are disappointingly sparse. Nevertheless, these reservations aside, the authors are confident that all persons with a legitimate (even though in some cases involuntary) claim to membership are sketched.

MANUSCRIPTS

Clay, Clement C. Papers, Duke University, Durham, N. C.

Clingman-Puryear Papers, Southern Historical Collection, University of North Carolina Library, Chapel Hill.

Graham, William A. Papers, North Carolina Department of Archives and History, Raleigh.

Harrison, James T. Papers, Southern Historical Collection, University of North Carolina Library, Chapel Hill.

Hilton, Robert B. Diary, University of Florida Library, Gainesville.

Mallory, Stephen R. Papers, Southern Historical Collection, University of North Carolina, Chapel Hill.

Pickett, John T. Papers, Manuscripts Division, Library of Congress, Washington, D.C.

Stephens, Alexander H. Papers, Manuscripts Division, Library of Congress, Washington, D.C.

Turner, Josiah. Papers, Duke University Library, Durham, N. C.

Vance, Zebulon B. Papers, North Carolina Department of Archives and History, Raleigh.

Walser, Zebulon V. Papers, Southern Historical Collection, University of North Carolina Library, Chapel Hill.

Yancey, William L. Papers, Alabama Department of Archives and
History, Montgomery.

NEWSPAPERS

Arizona Citizen (Tucson)
Arizona Republican (Phoenix)
Arizona Sentinel (Yuma)
Arizona Weekly Enterprise (Florence)
Arizonian (Tucson)
Arkansas State Gazette (Little Rock)
Atlanta *Southern Confederacy*
Augusta (Ga.) *Tri-weekly Constitutionalist*
Austin *Gazette*
Baltimore *Sun*
Baton Rouge *Gazette and Comet*
Brunswick (Ga.) *Advertiser*
Charleston (Mo.) *Enterprise*
Charleston (S.C.) *Mercury*
Chattanooga *Times*
Clarksville (Tex.) *Standard* (later *Northern Standard*)
Cleveland (Tenn.) *Banner*
Cleveland (Tenn.) *Tribune*
Cleveland (Tenn.) *Weekly Herald*
Columbus (Mo.) *Herald*
Copiah County (Miss.) *News*
Dallas *Herald*
Dallas *News*
El Paso *Herald*
Georgetown (Ky.) *Times*
Giles County (Tenn.) *Democrat*
Jackson (Miss.) *Daily Clarion-Ledger*
Jackson (Miss.) *Daily News*
Jackson (Miss.) *Weekly Mississippian*
Jacksonville *Florida Times Union*
Jefferson City (Mo.) *State Tribune*
Louisville *Commercial*
Louisville *Courier-Journal*
Louisville *Daily Democrat*
Louisville *Daily Ledger*
Louisville *Evening Post*
Marietta (Fla.) *Family Friend*
Memphis *Daily Appeal*
Memphis *Daily Avalanche*

Mesilla (N.M.) *Times*
Mobile *Daily Register*
Montgomery *Advertiser*
Moulton (Ala.) *Advertiser*
Mt. Sterling (Ky.) *Advocate*
Nashville *Tennesseean*
New Orleans *Daily Delta*
New Orleans *Daily Picayune*
New Orleans *Times-Democrat*
New York *Times*
Niles National Register
Opelousas (La.) *Courier*
Paris (Tex.) *Morning News*
Paulding (Miss.) *Western Clarion*
Petersburg (Va.) *Index*
Phoenix *Herald*
Pulaski (Tenn.) *Citizen*
Raleigh *Standard*
Richmond *Daily Enquirer*
Richmond *Daily Examiner*
Richmond *Dispatch*
St. Louis *Republican*
St. Martinville (La.) *Weekly Messenger*
San Antonio *Daily Express*
Savannah *Morning News*
Savannah *Republican*
Shreveport (La.) *News*
Sparta (Tenn.) *Expositor*
Stockton (Calif.) *Record*
Talladega (Ala.) *Reporter and Watchtower*
Tallahassee *Sentinel*
Tucson *Star*
Wilmington (N.C.) *Journal*
Wilmington (N.C.) *Morning Star*
Yorkville (S.C.) *Enquirer*

OFFICIAL GOVERNMENT RECORDS

Biographical Directory of the American Congress, 1774–1961. Washington, D.C., 1961.

Heitman, Francis Bernard. *Historical Register of the United States Army, from Its Organization, September 29, 1789, to September 29, 1889*. 2 vols. Washington, D.C., 1903.

Journal of the Congress of the Confederate States of America, 1861–1865. 7 vols. Washington, D.C., 1904–1905.

Matthews, James M., ed. *Public Laws of the Confederate States of America, First Congress, Sessions 1–4; Second Congress, First Session.* Richmond, 1862–64.

———. *Statutes at Large of the Provisional Government of the Confederate States of America.* Richmond, 1864.

Ninth Annual Report of the Commission to the Five Civilized Tribes to the Secretary of the Interior for the Fiscal Year Ended June 30, 1902. Washington, D.C., 1902.

War of the Rebellion: A Compilation of the Official Records of the Union and Confederate Armies. 70 vols. Washington, D.C., 1880–1901.

The authors have scanned all journals of the secession conventions and the state legislatures for information on elections. Those in print are easily accessible and need not be listed herein. The following are on microfilm at the University of North Carolina at Chapel Hill: Arkansas, 1861–62; Florida, 1860–64; Louisiana, 1861; Tennessee, 1861–62; and Texas, 1861–64.

COLLECTED SOURCES

Candler, Allen D., comp. *The Confederate Records of the State of Georgia.* 5 vols. Atlanta, 1909–11.

Hull, A. L., ed. "Correspondence of Thomas Reade Rootes Cobb, 1860–1862." *Southern History Association Publications*, XI (1907), 147–85, 233–60, 312–28.

———. "Thomas Reade Rootes Cobb: Extracts from Letters to His Wife, February 3, 1861–December 10, 1862." *Southern Historical Society Papers*, XXVIII (1900), 280–301.

"Proceedings of the Confederate Congress." *Southern Historical Society Papers*, XLIV–LII (1923–59).

Ramsdell, Charles W., ed. *Laws and Joint Resolutions of the Last Sesssion of the Confederate Congress (November 7, 1864–March 18, 1865) Together with the Secret Acts of the Previous Congresses.* Durham, N.C., 1941.

Reese, George H. ed. *Proceedings of the Virginia State Convention of 1861.* 4 vols. Richmond, 1965.

Smith, C. C. "Some Unpublished History of the Southwest." *Arizona Historical Quarterly*, IV–VI (1933–35), *passim.*

PERSONAL NARRATIVES, DIARIES, AND LETTERS

Bay, William Van Ness. *Reminiscences of the Bench and Bar of Missouri.* St. Louis, 1878.

311

Bell, Hiram P. *Men and Things*. Atlanta, 1907.

Bell, John W., *Memoirs of Governor William Smith of Virginia*. New York, 1891.

Browne, Junius H. *Four Years in Secessia*. Hartford, Conn., 1865.

Chesnut, Mary Boykin. *A Diary from Dixie*. Ed. Ben Ames Williams. Boston, 1949.

Davis, Jefferson. *The Rise and Fall of the Confederate Government*. 2 vols. New York, 1881.

DeLeon, Thomas Cooper. *Four Years in Rebel Capitals*. Mobile, 1890.

Duke, Basil Wilson. *Reminiscences of General Basil W. Duke, C.S.A.* New York, 1911.

Fleming, Francis P. *Memoir of Capt. C. Seton Fleming of the Second Florida Infantry*. Jacksonville, 1884.

Foote, Henry S. *Casket of Reminiscences*. Washington, D.C., 1874.

Goode, John. *Recollections of a Lifetime*. New York, 1906.

Jones, John B. *A Rebel War Clerk's Diary at the Confederate States Capital*. Ed. Howard Swiggett. 2 vols. New York, 1935.

Kean, Richard Garlick Hill. *Inside the Confederate Government: The Diary of Richard Garlick Hill Kean*. Ed. Edward Younger. New York, 1957.

Reagan, John H. *Memoirs, with Special Reference to Secession and the Civil War*. New York, 1906.

Smith, Willilam R. *The History and Debates of the Convention of the People of Alabama, Begun and Held in the City of Montgomery, on the Seventh Day of January, 1861*. Montgomery, 1861.

Sterling, Ada, ed. *A Belle of the Fifties, Memoirs of Mrs. Clay of Alabama*. New York, 1905.

Wiley, Bell I., ed. *Letters of Warren Akin, Confederate Congressman*. Athens, Ga., 1959.

LOCAL AND FAMILY HISTORY

Barksdale, John A. *Barksdale Family History and Genealogy*. San Rafael, Calif., 1940.

Battey, G. M., Jr. *History of Rome & Floyd Co*. Atlanta, 1922.

Butler, John C. *Historical Record of Macon and Central Georgia . . .* Macon, Ga., 1958.

Christian, W. Asbury. *Richmond: Her Past and Present*. Richmond, 1912.

The City of Petersburg, Virginia: The Book of Its Chamber of Commerce. Petersburg, Va., 1894.

Coffman, Edward. *The Story of Logan County* [Ky.]. Nashville, 1962.

Cook, Anna M. G. *History of Baldwin County, Georgia*. Anderson, S.C., 1925.

Eno, Clara B. *History of Crawford County, Arkansas*. Van Buren, Ark., 1951.

Escott, George S. *History & Directory of Springfield & North Springfield*. Springfield, Mo., 1878.

Fairbanks, Jonathan, and Clyde Edwin Tuck. *Past & Present of Greene County, Missouri* . . . Indianapolis, 1915.

Gaines, B. O. *History of Scott County* [Ky.]. N.p., n.d.

Garrett, Franklin. *Atlanta and Its Environs*. New York, 1954.

Hayden, Horace E. *Virginia Genealogies*. Washington, D.C., 1931.

Heyward, James B. *The Genealogy of the Pendarvis-Bedon Families of South Carolina, 1670–1900*. Atlanta, 1905.

History of Cass and Bates County, Mo. St. Joseph, Mo., 1883.

History of Ray County, Mo. St. Louis, 1881.

Holcombe, R. I. *History of Greene County* [Mo.] St. Louis, 1884.

Hyde, William, and H. L. Conard. *Encyclopedia of the History of St. Louis*. St. Louis, 1899.

Langford, Ella Malloy. *Johnson County, Arkansas: The First Hundred Years*. Clarksville, Ark., 1821.

Lewis, W. T. *Genealogy of the Lewis Family in America*. Louisville, 1893.

McGuffey, Charles D. *A Standard History of Chattanooga*. Knoxville, 1911.

Nuremberger, Ruth K. *The Clays of Alabama: A Planter-Lawyer-Politician Family*. Lexington, Ky., 1958.

Perrin, W. H., ed. *County of Christian, Kentucky*. Chicago, 1884.

———, ed. *History of Bourbon, Scott, Harrison and Nicolas Counties* [Ky.]. Chicago, 1882.

Raffalovich, George, comp. *Dead Towns of Georgia*. Atlanta, 1938.

Rea, Ralph R. *Boone County and Its People*. Van Buren, Ark., 1955.

Register, Alvaretta Kenan, comp. *The Kenan Family and Some Allied Families*. Statesboro, Ga., 1967.

Sherrill, William L. *Annals of Lincoln County, North Carolina*. Charlotte, N.C., 1937.

Sims, Carlton C., ed. *A History of Rutherford County* [Tenn.] . . . Murfreesboro, Tenn., 1947.

Stevens, Walter B. *St. Louis, the Fourth City, 1764–1909*. St. Louis, 1909.

Temple, Sarah Blackwell Gober. *The First Hundred Years: A Short History of Cobb County, in Georgia*. Atlanta, 1935.

Thomas, David Y. *Arkansas in War and Reconstruction, 1861–1874*. Little Rock, 1926.

Tyson, John A. *Historical Notes of Noxubee County, Mississippi*. Macon, Miss., 1928.

Wardlaw, Joseph G., comp. *Genealogy of the Witherspoon Family*. Yorkville, S.C., 1910.

Waters, Phileman Berry, comp. *A Genealogical History of the Waters and Kindred Families*. Atlanta, 1902.

Williams, S. C. *History of Johnson City, Tennessee, and Its Environs*. Johnson City, Tenn., 1940.

Wooten, John M. *A History of Bradley County* [Tenn.]. Cleveland, Tenn., 1949.

BIOGRAPHIES AND BIOGRAPHICAL COLLECTIONS

Appleton's Cyclopedia of American Biography. 6 vols. New York, 1898.

Armstrong, Zella, comp. *Notable Southern Families*. Chattanooga, n. d.

Ashe, Samuel A., *et al.*, eds. *Biographical History of North Carolina: From Colonial Times to the Present*. 8 vols. Greensboro, N.C., 1905–17.

Biographical and Historical Memoirs of Mississippi. 2 vols. Chicago, 1891.

Biographical and Historical Memoirs of Northeast Arkansas. Chicago, 1889.

Biographical Cyclopedia of the Commonwealth of Kentucky. N.p., 1896.

The Biographical Encyclopedia of Kentucky. Cincinnati, 1878.

Brewer, Willis. *Alabama: Her History, Resources, War Record and Public Men*. Montgomery, 1872.

Caldwell, J. W. *Sketches of the Bench and Bar of Tennessee*. Knoxville, 1898.

Capers, Henry D. *The Life and Times of C. G. Memminger*. Richmond, 1893.

Charter, Rules, Regulations, and By-laws of the Elmwood Cemetery Association of Memphis. Memphis, 1874.

Chitwood, Oliver P. *John Tyler: Champion of the Old South*. New York and London, 1939.

Connor, R. D. W., *et al. North Carolina Biography*. Chicago and New York, 1919. Vols. IV–VI of R. D. W. Connor *et al.*, *History of North Carolina*. 6 vols. Chicago and New York, 1919.

Cyclopedia of Eminent and Representative Men of the Carolinas of the Nineteenth Century. 2 vols. Madison, Wis., 1892.

Davis, Charles S. *Colin J. McRae: Confederate Financial Agent*. Tuscaloosa, Ala., 1961.

Dowd, Jerome. *Sketches of Prominent Living North Carolinians*. Raleigh, 1888.

Fancher, Frank T. *The Sparta* [Tenn.] *Bar*. Milford, N.H., 1950.

Fleming, Francis P., ed. *Memoirs of Florida . . . by Rowland H. Rerrick*. 2 vols. Atlanta, 1902.

Flippin, Percy S. *Herschel V. Johnson of Georgia: State Rights Unionist*. Richmond, 1931.

French, S. Bassett. "Biographical Sketches" (MS in Virginia State Library, Richmond).

Gaines, William H. *Biographical Register of Members, Virginia State Convention of 1861, First Session*. Richmond, 1969.

Garnett, James M. "Biographical Sketch of Hon. Muscoe Russell Hunter Garnett." *William and Mary College Quarterly*, XVIII (1909–10), 17–37, 71–89.

Garrett, William. *Reminiscences of Public Men in Alabama, for Thirty Years*. Atlanta, 1872.

Green, J. W. *Laws and Lawyers*. Jackson, Tenn., 1950.

Hallum, John. *Biographical and Pictorial History of Arkansas*. Albany, N.Y., 1887.

Hill, Louise B. *Joseph E. Brown and the Confederacy*. Chapel Hill, N.C., 1939.

Historical Catalogue of the University of Mississippi, 1849–1909. Nashville, 1910.

Johnson, Allen, *et al.*, eds. *Dictionary of American Biography*. 20 vols. New York, 1928–44.

King, Alvy L. *Louis T. Wigfall: Southern Fire-eater*. Baton Rouge, 1970.

Kittrell, N. G. *Governors Who Have Been, and Other Public Men of Texas*. Houston, 1921.

Levin, H., ed. *The Lawyers and Lawmakers of Kentucky*. Chicago, 1897.

Mason, Virginia. *The Pub. Life and Diplomatic Correspondence of James M. Mason, with Some Personal History by His Daughter*. Roanoke, Va., 1903.

Meade, Robert Douthit. *Judah P. Benjamin, Confederate Statesman*. New York, 1943.

Memoirs of Georgia. 2 vols. Atlanta, 1895.

Montgomery, Horace. *Howell Cobb's Confederate Career*. Tuscaloosa, Ala. 1959.

National Cyclopedia of American Biography. 37 vols. New York, 1892–1951.

Northen, William J., ed. *Men of Mark in Georgia*. 6 vols. Atlanta, 1907–12.

Oldham, Williamson Simpson. "Memoirs of a Confederate Senator, 1861–1865." MS in University of Texas Library, Austin.

O'Rear, Edward C. *A History of the Montgomery County* [Ky.] *Bar*. Frankfort, Ky., 1945.

Owen, Thomas M. *History of Alabama and Dictionary of Alabama Biography*. 4 vols. Chicago, 1921.

Patrick, Rembert W. *Jefferson Davis and His Cabinet*. Baton Rouge, 1944.

Pearce, Haywood J. *Benjamin H. Hill: Secession and Reconstruction*. Chicago, 1928.

Perrin, W. H., ed. *Southwest Louisiana: Biographical and Historical*. New Orleans, 1891.

Ranck, James B. *Albert Gallatin Brown: Radical Southern Nationalist*. New York, 1937.

Register of Graduates and Former Cadets, United States Military Academy, 1802–1948. New York, 1948.

Reynolds, Emily B., and Joan R. Faunt, comps. *Biographical Directory of the Senate of the State of South Carolina, 1776–1964*. Columbia, S.C., 1964.

Rice, Jessie Pearl. *J. L. M. Curry: Southerner, Statesman, Educator*. New York, 1949.

Shinn, Josiah Hazen. *Pioneers and Makers of Arkansas*. Chicago, 1908.

Speers, William S. *Sketches of Prominent Tennesseeans*. Nashville, 1888.

Thompson, William Y. *Robert Toombs of Georgia*. Baton Rouge, 1966.

Tyler, Lyon G., ed. *Encyclopedia of Virginia Biography*. 5 vols. New York, 1915.

United States Biographical Dictionary and Portrait Gallery. N.p., n.d.

Von Abele, Rudolph R. *Alexander H. Stephens: A Biography*. New York, 1946.

Wheeler, John H. *Reminiscences and Memoirs of North Carolina and Eminent North Carolinians*. N.p., 1878.

White, Laura A. *Robert Barnwell Rhett: Father of Secession*. New York and London, 1931.

GENERAL AND SPECIAL STUDIES

Abel, Annie H. *The American Indian as Participant in the Civil War*. Cleveland, Ohio, 1919.

———. "The Indians in the Civil War." *American Historical Review*, XV (1909–10), 281–96.

Alexander, Thomas B., and Richard E. Beringer. *The Anatomy of the Confederate Congress*. Nashville, 1972.

Battle, J. H., W. H. Perrin, and G. C. Kniffin. *Kentucky: A History of the State*. Louisville, 1885.

Beringer, Richard E. "Political Factionalism in the Confederate Congress." Ph.D. dissertation, Northwestern University, 1966.

Biographical Souvenir of the State of Texas. Chicago, 1889.

Booth, Andrew B. *Records of Louisiana Soldiers and Louisiana Confederate Commands*. New Orleans, 1920.

Brown, John Henry. *Indian Wars and Pioneers of Texas*. Austin, n.d.

Bryan, T. Conn. *Confederate Georgia*. Athens, Ga., 1953.

Catton, Bruce. *The Coming Fury*. New York, 1961.

Cauthen, Charles E. *South Carolina Goes to War*. Chapel Hill, N.C., 1950.

Clauset, Martha B. "Josiah Turner, Jr.: Portrait of a North Carolina Whig, 1821–1865." M.A. thesis, Wake Forest University, 1967.

Cleland, Robert. "Jefferson Davis and the Confederate Congress." *Southwestern Historical Quarterly*, XIX (1915–16), 214–31.

Collins, Lewis, and Richard H. Collins. *History of Kentucky*. Covington, Ky., 1874.

Coulter, Ellis M. "The Movement for Agricultural Reorganization in the Cotton South during the Civil War." *North Carolina Historical Review*, IV (1927), 22–36.

Craven, Avery O. *The Growth of Southern Nationalism, 1848–1861*. Baton Rouge, 1953. Vol. VI of Wendell Holmes Stephenson and E. Merton Coulter, eds. *A History of the South*. 10 vols. Baton Rouge, 1949–

Cunningham, H. H. *Doctors in Gray: The Confederate Medical Service*. Baton Rouge, 1960.

Chronicles of Oklahoma. Autumn, 1965.

Davis, Reuben. *Recollections of Mississippi and Mississippians*. Boston, 1889.

Davis, William W., *The Civil War and Reconstruction in Florida*. New York, 1913.

Evans, Clement Anselm, ed. *Confederate Military History: A Library of Confederate States History*. 12 vols. Atlanta, 1899.

Farish, T. E. *History of Arizona*. Phoenix, 1915.

Freeman, Douglas Southall. *Lee's Lieutenants: A Study in Command*. 3 vols. New York, 1942–44.

Goode, John. "The Confederate Congress." *Conservative Review*, IV (1900), 97–112.

Green, John W. *Law and Lawyers*. Jackson, Tenn., 1950.

Handbook of Texas. Austin, 1952.

Hempstead, Fay. *A Pictorial History of Arkansas, from Earliest Times to the Year 1890*. St. Louis and New York, 1890.

Henderson, Archibald. *North Carolina: The Old North State and the New*. Chicago, 1941.

Hill, Luther B. *A History of the State of Oklahoma*. 2 vols. Chicago, 1909.

History of the Baptist Denomination in Georgia. Atlanta, 1881.

Johnson, L. F. *Famous Kentucky Tragedies and Trials*. Louisville, 1916.

Johnson, R. U., and C. C. Buel, eds. *Battles and Leaders of the Civil War*. 4 vols. New York, 1887–88.

Jones, Charles Edgeworth. *Georgia in the War, 1861–1865*. Atlanta, 1909.

Keleher, William A. *The Fabulous Frontier*. Albuquerque, 1962.

Knight, Lucian Lamar. *Georgia's Landmarks, Memorials and Legends*. Atlanta, 1913.

––––––. *Georgia's Bi-Centennial Memoirs and Memories*. N.p., 1932.

Long, Everette B. *The Civil War Day by Day*. New York, 1971.

May, John Amasa, and Joan Reynolds Faunt. *South Carolina Secedes*. Columbia, S.C., 1960.

Moore, Albert B. *Conscription and Conflict in the Confederacy*. New York, 1924.

Morrison, W. B. *Military Posts and Camps in Oklahoma*. Oklahoma City, 1936.

Neville, A. W. *The Red River Valley Then and Now*. Paris, Tex., 1948.

Paisley, Clifton. *From Cotton to Quail . . .* Gainesville, Fla., 1968.

Pollard, Edward A. "The Confederate Congress." *Galaxy*, VI (1868–69), 749–58.

Ridley, Bromfield L. *Battles and Sketches of the Army of Tennessee*. Mexico, Mo., 1906.

Robbins, John Brawner. "Confederate Nationalism: Politics and Government in the Confederate South, 1861–1865." Ph.D. dissertation, Rice University, 1964.

Rowland, Dunbar, ed. *Encyclopedia of Mississippi History*. Atlanta, 1907.

––––––. *Mississippi, Comprising Sketches of Counties, Towns, Events, Institutions, and Persons . . .* Atlanta, 1907.

––––––, ed. *The Publications of the Misssissippi Historical Society*. Jackson, Miss., 1918.

Sacks, B. *Be It Enacted: The Creation of the Territory of Arizona*. Tucson, 1964.

Shanks, Henry T. *The Secession Movement in Virginia, 1847–1861*. Richmond, 1934.

Sikes, Enoch Walter. *Confederate States Congress*. Raleigh, 1903.

Sonnichsen, C. L. *Tularosa*. New York, 1963.

Spencer, J. H. *A History of Kentucky Baptists from 1769 to 1885*. Cincinnati, 1885.

Starr, Emmett. *Encyclopedia of Oklahoma*. Claremore, Okla., 1912.

Todd, Richard C. *Confederate Finance*. Athens, Ga., 1954.

Thompson, Ed Porter. *History of the First Kentucky Brigade*. Cincinnati, 1868.

————. *History of the Orphan Brigade*. Louisville, 1898.

Wallace, John. *Carpetbag Rule in Florida*. Gainesville, Fla., 1964.

Warner, Ezra J. *Generals in Gray: Lives of the Confederate Commanders*. Baton Rouge, 1964.

Wright, Marcus J. *General Officers of the Confederate Army*. New York, 1911.

————, comp. *Texas in the War*. Hillsboro, Tex., n.d.

Yearns, W. B. *The Confederate Congress*. Athens, Ga., 1960.